Gender in a Changing World

Marc Shimazu

with editorial assistance from Lena Ericksen

Western Washington University

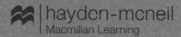

haydon-mcneil
Macmillan Learning

Macmillan Learning Curriculum Solutions
14903 Pilot Drive
Plymouth, MI 48170
www.macmillanlearning.com

Ericksen 1123-0 S19

Sustainability

Hayden-McNeil/Macmillan Learning Curriculum Solutions is proud to be a part of the larger sustainability initiative of Macmillan, our parent company. Macmillan has a goal to reduce its carbon emissions by 65% by 2020 from our 2010 baseline. Additionally, paper purchased must adhere to the Macmillan USA Paper Sourcing and Use Policy.

Hayden-McNeil partners with printers that use paper that is consistent with the environmental goals and values of Macmillan USA. This includes using paper certified by the Forest Stewardship Council (FSC), Sustainable Forestry Initiative (SFI), and/or the Programme for the Endorsement of Forest Certification (PEFC). We also offer paper with varying percentages of post-consumer waste as well as a 100% recycled stock. Additionally, Hayden-McNeil Custom Digital provides authors with the opportunity to convert print products to a digital format to use no paper at all. Visit http://sustainability.macmillan.com to learn more.

For Rebecca C.

Introduction

· ·

The noted twentieth-century philosopher Wittgenstein (1953) was very concerned about what can be known and what can be communicated. If a person had a completely different point of view from our own, he wondered, would we be able to hear what that individual had to say? If the statements expressed by the person were alien to our experience, would we be able to understand anything that was uttered?

A different view of the world can be more than disorienting. It can be incomprehensible.

Gender is a condition of human existence that is like a window through which we stare out upon a landscape colored by hopes and fears, with confusion and clarity, with perhaps love and hate. These projections of personal feelings, both positive and negative, assume a certain texture and substance that pervade our personal worldview of relationships with other individuals so that for some, no matter how beautiful the landscape might be, only desolation is seen. No matter how unjust the act, there are those who see only normality.

The attitudes we hold in our thoughts and feelings act like a lens through which all images pass. The lens may concentrate what passes through or the lens may diffuse it. Either way, it distorts.

It is not possible to put aside all attitudes and preconceptions about such a loaded and personal matter as gender. We all have our baggage of collective hurts and misgivings, personal triumphs and tragedies that come from our life experiences. It is highly unlikely—perhaps impossible—to approach this subject with a completely open mind.

But in order to understand or, to use Wittgenstein's approach, hear the meaning of gender in a changing world, it is necessary to adopt, or at least consider, many different perspectives. As you will read in the following chapters, many important insights can only be gained through frames of reference and points of view that may seem far removed from everyday ways of viewing gender and gender relations. The trick is in being open to new perspectives—to see the world in new ways.

According to anthropologists, since the dawn of our species, a hundred billion people have lived. Currently, seven percent of that enormous number is alive today (Ferguson, 2011). Among all those teeming individuals, all manner of interpersonal relationships have formed out of the wellspring of emotion and the hard edge of circumstance. Some were as ephemeral as a passing breeze, others as enduring as the stars, but much of the quality of each relationship was contingent in one way or another upon gender, the sense of being (as we shall see in the coming chapters) either a guardian of tomorrow or a citizen of the moment.

Gender is our gateway to the world of courtship and friendship, of commitment and competition, of lasting love and fleeting contact. It is a fundamentally personal part of our humanity and should not be denied, no matter its character.

REFERENCES

Ferguson, N. (2011). *Civilization: the west and the rest*. New York: The Penguin Press. p. xix.

Wittgenstein, L. (1953). *Philosophical Investigations*. New York: Prentice Hall. p. 223.

Chapter 1

Toward a Positive View of Gender

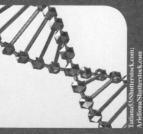

Chapter 1

gender
Mora
Roles
Attitu
ealousy
an
feelings
mpetitiveness
behavi
male/female
gr
HA

We live in an extremely complex world. Everything is changing. Nothing is constant. People find themselves struggling to make sense of altered economic conditions, disruptive technologies, and ever-shifting job prospects. What works today may be out of date tomorrow. What will work in the future may not be discernible to even the people at the leading edge of change. Nothing is certain anymore.

What questions do you have about men and women and interpersonal relationships?

. . . .

And when it comes to the way people interact with each other, uncertainty is there too. How should people behave? How should men treat women? How should women treat men? Is there a "right" way of being a girl or a guy? What are women really looking for in relationships? What do men really want? What does it mean to be a man? What does it mean to be a woman? What is up with everyone?

Do intimate relationships always have to be so complicated?

There are so many conflicting messages coming from so many different views on gender issues. More questions are generated than answers. Is there really a patriarchy out there bent on subjugating women? Is there any truth in the saying "boys will be boys and girls will be girls"? Is conflict always a part of relationships? Is sex a weapon? The term "sexist" and worse are all too often used to label competing views of gender and sex—a practice that tends to create broad divisions and makes any thoughtful conversation about the nature of being a gendered person difficult.

FIGURE 1-1. Why are men more likely to perform stunts like this?

FIGURE 1-2. Why are women usually the ones engaged in conversation?

We humans have a strong tendency to actively note the differences between groups of individuals and then use those differences to gain influence and power (Hogg et al., 2000). During times of war, the enemy is always portrayed as different, as alien. During elections, candidates and political parties seldom point out the similarities they share with each other, but instead emphasize their differences. In advertising, the superiority of those who buy a particular product over those who do not is often the underlying message. And once these differences have been firmly planted in the minds of people, they are then used to establish a boundary line that segregates one group from another (Tajfel, 1970). On one side are the good guys; on the other are the bad guys.

This candidate is a patriot; that one is a traitor. Buy this product and you will be a winner; buy that product and you will be a loser.

Differences in ethnicity, race, religion, ancestry, citizenship, socioeconomic status, occupation, tastes, habits, opinions, skin color, even hair length, have been used to draw lines between groups of individuals. The many wars of the previous century that produced death tolls counted in the tens of millions were all impelled by some variation of the difference between them and us, and upon some division that separated one group from another (Ferguson, 2006). The present is littered with the aftermath of conflicts fought over differences.

Very often the purpose of this tendency to divide people into in-groups and out-groups, into allies and enemies, into friend and foe, is to empower those who emphasize these differences. And this is the root of the matter: we humans are obsessed with power (Buss et al., 1996). We can turn just about anything into a play for power. A friendly gathering of adults can easily turn into a power struggle over who will dominate the conversation. An offhand entry on a blog can spark a firefight of words, with everyone choosing sides. A family dinner can be a tinderbox for inflammatory power displays. Struggles can be as overt as a fistfight or as subtle as the direction the butter knife is facing.

FIGURE 1-3. Why is conflict so common between men and women?

If there is one subject that can swiftly rouse the fires of "us versus them," it is gender. There is a tendency for people to quickly jump onto one side or another of the divide that many wish to draw between individuals based upon gender and advocate for a particular side. Indeed, it is fortunate that English has enough gender-neutral parts of speech that it is possible to make these statements without unintentionally implicating anyone.

Gender is such a hot-button topic. The term itself has become a loaded word. Any claim made about the nature of the genders or of the nature of their interactions is likely to be scrutinized and judged with a terrible intensity for any hint of justifying past injustices, for supporting the oppression of any group, or for any possible bias.

2.

Do you try to avoid appearing sexist?

. . . .

One small unintentional consequence of the tumult surrounding the issue of gender is that it is now customary to use the gender-neutral plural pronoun, *they*, in place of the gender-specific singular pronouns, *he* and *she*. So conscious have we become not to express any biased leanings. (Here is an example of the practice of using "they" instead of "he" or "she": *If a person wants to avoid appearing sexist,* they *should choose* their *words carefully.* The subject of the sentence is "a person," so a pronoun should be used that refers to a single individual, either "he," "she," or "it," followed in the sentence by the corresponding possessive pronoun "his," "her," or "its." But because it is now commonplace to avoid showing preference for one gender over the other, the use of the plural pronoun "they" and the possessive pronoun "their" have come to be the norm, even though technically it is grammatically incorrect. The easiest way of making this sentence grammatically correct would be to change the subject to the plural form "people." *If* people *want to avoid appearing sexist, they should choose* their *words carefully*.)

The human concern with power certainly encompasses gender and its partially associated biological root: sex. Though through the lens of biology sex can be viewed mainly as a matter of reproduction, we humans attach a great deal to it beyond simply continuing our kind (Miller, 2000). All kinds of social, political, religious, legal, economic, artistic, scientific, ethical, and moral factors have been connected to this elemental part of our lives. And out of this mind-numbingly complex interplay of contesting views and positions, so much discord and distrust has been generated that many people have developed a reluctance to openly discuss the matter.

Gender studies have the feel of a battlefield (Faludi, 2010).

3.

Do you feel it is easy to talk about the differences between men and women?

This is unfortunate because a new generation of people, all born long after the 1960s, 70s, and 80s, after the formative years of the debate over the roles and nature of the sexes and the genders, are facing a future markedly transformed by social, economic, and technological innovations. Human interpersonal relationships are changing rapidly (Turkle, 2011). There is now so much confusion and angst about intimate relationships. So many of the young have watched their parents divorce and remarry, so many have experienced the loss of their childhood home, and so many have entered adolescence and early adulthood unsure about their sense of being a gendered human being.

The underlying goal of this book is to present a view of gender that is informative—free of the

hostility that surrounds so many discussions of this aspect of our humanity. Gender, and the issues that relate to it, will be examined from the point of view of the biological and the behavioral sciences. Inevitably, some bias or other will appear in this discussion. Science is not the perfect way of approaching the issue of gender, nor is it the only way. But one of its virtues is that the view it offers of gender is broad enough to include everyone.

4.

Can you think of other ways of approaching this subject that will shed light without producing too much heat?

The scientific enterprise is a very human way of trying to understand ourselves, and the world around us (Bronowski, 1973). Science is not definitive. It is not the final word on any matter of study. Its findings are our recent insights and these insights may be swept away and invalidated with the next observation or experiment. The theories and conjectures that we use to make sense of the things we see and experience are not written in stone and are always subject to revision. We make mistakes; we sometimes come to dead ends. Sometimes the conclusions that are drawn are not what we expect and sometimes not what we want. Inevitably there is bias. Science has never offered nor will it ever offer certainty. Indeed, the very nature of the Universe itself probably precludes the possibility of certainty (Heisenberg, 1971).

But this does not mean that science is useless. For better and worse, it has profoundly shaped the path of collective human development. For better and worse, we have gone from being hunter-gatherers to post-industrialists in less than ten millennia. The standards of living we enjoy today and the opportunities we have for growth and understanding would not be possible without science.

This book is also an attempt to examine gender with a view to living in a world that is rapidly changing. Though we humans are among the most adaptive of species, the rate at which change is occurring in the present is putting enormous pressure on our ability to adapt. Consequently, it is important to look to the past to see how others lived and dealt with change as well as how the past shapes our current understanding of gender.

By looking to the past, insight can also be gained about why individuals are predisposed to behave in a certain way in the present. Generalizing human behavior does not mean that we are all destined to act in the same way and suffer the same fate. Nor does it justify unacceptable behavior. But it sheds light on the larger behavioral trends that got our ancestors through difficult times. Does this mean that we must follow in our forebearers' footsteps? Certainly not, but to turn a blind eye upon the past because we do not like what happened is not only unhelpful; it denies us our human-ity—warts and all.

History is in many respects horrific. The noted Irish writer, James Joyce (1922) wrote, it "…is a nightmare from which I am trying to awake." For many, the present is just as disturbing, if not frightening, but we are going to get through these times not by closing our eyes to it, but by waking up, dealing with the world in which we live, as well as its past, and perhaps trying to improve our collective well-being.

What is different about gender studies is that it is not a detached field of inquiry. Unlike research into the chemistry of distant planets or the study of plant biology, gender is about a significant and immediate part of your life. To put it bluntly: it's in your face. It touches everyone's life. From the way we flirt, to the shifting uncertainties of fleeting or lifelong intimate relationships, to the way we raise our children, gender is an integral part of living among others. And the hope is that the find-ings that come from research into this field can potentially be used to improve the quality of life for everyone.

Consequently, many people argue that we should use what we have learned about gender to changes things for the better. Historically, gender studies have been an integral part of the women's movement and the push to eliminate sex-based bias from all parts of human society. Gender studies have also contributed greatly to the lesbian, gay, bisexual, and transsexual (LGBT) movements for acceptance and civil and legal equality. Awareness of gender issues has also affected educational policy, family law, workers' rights, and much, much more. And underlying the various positions that have been put forward by advocates of reform are a diverse mix of worldviews that order how we interpret gender and human behavior.

It is important, therefore, to be aware of the worldviews that are used to interpret the findings of science and of history, and which form the foundation of the many social move-ments and initiatives that shape our world. Information about our biological nature, our behavioral qualities, and how these unfolded in the context of history is just so many bits of data unless it is placed into some larger theme from which to make sense of what it all means. So, it will be important to consider the worldviews that are used to structure our understanding of gender.

But first, there is the matter of gender itself. What is it?

FIGURE 1-4. Worldviews: There are many ways of understanding gender. What global view orders your thoughts and feelings?

WHAT IS GENDER?

5.

Which box gets your check mark: male ☐ female ☐?

· ·

Who are you?

Out of this simple, three-word question an incredibly rich, complex answer is likely to emerge. Your name, your family ties, your ethnicity, cultural background, beliefs, interests and inclinations, all the characteristics that are important to you and make you *you* would probably come in response to this question. In short, you are identifying yourself. No other person in the world would likely describe him or herself in exactly the same way you would. And somewhere in your answer you would probably directly or indirectly state your gender.

However, if you glance at your driver's license or other official identification offered in the United States and many other countries, you will find somewhere on it reference to your sex, with either an "M" for male or an "F" for female. (In a later chapter we will examine the practice in some countries of recognizing more than two sexes.)

So what is the difference between being an "F" or an "M" and gender?

This is where things get complicated.

We humans are living, breathing biological beings. From the perspective of biology, of the many activities all of us are inclined to do, like eating and sleeping, one of the most important is reproduction—having children. You would not be reading these words if it weren't for this biological aspect of human existence. Making more of ourselves is what makes possible the continuation of our kind—and irrespective of how you might feel about this issue it is a fact of life that significantly shapes your personal development.

There are many creatures in the world around us that produce offspring by simply cloning themselves. In other words, many microorganisms, as well as large forms of life like some plants, reptiles, and insects, can make more of themselves without engaging in sex (Zimmer, 2001). But most life forms on Earth are not mere copy machines; they mix the genes of two parents to produce unique offspring. We humans are gene-mixers. We reproduce sexually. (That we use the same word "sex" for the act that may initiate reproduction, as well as for the category into which an individual is conventionally designated male or female, indicates the strong connection between these two issues.)

As we will see in the next chapter, there are several factors that come together to determine a person's sex. But despite this complexity, we often generalize our biological reproductive characteristics into a simple binary: some individuals are female and some are male.

Adults usually identify themselves as either men or women. In most people's minds, it seems such an obvious and straightforward thing that it does not require further consideration. The conventional view is that if you are born female you will grow into a woman; if you are born male you will grow into a man. Roughly half the world's population is composed of females and roughly half is composed of males. Children are either boys or girls, and that is that. To go further, it is commonly believed that females behave in a feminine manner and males behave in a masculine manner. Hence the view that boys will be boys and girls will be girls. In other words, most people maintain a strictly biological view of gender. To put it simply, sex = gender. This is the tidy correspondence that tends to order most people's thoughts about gender.

But is gender really determined solely by biology?

6.

Which sign are you: ♀ or ♂?

. . . .

When you think about how complex the world is, it is actually rather strange that we are likely to think about gender in such a simple manner. Think about the complexity of the car you drive or the computer you use. Think about the manufacturing processes and the networks that support their operation. Consider the practical knowledge, the sophisticated mathematics, and physical science that make every engine and microprocessor possible. Yet as complicated as cars and computers are, the human mind and body are far more intricate.

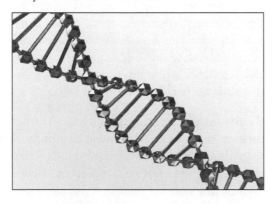

FIGURE 1-5. This is DNA (deoxyribonucleic acid). It contains the genetic instructions used in the development and functioning of all known living organisms and is in the nucleus of every one of the cells of our body.

Billions and billions of molecular base pairs—the chemical components that compose your DNA—are in the nucleus of each of the multitudes of cells that make up your body. The amount of information they encode is staggeringly large. If your DNA were printed out as books as long as this one, they would fill 5,000 volumes (Ridley, 1999). All the biochemical activity DNA activates, moderates, and initiates in response to an enormous variety of signals and cues is even more complex.

The human brain, the organ that generates the distinctive consciousness that distinguishes

you from all the other people of the world, is also fantastically complex. The human capacity for learning and creativity that produces the teeming diversity of cultures and experiences that surrounds us all springs from that compact but labyrinthine neural mass that resides in each of our heads.

The world we live in is certainly complex. Our relationships with family, with friends, with acquaintances, with co-workers and with many others are full of nuances and subtleties that change with time and circumstance. The physical and economic infrastructure that supports many of our daily activities, from providing the energy to heat the water for that morning shower to the long chain of production and distribution that puts dinner in front of us to eat, is also incredibly intricate.

So why should gender be a simple matter of labeling a person male or female?

Well, it isn't so simple.

While sex is conventionally designated using an either/or approach (either female or male), gender is rather like characterizing movies or books. Here the related term *genre* offers insight. Some movies or books are romances, some are action/adventures, some are westerns, some are documentaries, some are comedies, and some are dramas. There are hybrid genre forms like romantic comedies, or science fiction action/adventures, or historical dramas. Genres tell you something about the prevailing themes of the films or books you might want to view or read. You are likely to have certain expectations about a book that belongs to a particular genre.

Using just sex to describe people is like differentiating all books and movies into fiction or non-fiction. It would be rather odd to place movies like *Gone With the Wind* and *Dude, Where's My Car?* into the same category just because they are both fictional. Why then should a person, who is much more complex than any book or movie, be pigeonholed into one of two categories?

Gender in individuals is rather like genre in books and movies. Gender is about a person's identity and sense of self. A person's sex is certainly an important part of that identity, but gender also encompasses all the associated roles and behaviors (West and Zimmerman, 1987) that are uniquely configured by the particular experiences and heritage that inform the life of the individual. Gender also characterizes the way an individual is physically present in the larger world beyond the self.

The sex you perceive yourself to be is just the starting point from which your personal gender identity arises. Gender is much more than knowing which bathroom to use at a restaurant. The sense of being a gendered individual is central to your sense of self—it shapes your worldview of so many things, it influences the nature of your life, and it can bias your likes and dislikes.

Another layer of complexity is added to gender when we deal with family and friends and with the larger society and culture in which we live. Stereotypes and expectations about the nature and character of specific genders swirl around us all the time. Some views of gender maintain that boys should participate in rough-and-tumble play while girls should engage in nurturing play with dolls and stuffed animals, or that men should be autonomous and women should be dependent. Many people view these broad stereotypes as limiting and sexist. But irrespective of the judgments placed upon particular conventions about the nature of females and males, gender identity does not exist in a vacuum. It has a social as well as a psychological dimension.

FIGURE 1-6. Stereotypes and expectations based upon gender exist both within and outside families.

ABOUT FRAMES OF REFERENCE

According to the biological and anthropological sciences, we are all one species, *Homo sapiens* (Sykes, 2001). You and me and every human being alive today, and who has ever lived in the past, all belong to the same family. Every person you know, have known, and will ever know is related to you. Even if you encounter a person who speaks a language that is entirely unintelligible to you, is from a culture completely unfamiliar to you, has physical characteristics that appear very different from your own, that person is a distant relative. Go back far enough through time and you will find a common ancestor that you share with any person alive today and with any person who ever lived in the past. We are all one big family.

FIGURE 1-7. We all belong to the same family—the human family.

From this genealogical frame of reference to human relatedness, there are no foreigners. The notion that a person who is your distant cousin can be a foreigner arises from cultural or legalistic practices. According to biology and anthropology, we are all human inhabitants of Earth, and if there is one place where our kind can be regarded as native, since the origin of our species can be traced to that place, it is Africa.

The point of these references to biology and to anthropology is not to change your political beliefs, but to make you aware that different approaches to gender may reveal different information. In other words, it is important to be aware of how the references we use affect the way we see and understand the world around us.

Gender is a complicated issue because it can be looked at from so many different points of reference. If you use the law as a reference point to understand gender, you may discover that it does not necessarily match what biology or anthropology has to say on the matter. (The law certainly does not match these sciences when it comes to the definition of citizenship and what makes a person a foreigner.) The legal reference can enter into issues like how your gender may determine whether you can marry the person you wish to wed, or your responsibility to your spouse, something biology does not address. Politicians sometimes use legal referents on aspects of gender to make distinctions between groups of people. More often, they use cultural references about what is generally perceived as "normal" to make distinctions about gender matters. As a result, these norms may profoundly affect your life's path. From the reference of some religions, your gender can determine whether you can participate in certain acts of faith. When gender is referenced from an educational or developmental perspective, it is viewed as a part of the self that changes with time. For example, the sense children have of being male or female changes with maturation, particularly during puberty, with the transition into sexual maturity. Educational referents may overtly or covertly predispose you to receive instruction in certain fields over others.

7.

A point of reference that focuses on you?

. . . .

When gender is referenced from the point of view of psychology and its role in the life of the individual person, all the referents come together. Psychology is a branch of the behavioral sciences that focuses on the individual. Unlike sociology, which views human behavior

from the perspective of the social interaction of groups of individuals, or anthropology, which is concerned with humanity in terms of culture and its physical evolution, psychology tries to look at *all the inputs* that shape the mental characteristics of the individual. Knowing the frame of reference that informs a particular influence (for example, your gender can predispose you for certain illnesses, this being a biological aspect of gender), which affects a person's sense of self, is important.

To understand gender we have to take into account several points of reference. It can be quite disorienting, especially when the information that is revealed by one frame of reference runs contrary to another, or to your expectations. But as we examine the many elements that come together to generate gender identity, a broader picture will begin to emerge about a fundamental part of ourselves.

DUELING WORLDVIEWS

Gender identity, that sense of ourselves we all have that sometimes includes being a specific sex, has enormous consequences for the individual. Educational and occupational opportunities, lifestyle choices, social mobility, and much more can be affected by one's gender. As a result, there is much debate over whether we have any choice about our gender identity. Do we have any control over our sense of being a particular gender? This leads to the larger question: what really determines our gender identity?

8.

Think about how your freedom to choose is connected to your sense of empowerment.

. . . .

Many of the most controversial issues of our time are about matters relating to personal choice. Whether it is reproductive rights, gun ownership, plastic bag use at the supermarket, or the continued availability of incandescent lightbulbs, the element of choice is central because choice is ultimately about power—and as we shall see, power is something that fascinates us all.

There is a strong bias in our outlook in Western cultures: we want to believe we have control. And gender identity is no different. The underlying concern for control has generated a lot of debate about what determines our personal sense of being a gendered individual. Are we innately male or female, or are we taught to be male or female? Is our personal gender identity a product of culture or something we are born with?

What's at stake is the degree to which we can shape our own lives.

So what are the main points of view on this aspect of gender?

9.

Keep in mind that, since we are interested in how gender affects our personal sense of self, these points of view are the ones used in psychology. Do you think they could be used to understand other parts of our lives?

In a nutshell, some people argue that gender is principally a matter of biology. Your gender identity is primarily shaped by your inborn qualities and predispositions. This view of gender is generally termed *essentialist* (Keller, 2005).

Some argue that gender is something that is learned. That is, you learn to behave for example in a feminine or a masculine manner and are playing a role assigned to you by the prevailing customs of the society into which you were born. Your identity is entirely constructed out of the information you receive from your surroundings. This is the *social constructivist** view (Marecek, 2004; Gergen, 1985).

There are also some who argue that both biology and culture interact to create gender identity. From this perspective, your inborn tendencies and the environment in which you live shape your gender identity. This is the *nature via nurture* view (Ridley, 2003).

These distinctive ways of looking at the character and origin of gender are at the heart of debates on issues as diverse as the legitimacy of gay and lesbian marriage, to whether violent video games cause teenage males to act in an overly aggressive manner, to educational policy. Even answers to such questions as why weight loss is such a struggle for so many people, and how best to deal with the increasing incidence of obesity, depend on whether you approach the matter from an essentialist, a social constructivist, or a nature via nurture point of view.

At the core of these three differing perspectives is an intense debate over whether our biology controls our lives, whether the environment makes us who we are, or if we are the product of an intricate dance between these two forces. The arguments between proponents of these three views can become quite heated. Ultimately, the reason for this is that each approach places the power and the responsibility for personal and social matters in different hands.

For example, do violent video games cause teenage males to behave violently?

An essentialist could argue that boys are inherently aggressive—they are biologically just that way. We know that the hormone testosterone floods their bodies during puberty and adolescence, which causes aggressive behavior. So they are strongly inclined to violent behavior. It is not the violence in the video game that

---

* The concept of "social construction" takes many forms in the sciences, and there are many subtle and not so subtle differences between its specific applications in specific fields of study. However, in order to minimize confusion, the generalized term *social constructivism* is used to encompass all its various forms.

makes them violent. They are drawn to violent video games because the content mirrors their own emotional state. Getting rid of violent video games would make no positive difference. In fact, the elimination of violent video games may make matters worse because a safe channel for dissipating aggression would no longer be available to young males.

A social constructivist could make the counter-argument that young males are taught to behave in an aggressive manner by the demands and expectations placed upon them by the surrounding culture. Violent video games are a powerful source of cultural information about how a male is expected to behave. Additionally, the way the games are set up rewards the user for aggressive play, thus reinforcing violent behavior. We know that testosterone levels increase when youngsters engage in such activity. Thus violent video games are a particularly potent element in the social environment that shapes the gender identity of males during a critical developmental period, adolescence, which precedes adulthood. The elimination of violent video games would do much to moderate male youth violence.

The nature via nurture advocate could argue that young males are inherently predisposed to aggression—they were evolved to be. In the ancestral hunter-gatherer societies in which our human characteristics developed, when boys reach about six years of age, the men of the village begin to train them to be hunters (Mayberry-Lewis, 1992). In the post-industrial world we live in, we no longer formally train boys to hunt, but that window for learning still exists in the young. Unintentionally, videogame makers may be taking over the role of the older men in hunter-gatherer societies. From this perspective, whether we like it or not, the predisposition for aggressive behavior, which could turn violent, is present in young males (and young females too), but whether the video games themselves are the cause of violent behavior is not clear. However, what is clear is that young boys need to learn how to appropriately channel their innate aggressive inclinations in positive ways.

You may have noticed that when describing how a proponent for each of these viewpoints would address the issue of video games and violence, the term "could" is used preceding the respective position. The reason is that there is a lot of variation even among those who advocate for each view. There is no single definitive essentialist, social constructivist, or nature via nurture response to this or any other matter. But what is important to understand are the consequences that arise from each of these worldviews.

10.

What are the consequences of these different worldviews?

FIGURE 1-8. In its purest form, the essentialist position is that our brains come preloaded with what is needed for survival.

THE ESSENTIALIST VIEW

Many who view violent behavior among young males from an essentialist view would likely advocate to keep violent video games available. From their point of view, legislation banning such games would be counterproductive. It might generate bootleg trade in illicit games, deprive video game producers of an important revenue source, and might even infringe upon free speech rights. The cost of dealing with violent behavior might increase because young males would no longer have access to this method of channeling their aggression.

The objection that many have to the essentialist view is that it suggests that there is not much that we can do to change human nature. The way we behave, the way the sexes interact, the nature of conflict between individuals, and the character of our gender identity are difficult, if not impossible, to change. This seems to ignore the incredible diversity that can be found within and across the human cultures of the world. The essentialist approach is often interpreted to imply a kind of mechanistic view of human behavior and development; we are slavishly following a preset program that allows us few options. Yet even a cursory study of the wide variety of customs and behaviors that people have adopted around the world should reveal that we are not following a rigid program. In response, the essentialist might argue that the variations are not great and that the essential themes of human behavior are universal. There is also the implication that the established ways of doing things—as much as we might object to them—have worked in the past, and that human nature has been tried and tested over countless generations. Therefore, any changes we attempt to impose on our fundamental nature should be done with caution.

FIGURE 1-9. In its purest form, social constructivism claims that our minds begin as blank slates and that all our characteristics are learned from the environment.

THE SOCIAL CONSTRUCTIVIST VIEW

From a social constructivist position, the prohibition of violent video games would likely be received as a positive development. A significant socializing element in the lives of young males that modeled negative behavior would be eliminated. They would maintain that the financial losses resulting from the ban on such games would be more than recovered from the absence of costs associated with dealing with violent activity and its aftermath. It would be a net gain for society if such entertainment were completely absent.

The social constructivist position is based upon the assumption that we humans are extremely plastic and changeable, and are principally shaped by our social context. In other words, a person's gender identity is entirely constructed from the lessons, messages, and feedback that we receive, particularly during childhood. We consciously or unconsciously absorb the cultural conventions that surround us during our lives. It suggests that we are born blank slates and can, through socialization and formal instruction, be made into a male or a female, no matter what our biology indicates. Among many individuals, social constructivism has been the foundation from which they have advocated for the reform of traditional sex roles, family structures, the legal system, educational institutions, and the workplace as a means to ensure equality among the sexes. Overall, the social constructivist view implies that the biological aspects of our humanity are largely irrelevant. Consequently, the reform of the prevailing social environment is perceived as the best way to remedy a variety of issues. Many object to the social constructivist view because it seems to ignore the cultural norms and experiences of people who are not Western Europeans. This is based upon the stance, for example, that gender equality is a goal that justifies the elimination of all social systems that are in any way discriminatory. Advocates of the social constructivist view frequently maintain that the old ways of doing things are no longer appropriate in a world deeply altered by social, economic, and technological innovations, even if a given culture does not recognize or accept those changes. The liberation of the individual from cultural conventions structured around essentialist views is necessary from this point of view. Social constructivism also appears to ignore the similarities that are common to all human cultures.

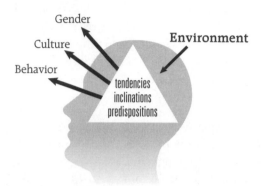

FIGURE 1-10. The environment in which we live is interpreted by our inborn mental characteristics; together, our surroundings and our inborn mental traits interact to generate behavior.

THE NATURE VIA NURTURE VIEW

The nature via nurture stance might be more nuanced. Instead of attempting to legislate the problem away by making the creation, distribution, and sale of violent video games illegal, the emphasis should be placed on offering young males alternatives that would be inherently appealing to them while directing them to more desirable activities. Through education and appropriate reinforcement, adolescents might be persuaded to engage in more pro-social activities. From this perspective it could be argued that simply banning violent video games, like banning alcohol, would not work in the long run, because it does not change the underlying motives that drive individuals to consume these items. Though we humans are not destined by our biology to act in specific ways, our biology inclines or predisposes us to behave in certain ways. What is needed is to redirect old impulses along new behavioral paths.

The nature via nurture view is also known as the epigenetic approach. As the word epigenetic implies, human behavior is shaped by nurture *upon genes*. In other words, our personal life experiences affect more than just our minds; they affect the behavior of our genes.

If you could closely examine your DNA, you would discover specific molecular markers on it that respond to environmental cues, which activate or deactivate sections of your genes. From the moment of your conception to your present life condition, an array of these epigenetic markers have been turned on or off in response to your exposure to, and interaction with, the environment. Though our understanding of these genetic on/off switches is still in its infancy, it has been determined that behavioral predispositions and tendencies are subtly shaped by these genetic activations and deactivations. Your taste for certain kinds of food, for certain sorts of activities, your outlook on life, and even who you are inclined to associate with all have epigenetic components (Bosson et al, 2019).

To a large degree, this framework for understanding gender identity has been informed by evolutionary psychology. Though it is commonly thought of as essentialist (Brannon, 2008), evolutionary psychology takes into account the environment's effect on personal development (Buss, 2012). In this respect it attempts to bridge the essentialist and the social constructivist views together in a new synthesis. Many who object to the nature via nurture or epigenetic perspective argue that its reliance on a genetic understanding of human behavior is essentialist and simply wrong, since they claim that it is not possible to pair specific behaviors with specific genes. Advocates of nature via nurture counter that genetic characteristics only broadly predispose us to behave in certain ways. It is the particular social and cultural setting that surrounds us that shape these inclinations into specific behaviors. For example, we are all predisposed to like high calorie, tasty foods, but education and the norms we have absorbed from our experiences may keep us on a diet that promotes good health. Our taste for high calorie munchies was inherited from our ancestors who lived in a setting where such food was scarce. But now that that predisposition is no longer good for us in a world where fast food is cheap and easily available, we can learn to alter that impulse. However, the mediating force that ultimately determines what behaviors will persist is the environment. In other words, over the long run, things people do that contribute to their survival will continue, while those that do not benefit them will not. This dynamic interaction of epigenetic behavioral tendencies tested by beneficial or detrimental outcomes clearly illustrates the evolutionary processes that shape our genes—and by extension, their epigenetic traits. Social constructivism runs contrary to this view on many grounds, but mainly because it implies that social justice may not be achievable from the framework of epigenetics.

11.

What are these three perspectives on gender trying to determine?

. . . .

These are the main contesting views that inform the study of gender. If this area of study were just a matter of understanding our personal sense of being a particular sex without concern for all the effects and counter-effects of life in a changing world, it would be a simpler matter. But because gender is in many ways the most fundamental characteristic that shapes our interactions with other people and with the larger world beyond ourselves, additional social, political, moral, ethical, and cultural dimensions are heaped onto it. The essentialist, social constructivist, and nature via nurture views—if you think about them for a moment—come from our desire to define the limits of our power over our lives. Are we fated to live a certain way, and how much of our destiny is determined by our gender? Or do we have the power to make a life for ourselves that is entirely of our own making? Does our

ancestry, our links to our parents and grandparents and great-grandparents, play any role in our personal sense of gender? How much does the past contribute to the present and the future? And why is this all so complicated?

As we consider the answers to these questions in the coming chapters, let us first ask the more basic question: how did this all start?

FIGURE 1-11. Do you think these worldviews have anything in common?

SUGGESTED DOCUMENTARY TO ACCOMPANY CHAPTER 1:

National Geographic. (2009). *Sex, Lies and Gender*. www.nationalgeographic.com

REFERENCES

Bosson, J. K., Vandello, J. A., Buckner, C. E. (2019). *The psychology of sex and gender*. Thousand Oaks: SAGE Pub. p. 79.

Bronowski, J. (1973). *The ascent of man*. Boston: Little, Brown. p. 374.

Buss, D. M. and Malamuth, N. M. eds. (1996). *Sex, power, conflict: evolutionary and feminist perspectives*. Oxford: Oxford University Press.

Buss, D. M. (2012). *Evolutionary psychology: the new science of the mind, 4th ed.* Boston: Allyn & Bacon. pp. 35–68.

Faludi, S. (2010). "American electra: feminism's ritual matricide." *Harper's Magazine*. 321, October 2010. pp. 29–42.

Ferguson, N. (2006). *The war of the world: twentieth century conflict and the descent of the west*. New York: The Penguin Press.

Gergen, K. J. (1985). "The social constructionist movement in modern psychology." *American Psychologist*, 40, 266–275.

Heisenberg, W. (1971). "Positivism, metaphysics and religion." *Physics and beyond: encounters and conversations by Werner Heisenberg*. New York: Harper & Row.

Hogg, M. A. and Williams, K. D. (2000). "From I to we: social identity and the collective self." *Group Dynamics: Theory, Research, and Practice*. 4:81 (http://dx.doi.org/10.1037%2F1089-2699.4.1.81).

Joyce, J. (1922). *Ulysses*. New York: Vintage International.

Keller, J. (2005). "In genes we trust: the biological component of psychological essentialism and its relationship to mechanisms of social cognition." *Journal of Personality and Social Psychology*, 88, pp. 686–702.

Marecek, J., Crawford, M., and Popp, D. (2004). "On the construction of gender, sex, sexualities." *The psychology of gender, 2nd ed.* New York: Guilford Press. pp. 192–216.

Maybury-Lewis, D. (1992). *Millennium: tribal wisdom and the modern world*. New York: Viking Press. pp. 137–140.

Miller, G. (2000). *The mating mind: how sexual choice shaped the evolution of human nature*. New York: Doubleday.

Ridley, M. (1999). *Genome: the autobiography of a species in 23 chapters*. New York: Harper Collins. p. 7.

Ridley, M. (2003). *Nature via nurture: genes, experience and what makes us human*. New York: Harper Collins.

Sykes, B. (2001). *The seven daughters of Eve: the science that reveals our genetic ancestry*. New York: W.W. Norton.

Tajfel, H. (1970). "Experiments in intergroup discrimination." *Scientific American*, 223, pp. 96–102.

Turkle, S. (2011). *Alone together: why we expect more from technology and less from each other*. New York: Basic Books.

West, C. and Zimmerman, D. H. (1987). "Doing gender." *Gender and Society*, 1, pp. 125–151.

Zimmer, C. (2001). *Evolution: the triumph of an idea*. New York: Harper Collins. pp. 230–231.

Name   Date

1. What is gender?

2. How is cloning different from sexual reproduction?

3. What is DNA?

4. How do different points of reference affect the way we understand issues relating to gender?

5. Define essentialism.

6. Define the social constructivist view.

7. Define nature via nurture.

8. How do these three perspectives differ on the issue of gender?

9. Based upon your own experience, do you think our behavior is determined by our biology, shaped by our environment, or a mix of both biology and our surroundings?

10. Can you think of behaviors you have witnessed that can be accounted for primarily from an essentialist, a social constructivist, or an epigenetic point of view?

Chapter 2

Our Beginnings

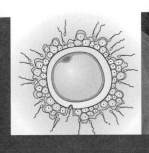

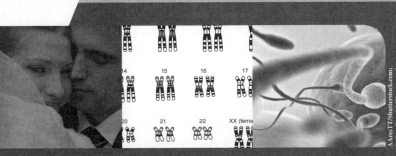

AAresTT/Shutterstock.com;
Joshua Resnick/Shutterstock.com;
Clara/Shutterstock.com

WHY IS SEX SO CENTRAL TO LIFE?

You have been invited to celebrate your cousin's wedding. The reception is at a fancy hotel in town beginning at 5 pm. Dinner will be served at 7 pm. When you arrive at the hotel, music can be heard throbbing from the open doors of the ballroom located down one of the corridors that radiate from the lobby. Peoples' voices can be heard as you go down the hall. Young and old mingle together; laughter and excited cries pop like champagne corks. As you come to the entrance you see familiar faces as well as unfamiliar ones. Your uncle welcomes you. Your aunt greets you warmly and thanks you for coming, while one of your other cousins gives you a friendly smile. People who you don't know glance your way. Some introduce themselves. Others remain standoffish. You take in a view of the gathering. So many people are present. Many have already found their assigned seats and are standing around their respective tables making small talk. A few couples are tentatively dancing in front of the band. Grandpa is telling his usual stories in a corner of the room.

Taking a deep breath, you let it all wash over you, the living tide of family and friends all gathered to share in the joy of the joining of two into one.

Where did these traditions come from? What do they mean?

Have you ever reflected on these questions?

FIGURE 2-1. Two are now one.

In a very real sense, the marriage of two individuals and the rituals that go with this change in their relationship to the wider world echoes something that happened long, long ago. It was an event that revolutionized the nature of life on planet Earth and made much in the realm of living things, including you and me, possible.

HOW IT ALL BEGAN—OR MAYBE *WHY* IS MORE ACCURATE

In any discussion about gender issues, there are always some who feel that the whole matter of sex is overdone. Many people feel that there are simply too many allusions to it both in the study of this subject and in society in general. Everywhere you turn there is always some reference to sex, they say. In commercials, in movies, in books, in conversation at home and in the office, there is inevitably some sexual reference or innuendo lurking in the background.

When it comes to the origin of sex, however, there is nothing particularly enticing or sultry about it. This is a broad simplification of its practical biological function, but as far as researchers have been able to determine, sexual reproduction proved adaptive, not only because it worked as a way to produce offspring, but more importantly, as a strategy for dealing with parasites (Ridley, 1993).

The usual image associated with the word *parasite* is of critters like fleas and heartworms that might have you taking your dog or cat to the veterinarian for treatment. And while fleas and heartworms are very definitely parasites, the word itself also refers to a particular relationship between organisms. Parasitism denotes an arrangement in which one organism obtains benefit from another and often causes injury in the process. The organism that is exploited is the host. The organism that receives the benefit is the parasite. We humans have pretty much eliminated mega-fauna predators like big cats and roving packs of wolves that can threaten us, but many microscopic ones still stalk us. For example, the common cold virus is a parasite that occasionally plagues us. It gets inside us, invades our bodily cells, uses the contents of our cells to make copies of itself, and in the process destroys the infected cells. We feel sick while this is going inside of us. If our immune systems are not functioning properly, it could kill us.

According to some biologists, the mixing of genes from two separate and unique individuals—which is the essential part of sexual reproduction—was an adaptation that made life for parasites much more difficult (Zimmer, 2001, pp. 230–233).

2.

Ever thought about having children without having sex?

To understand the benefits of sexual reproduction, we have to consider the implications of not having sex to have offspring. Life has existed on Earth for more than three and a half billion years, and for all of that time, up to this very day, there have been creatures that reproduce without sex. There are lizards in the American southwest, for example, that are all female (Roughgarden, 2009, p. 16). They lay eggs that contain just their genes and, when the eggs hatch, reveal offspring that are replicas of the single parent and are all daughters. This contemporary method of asexual reproduction hearken back to the original way the earliest microorganisms reproduced. All early single-celled organisms made more of themselves by dividing into two cells (Tudge, 2000). After each cell grew large enough to support the replication of its DNA and its parts, it divided again, making yet another clone of itself.

3.

What are the advantages of having offspring without having sex? Would you like to have children who are clones of you?

When you think about, reproducing this way is a lot more efficient than the way we do it. There's no search for a suitable mate, no courtship, no potential rejection, no sharing of labor and resources to raise the young, and no concern about infidelity. If you think about it even more deeply, beings that clone themselves would outnumber any sexually reproducing beings fairly quickly. Among the "cloners" everyone can have offspring, while among the "sexual reproducers" only half the population—the females—can have children.

Yet less than 1 percent of all vertebrate species (animals with backbones) clone themselves (Zimmer, 2001, p. 231). The reason for this is that clones suffer from one enormous disadvantage. They are all identical.

4.

What would happen if all of us were identical?

Imagine a population composed entirely of identical people during an epidemic outbreak. Say a deadly strain of influenza virus developed that could completely overwhelm the immune systems of these individuals. With no variations in their ability to fight disease, the virus would spread rapidly and the result would very likely be the same in every case—death. In the fourteenth century, the Black Death—which was an outbreak of bubonic plague—ravaged Europe (Tuchman, 1978). The particular strain of bacteria involved often killed those it infected in a matter of a day or two. Some towns lost half or more of their populace, and yet, despite the virulence of this disease, there were infected individuals who survived. This would suggest that a sizeable fraction of the population had immune systems that could repel the onslaught of the bacillus. (Very possibly you are a direct descendant of these fortunate men and women, and may have inherited some of their ability to resist this disease.) Now think about what would have happened if everyone had the same immune system and it was the version not able to deal with the plague. The mortality rate might have reached 100 percent and no one would have survived to record the horror of the Black Death.

This is what can happen to species that are composed of clones. With no variation in the population, the occurrence of a single type of parasite could render a cloned species extinct very easily. And no doubt this happened in the past—imagine whole populations of cloned creatures being utterly defenseless against some parasitic onslaught. Such events made asexual reproducers rare.

The great virtue of swapping genes with another non-identical individual, which from the frame of reference of biology is what defines sex, is that the mixing of genes from the two parents produces a completely new person. From two non-identical parents comes a third unique individual. And because the little family that results from even one generation of successful sexual reproduction has at least three different individuals in it, the likelihood of a particular parasite, being able to easily wipe out all three would be significantly reduced.

As in the case of an outbreak of plague like the Black Death, all the differing immune systems that might exist in a population of townspeople would produce varying degrees of resistance. In the fourteenth century, before the development of medications like antibiotics, the individuals whose immune systems could cope with the disease survived and so they could perhaps pass this characteristic on to their descendents.

Reproduction through sex creates biological diversity (Gould, 1989). It can be thought of as a savings account of different genetic characteristics. Like a rainy-day fund, biodiversity can make species less vulnerable to the most common external active threats to their continued existence. Due to the fact that it is often not possible to foresee what adversities like disease or climatic change may come in the future, the more genetic variety there is in the population, the greater the likelihood that even in the direst of situations, some individuals will possess the characteristics needed to survive. Among cloned creatures, this lack of variety means that any threat that is fatal to one individual in that species is very likely to be fatal to all.

That there is still a tiny minority of non-sexually reproducing animals in the world indicates that there are environmental niches, and living strategies that these creatures use, that make this method of reproduction adaptive. But by and large, variety is more than the spice of life; it helps ensure survival.

5.

Why is the biology of sexual reproduction viewed as deterministic from a social constructivist standpoint?

. . . .

The primary criticism that this account of the advantages of sexual reproduction someone might draw from a social constructivist view is that it is deterministic. Biological explanations of this sort, which are deemed essentialist from a social constructivist view, seem to suggest that there is only one "right" way for animals to develop. Consequently, learned behavior has no place in this scheme. There is also the implication that sexual reproduction is an inevitable adaptation to an environment in which parasites are common. Building upon this view, the judgment could be made that those creatures that are not characterized by the ability to reproduce sexually are somehow not as well adapted. Additionally, it might be construed that all animals, including humans, are unchangeable (or should not be changed) because of the purported advantages of their adaptations. In other words, all creatures are the way they are because they have all been "fitted" into their respective environment. From the social constructivist view, this might be interpreted as deterministically essentialist.

Examining the origin of sex from a biological referent is based upon the view that the exchange of genes between two non-identical parents to produce offspring was an ancient innovation that happened spontaneously, but there was nothing inevitable about it. Other reproductive methods could have evolved, but it was sex that turned out to work best for organisms that had to deal an environment that featured parasites. Sex was advantageous in such a setting and was selected for by the pressure exerted on species preyed upon by parasites. If a new, more advantageous form of reproduction were to develop, sexual reproduction might disappear over time. Evolution

is not a perfection seeking process. Asexual reproduction is just as advanced as the sexual variety; it is just that in certain settings it is less adaptive. From the biological view, change is not only possible, it is always happening.

6.

How is sexual reproduction viewed from the epigenetic or nature via nurture perspective?

. . . .

The epigenetic, or nature via nurture worldview, would emphasize the interaction between the environment and the inherent nature of living organisms. The interesting thing is that from the starting point of sex came, through the interplay of evolution and biological mutation, all the fantastic plant and animal diversity found in the world today. Within the context of gender studies, as we will see in following chapters, our ancestral environment greatly shaped our characteristics. Our evolutionarily derived fixation on sex generated human cultures in which everything from lipstick to luxury cars, childcare to college, from holding hands to founding empires are all motivated by the impulse for survival.

But before we delve into these more expansive matters, we need to consider a few more nittygritty issues first.

GETTING TOGETHER

Once the recombination of the shared genes of two individuals emerged as an adaptation to counter parasites, the advantage it gave to those organisms that do *it* was so dramatic that they were soon more common than the non-sexual reproducers. But one of the great physical complications of sexual reproduction remained: getting the DNA, the genetic material, of one individual together with the DNA of another, to swap genes. As mentioned earlier, the amount of information encoded in DNA is fantastically large, but despite the enormity of its data storage capacity, DNA is itself fantastically small. When DNA is configured for sexual reproduction, it is enclosed in sex cells called gametes; in humans these are referred to as sperm and eggs. It is theorized that in the past early sexual reproducers simply cast their gametes out into the surrounding environment, much as many fish still do, which made it problematic for these cells to find each other (Zimmer, 2001, p. 234).

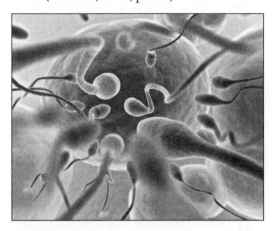

FIGURE 2-2. Sperm carries DNA from the male. The sperm that swims fastest through the acid uterine environment may be the one that penetrates the egg.

A mutation that may have greatly aided the sex cells finding each other was a change in which one gamete was stationary. Like a search party looking for a lost hiker, it is better if the lost person remains in one place, thus making the number of places he or she can possibly be over time fewer, thus increasingly the likelihood of being found. This adaptive mutation, in which one gamete is stationary and the other gamete is an active searcher, helped lay the foundation for the formation of the sexes.

For stationary gametes, size was no longer a critical characteristic, since mobility was not an issue. So when a mutation that endowed the stationary gamete with the capacity to store more nutrients needed for later growth occurred, its lack of movement helped to reinforce this change. This increased nutrient storage capacity resulted in this gamete becoming enormous compared to the gametes that remained mobile. The stationary gametes in humans became what we call eggs.

For the gametes that moved about, size mattered a great deal. The smaller they were, the less energy was required for movement. This allowed them to cover more territory, thus improving the chance they would encounter the egg. So the mutations that would have reduced these sex cells down to mere containers of genetic information were favored. Like track and field athletes they are lean, and in humans, the mobile gametes are a millionth of the size of eggs (Roughgarden, 2009, p. 29). Another important mutation was the increase in their numbers. The bigger the search party is, the greater the likelihood of success. In humans the mobile gametes became tiny and numerous. This is why human sperm are so small and made in such vast numbers.

Among all the sexual reproducers in the world, the closest we can come to a universal definition of the difference between the sexes is this: females make big gametes and males make small gametes (Roughgarden, 2009, p. 23). In humans, the big gametes are the single largest cell in females, and the small ones are so numerous that the sperm produced during the lifetime of one male could easily fertilize every human egg in the world many times over.

The adaptive edge sexual reproduction gives to organisms over the parasites that literally plague them, plus the size differences in gametes, are the starting point of sex and gender. These are the important insights offered by biology's study of the long history of life that helps us begin to understand human gender issues.

7.

What does this all mean?

. . . .

If a person who saw things from an essentialist or a nurture via nature point of view on gender issues could travel back perhaps a billion years—long, long before humans appeared—and confirm the beginnings of sex and of differences in gamete size, that person would probably be awestruck knowing how these two characteristics would play themselves out over the eons. The origin of sex and the sexes is when the intricate dance of life that led to first glances and first dates, to the crying of babies and the effort of child rearing, all began.

OF X AND Y

What does it mean to be female or male?

From a strictly biological frame of reference, males and females are components of a species that each contributes their genes to generate unique offspring. But among the various animals—and plants—that reproduce sexually, there are no hard-and-fast rules that define the characteristics of males and females. In other words, there is no single way of being a male or a female in the plant and animal kingdoms.

There are animals in which the males carry the eggs till they hatch. It is common among plants and some animals to be both male and female sometimes, and one or the other sex at other times (Roughgarden, 2009, pp. 27–28). There are animals in which the male appears to be little more than a tiny clinging parasite attached to an enormous female (Gould, 1983, pp. 26–28). In some species of fish there is more than one form of the male sex (Roughgarden, 2009, p. 78–79). There are female animals that have penis-like organs and there are species in which the male and female are externally indistinguishable (Gould, 1983,

p. 148–150). Sometimes the male is the flashy attractive one while the female is drab and unassuming. Not all males are sexually promiscuous, while some females are so inclined (Roughgarden, 2009, p. 28).

There is no prevailing pattern that orders the characteristics of the sexes among the living things of this world. There are many ways of negotiating the often-complex terrain of survival. What proves adaptive persists, what does not disappears. And apparently in the billions of years that life has existed no single approach to being female or male has ever come to dominate the environment.

The First Nudge: The Recombination of Our Parents' Chromosomes

From the reference point of *human* biology, the elements that contribute to our sense of being a gendered individual are many. Though we are apt to think that the particular genes we acquire from our parents is the sole determiner of gender identity, the reality is much more complicated.

During your development in your mother's womb, you went through five critical stages that greatly contributed to the formation of your particular biological gender identity. If along these stages things had gone a little differently, you might not be your present gender. (You may have noticed that the word *gender* is now being used where in previous paragraphs the term *sex* was used. The reason for this is that we have gone beyond just discussing the simple biological binary of male or female. We have entered the more complex realm of the way in which a person's sex is physically and psychologically expressed in relation to the configuration of a person's genes.)

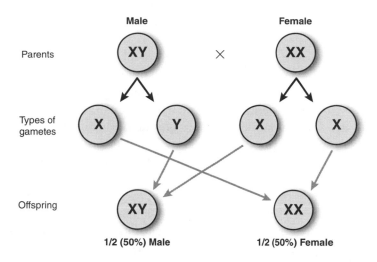

FIGURE 2-3. We either got an XY or an XX from the recombination of our parents' chromosomes.

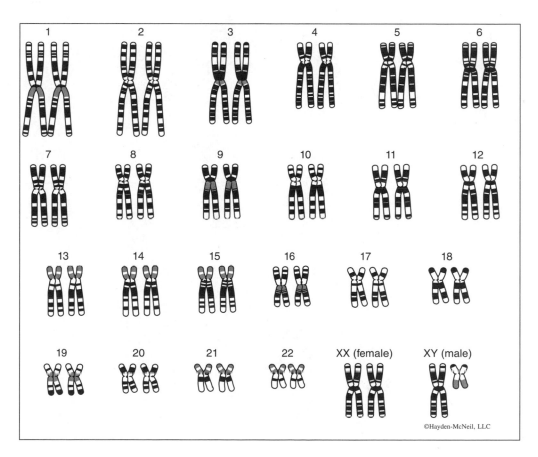

FIGURE 2-4. The 23rd chromosomes are either XX or XY.

Humans have 23 pairs of chromosomes that reside in the nucleus of every cell except in the sex cells, in eggs and sperm, where they are not paired. It is when they become combined with the DNA of another individual that they become paired and form a new combination and conception occurs. You may be aware that among our kind, the 23rd chromosome generally occurs in two versions. Typically, a person has either a pair of X chromosomes or an X and a Y chromosome. (There are other configurations, which will be discussed later.) In humans the XX configuration is designated female and the XY is designated male. If you are interested, there are animals in which the XX is male and the XY is female. This is the case with birds—remember that when you have chicken for dinner next time (Roughgarden, 2009, p. 27). In humans, the father's sperm carry either an X or a Y chromosome for the 23rd chromosome pairing. If the sperm that enters the egg to fertilize it carries an X, the zygote (which is the term for the single cell that results from the union of gametes) has the XX genetic configuration. If the sperm that enters the egg to fertilize it is a Y, the zygote is an XY. Mothers always contribute an X chromosome for the 23rd chromosome pairing. So it might be a good idea to tell the father who is disappointed with the arrival of a son or a daughter, "Dude, it was your contribution to your child's DNA that determined whether the genes of your child was XX or XY."

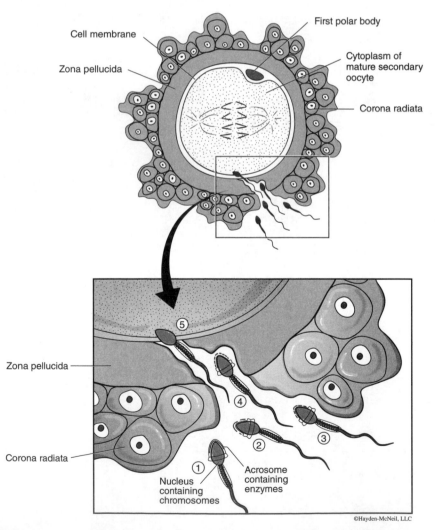

FIGURE 2-5. The act of fertilization: a sperm penetrates the egg. Note how tiny the sperm is compared to the egg in this diagram (in reality, the sperm is even smaller).

The recombination of our parents' genes and the resulting formation of an XX or an XY chromosome is the first nudge we received during our development toward being a specific gender.

ARE WE ALL FEMALE IN THE BEGINNING?

The Second Nudge: The Formation of the Gonads, and The Third Nudge: The Release of Hormones

During the first six weeks of prenatal development we are neither male nor female, though the potential for being either is in our anatomy (Brannon, 2008, p. 78–81). Nevertheless, it is not unusual for some to claim that during this initial period of prenatal development we are all female.

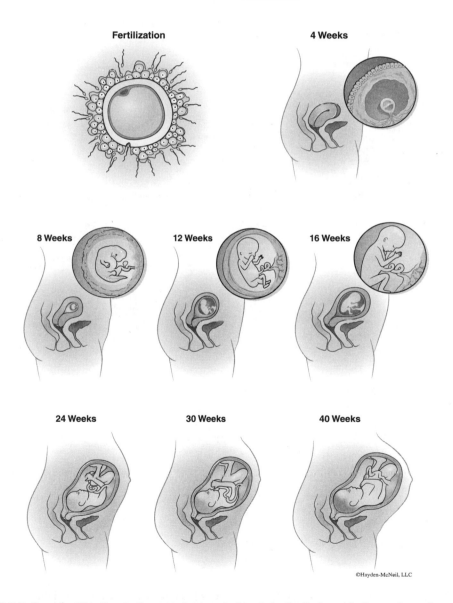

©Hayden-McNeil, LLC

FIGURE 2-6. From fertilization to the germinal period ends in the 2nd week, the embryonic period extends from the 3rd to the 8th week, and the fetal period extends from the 9th to the 40th week.

8.

Have you ever wondered about the claim that we all began life as females?

The reasoning behind the view that we are all initially female is based upon the seeming divergence of male embryos from the main path of development. It all starts six weeks after the formation of the zygote, which is the cell that result from the joining of the two gametes. The presence of a Y chromosome stimulates the development of testes, which are the male gonads (the female gonads are the ovaries), and begins to produce hormones called androgens. Incidentally, the formation of the gonads is the second nudge we receive toward being a particular gender.

The hormones that gonads secrete are powerful biochemicals that influence the body's function and activities. Once the hormones begin to influence the development of the embryo, the third stage of gender development has begun. During this stage of development, androgens are the hormones involved in the formation of male reproductive organs.

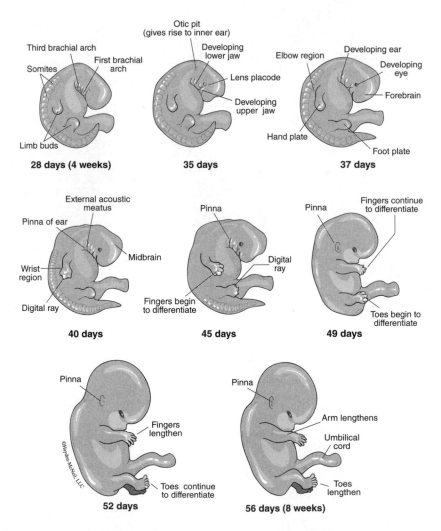

FIGURE 2-7. Week 4 to week 8: The embryonic phase is the most sensitive prenatal developmental period because internal organ development occurs during this time.

The most important of the hormones that are associated with males, as you probably already know, is testosterone. Previous to the time in which exposure to hormones occurs, all human fetuses have organs that have the potential to be male or female. Androgens kick off the sequence of development that promotes what is called the *Wolffian system*, which stimulates the formation of the male pattern of reproductive organs while, at the same time, inhibiting the *Müllerian system*, which is involved in the formation of the female pattern of reproductive organs.

On the other hand, female reproductive organs do not require a significant input of female hormones (you may already know that this is estrogen) to initiate their development. It is this dependence on the introduction of androgens to foster the development of male reproductive organs, and the lack of such a hormonal event to develop the female pattern, that seems to imply that males diverge from a kind of "default" pattern. The default pattern, from this interpretation of early development, would appear to be female.

9.

What do you think? Are we all female during the first few weeks?

This is when the term *gender* first begins to really become relevant from a developmental point of view. The genes of an embryo may indicate a particular sex but its specific embryonic physiology may not necessarily correspond, according to our conventional point of view about what determines gender. At six weeks all embryos have the potential to be either sex, and it is the introduction of male hormones, androgens, that simultaneously stimulates one system that leads to male reproductive organs and the degeneration of another system that would have led to female organs in XY embryos. Does this divergence really indicate that we are all female during the first weeks of prenatal development?

In the biological sciences, the difference between what genes indicate and the way the genes are actually expressed can be significant, and is one of the reasons the terms *genotype* and *phenotype* are used to refer to these differences (Hrdy, 1999). Genotype refers to the genetic characteristics of a particular organism or species, while phenotype refers to the actual physical expression of the genes in the environment.

In the case of humans, during the first six weeks of life, even if our genotype indicates we are male, our phenotype is neither female nor male. Without androgen hormonal introduction, development would continue toward the female reproductive organ pattern. Some argue that this early characteristic of prenatal development is an indication that the default sex is female and that we are all female during the first six-week stage of prenatal development. On the other hand, some would take the position that this is merely a matter of interpretation and that from a biological view there is no default sex since the embryo during the first six weeks displays no single phenotypic sex characteristics. Whichever way this aspect of our earliest weeks of existence is interpreted, it is clear that from the reference point of biology, sex and gender are complex matters.

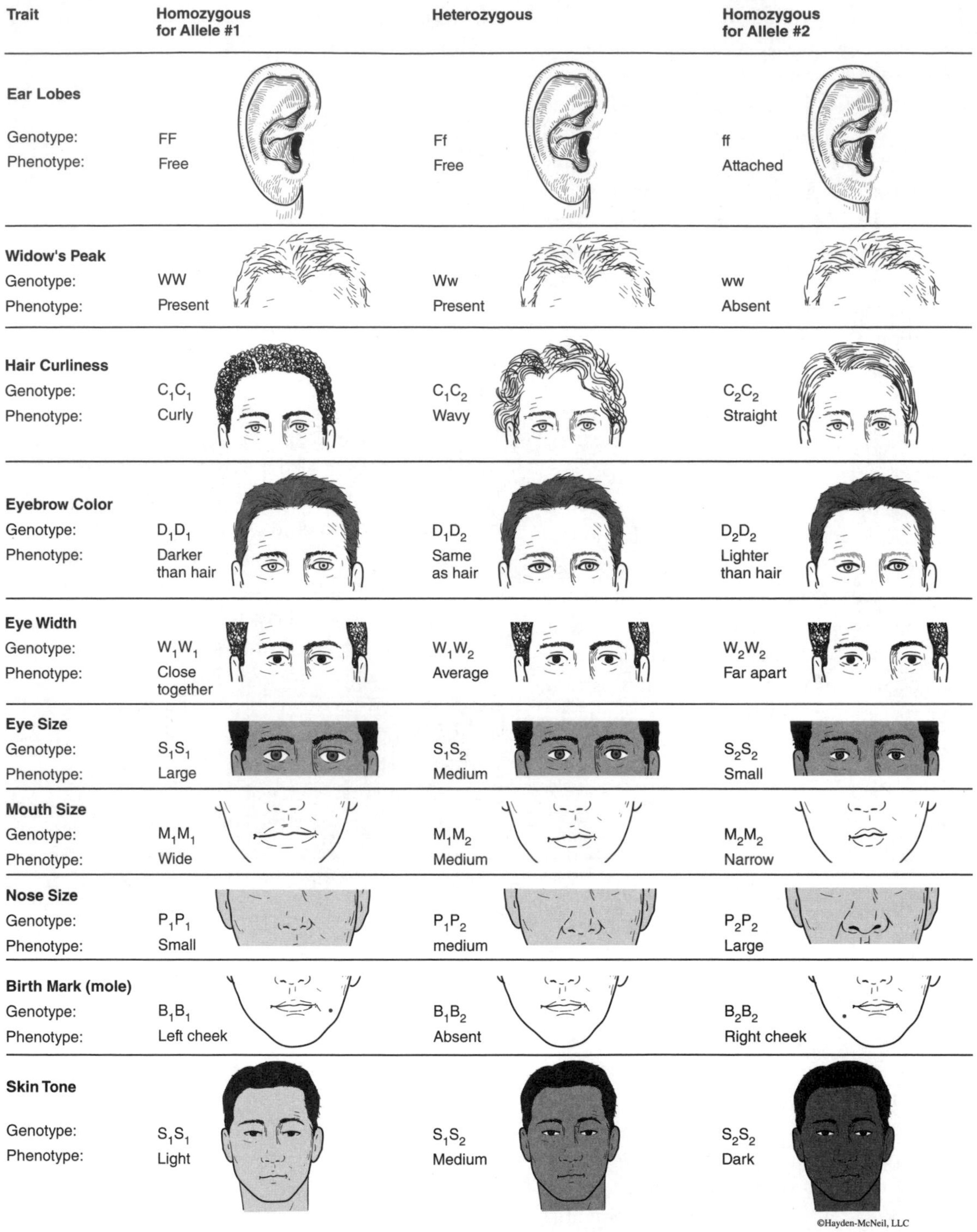

Trait	Homozygous for Allele #1	Heterozygous	Homozygous for Allele #2
Ear Lobes Genotype: Phenotype:	FF Free	Ff Free	ff Attached
Widow's Peak Genotype: Phenotype:	WW Present	Ww Present	ww Absent
Hair Curliness Genotype: Phenotype:	C_1C_1 Curly	C_1C_2 Wavy	C_2C_2 Straight
Eyebrow Color Genotype: Phenotype:	D_1D_1 Darker than hair	D_1D_2 Same as hair	D_2D_2 Lighter than hair
Eye Width Genotype: Phenotype:	W_1W_1 Close together	W_1W_2 Average	W_2W_2 Far apart
Eye Size Genotype: Phenotype:	S_1S_1 Large	S_1S_2 Medium	S_2S_2 Small
Mouth Size Genotype: Phenotype:	M_1M_1 Wide	M_1M_2 Medium	M_2M_2 Narrow
Nose Size Genotype: Phenotype:	P_1P_1 Small	P_1P_2 medium	P_2P_2 Large
Birth Mark (mole) Genotype: Phenotype:	B_1B_1 Left cheek	B_1B_2 Absent	B_2B_2 Right cheek
Skin Tone Genotype: Phenotype:	S_1S_1 Light	S_1S_2 Medium	S_2S_2 Dark

©Hayden-McNeil, LLC

FIGURE 2-8. Genotype refers to genetic traits while phenotype refers to the way the genotype is actually expressed. The chart above illustrates various traits genotype/phenotype relationships.

10.

In terms of gender, how different are we from each other?

A NOTE ABOUT SEX DIFFERENCES

It is not uncommon to hear people say that males are the "opposite" sex of females. And as we will see in a later chapter, this notion of the opposition between the sexes is a relatively recent idea that can be traced back to a Greek philosopher who lived more than two millennia ago (Allen, 1985). But from a biological point of reference—and from the point of view of many cultures—females and males are not opposite in relation to each other but are instead complementary beings. Together they form a greater whole, like the yin and yang symbol found in Asian cultures (Lewis, 1992).

An implication of the complementary nature of the sexes is that they are similar, yet each has their own characteristics. During the third nudge toward a particular gender, prenatal hormone exposure contributes to the differing physical traits of each. It is during this third stage of gender development that *sexual dimorphism* begins to become readily apparent.

11.

What is sexual dimorphism?

From the biological referent, in many animals and plants, the sexes physically differ; that is to say, sexual dimorphism is evident in many species. For example, among our nearest primate relatives, chimpanzees and bonobos, one aspect of sexual dimorphism is readily apparent: the males are larger than the females (Plavcan, 2001). Similarly, we humans are also sexually dimorphic in this way: on average, male humans are slightly larger than females.

What this means is that if you were to randomly select a large sample of people and measure their heights and weights, on average you would find that males are taller and heavier than females. However, as in so many measures used to characterize the sexes, you should have no difficulty finding individuals who do not conform to this generalization. There are many individual women who are taller and heavier than many men. But on average, for example, when you add up the weights of each sex and divide by the number of subjects you measured, males will come out heavier. This is why it is so important to understand what is meant by the generalizations used to describe female/male differences. These statistical measures can tell you something about a sample set of people but it may not necessarily tell you much about the individual, except perhaps in relation to the overall sample. (In other words, it would be pointless to try to accurately determine the height of a male or a female professional basketball player using statistics of height based upon the general public. The best you could do is say that WNBA and NBA players are on average taller.)

12.

What kind of information do statistics provide?

Many physical characteristics that are cited to establish sexual dimorphism in humans are reliant on these statistical measures. The physical size of organs, like the heart and lungs, measures of performance, like running speed or throwing distance, or aptitude in certain academic activities are all analyzed on a statistical basis. There are always individuals who do not fit into the average measures for a particular gender, but the point of recognizing sexual dimorphism is not to claim that one is better than the other, but rather, that there are *on average* differences between the genders.

HORMONES AND THE BRAIN

Besides promoting or inhibiting the development of specific reproductive organs along certain sex patterns, hormones also influence the respective physical and physiological characteristics of male and female fetuses.

13.

Do big heads indicate greater intelligence?

. . . .

One of the organs affected by hormone exposure during prenatal development is the brain. On average males develop slightly larger brains even when taking into account their larger overall body size (Roughgarden, 2009, p. 226). The claim is sometimes made that size equals brainpower, and that men are therefore more intelligent than women. This is a rather simplistic view and fails to take into account the effect the environment has on personal intellectual development even during the months in the womb and certainly in the years that come after birth. Additionally, the functioning of the human brain is awesomely complex, and to imply that its capacities and capabilities can be summarized by so crude a measure as size is ridiculous. And until there is a clear definition of what exactly intelligence is—even psychologists cannot agree among themselves about its nature—such gender generalizations are meaningless (Gould, 1981).

Despite differing hormonal exposures during development in the womb, male and female human brains are quite similar (Roughgarden, 2009, p. 226). It is very difficult to accurately discern the causes of the changes that occur in the brain during prenatal development: do hormones actually cause changes in the brains of male and females or do hormones merely sensitize or prepare brains for changes initiated by environmental stimuli that come after birth? There are certainly differences between male and female brain development in the womb, but how they contribute to gender differences is not entirely clear.*

For example, during the last ten weeks of pregnancy, the presence of testosterone slows the death of nerve cells. When the brain is first forming it is endowed with far more nerve cells than are needed. There is a period when a kind of pruning process takes place in which many of these excess cells die; however, testosterone inhibits the process of cell death. Consequently, females have fewer neurons at birth than males. How this event affects us in the long run and how it relates to differences between males and females is not known (Roughgarden, 2009, p. 228).

Science has only begun to reveal the intricacies of hormones on the developing human brain, and no doubt future research will shed more light on this issue.

BENEATH THE SKIN
The Fourth Nudge: The Development of Female and Male Internal Anatomy

14.

What are the male and female internal reproductive organs?

. . . .

The fourth nudge in the formation of personal gender is the development of the internal organs that characterize female and male anatomy. As noted above, the female reproductive

---

* If you would like to know, the physical differences in male and female brains are: a tiny cluster of cells in the preoptic area of the hypothalamus called the SDN-POA is bigger in males; a minute cluster of nerve cells called the BSTc that is part of the brain called the septum that is associated with sexual function is bigger in males; another tiny cluster of nerve calls called VIP-SCN of unknown function is larger in males; the shape of the corpus callosum, the bridge that connects the hemispheres of the brain, is shaped differently in males and females; and finally, the density of neurons and their connections of the cerebral cortex differ between females and males (Roughgarden, 2009, pp. 226–228).

organs develop from the undifferentiated structures that exist in the fetus at six weeks of age without a surge of hormones. The ovaries, the uterus, the fallopian tubes that connect them, and the upper vagina are the internal female reproductive organs. The male internal reproductive organs are the testes, seminal vesicles, vas deferens, and prostate gland.

APPEARANCES
The Fifth Nudge: The Formation of External Female and Male Anatomy

 15.

What are the male and female external reproductive organs?

. . . .

The fifth prenatal differentiating physical development is the formation of the external sexual organs. For females this entails the formation after the seventh week of the clitoris, urethra, vagina, and labia. For males, between the 8th and 12th week, the penis forms and the scrotum is produced.

Over the millions of years that humans have existed, it is the fifth nudge that has been used as the principal indicator of a person's sex. Indeed, it was the only nudge that our ancestors knew about.

NOTIONS OF NORMALCY AND OTHER NUDGES IN THE WOMB

The five stages (or nudges) in prenatal developed that were described above—the genetic configuration of the zygote, the appearance of gonads, the role of hormones, the formation of internal reproductive organs and the development of external genitalia—all culminate in the cry of "You have a baby girl!" or "You have a baby boy!" on the occasion of a child's birth.

But are these the only factors that determine personal gender while in the womb? Are there other outcomes that can result from the complex interplay of genes, hormones, the environment, and even chance?

The answer is very definitely yes. But before we get to this, a word about points of view is again in order.

It is customary to feel that the five nudge sequence of gender development, as previously described, is the norm and that any deviation from it is abnormal. Indeed, it is generally held by the medical community that this is the correct and desired sequence of sexual differentiation. An unfortunate and unintended consequence of this judgment is that individuals who experience differing prenatal nudges might themselves be regarded as somehow abnormal.

16.

Can you imagine any new variations that might evolve in the future?

. . . .

From the referent of the biological sciences, normal and abnormal are categories created by humans, not nature. Changes that might occur at any stage of gender development are mutations. Granted, most mutations do not appear advantageous, but it is impossible to determine, before a mutation has played itself out over time, which are adaptive and which are not. Think about how unlikely many of our human characteristics are: we don't have claws for hunting or defending ourselves, we're not very fast compared to other animals, we don't reproduce very quickly, childbirth can be extremely dangerous for mother and child, our young take a long time to reach maturity and stay dependent for even longer. Yet the human pattern is adaptive—for now. Changes in the environment can come at any time and can take any form, so judging what is normal or abnormal, beneficial or detrimental is difficult to determine from a strictly biological point of view.

17.

How is "normal" viewed from a social constructivist point of view?

. . . .

From the perspective of social constructivism, the notion of normal and abnormal in gender development are fabricated social categories that may be used to divide individuals into in-groups or out-groups, as allies or aliens. By extension, the interpretation of abnormality could be used to suggest that some individuals are inherently inferior or even defective. In the past, as we will see, whole groups of individuals were classified as inferior or deemed incapable of handling their own affairs because of artificially structured norms (Gould, 1981). As a result, from this view, alternative developmental paths that are deemed deviant may be regarded as an attempt to reinforce existing biases or to create new ones. There is also the matter that in other societies or in other cultural contexts, alternative prenatal gender development may be interpreted in a completely different way. This indicates again that the categories of normal and abnormal are undoubtedly products of prevailing attitudes.

18.

How is "normal" viewed from the epigenetic of nature via nurture point of view?

. . . .

From the epigenetic view, differing prenatal gender development is neither normal nor abnormal. What is interesting is the interaction of nature (the particular gender identity that emerges out of the nudges the individual receives in the womb) and nurture (the cultural and physical environment in which the individual lives). The mix of these two aspects of an individual's life is a dynamic process whose outcome cannot be predicted and whose value to humanity cannot be ascertained in advance.

Also within the purview of the nature via nurture perspective is the historical question of why certain norms or views about variations in gender development are established in the first place.

This is one of the instances in which the three perspectives on gender issues discussed in this book are in general agreement: notions of normalcy are cultural creations.

GENETIC/GONAD VARIATIONS

But to return to the matter of prenatal sex development and factors that can affect gender identity formation: there are variations in genes, gonad development, hormonal variations, and the formation of internal and external reproductive organs.

To begin at the chromosomal level, the XX and XY genotype of the 23rd chromosome are not the only configurations that can occur. At this initial, fundamental level of development in the womb, many of the alternative chromosomal arrangements that occur are highly disadvantageous to the fetus and can result in complications and disabilities that affect not only the reproductive organs but also patterns of growth and intellectual development. At this stage of gender formation, when genotypes significantly differ from the XX and XY configuration, it could be argued that socially constructed notions of detriment to the individual correspond with some of the outcomes that follow.

19.

Can an individual have an unpaired sex chromosome?

. . . .

On occasion a zygote does not have an XX or an XY, but only one X. This is known as Turner's syndrome and the notation for this gene configuration is X0 (X zero). Possessing only a female gene, the fetus appears to follow the female configuration; however, functioning ovaries do not form and there are subtle variations in the brains of X0 individuals (Sybert et al., 2004). At birth, infants with Turner's syndrome appear female. Over time, without ovaries that produce estrogen, these individuals do not sexually mature. Estrogen can be administered to these individuals, which makes them appear female, but they will not be able to have children.

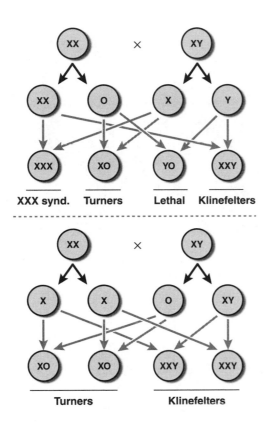

FIGURE 2-9. The formation of XXX, X0, Y0, and XXY genotypes is illustrated.

There also are females who have three Xs. In the womb, these individuals develop as females. Sometimes difficulties result from the XXX genotype, which adversely affect later intellectual development. However, sometimes these individuals do not experience any problems. After reaching sexual maturity, some of these women have irregular periods or do not menstruate at all. The latter are unable to have

children. However, some XXX women experience no difficulty having children (Brannon, 2008, p. 88).

There are individuals with four, even five, X chromosomes. The incidence of severe developmental difficulties is common among these females. Most are disabled and unable to have children.

20.

What does an XXY genotype indicate?

Some zygotes form from two gametes with an XXY configuration. Known as Klinefelter's syndrome, the XXY configuration is the most frequently occurring sex gene variation, with this genotype occurring on average once in every thousand among the general population (Bock, 1993). Individuals with the XXY genotype appear male internally and externally; however, their testes are small and usually do not produce sperm, consequently making them sterile. They may suffer from developmental disabilities. During puberty, breasts may develop and their overall body may appear to follow the feminine pattern.

There are individuals with XXXY and XXXXY genotypes. Severe skeletal, reproductive organ, and developmental disabilities result from these variations.

There are individuals who possess one X and two Y chromosomes. This is Jacob's syndrome. These XYY genotype individuals were once thought to be excessively aggressive males due to the presence of two male Y chromosomes. However, further research has revealed that this is not the case, though developmental disabilities are more common among XYY individuals (Brannon, 2008, p. 88). Learning disabilities and delayed emotional maturity are common symptoms of Jacob's syndrome. These males are usually tall, thin, and often suffer speech and reading difficulties. Many XYY males are fertile. This particular gene configuration occurs in about one out of a thousand male births (Kim et al. 2013, p. 188–196).

21.

Are there XX males and XY females?

· ·

There are also variations that occur within the chromosomes themselves, rather than the appearance of extra copies of X or Y in the 23rd chromosome, as in de la Chapelle's syndrome. Here an individual has the XX female genotype but has the phenotype of a male (Vorona et al., 2007). This happens when the father's contribution of an X chromosome (remember, it is the father's sperm that determines the sex of the zygote) has the active genes of a Y chromosome in it. So despite the presence of two Xs in these individuals' genes, these individuals develop as males. According to research findings, these XX males usually have small testes and are sterile (de la Chapelle, 1972). These individuals develop breasts, female pubic hair pattern on their bodies, display little beard growth, are tall in stature, and have no sex drive. Approximately one in twenty thousand individuals has this genetic trait.

If there are XX males, then are there XY females? Yes. In Swyer's syndrome an individual has the XY male genotype and is female in appearance (Michala et al., 2008). A range of different genes on the Y chromosome may not activate the formation of fetal testes; as a result, no androgens are produced. As mentioned earlier, the absence of androgens causes embryonic development to follow the female pattern. Individuals with Swyer's syndrome appear female at birth and are often not determined to have the male genotype until puberty when they do not begin to have their period and do not develop mature female physical characteristics, like breasts and widening hips. These individuals can receive hormone replacement

therapy to promote the development of mature female physical characteristics; however, without ovaries (because of the XY genotype), these individuals do not produce eggs.

22.

Can a person have more than one genotype?

· ·

FIGURE 2-10. This is an example of mosaic art. Made of several different colored pieces, an image emerges from differing components. Similarly, a person can be whole yet made of different genotypes.

Now if all these variations weren't complicated enough, hold on to the concept of genotype in your thoughts as we consider mosaicism. Mosaic genes are what the name suggests: the populations of cells within the body have different genotypes, thus forming a mosaic (Conlin et al., 2010). Individuals with mosaic genes may have XX genes and XY genes present in the cells of their bodies. After the formation of the zygote (the fertilized egg), cell division occurs as it grows. Different configurations of the sex genes can result during cell division, thus generating two different sex genotypes. Such individuals possess both such genotypes. How these individuals appear at birth varies according to the particular manifestation of physical development unique to that individual that the genes initiate.

23.

Can a person be a fusion of two separate eggs in the womb?

. . . .

And then there is chimerism. In this condition, two separate fertilized eggs fuse to form a single individual (Conlin et al., 2010). If these two fertilized eggs have different genotypes for sex (one is XX and one is XY), depending at what stage of development the fusion occurs, it may be possible that the embryo will develop ambiguous reproductive organs or develop the genitals of both sexes, either as ovary and testes or as an ovotestes (a gonad with the characteristics of both ovary and testes).

SUMMARIZING ALL THE GENETIC VARIATIONS

To summarize, X0, XXX, XXXX, XXXXX, XXY, XXXY, XXXXY, and XYY (an egg cannot develop with only a single Y chromosome) are all genotypic variations of the most frequently occurring genotypes of XX and XY. Swyer's and de la Chapelle's syndromes result from mutations within the X or Y genes, while mosaicism and chimerism indicate the presence of more than one genotype in an individual. From the point of view of most of the individuals with these genotypes, and of the medical community, as we have seen, these variations in the sex chromosomes are often not advantageous. They all produce complications at the very least and serious disabilities at worst, but it does not serve the interests or the humanity of these individuals to be labeled with socially constructed terms like abnormal or deviant. Rather, it would be best to use our understanding of the genetic nature of these variations in order to accept these individuals for who they are, and in a manner that upholds their dignity.

GENETIC/ENZYME VARIATION

There is a genetically determined gender variation caused by a deficiency in an enzyme called 5-alpha-reductase. An enzyme is a biochemical synthesized from information in the DNA that regulates chemical reactions in the body. This enzyme deficiency affects the development of male external genitalia in male fetuses (Thiele et al., 2005). At birth, individuals with this variation may have either male external reproductive organs, or ambiguous (not clearly male or female) genitals, or female genitals. They are born with male gonads but usually follow the female physical pattern during prenatal development. Consequently, many of these individuals are not identified at birth as males and are raised as females. During puberty, these individuals respond to the increased presence of androgens (the male hormones) and develop male physical characteristics. Individuals born with ambiguous genitals tend to have either an enlarged clitoris or a small penis. Most individuals who have the 5-alpha-reductase enzyme condition are capable of producing sperm, though their internal and external reproductive organs may not be suitable for intercourse. These genetically male individuals, though they are often unintentionally raised as females, usually have a sense of being males and often later develop male gender identities (Brannon, 2008, p. 90).

HORMONAL VARIATIONS

As complicated as gender variation is at the genetic stage, at the hormonal stage of prenatal gender formation, the relationship between genotype and phenotype begins to grow even more complex.

24.

Consider how hormones affect the relationship between genotype and phenotype.

· ·

As was discussed earlier, the presence of testosterone is crucial to the formation of the male pattern in fetuses with XY chromosomes. The testosterone in this circumstance is produced by the fetus's own testes. There are situations, however, in which XX fetuses (who are therefore genetically female) may be exposed to testosterone. A variation called *congenital adrenal hyperplasia* (CAH) can occur when the adrenal glands of the female fetus produces excessive amounts of testosterone (Brannon, 2008, p. 89). This results in what is termed the "masculinization" of female external genitals; specifically, the clitoris appears to develop into a small penis. In addition to affecting this anatomical feature of the female fetus, research indicates that the brain may also be altered by exposure to androgens (male hormones).

Parents of girls born with this variation in prenatal hormonal exposure are very often advised by their physicians to have their infant daughters undergo surgery to make their genitals conform to socially accepted norms. However, such procedures are not without risks, as nerve damage resulting from surgery may impair later clitoral function.

In the case of CAH, if the genotype of the individual is female, the phenotype, in terms of the appearance of external genitalia, may at birth be unclear or ambiguous. Research also suggests that during childhood, girls with CAH are more inclined to engage in play behavior typically associated with boys.

From the social constructivist perspective, these claims are of little value because concepts like "play typical of boys" and even "heterosexuality" are social conventions and may not be the result of genes or hormones. Additionally, from this view, it is difficult to determine if the behavior of CAH females are the result of prenatal hormonal exposure or due to socialization during their childhoods. Just because there might be a correlation between play behavior and the appearance of ambiguous genitalia at birth associated with CAH does not establish a link of causation.

Another hormonal variation is *androgen insensitivity syndrome* (Hughes, et al., 2006). This occurs when an XY genotype male has cells whose receptors are insensitive to androgens (male hormones). As a consequence of this variation the bodily cells of the fetus do not respond to the presence of the androgens that are produced by the testes, thus the formation of the male pattern does not occur (Brannon, 2008, p. 89–90). As you may recall, no infusion of hormones is required for the female body pattern to develop in the womb. Such individuals are genetically male, but at birth, their phenotype is female. The internal reproductive organs, however, are not female since the testes did form, though these organs remain in the body, unlike the male pattern of being located in the external genitals.

Individuals who are androgen insensitive usually go undetected at birth and through childhood. These individuals are perceived as female from birth and are raised as girls, though they are genetically male. Only at puberty does it become apparent that their genotype and phenotype do not correspond. With no ovaries, menstruation cannot occur. Additionally, androgens affect the growth of pubic hair, and being insensitive to these hormones, these individuals never grow any such hair. The testes do however produce some estrogen to which these individuals are not insensitive, which contributes to the development of breasts.

A gynecological examination would quickly reveal the absence of internal reproductive organs. Since there is no way to sensitize these individuals to androgens, there is no medical intervention that can match genotype to phenotype. Also, after years of being raised as girls and being socialized as females, these individuals find it difficult to conceive of themselves as males. Research indicates that over time these individuals typically live their lives as women and regard themselves as such even though they have the XY male genotype.

25.

How do all these variations affect the concept of male and female?

. . . .

ARE THERE MORE THAN TWO SEXES?

During this discussion of the variations in the nudges that an individual can receive during development in the womb, you may have begun to wonder if there is anything really definitive about the concepts of male and female. Is our sex and sense of gender really a simple matter of genes? If so, what does it mean, for example, to have a male genotype but have a female phenotype? Should we draw the line at the level of the X and Y chromosomes and declare that this determines sex? But what about X chromosomes that act like Y chromosomes? Should we make a judgment and define one form of these chromosomes as "normal"? Should we discount the effect that gonads and hormones have on the formation of gender? Should we even trust the appearance of a newborn's external genitalia as a true indication of its sex? If not, does this mean that a genetic test should be done on every child? And what if the results are ambiguous—how then should sex be defined?

This is where science, medicine, and culture come charging at each other. Particularly the cultural dimension impresses its demands on the matter of defining gender. People want to know where they stand. Whether we like it or not, our identity is fundamentally structured around our sense of being a gendered person.

Keep in mind that many of the opinions held by the general public about what is male and female are based upon views that developed long, long ago. For most of human history, the only way people could discern the sex of a newborn was through visual or behavioral cues. The general size and shape of a newborn's body, the presence of genitals that characterized male or female, the child's overall behavior and disposition these were the ways in which the sex of the young was ascertained over countless millennia.

©Hayden-McNeil, LLC

FIGURE 2-11. Gregor Mendel, 1822–1884, the father of genetic science.

Only very recently with the rise of science, modern medical practice, and most crucially, our knowledge of genetics and evolution, have deep insights into the complex nature of sex and gender emerged. The first groundbreaking publication of genetic research, done by a monk named Gregor Mendel, dates back to only 1866, and at that time his work was not understood, much less appreciated (Bronowski, 1973). We have known about the actual structure of DNA, in which information about the workings of the body are encoded, only since the 1950s (Watson, 1968). Much of the research into the genetic and hormonal nature of the variations in sex formation is at most only a few decades old. And even then, there is still much more study and research that needs to be done in order to fully encompass the biological foundations of sex and gender.

However, understanding the ancient origins of our conventions about sex and gender does not justify the discrimination, the negative stigmas, and the violence suffered by individuals who did not fit into generally accepted views of gender. In our legal system, ignorance is not an excuse. On the other hand, it must be acknowledged that it takes time for new knowledge to settle into the collective conscious of the general populace and affect its outlook. Our socially constructed definitions of male and female, and of gender in general, have not kept pace with the rapid rate of scientific discovery.

Researchers who study the phenomena of variations in sex formation claim that among the general populace of any human society, individuals who possess the genetic and anatomical characteristics of both male and female may constitute anywhere between .37 to 4 percent of the population (Asma, 2011). That means that over the course of a typical day (or among your many Facebook friends), you may very possibly have at least passing contact with individuals who are *intersex*.

Intersex is the term used to describe individuals who, because of their genes, their exposure to certain hormones during prenatal development, or some other factor, were born with intermediate forms of, or some combination of, the physical characteristics that conventionally differentiate males and females. Many of these individuals do not identify themselves as female or male; they are in fact from a biological perspective neither one nor the other, but are a third sex (ISNA.com).

For quite some time the medical community has approached this matter by advising parents of intersex children to have the physical appearance of their children's external

reproductive organs surgically altered. The purpose of this procedure is to ensure that these children would be viewed as "normal" as they grow to maturity (Diamond, et al., 1997). The underlying assumption was that newborns are not born with an innate sense of being a specific gender; in other words, babies are blank slates who are taught to be whatever gender the surrounding society instructs them to be. This is social constructivism applied to childhood gender development. Consequently, if, for example, a boy is made into a girl because he has ambiguous genitals, he can be socialized to possess a female gender identity.

26.

Do we possess an inborn (essentialist) sense of personal gender?

However, a problem may arise if the individual does not feel that the sex assignment or reassignment received in early childhood corresponds with the gender identity that is felt by that individual to be the authentic one. And it is here—at the intersection of psyche and body—that much of the controversy that surrounds the issue of gender assignment as well as the larger issue of gender development itself originates. Is there an unchanging, inborn, essential gender identity that we each possess? Or is our gender identity a product of the circumstances in which we live?

As in so many aspects of our lives, things are changing so rapidly around us that it is difficult to keep up. Knowing how complex the prenatal nudges are that contribute to our gender biology, how should we order our understanding of this important part of every individual's personal sense of self?

This is the challenge of gender studies in a changing world.

SUGGESTED DOCUMENTARY

National Geographic. (2006). *The Biology of Prenatal Development*. www.nationalgeographic.com

SUGGESTED READING

Le Guin, Ursula K. (1969) *The Left-Hand of Darkness*. New York: Ace.

REFERENCES

Allen, S. P. (1985). *The concept of woman: the aristotelian revolution, 750 b.c.-a.d. 1250*. Grand Rapids, MI: Eerdmans. pp. 119–121.

Asma, S. T. (2011). "Gauging gender." *The Chronicle of Higher Education*. October 30, 2011.

Bock, R. (1993). "Understanding klinefelter's syndrome: a guide for XXY males and their families." National Institutes of Health, 93–3203.

Brannon, L. (2008). *Gender: psychological perspectives*. Boston: Pearson.

Conlin, L. K., Thiel, B. D., Bonneman, C. G., Medne, L., Ernst, L. M., Zackai, E. H., Deardorff, M. A., Hakonarson, H., & Spinner, N. B. (2010). "Mechanisms of mosaicism, chimerism and uniparental disomy identified by single nucleotide polymorphism array analysis." *Human Molecular Genetics*, 19 (7), January 6, 2010, pp. 1263–1275.

de la Chapelle, A. (1972). "Analytic review: nature and origin of males with XX sex chromosomes." *American Journal of Human Genetics*. 24(1), January 1972. pp. 71–105.

Diamond, M. & Sigmundson, K. (1997). "Sex reassignment at birth: a long term review and clinical implications." *Archives of Pediatrics and Adolescent Medicine*. 151, March 1997.

Gould, S. (1981). *The mismeasure of man*. New York: W. W. Norton.

Gould, S. (1983). *Hen's teeth and horse's toes: further reflections in natural history*. New York: W. W. Norton.

Gould, S. (1989). *Wonderful life: the burgess shale and the nature of history*. New York: W. W. Norton. p. 310.

Hrdy, S. B. (1999). *Mother nature: a history of mothers, infants, and natural selection*. New York: Pantheon. p. 55.

Hughes, I. A. & Deeb, A. (2006). "Androgen resistance." *Best Practice & Research Clinical Endrocrinology & Metabolism*. 20 (4), December 2006, pp. 577–598.

Intersex Society of North America. ISNA. com

Kim, I. W., Khadilkar, A. C., Ko, E. Y., Sabanegh, E. S. Jr (2013). 47, *XYY Syndrome and Male Infertility*. Rev Urol. 15: 188–196.

Lewis, D. M. (1992). *Millennium: tribal wisdom and the modern world*. New York: Viking. pp. 131–133.

Michala, L., Goswami, D., Creighton, S. M., Conway, G. S. (2008). "Swyer syndrome: presentation and outcomes." *BJOG An International Journal of Obstetrics and Gynaecology*. 115, pp. 737–742.

Plavcan, J. M. (2001). "Sexual dimorphism in primate evolution." *American Journal of Physical Anthropology*. Supplement 33, pp. 25–53.

Ridley, M. (1993). *The red queen: sex and the evolution of human nature*. New York: MacMillan. pp. 66–87.

Roughgarden, J. (2009). *Evolution's rainbow*. Berkeley, University of California Press.

Sybert, V. P. & McCauley, E. (2004). "Turner's syndrome." *New England Journal of Medicine*. 351, September 16, 2004, pp. 1227–1238.

Thiele, S., Hoppe, U., Holterhus, P.-M., Hiort, O. (2005). "Isoenzyme type 1 of 5alpha-reductase is abundantly transcribed in normal human genital skin fibroblasts and may play an important role in masculinization of 5-alpha-reductase type 2 deficient males." *European Journal of Endocrinology*. 152, June 1, 2005, pp. 875–880.

Tuchman, B. (1978). *A distant mirror: the calamitous 14th century*. New York: Knopf. pp. 92–125.

Tudge, C. (2000). *The variety of life: a survey and a celebration of all the creatures that have ever lived*. Oxford: Oxford University Press. pp. 550–551.

Vorona, E., Zitzmann, M., Gromoli, J., Schüring, A & Nieschlag, E. (2007).

"Clinical, and epigenetic features of the 46, XX male syndrome, compared with 47, XXY klinefelter partients." *Journal of Clinical Endrocrinology & Metabolism*. September 1, 2007, 92, no. 9.

Watson, J. D. (1968). *The double helix*. New York: Atheneum.

Zimmer, C. (2001). *Evolution: the triumph of an idea*. New York: Harper Collins.

Name   Date

1. What do parasites and the origin of sexual reproduction have to do with each other?

2. Why is reproduction through cloning so disadvantageous?

3. What are gametes?

4. What is a zygote?

5. What are the five prenatal nudges that contribute to the formation of a person's sex and gender?

6.   What are the typical genetic configurations for females and males?

7.   What are hormones?

8.   Define genotype.

9.   Define phenotype.

10. What is sexual dimorphism?

11. What is Turner's syndrome?

12. What is Kleinfelter's syndrome?

13. What is Jacob's syndrome?

14. What is Swyer's syndrome?

15. What is de la Chapelle's syndrome?

3

Chapter 3

How WE KNOW

The Scientific Method

Observation or Question
what where, when, why, how)

↓

Tentative Explanation
(hypothesis)

↓

Testable Prediction

Why is the desire to have sex so strong at the time in your life you are told you are not ready to have sex? Why do "pig" and "bitch" get yelled when anyone says something about relationships that someone else does not agree with? What is up with girls kissing each other at parties? What is up with guys being such jerks? At a time when everyone is supposed to be conscious of women's rights and feminism, why is pornography more common than ever? Why do girls hate it when guys stare at an attractive girl and guys hate it when girls talk about guys with money? Whatever happened to all that talk about being a good person and having a nice personality?

Double standards and triple standards, unequal rights and privileges, overt power and covert power, "no" in public and "yes" in private—many people would say that none of it makes any sense, all of it is hypocritical and is just plain stupid. Frustration, angst, despair, and outright anger are frequently present when people talk about the conflicts that often come with trying to get some happiness in their lives.

Are these feelings familiar to you?

· ·

It seems all so complicated and confusing.

How did it come to this? Can the behavioral sciences really say anything meaningful about gender issues that often generate so much bad feeling, so much hostility, in so many people? Is there any way of cutting through all the arguments and disagreements and get to some kind of truth?

Let's try.

In psychology books, among the opening chapters there is usually a section about something called methodology. In other words, an explanation is offered about the techniques used by people who study the way we behave to make sense of what is going on inside our minds.

For many people, reading about how psychological research is done is not particularly interesting. The scientific method, hypothesis formation, rules of investigation, have a formality to them that stands in stark contrast to the way we make sense of things in our day-to-day lives. So perhaps more insight can be gained about the whole process of understanding gender issues by examining not just the most recently developed methods. We need to also consider the more conventional ways we humans comprehended the world.

THE PAST THAT IS STILL PRESENT

We may think of ourselves as fully up-to-date, modern (or postmodern) individuals, adept at wielding the latest technology, knowledgeable about leading-edge ways of thinking and behaving. But no matter how recently our mental software (to borrow a concept from computer science) has been updated, the past always forms a foundation upon which the present rests. For example, though we may be aware of cutting-edge trends in what to wear, the transactions we engage in to purchase what we want are based upon concepts of exchange and trade that date back thousands of years (Cameron, 1989). The wireless connections we rely upon to text and talk with others and that we use to buy things are still relatively new, but the basic physics behind it have been known since the nineteenth century (Harman, 1998). And when gender-related issues are considered, the basis for the attitudes and conventions that we still live with date back literally hundreds of thousands, if not millions of years (Maybury-Lewis, 1992; Stringer et al., 2012, pp. 208–229).

Indeed, it can be argued that one of the reasons we have such strong feelings about gender matters—about interacting as males or females or, more recently, as intersex individuals with others—stems from the fact that we humans have been living together and relying upon each other for survival for as long as our species has existed. So long, in fact, that we are not aware of the original reasons and motivations that formed the basis for our notions of being gendered individuals. In other words, many of the conventions we take for granted about gender matters are like echoes from the past, when people lived in ways quite unlike the way we do today.

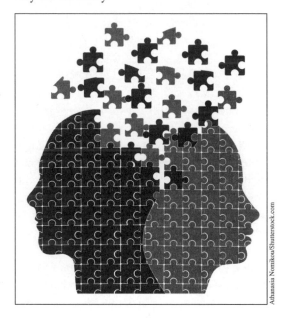

FIGURE 3-1. The past still influences the future.

OLD WAYS OF KNOWING

Your parents grew up without mobile communications devices. Your grandparents can remember when black and white television pictures were the norm and color TV was a novelty. Your great-grandparents lived at a time when war raged over the entire world and the most high tech thing they might have in their home was a radio or a record player. If you go back even further into the past, your forebears lived without electric light or indoor plumbing. They never encountered anything made of plastic. They were considered elderly when they were forty years old.

2.

Can you imagine what it "felt" like to live in the world your grandparents knew, or for that matter, the world of your distant ancestors?

• •

If you look back more than ten thousand years, there wasn't a single city in the entire world yet. Money did not exist. The most common "high tech" things the average person might have were digging sticks, needles made of bone, and stone arrowheads and axes. There was no writing, so people had to rely upon their memory for data storage.

When you cast your thoughts back to a period when there were no cities, you have passed an important threshold. Before this time people lived with a worldview that did not commonly feature what we call scientific thought. When you get into an argument with someone today and try to use reason with that person to make a point to support your position, you are using a way of thinking logically that had not been formalized until about two and a half thousand years ago.

FIGURE 3-2. Many features of our lives are relatively new: traffic jams are a very recent phenomenon.

We humans have been around in our various forms for millions of years, and only during less than the last one percent of our collective existence have we had available to us what we can call structured rational thought (Burke, 1985, pp. 42–44). How then did we function mentally for almost all of the history of humanity? The old ways of responding to the environment can be glimpsed every time a commercial comes into view.

Watch a political ad on television or on the Internet, and images and statements will be presented in such a way that feelings will emerge within you. If the ad is done well you may feel a rush of anger ("my opponent is an advocate of what you despise"), a wave of fear ("you will lose everything if my opponent is elected"), a twinge of nausea or disgust ("my opponent is not like you"), or perhaps feelings of patriotism and sympathy for a particular candidate ("he or she fought for our freedom"). If you see an advertisement for a car you may feel excitement or desire or envy ("this baby will take your neighbors' breath away"). Notice how pizza commercials aired at night make you feel hungry ("extra cheese on a warm bread crust"). Observe your reaction to such advertising carefully, and very likely you will notice not an intellectual reaction within your mind but an emotional one in your gut.

3.

Can you recall a commercial that motivated you to get the product it was pitching? Remember how you felt?

. . . .

Advertisers have known for a long time that the way to effectively connect with a targeted audience of consumers or voters is to produce an emotional reaction within viewers. Observe your own reaction to a political ad that states, "My administration will focus on raising industrial output and improving levels

of employment, thus obviating the need for continued intervention from central banks." Or consider an ad for a car that stated, "The hybrid engine in this vehicle is designed to minimize carbon emissions." Dull thud, and the reason you are likely to respond in this manner, despite the fact that both of these statements are actually much more informative than the short emotion-inducing quips in the previous paragraph, is because thinking analytically about "raising industrial output" does not come as easily as emotionally reacting to "you will lose everything." Feelings emerge without effort. Thinking in a systematic manner is work. This is why, while reading this, there is very likely a part of you that would much rather be texting or talking, shopping, or playing a video game. Your interest naturally gravitates to activities that effortlessly produce feelings, rather than doing the hard slog of interpreting words and assimilating their meaning.

Don't feel bad; this is natural. It is a consequence of the long history of our kind. For millions of years our ancestors lived without the benefit of the kind of logical thought that underlies the law, or high technology, or democratic government. Thinking about things in a systematic, logical manner—in the way of the sciences—is such a new way of using our intellects that it still requires concentration and effort. In a lot of ways it is like the difference between speaking and reading. Speech comes easily. Reading, on the other hand, takes years to learn and requires constant practice. Again, this is natural. We humans have been gabbing away for much longer than we have been scribbling. Verbal communication probably dates back hundreds of thousands, maybe millions, of years, while the oldest known writing is only a few thousand years old (Pinker, 1994).

4.

Be honest! Would you rather be talking to friends or reading a book right now?

· ·

FIGURE 3-3. For some people, reading and learning are enjoyable activities.

The old ways of responding to our environment are still very much with us. Indeed, we are still more inclined to react with feelings than we are with reasoned analysis. And this is certainly true when it comes to issues relating to human relations and gender matters.

FUNCTIONAL FEELINGS?

But let's not diss feelings. Emotions have served—and continue to serve—humanity well. Feelings motivate us. They often focus our attention on matters that are crucial to our well-being. They make us aware of hazards in our surroundings as well as opportunities to improve our lives. When was the last time you were deeply moved to consider the suitability of your community based upon statistical measures of income distribution or property valuation? But if you saw foreclosure sale signs spring up all over an increasingly vacant neighborhood or a series of shootings and robberies on your block, you would probably feel some urgency about reevaluating your living situation.

The old way of interpreting the world around us is still adaptive. The problem is that this way of relating to our surroundings is not very effective when dealing with new developments or with complexity.

FIGURE 3-4. A same-sex couple getting married on the beach.

WHAT!

Same-sex marriage is a hot button topic these days. Very strongly polarized views dominate the debate that surrounds this issue. Some individuals argue that marriage should be strictly limited to a union between a man and a woman. Others argue that such limits undermine the dignity and rights of same-sex couples who want their relationships accorded the same legal status as traditional unions. A wide variety of legal, ethical, religious, cultural, social, psychological, and biological claims are put forward to support both positions.

At the heart of this debate, however, are strongly felt convictions about what should or should not be regarded as normal. In Western cultures, the tradition that views marriage as the basis for the foundation of family dates back to its beginnings more than two thousand years ago, which are based upon traditions that are older still (Veyne, 1987). The notion of marriage based upon romantic love, upon ties of affection, between two consenting individuals as we currently view marriage in the West, however, is a convention that is much more recent, going back only a few hundred years (L'Hermite-Leclercq, 1992; Maybury-Lewis, 1992, pp. 94–100). Before this time most marriages were arranged between two families, or the individuals involved in the union viewed it as a bond more concerned with economic issues of labor, inheritance, and survival than of ties based on love. The feelings of the individuals involved in the arranged marriage were often secondary considerations. In the past, when most people worked as farmers and shepherds, creating a labor force that could assist in the tending of fields and the care of livestock meant having many children was a priority. Thus, reproduction was central to marriage and family.

FIGURE 3-5. Bridal decoration from a Hindu arranged wedding.

Today, most people in the West react very negatively toward the practice of arranged marriage with overt concern for economic matters. Self-determination and personal freedom of choice are central to our notion of how interpersonal relationships should be structured. Many women and men are also repelled by the focus placed upon reproduction in such arrangements, with its apparent view of females in such traditional relationships as being little more than baby-machines.

And rightly so, for we in the West now live in a legal context in which the right of the individual to freedom of choice is almost never questioned and rarely challenged. Looked upon from a cultural perspective, the power of the individual today, irrespective of sex or gender, is so great that the personal right to choose takes priority over almost everything. This is remarkable compared to what has been the norm for most of human history.

FIGURE 3-6. Even today, most people struggle to eke out a living from the soil.

For most of the history of Western civilization, only a tiny minority of individuals—principally landowning males—had many of the rights that we take for granted. For the vast majority of women *and* men, life was a constant struggle against cold and hunger, disease and poverty. Freedom of choice and of self-determination simply did not figure into their lives. Until the Industrial Revolution a little more than a couple of centuries ago, nearly everyone eked out a living as peasant farmers trying to grow enough to eat (Nasar, 2011). In an agricultural setting, good soil, steady sources of water, good weather, and labor were the immediate ingredients for survival. Of these, about the only element that pre-industrial agriculturalists had any control over was labor. And this meant that large families were desired.

From a purely economic point of view, combined with religious doctrine, it can be argued that these are the motivating rationales that underwrote the traditional marital configuration of a man and a woman. In the West, until very recently, reproduction was central to marriage and essential to survival.

However, when changes occurred in the economic and cultural environment, the old ways and the new innovations that sprang from those changes clashed. Beginning in the last century, advances in health care lowered the infant mortality rate, mechanization altered the nature of labor, and the cost of raising children rose significantly. These changes, and many others, drastically reduced the incentive to have large families. So profound have these changes been that having children is no longer necessarily a priority in relationships anymore. Add to this mix the right of individuals to assert their own personal desires for happiness and fulfillment, and we enter a radically altered environment. And in this new context, marriage takes on new characteristics.

FIGURE 3-7. Industrial workers rioting for better wages and living conditions in 1868. Their efforts helped create the world we know today.

The problem is that our worldviews, and the emotional attachment we have to them, take time to change. Indeed, for those individuals whose sense of what is normal and acceptable was established before these changes occurred, it is disorienting and disturbing. The ground upon which the foundations of normalcy and morality are based feels as though it is losing its substance.

FIGURE 3-8. Can a person be happy without having children? Is happiness found living in a house in the suburbs?

Another factor that intensifies the clash of the old and the new is the sheer velocity of change today. Everything is being altered by the application of powerful new technologies and even more powerful new ideas. For example, we have gone from brick-and-mortar mom-and-pop stores to bustling malls to Internet shopping in just a few decades. When was the last time you went to a store that sold only new music recordings? Think about cash. How regularly do you buy things with paper bills or metal coins anymore? And these are just the obvious mundane changes that have come about in the last decade or so.

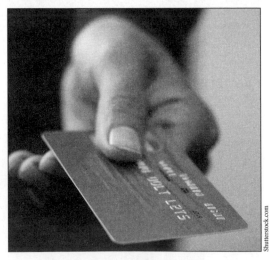

FIGURE 3-9. What unforeseen changes lie behind the new ways we buy things?

5.

Can you think of changes that have occurred in your lifetime?

. . . .

It is perhaps inevitable that matters like same-sex marriage generate so much controversy and heated emotional debate. From a *social constructivist* perspective, it could be argued that it signals the transition from one cultural context (male/female marriage with the view that reproduction is a significant part of such a relationship) to another (marriage defined by the individuals in it) that motivates such vigorous debate. From a *nature via nurture* point of view, though reproduction is an elemental part of being human, how it is achieved is being redirected by changes in the environment. In this case the linkage between reproduction and marriage is becoming less significant. The *biological essentialist* view would likely take the view that marriage is a creation of culture, and whether reproduction takes place in it or not is immaterial. Reproduction is an inherent part of our species' pattern of behavior and will likely persist even if the formal institutions that once supported it are altered. (See Chapter One for the defining perspectives of these three approaches to understanding gender.)

And the clash of the old and the new is not limited to feelings about changes occurring in established conventions like marriage. New findings can critically undermine the very structure of these conventions. For example, as we have learned in Chapter Two, there are many nudges that contribute to the formation of sex and gender. There are also many variations in these stages of development. Therefore, before the invention of genetic testing and effective internal scanning of the human body, there must have been many individuals in the past that lived their entire lives not knowing that their phenotype (their physical appearance) did not correspond with their genotype (their actual genes).

How meaningful is the prohibition of same-sex marriage when many husband/wife couples may actually have been genetically, or in terms of internal anatomy, same-sexed? It also raises the possibility that some same-sex couples may actually be non-same-sex couples. Which raises the larger question, if the prohibition of same-sex marriages is to be maintained, upon what criterion should sex defined? As discussed in the previous chapter, should sex be defined by XX and XY gene patterns or by prenatal hormonal exposure? Does this mean that every couple should be genetically screened and submit to an internal imaging scan to confirm their sex? Or should sex be determined by phenotype? There's even a larger question: is sex—and therefore gender—merely a social construct?

6.

Think about the consequences of sex and gender being nothing more than social constructions.

. . . .

Since we no longer consider marriage principally as an arrangement to facilitate reproduction, this means that we are removing a primary biological component from marriage. The elimination of reproductive behavior as a primary distinguishing characteristic of marriage means that such a union is simply whatever we choose to say it is, or to be more precise, whatever a couple chooses to say it is. Consequently, if marriage no longer has a basis in biology, and the connection between biology and how we identify the sex and gender of an individual is becoming so complex that it may be necessary for us to create an artificial definition for it, the entire rationale for the traditional view of marriage disappears.

This is what is meant by the earlier statement, "The ground upon which the foundations of normalcy and morality are based feels as though it is losing its substance."

For many, the emotional reaction that follows is: What?!

THE LIMITS OF FEELING

When we rely upon our feelings for guidance, we soon fall into a state of confusion and anxiety when the conventions we took for granted are challenged by new information that weaken their foundations. To continue the above example, how can the prohibition on same-sex marriage have any meaning when it is not entirely clear how to determine the gender of an individual? In the past, if there were married couples that were unknowingly the same sex, has there actually ever been an effective ban on such marriages? Should couples that appear to be the same sex, but who are actually not same-sex couples, be allowed to marry? It gets complicated—and it is with complex issues that emotion-based reactions lose their effectiveness.

When our ancestors lived lives that were relatively simple, as hunter-gatherers moving from place to place, before the rise of civilization, relying upon gut reactions for guidance was sufficient. Possessing neither physical property nor citizenship in some larger political system, they probably got by with the array of feelings that we still have today through times of plenty and periods of want. But when our ancestors began to organize themselves into cities, and later nations, more sophisticated systems developed to deal with increasingly complex circumstances (Diamond, 1997).

Among researchers concerned with the origins of human civilization, there is much debate about what motivated the creation of the first civilizations. War (Fukuyama, 2011), resource use and commerce (Burke, 1978), religion (Wood, 1992), and there are no doubt many more possible causes, have been cited as the prime motivators for the founding of the first cities and—most significantly—the institutions that support their operation.

What would it be like to live in a country in which feelings governed everything?

FIGURE 3-10. How could a society function with no laws to help arbitrate disputes among its citizens?

Imagine for a moment if our cities were run using structures of governance based not upon logically derived legal principles but emotionally driven family ties like those that ordered the lives of our ancient ancestors. The general populace would quickly divide themselves into small groups for self-protection as the boundaries of who-is-a-family-member and who-is-an-outsider would assert themselves. Conflict would easily break out as competing groups fought over resources. It would be very difficult for cities and towns, much less commerce and business, to function properly under such circumstances. What authority would run the water supply, sewage system, the electrical system, communications networks, or maintain the roads, the railroads, the airports, and the ports? Who would have the authority to maintain the peace, enforce the laws, run the courts, employ the police, collect revenues, or establish the concept of the rule of law in the first place?

Feelings are not equal to the task of dealing with complexity beyond the level of hunting and gathering social units. Would you want wages and prices for goods and services to be determined by whether you were viewed as a family member (an insider) or an outsider? Would you like your course grades to be determined on the basis of feelings? Of course not—we want an objective measure to be used. We want consistency and reliability to order our communities and our lives.

REASON AND LOGIC

If you listen carefully to the arguments that people get into, you may notice a common thread that runs through most of them. The conflict between the individuals involved could be about work, or money, or who is supposed to do this or that, but beneath the details of the argument is there is often a constant underlying theme.

8.

What do you think is the underlying theme of most arguments?

· ·

Many people in their early twenties have vivid memories of their parents fighting. Dishes smash onto the floor, fists strike walls and tables, voices are raised into howls of anger or despair. Betrayals, ruinous expenditures, incompatibilities of taste and morals, differing notions of what is and is not acceptable are laid bare. Tears, piercing silences, tortured stares, vacant gazes express the intensity of feeling that permeates these outbursts. Statements like, "Can't you see what you've done?" and "Don't you understand?" echo and re-echo like waves spreading across a pond that cannot be stilled.

If you could strip away the details of the infidelities, the incautious spending, the reckless behavior, the thoughtless choices, what often emerges is a conflict that is a product of two different personal feelings about right and wrong, of what is justifiable and unjustifiable, of what one person wants and what another person wants. In essence, fights are often about two divergent worldviews.

Almost eight hundred years ago, during the thirteenth century, a priest called Thomas Aquinas (Aquinas was not his last name, it was the name of city with which he was associated) was struggling with a very complex conflict. For the better part of a thousand years Europe had relied upon the authority of the Roman Catholic Church to maintain order. Ever since the fall of the Roman Empire in the fifth century, church dogma, and in particular the dictates of the Pope as the head of the Catholic Church, were the sole determiners of the truth. The problem was that a new way of thinking was beginning to threaten that authority (Spade, 1994).

This clash of thought had its origins at the end of the eleventh century; Pope Urban II had decreed that knights, noblemen, and other fighting men should travel to what is now Israel to take Jerusalem back from the Muslims who controlled the area at the time. During these journeys to the Holy Land and to other sites in Europe controlled by the Muslims, the Crusaders rediscovered the writings of the ancient Greek philosophers that had been lost with the fall of Rome (Cantor, 1993).

FIGURE 3-11. Painting of the Roman Forum in decline.

When the Roman Empire was in decline there had been a spiritual backlash against what we would call intellectual activities. The knowledge the Romans had accumulated over its long history through its own efforts at civil engineering and through the absorption of Greek and Egyptian learning when it made these nations part of its empire, was suddenly shunned. To many Romans, the disciplines of practical knowledge and philosophical thought had failed them as their empire fell into chaos and wave after wave of marauding tribes from outlying lands raped, pillaged, and plundered. Influenced by the writings of St. Augustine, Romans became inward-looking and culti-vated an anti-materialist spiritualism. They turned their backs on the knowledge that had taken centuries to develop. Much of the works of learned individuals were lost or destroyed (Burke, 1985, p. 20).

However, during the European Dark Ages that followed the fall of Rome, the Muslim peoples of what we now call the Middle East retained an interest in all learning. They trans-lated the Greek and Latin texts into Arabic and so preserved the works of Greek thinkers like Plato and Aristotle, whom the Romans had once held in high regard, as well as many other important scholars and philosophers. When the European Crusaders entered the lands inhabited by the Muslims in the eleventh and twelfth centuries, they came upon the lost intellectual legacy of ancient Rome, Greece, and Egypt (Greenwood, 2009, p. 78–80).

FIGURE 3-12. Aristotle (384 BCE–322 BCE) contemplating the bust of Homer.

The problem for the thirteenth century Catholic Church was principally the works of the Greek philosopher, Aristotle. And in a very real sense, Aristotle's contribution to Western civilization is still causing controversy to this day. For it was this individual, born almost four hundred years before Christ, who it can be argued initiated the approach to understanding the world that we now call science. This is an over-simplification, but the basic threat that Aristotle posed to the authority of the church was his practice of using reason and logic to understand all things. Aristotle's way of trying to understand the Universe was concrete and practical. Magical supernatural forces had no place in his study of phenomena. Basically, his approach rested on the notion that reason could reveal truths independent of religious belief and doctrine. In a very real sense, he fostered the idea that the individual could through the application of logic, comprehend everything, thus potentially threatening the power of those who claimed divine access to the truth. The saying "Question authority," it could be said, started with the challenge posed to church doctrine by Aristotle's way of exam-ining the Universe (Burke, 1985, pp. 42–45).

9.

How do you deal with issues that can be understood from more than one point of view?

Thomas Aquinas was essentially trying to bring peace to two parties who were arguing from two distinct points of view (Spade, 1994, p. 89). The issue in question was the truth. What is it, and which approach to it was the most valid. Thirteenth-century Catholic lead-ership believed that divine revelation led to the truth. However, a growing body of thinkers argued for freedom of thought and the use of logic and reason rediscovered in the works of the Greek philosophers like Aristotle to ascertain the truth.

Eight hundred years after Thomas Aquinas put his mind to this task we still live with the outcome of his efforts. He formalized the dualism we still live with today in which matters of faith are governed by spiritual contact with divine revelation and the material world is the realm of scientific inquiry (Greenwood, 2009, p. 84–85). It is important to understand, that before Thomas Aquinas' work, in the Christian West, everything was comprehended through the lens of religion. After Thomas Aquinas' careful philosophical and theological examination of the conflict between faith and logical approaches to knowledge, the world was divided into two realms: the divine and the material. In the thirteenth century, the material world was seen as inferior to the spiritual dimension, a place where death and decay predominated. The material world was perceived as corruptible, while the divine spiritual realm was incorruptible, pure and beyond the reach of reason and logic (Meeks, 1993).

It is where faith and science meet today that so much debate is generated. Issues of morality and ethics, of life and death, of our identity as either spiritual beings made in the image of God or as descendents of earlier forms of animal life are at the heart of many of the arguments that split people in the Western nations of the world. It could be argued that St. Thomas Aquinas (he was made a saint by Pope John XXII forty-nine years after his death) created the setting of this conflict, but it could also be said that he opened the door to the technology-based world whose benefits we now enjoy by accommodating Aristotle into the prevailing orthodoxy, while maintaining the spiritual and moral foundations that attempt to moderate human behavior.

10.

Think about how important it is to approach difficult issues with an open mind.

. . . .

By reconciling logic-based thought with religious belief, Thomas Aquinas created boundaries around these two seemingly incompatible approaches to the truth. This is an important point to consider in the study of gender. Formal inquiry into the nature of the physical world, what we call science (which is one of the legacies of the ancient Greek philosophers to us) has its limitations. One fundamental limitation on the search for the truth, from the perspective of Western science, is that it must be done as objectively as possible. To be valid, those who seek the truth—conduct the research—must not be affected by their own biases about the nature of the Universe. An open mind is a vital prerequisite to the operation of science.

In the first chapter, the anthropological view that all people are members of one species was discussed. Every human being who has ever lived, irrespective of their particular cultural or physical characteristics, are our relatives. If we adopt this perspective for a moment, it casts a very questionable light on the validity of research that has been conducted about the inherent superiority or inferiority of various groups of individuals based upon racial-ethnic lines.

Just as Thomas Aquinas's work philosophically ascertained the limits of the reach of scientific inquiry, social constructivism identifies an important limit that must be recognized in studies about the world around us. In this instance, what makes inquiry into the superiority or inferiority of any given racial-ethnic group problematic is the fact that the concepts of race and ethnicity are fabrications—are social constructions.

One of the unusual aspects of research into matters relating to people in the behavioral sciences is the use of what are called *operational definitions* (Greenwood, 2009, p. 20). For example, when racial-ethnic differences are examined, researchers may or may not be aware that they are, from an anthropological and from a biological point of view, studying artificial distinctions. In other words, the concept of racial-ethnic differences cannot be objectively defined—it is a product of culture. Race and ethnicity are social constructions. Since all people are human, race and ethnicity have no basis in biology or genetics. When, for instance, after the genocidal war that engulfed Bosnia in the 1990s had ended and the bodies that had been buried in mass graves were exhumed and identified using DNA testing, such examination could reveal the identity of individuals, but could not tell to which group any of the individuals belonged. DNA testing could not determine who was a Croat, a Muslim, or a Serb (Ferguson, 2006, p. 630). In other words, there is no biological basis for racial-ethnic identities, even though people *feel* that these distinctions are real. Nature does not recognize race and ethnicity as anything more than tiny variations among humans. It is probably safe to say that dogs and cats do not distinguish between people by skin color, nationality or religious affiliations either—only people do.

When scientific research is done, we need to ask if what we are studying is a real natural phenomenon or if what we seek to understand is something that is a product of our own preconceptions. When research on racial-ethnic differences is performed, those doing the study must proceed from operational definitions because the characteristics they are examining are real only from a very limited point of view. That is, they have to intentionally create descriptions of different races and ethnicities that may not necessarily reflect distinctions that actually exist in nature (Greenwood, 2009, p. 20).

FIGURE 3-13. This mouse is "thinking outside the box"; how should we regard its intelligence?

For example, intelligence tests have been used to try to prove that certain racial-ethnic groups (as well as males and females within these groups) are inherently more or less intelligent compared to other groups. From the social constructivist and the biological essentialist view, there are many problems with this activity. First, since there is no objective definition of smarts, intelligence must be operationally defined. Its definition can be found in the intelligence test itself. The items in the test are based upon attributes the researcher regards as indicative of intelligence. If, for example, there are math problems in the test, then intelligence is very likely being defined by mathematical abilities. Second, the subjects being studied are also operationally defined. If the research is concerned with determining which racial-ethnic group is the most intelligent, then some mix of cultural and political designators have to be used to divide the population of subjects into racial-ethnic groups, since there are no definitive genetic or biological ways of distinguishing between individuals. Third, whatever results come from this investigation must be clearly presented as being the product of artificial, socially constructed, operationally defined methods. In other words, if intelligence is defined in a particular way, and if the test itself is an accurate measure of operationally defined intelligence, and if race and ethnicity are defined in a particular manner, then it needs to be clear that the particular findings derived from these definitions is strictly limited to these definitions. The context these definitions form is what is often missing when research of this type is undertaken and its findings presented (Kagan, 2012). It is highly unlikely that the conclusions derived from research structured in this manner can be generalized in any meaningful way to the whole of humanity.

Knowledge, under these circumstances, is what the researcher says it is, because much is contingent upon initial assumptions. By creating a given set of questions for a test of intelligence, the researcher has already predetermined what data is being sought in the test. This indicates that the researcher is essentially blind to any other potential indicator of intelligence (Burke, 1985, p. 303–337). Consequently, research based upon social constructions will likely have little correspondence with objective reality and will yield results that are only relevant within the narrow confines of the artificialities of the investigation.

Gender as a field of inquiry is very problematic for this reason, because gender is itself a social construction.

IS REALITY REAL?

At the center of the debate about gender is a simple but profound question: Is the real world real?

11.

What makes the world real for you?

· ·

You may think this is a rather strange question to ask. Most people would respond, of course the world is real. We all live in it. We work from day to day trying to get ahead in it. We devote our lives to doing what we think will make ourselves happy in it. The world

of people and places and events are real. If we blindly run out into traffic we will likely get run over. If we break the law there will be consequences.

In March 1999, the movie *The Matrix* was released. Though it was set in a future in which individuals live either beneath the ruins of a ravaged Earth or plugged into a computer-generated reality, the tale is actually an elaboration of the thoughts of another of the ancient Greek philosophers, Plato. Roughly 2,500 years ago, this one-time student of Socrates and later teacher of Aristotle put forward the idea that most of us do not perceive the "real" world, but instead mistake illusion for reality. The image he used to illustrate his point was of people chained to the floor of a dark cave in which a fire burns and projects shadows on a wall. The flickering shadows moving and playing on the walls of the stone enclosure are perceived by the imprisoned individuals as the world of the real. Plato argued that if they were freed of their bonds and allowed to exit the cave to live in the real world, they would not be able to perceive it, because the light of the sun would blind them (Plato). In other words, they would be so accustomed to perceiving fire-lit shadows as the real world that they would not be able to experience the real thing. Transpose Plato's Allegory of the Cave onto a future computer-produced virtual reality, and a compelling tale of people chained to machines arises quite readily.

FIGURE 3-14. Statue of Socrates in Athens, Greece. Plato (423 BC–347 BC) was a student of Socrates (469 BC–399 BC). Plato, in turn, was Aristotle's (384 BC–322 BC) teacher. Socrates gave us the immortal statement: "Know thyself."

But some behavioral scientists would argue that we do not need tera-flopping networked computers churning out virtual reality to chain individuals to illusions. People are already enthralled by illusions, like the belief that men and women have inherently different characteristics that make one sex better at any given task than the other and that this proves the superiority of one sex over another (Fausto-Sterling, 1985). All that is required to construct social illusions is to establish attitudes and values that reinforce these beliefs. Condition people to "see" the world in the required way and they will come to feel and think and perceive all things in that way.

For example, twenty-five hundred years after Plato lived, Greeks living in the opening years of the second decade of the twenty-first century are wondering if the economic system they live with in Europe is the only one that can order their lives. As the massive debts owed by the Greek government strangle that nation's economy and the Greek people are forced by banks in other nations to live with drastically lowering standards of living, many are asking if the reality of their situation can be changed (*The Economist*, 2011). Is capitalism, as it is practiced in the Euro-zone, a play of light and shadow to which they are economically chained? Have they simply been trained

to see money as a reality and allowed this man-made abstraction to completely control their destinies? After all, it could be argued, money does not exist in nature. If bills aren't paid, the sun still rises and the rain still falls. Many Greeks ask why so many of them must go hungry and homeless to maintain the value of the euro (the currency of the participating nations of the European Union).

FIGURE 3-15. The former Greek currency, the drachma, was first introduced in 1832 and replaced by the euro in 2001.

It can be argued from the social constructivist point of view that, like the Greek debt situation, the views we have about women and men are creations of our social systems—artificial contrivances. Money is something people created. There are no capitalist insect communities, no market-oriented monkey colonies, no coin-carrying wolf packs, and in the same vein, there are no natural distinctions that mark one sex as better or stronger or smarter or fitter than the other. Notions of better, stronger, smarter, and fitter are human concepts created by collective human attitudes.

12.

Is reality what we say it is? Does our view of things determine our reality? How do the three perspectives introduced in Chapter One affect our perception of the truth?

· ·

If you think about it, this perspective puts forward the view that if there is a real world "out there" beyond the boundaries of the individual mind, all its qualities and characteristics are what we say they are. To put it bluntly, reality—as we know it—is what we collectively say it is. A blue bird is only a blue bird because we have learned what "blue" and "bird" are. A person deprived of color vision might be able to discern "bird," but the concept of "blue" would be meaningless. For a newborn, a blue bird is a fuzzy object in his or her field of view that moves and makes sounds. For a wild cat, a blue bird is a potential meal and the human conceptual categories of "blue" and "bird" are as meaningful to it as the drachma (the money the Greeks used before they adopted the euro currency) is to the central banks of the Euro-zone.

If the real world is what we say it is, can we say anything meaningful about it? Is everything we say lacking in objectivity? Is there such a thing as truth? Is there a "real" world out there to study?

The biological essentialist view and the nature via nurture view would argue that yes, there is a real world "out there" that exists independent of us and we can discern, within limits, the truth about it. This is referred to as *logical positivism* (Greenwood, 2009, p. 479). The social constructivist perspective can be roughly divided into two outlooks on this matter. What could be termed *strict* constructivism would say, no, the real world does not have an independent existence from us, and what we perceive is hopelessly distorted by our biases

and is essentially an illusion built up from what we want to see. Social constructivism would say, yes, the real world exists but it is difficult, perhaps impossible, for us to perceive it in a completely unbiased way. We observe the world through glasses tinted with preconceptions and prejudices that we learn from those around us, and these acquired views cannot be removed.

A MODEL UNIVERSE

Seeing and understanding the world around us in an entirely objective way is one of the goals of scientific inquiry. In order to achieve objectivity, formalized systems of measuring and examining and thinking about phenomena have been developed. It is an approach that requires those engaged in research to accept whatever findings are derived from their investigation—even if it runs counter to their expectations.

For example, flying is one of the safest modes of transportation. According to statistics (which is regarded as an objective way of interpreting numerical data) compiled over decades of passenger travel, it is far safer to fly than it is to travel by car. Yet many people still feel some level of unease when they enter a passenger airliner. The old adage, "If God had meant for man to fly, he'd have given him wings," comes to mind. No doubt, the novelty of flight contributes to this feeling. Cars are a common part of most people's lives in the West, while few of us have airplanes in our garages or carports. But despite the overwhelming statistical evidence, many people cannot bring themselves to feel that it is an entirely safe mode of travel.

If you are anxious about flying and you cannot find comfort in statistics, it may help to know that the amount of study that goes into the design and construction of aircraft is enormous. One of the techniques used in the initial design of new aircraft is the testing of scale models. Miniature three-dimensional copies of the plane are placed into wind tunnels and subjected to forces and conditions that mimic those that the real aircraft would encounter over its life. Using this method, any potential deficiencies or problems can be identified and remedied long before the first passenger sets foot inside a new plane. Nevertheless, even after rigorous testing of models, aeronautical engineers test components and systems throughout the design and construction of aircraft.

There is a reason that testing continues even after the models have proven to be free of faults. And you can take comfort in this; engineers always keep in mind that models are nothing more than approximations of the real thing. Models may serve as guides for projecting real performance, but it has its limitations. A model is not the real thing.

13.

Psychological research is based upon mental models of human behavior.

· ·

This fact is seldom mentioned in psychological research. Every formal investigation of human behavior is actually a study based upon models. Remember this. Every theory of human behavior is based on a mental model of how we behave.

There are two paths that are generally accepted in scientific methodology to advance our understanding of things in the environment. Either an individual develops a notion of how things work or of the characteristics of a particular subject through observation, or an individual comes up with a notion of how things work or of the characteristics of a particular subject and then designs experiments to prove the truth of the notion. To use the formal terminology of the scientific method, these are the two ways that hypotheses are generated. The first way is referred to as the *inductive method* and the second is the *hypothetico-deductive method*. But whichever method is used, these notions or hypotheses are mental models—and are the products of individual creativity (Greenwood, 2009, p. 21). Like a painting or any other creative work, they are representations of reality (and once again a medium for potential personal bias to express itself).

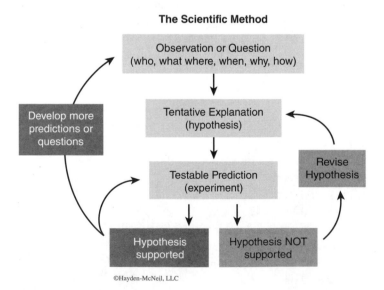

The Scientific Method

©Hayden-McNeil, LLC

FIGURE 3-16. The hypothetico-deductive scientific method.

The task that confronts researchers, then, is to confirm the accuracy or validity of the mental models and the hypotheses that they develop from them—and by extension the theories that are built upon these hypotheses by comparing them to the real world. This again rests upon the view that there is a real world "out there" that has an independent existence from the individual studying it, and is the basis of *empiricism*.

In the behavioral sciences there are a number of different ways of empirically comparing hypothesis with reality. In an effort to emulate fields of study like physics and chemistry, *quantitative* research has been emphasized in behavioral sciences like psychology, sociology, and economics. In gender studies a researcher might ask subjects to use a numerical scale to rate their impressions of interactions with individuals who are not of the same sex as the subject. The scores that result from these ratings can then be statistically analyzed and used to support a given hypothesis. This is an attractive course to pursue in research because the use of quantitative methods enforces a certain degree of rigor through the statistical relationships that are derived and thus appear more objective.

FIGURE 3-17. Is solving this puzzle in a given time reification of intelligence?

14.

Can we really turn everything into numbers?

However, the problematic element lies in the act of *reification*. In order to do quantitative research, operational definitions must be established to pair a particular attribute with a particular score. One of the most well-known examples of reification is the IQ score. Here an abstract concept, intelligence, is paired with a numerical score. In other words, smarts are reified into numbers. According to the operational definition of the scoring method employed in IQ testing, if an individual has a score of 100, it indicates that the subject's intelligence is average for the subject's chronological age. If the score is beneath 100, this indicates that the subject's intelligence is below average for the subject's age. Scores above 100 indicate above average intelligence for that particular age. But once again, the question of objectivity enters into the matter. As free of bias as quantitative analysis may appear, a weak link still exists wherein the researcher defines the relationship between whatever is being studied and the measures being used.

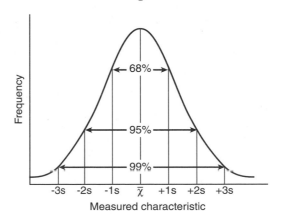

FIGURE 3-18. 100 IQ points are at the center of the curve. The average score on an IQ test is 100 points.

15.

The weak link in the quantitative approach to psychological research...

Imagine if a psychologist defined intelligence as the ability to reason in Latin as a prime indicator of intelligence. How would you score on a test written in Latin? That most English-speakers would probably score very low on such an IQ test would—according to the operational definition that underlay the rationale of the test—indicate that most Americans are highly unintelligent. Is this a valid finding? Of course it is not. This is a rather extreme illustration of definitional excess, but it shows how bias can easily enter into quantitative methods of study.

Numbers and the statistical relationships they describe follow from rigorous mathematical systems—the problem does not lie there. The problem rests with connecting the things being studied as well as certain underlying assumption to specific numbers. Put a little thought into the way IQ scoring works and you might realize that if you want to continue to maintain a specific level of intelligence according to the operational definition used in IQ testing, you are going to have to do better on the test with each passing year of your life in order to keep up with your advancing age. Do you think that eighty-year-olds who maintain average IQ scores are significantly more intelligent than averagely intelligent forty-year-olds?

This is not to say that quantitative methods are not appropriate for psychological research. The problem does not lie within the method itself. The difficulty arises from its specific application in research. When studying matters relating to gender using quantitative methods, great care has to be taken to ensure that researcher bias is minimized. Beyond this, there is also the matter of whether the design of the research is actually focused on the phenomenon in question.

16.

What are independent and dependent variables?

An experiment is a simulation of actual events and interactions. In an experiment, researchers attempt to create a controlled reality in which a particular element that is being studied is paired with another element that is believed to affect it, while trying to eliminate all other influences that might interfere with the expected result. For example, a researcher might design a study to prove that young males are excited by violent video games. When designing experiments (which again originate as mental models), researchers identify two important elements: the *independent variable* and the *dependent variable*. The independent variable is the component of the experiment that is manipulated by the researcher. In this case, it could be the video game. Either a golf video game or a violent action video game might be presented. The dependent variable would be a specific attribute of the subject, in this case a young male, which might indicate excitation. An increased heart rate could be defined as a reliable indicator of excitation. Thus the independent variable is the presentation of either a non-violent or a violent video game and the dependent variable is changes in the subject's heart rate.

In essence, the researcher tries to create a separate reality, in which all other influences are subtracted. It is also important to ensure that the independent variable and the measures or indicators designated as the dependent variable conform to the specifications of the hypotheses or theory. Similarly, the subject must also conform to the design of the study. In this case, is the golf video game truly devoid of violent content and does the violent video game adequately depict such activity? Does the subject fit the operational definition of a young male?

FIGURE 3-19. The independent variable is the push of the first domino; the dependent variable is the fall of subsequent dominoes.

17.

What confounding factors could affect this study?

. . . .

Ideally, when a researcher creates a model universe, the results are free of external influences that might affect the outcome of the experiment. For example, though the violent video game experiment may seem straightforward and likely to yield meaningful results, there are ways the outside influences might confound it. What if the subject is a frequent player of violent video games and has already played the one presented in the experiment many times? He might react to it with nothing more than a yawn. What if the subject has never been exposed to violent video games and reacts with fear? Is the increase in his heart rate indicative of the type of emotional excitation defined by the experimental design?

18.

Why is research into gender always problematic?

. . . .

Research into gender is always problematic because the researcher can never get inside the mind of a subject and determine the particular life experiences that shape personal views about the world, like the nature of men and women and their interactions. For example, if a researcher were to hypothesize about female reactions to male violence, then design an experiment to test that hypothesis, is it really possible to remove all external influences? The complexity of the individual and the uniqueness of personal experience and outlook make direct experimental study of gender challenging.

Another way of studying gender is to simply ask large numbers of people specific questions about issues relating to gender and then try to determine if there is a consensus about a particular topic. The greater the number of people queried, the greater the likelihood that the sample of responses received is indicative of the general view of a given populace.

The challenge for the researcher is to compose a set of questions and present them in such a way that they actually produce responses that reflect the real views of the person being polled. Here again the biases of the researcher can easily enter into the design of the study and affect the results.

Like the leading questions that attorneys use in court to manipulate a witness into delivering the kinds of answers that support a particular position, questionnaires can be composed to validate nearly any possible hypothesis or theory. Just as a question like "When was the last time you argued with your spouse?" predisposes the respondent to bias his or her thoughts and answers toward interpersonal confrontation in a trial, a similar query can color the nature of a questionnaire.

Other factors can affect respondents' reactions. Is the questionnaire presented as a list of questions with answers that respondents can choose from among? Can the respondent give open-ended answers? Is the respondent reading from a printed questionnaire, or is an interviewer asking the questions? If the questionnaire is printed, what typeface is being used? What color paper is it printed on? If an interviewer is asking the questions, what is his or her demeanor? How is he or she dressed? Is the interview being conducted in a private setting or in a public space?

FIGURE 3-20. How honest do you think most respondents are when responding to questionnaires? Can a respondent's honesty be determined?

All these variables do affect individuals when questions are put to them. There are also the added assumptions that participants are always going to fully comprehend the question, are always going to interpret it the way the researcher intended, and the most significant, that the response is authentic.

19.

Correlation does not indicate causation.

. . . .

Another way that researchers try to understand issues relating to gender is to study what are called correlations. Here researchers select two observable or measurable variables, operationally define them, hypothesize about their relationship to each other, try to isolate them from other influences, measure or record their occurrence in relation to each other, and then statistically characterize that relationship.

The classic example of the potential pitfalls of studies based upon correlations is ice cream sales and the incidence of crime relationship. In this particular study, the increase or decrease of the rate at which ice cream is sold is said to match very strongly the increase or decrease in the incidence of crime. The statistics are very straightforward, they come from sales figures for ice cream and police crime reports. These numbers are processed to determine the strength of their correlation that yields a figure that runs anywhere from +1.0 to 0 to −1.0. They are positively correlated if their increase or decrease occurs in unison. A perfect relationship is +1. If there does not seem to be any relationship between the two variables, then the result would be 0. If one variable increased and one decreased in unison, the negative relationship could be as high as −1. The idea behind these numbers is that if there is a high statistical relationship there must be some connection between the two variables—the desired finding is that one variable causes the other.

For the classic ice cream/crime rate relationship, though the statistics indicate a high degree of correlation, there is no doubt that the increase or decrease of both variables is a product of other variables, like the ambient air temperature during the day. Warms days find more people consuming ice cream, while the same conditions increase the likelihood of people being outdoors, getting together and potentially committing crimes. A naïve view of the ice cream/crime rate correlation might compel someone to suggest that the restriction of ice cream consumption would lower the crime rate. But as absurd as this sounds, less obvious meaningless correlations can easily produce statements—even public policies—that are based on illusory evidence.

Correlations do not necessarily indicate causation. Increased ice cream consumption does not cause an increase in crime, nor does increased crime cause increased ice cream consumption. It is not difficult to find all sorts of erroneous interpretations of correlations. For example, being born correlates perfectly with eventually dying. The relationship between birth and death is a perfect +1. Everyone who has ever been born has died. As a matter of public policy, does this mean then that we should eliminate death by eliminating birth? As ridiculous as this may sound, the way the media has portrayed the relationship between eating and obesity would seem to suggest that the only way to eliminate the latter is to stop doing the former.

In gender studies, correlation is used frequently. All kinds of research studies have been done on educating individuals about aspects of gender and then looking for changes in behavior. For example, are males who are aware of feminist issues less likely to engage in violent behavior against women? Again the problem is that it is very difficult to eliminate all extraneous influences on individual behavior. There might be a positive correlation between greater awareness and lower rates of violence, but to state with high degrees of confidence that one caused the other is not possible using just correlation.

Gender, like so many other aspects of being human, is such a rich and complex psychological facet of our personal existence. To reify any particular component of it down into a meaningful operational definition, then subject it to experimental study, then perhaps derive definitive statistical measures, and finally draw substantial actionable conclusions, is extremely difficult. The quantitative approach does enforce a high degree of rigor and formality to inquiry, but the problem of investigator bias manifesting itself at any stage—even if it is entirely unintentional—will always be a confounding element.

20.

Can any science be objective?

In the physical sciences, in what is arguably the most difficult and powerful of disciplines, quantum mechanics (the study of the realm of physics not covered by Einstein's Special and General Theories of Relativity), researchers admit that objectivity is impossible. They claim that the very act of making an observation changes the object under examination. Observation—never mind moving on to the next level, experimentation—will always have an element of subjectivity. In other words, at the subatomic level, certainty does not exist. There is only probability (Bronowski, 1973). Combine this with Einstein's finding that what any particular individual experiences is entirely contingent upon his or her personal frame of reference (Calder, 1979), and it becomes clear that observation—just describing what we personally "see"—is the closest we can come to accurately defining anything. Cause and effect is at best an approximation, at worse simply wrong. Relations and correlations may be just illusions, constructions derived from social norms and expectations.

FIGURE 3-21. Albert Einstein (1879–1955) was a German-born theoretical physicist who developed the theory of general relativity that revolutionized the study of physics.

And indeed, many behavioral scientists accept this limitation. Like the limitation St. Thomas Aquinas imposed on Aristotle and church dogma and social constructivism places on biological and epigenetic views of human behavior, some researchers restrict themselves to what are referred to as qualitative methods.

A QUALITATIVE UNIVERSE

In an attempt to remove as many artificial reconstructions of reality as possible, researchers who seek to understand whole social systems like anthropologists and, interestingly enough, people engaged in marketing and advertising, put aside operational definitions and reification and experimental design, and immerse themselves in what they wish to study. This is the qualitative approach to research.

Consider the different methods used in qualitative research.

· ·

In psychology, the *case study* is an effort by a researcher or therapist to know through interviews, interactions, and observations the details of a person's life. In the context of gender, the facts and features of an individual's background can yield important insights into the nature of living as a man, woman, or intersex person in a particular setting. In psychotherapy, that branch of psychology concerned with helping people achieve some degree of mental well-being, case studies are the foundation of diagnosis and the determination of treatment. That it is not based upon some numerical representation of behavior, some argue, makes it less rigorous. And certainly comparisons made between subjects of case studies have to be done with care and with an awareness of the pitfalls of generalizing one case across a larger population. Nonetheless, this approach does minimize the number of intervening reinterpretations of observable behavior that quantitative methods are based upon.

FIGURE 3-22. Sigmund Freud (1856–1939), an Austrian neurologist who founded the discipline of psychoanalysis by utilizing case studies.

In anthropology, the case study approach is expanded into what is known as *ethnography*. Like the student who works to achieve fluency in a foreign language by immersing him or herself in an environment in which only the particular language of study is spoken, anthropologists study cultures principally by living in them. By living, for example, as an aboriginal person of Australia lives, a researcher can really know and understand the nature and the quality of life in that cultural and environmental context. Similarly, psychologists can also employ this approach to learn about the influence of particular contexts on psychological states. For example, a researcher may achieve important insights into the psychology of homelessness by adopting this way of life for an extended period of time. Or in the case of gender studies, much can be learned by focusing on the culturally ascribed behaviors associated with being a male or a female in a society that is different from the one to which the researcher is accustomed.

FIGURE 3-23. Woman in a Peruvian market. How does she live? What gender roles define her identity?

Another method of acquiring information about the mental state of individuals is to do what advertising and marketing researchers do: gather a group of individuals together and interact with them. Though this method is not as naturalistic as the immersive approach, it can be conceived of a kind of group case study. Political campaign researchers often use a variant called a *focus group*, in which what is designed to be a representative group of people are brought together and asked to respond to ideas and statements put to them. Their responses are then used to tailor the political statements and policy positions of the candidate in such a way that the population of potential voters will react in the desired manner.

FIGURE 3-24. A person responding to a political speech, word by word, informing the researcher about how a speech is perceived (usually from highly positive, to very negative).

22.

What problems arise from the use of qualitative research methods?

Though many of the problems associated with quantitative research methods are absent in qualitative approaches, there are many new ones that arise. The objectivity and rigor conceptually implied by quantitative methods is very hard to achieve. The observer is hard pressed not to let his or her own previous life experiences, personal biases, and frames of reference interfere or color observation. The eye of the beholder can never be made to lose its subjective impressions. The desire to find, for example, a society in which men never act aggressively has clouded the objectivity of ethnographers in the past, just as the prejudices of witnesses have been known to affect their eyewitness accounts of crimes.

An over-riding shortcoming of all research methods is the obsessive way we humans discriminate between things. We always look for differences, seldom similarities. Nearly all research into issues relating to gender—no matter its method—is concerned with differences. Only very rarely does research center on the overlapping, shared characteristics of two or more groups. Whether it is males versus females, boys versus girls, one sexual orientation, lesbian, gay, or transsexual versus heterosexual, we are always prone to emphasize dissimilarities.

Contrast usually wins over comparison—it is probably part of the way we are wired. Which brings us to the question, is there a way to understand gender that minimizes the biases and prejudices that so limit our objectivity? Perhaps. And it has to do with the way we are wired.

AN EVOLUTIONARY VIEW

It may be possible to discern more universal truths about gender if we turn to more objective frames of reference like biology and anthropology, and study the processes that shaped our humanity. We have to look to the past, to a time when the social constructions and attitudes that so cloud our views of gender relations now did not yet exist. By doing this, we can attempt to put aside the contemporary biases and preconceptions that make discussion of gender issues so contentious.

To make sense of the present, we need to understand the past.

· ·

We have to cast our thoughts back to a time when men and women did not share their experiences on social networking sites, and brides did not dress in white and grooms did not wear tuxedoes, before money and writing existed, before we lived in communal settlements and knew how to grow crops that we could eat. We have to look back to our origins, when socially derived ideas about the equality of the sexes, much less the legal right to make personal choices, had not yet come into existence.

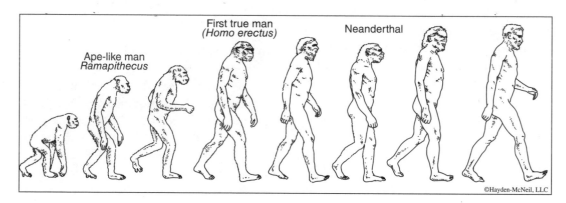

FIGURE 3-25. The timeline of human evolution. While human evolution begins with our common ancestry to all Earthly life, it generally refers to the evolutionary history of primates and in particular the genus *Homo*. The emergence of *Homo sapiens* signals the appearance of a distinct species of hominids ("great apes"). The study of human evolution is a major component of anthropology.

In the introduction, it was noted that roughly a hundred billion people have lived up to the present time, and that just seven percent of that number is alive right now. It makes you realize how many have lived in the past, despite the fact that the total number of people living at any one time has never been as high as it is in the present. What this means is that the amount of time that precedes the world we know is, in comparison, enormous. Our ancestors, the individuals who made us who we are today, can be traced back at the very least two and a half million years. If we use the cut off when our kind diverged from our primate relatives, we humans go back more than five million years (Stringer et al., 2012, p. 12). Compare that huge expanse of time with the age of human civilization, which is about ten thousand years. Now compare the age of our species to the amount of time we've lived with televisions and computers, malls and cars, and it is clear that the recent creations of our culture are a tiny, tiny fraction of the total amount of time we humans have existed.

For more than ninety-nine percent of human history, males, females, and intersex individuals lived in conditions that were very different from what we know today. Only in the last miniscule fraction of time have humans had the opportunity to live as we currently do. The branch of psychology that takes into account our vast ancestral past and places our postmodern gender issues into this larger context is evolutionary psychology.

DARWIN'S INSIGHT

FIGURE 3-26. Charles Darwin (1809–1882). In 1859, Darwin published *On the Origin of Species* in which he proposed a scientific theory that a "branching pattern of evolution" resulted from a process that he named natural selection.

Mathematics is a subject many people do not particularly enjoy. I have long had the suspicion that it is because numbers and the operations that govern them are far removed from the human realms of feeling and sentiment. The abstract nature of numerical systems makes them seem so stark and uncompromising and lifeless. They exist in some nether region, untouched by change. Two plus two always equals four.

Before Darwin came up with his theory of evolution, biologists also struggled with change. Take a stroll through a zoo and you will see enormous variety, elephants and otters, tigers and turtles, butterflies and birds. But you will not see any animals changing into something else. Yet walk through a natural history museum and you will see reconstructions of animals that lived in the past that were markedly different from the living critters in the zoo. All manner of dinosaur lived more than sixty-five million years ago. Go back roughly six hundred million years and really unusual creatures swam the ancient oceans, animals with body plans—five eyes and a single claw, for example—that are no longer found among living things today (Gould, 1989). Where did all this variety come from? How did all this change take place?

An important insight for biological inquiry into change came to light in 1798, when a paper was written about a very depressing fact. The rate at which animals reproduce (including humans) is always much higher than the rate at which the food supply increases (Malthus). The implication of this finding was that the threat of starvation and the specter of competition for resources are always going to be present. While the obvious reaction to this finding would be: that we have to somehow get people to have fewer children, Charles Darwin (1859) cleverly realized that this was the force that was driving biological change.

24.

Darwin's theory of evolution in a nutshell…

· ·

All living things are always competing for scarce resources. Those organisms that have characteristics that give them an edge over their competitors will be more likely to reproduce successfully. These organisms will leave more descendents. Offspring that inherent their parents' beneficial characteristics will in turn be more likely to reproduce successfully. Organisms that do not possess advantageous characteristics will consequently be less likely to reproduce and may over time disappear—in other words, go extinct. The environment acts as a kind of selective mechanism, favoring those organisms that have characteristics conducive to survival and reproduction in a particular setting, while those organisms that have less adaptive characteristics are less likely to survive.

Once in a while an organism is born with a variation caused by a random mutation in its DNA. Sometimes a new variation confers some advantage upon that organism, perhaps making it better able to get food or avoid hazards in the environment, like predators. Thus this slightly different individual might have more offspring who each possess this variation. Over generations individuals who possess this advantageous mutation may out-number those who do not possess the mutation. Eventually, those without the variation may completely disappear because they could not compete with those that have the mutation. Given enough time and selective pressures, the accumulation of mutations could change organisms to such a degree that they can no longer produce viable offspring with their non-mutated counterparts, thus making them a whole new species.

The force that drives evolution is everything in the environment that affects the lives of organisms. The climate can change, new predators can evolve, even changes in the output of the sun's radiation can alter natural selection. A species of organism that was once just getting by could suddenly have characteristics that are highly advantageous in the new setting, while a once favored species might find itself going extinct. This was the case with dinosaurs sixty-five million years ago when they disappeared, thus opening environmental niches for mammals to inhabit. Changes in the environment can also spur the development of new species.

25.

Two common misinterpretations of Darwin's theory of evolution…

. . . .

It should be noted, however, that biological change has two qualities that are often misinterpreted. The first is the notion that the "goal" of natural selection is to create a perfect organism; this is not true. It is an entirely mindless process. It merely acts upon whatever organisms with whatever characteristics that happen to exist at the time. There is no ideal form that life should take. The second is that evolution is a rapid process that is somehow "willed" by the organism. Change occurs—from our point of view—very slowly. The genetic unit of evolution is random mutation in the DNA of organisms—something that no living thing has any conscious control over. As a result, the pace at which organisms evolve is the rate at which generations occur; in other words, the rate at which an organism reproduces. In humans, a generation is counted as the number of years between the birth of an individual and the birth of that individual's children. Based on this criterion, a human generation has typically been about twenty years. If it takes, say, a thousand generations for natural selection to act upon a series of single tiny random DNA mutations to significantly alter a species that reproduces at the rate that we do, then twenty thousand years (1,000 generations × 20 years per generation = 20,000 years) may go by before any apparent phenotypic change might be observed. If the environment is fairly stable then change might proceed at an even slower rate. If the environment changes suddenly, sufficient time may not be available for natural selection to act and species may disappear (which is why so many plants and animals have gone extinct recently; human activity has become the cause of such rapid environmental change that species often cannot cope with the new conditions). It is not difficult, then, to realize that the amount of time involved in the evolution of organisms that reproduce at the rate that we do is enormous.

26.

It is important to understand that from an evolutionary perspective, our ancient ancestors differed in no meaningful way from ourselves.

. . . .

If you think about it for a moment, from the point of view of the rate of evolutionary change, it is extremely unlikely that we are in any meaningful way different, on a genetic basis, from our ancestors who lived before the development of civilization.

Darwin's theory of evolution offers a window into the process of biological change. It accounts for all the varieties of life that might be represented in a zoo that now inhabit the planet as well as all the forms cataloged in a natural history museum that are now extinct. Like the development of calculus that encompassed continuous change in mathematics and brought dynamism to seemingly static numbers, evolution altered the perception of living things as unchanging entities. Evolution is an on-going and necessary process for organisms if they are to persist on a planet where the environment is changeable.

AN EVOLUTIONARY VIEW OF THE MIND

Evolutionary psychology is in many respects the union of the biological essentialist and the epigenetic (or nature via nurture) perspectives. Based upon the systems of change that biology is structured upon, evolution, and the view that specific behaviors are expressions of evolved characteristics that arise in response to the particulars of the environment, evolutionary psychology blends our past with the present. This is very much in accord with the nature via nurture, or epigenetic, view, in the sense that nature (what we are endowed with at birth) is shaped and affected by nurture (the specific experiences we encounter over the course of our lives).

This approach to understanding human behavior is not without its critics. Social constructivists argue that because it relies on biological processes to account for behavior, it is deterministic, with the implication that we are merely mechanistically following preset behavioral programs. In the past and in the present, evolutionary theory has been misused to justify war, the oppression of women, the discrimination of individuals of differing sexual orientations, the occurrence of poverty, and the genocide of whole culturally defined populations. Evolutionary theory has enormous explanatory power, but it is very susceptible to misuse and misinterpretation. It is all too easy for individuals to project their personal biases through the lens of evolutionary theory to create rationalized explanations that seem to support their beliefs (Dennett, 1995).

Consequently, great caution has to be exercised in the use of evolutionary psychology to ensure that what is being studied has some real basis in human biology or human mental processes and is not something that is actually a recent product of our cultural biases. As noted earlier, the notion of the superiority of one sex over another is contingent upon culturally defined ideas of superiority expressed as operational definitions that may have no basis outside of our cultural situation. The social constructivist critique is in many respects an important check that acts to place appropriate limits on the uses of the biological and epigenetic perspectives on gender matters.

Evolutionary psychology is based on the view that the characteristics we humans evolved during our long past as hunter-gatherers still form the basic structure of our minds, our bodies, and our behaviors. However, we also evolved the ability to flexibly tailor these characteristics to the specific nature of the setting we find ourselves in. And through it all, selective forces are acting upon these characteristics, differentially favoring those that benefit our species, or at the very least do not detract from our survival, while pruning those that are not beneficial (Palmer et al., 2002).

27.

Evolution offers a different view of human behavior.

One of the aspects of evolutionary thought that makes it hard to comprehend and accept is what might be called its non-moral quality. Violence, for example, is highly destructive and appears to profoundly threaten our survival. Yet natural selection has not eliminated it from our behavioral repertoire. Indeed, violence seems to be a universal characteristic of our species no matter where or when people have lived.

28.

How do we reconcile our evolved predispositions with our current circumstance?

To apply evolutionary theory to this behavioral characteristic, it would follow that violence in the form that it took in the past (for natural selection cannot anticipate the future) must have conferred some reproductive advantage on those who possess this predisposition. We may ethically abhor violence—though judging by the popularity of violence in movies and video games, we are fascinated by it—but the inclination to engage in violent behavior must have had some overall benefit.

If we examine the behavior of other animals, it is clear that violent behavior is common. From chimpanzees raiding other chimp groups for food or mates, to bighorn sheep battling for dominance, to crocodiles ambushing wildebeests crossing a river, the use of violent behavior to acquire resources is common in nature. Taken from the perspective of natural processes, violence is neither good nor bad; it is merely a type of behavior that sometimes results when an organism attempts to secure food or reproductive opportunities for itself.

However, though the findings of evolutionary theory may yield important insights, it does not justify any particular behavior. Bending evolutionary theory to form a seemingly biology-based justification for violence—or any other behavior for that matter—is not appropriate. Concepts of right and wrong are entirely human conventions and, as we have seen, it is vital to respect the limits that the social constructivist critique (i.e., that social conventions are valid only in their respective cultural context) places on the various biological and epigenetic perspectives on human behavior. When these limits are ignored, as many groups seek to do by attempting to rationalize their misdeeds by incorrectly applying evolutionary theory, the results can be disastrous. From the intentional misreading of Darwin's theory by the Nazis to justify the annihilation of groups they deemed unfit for life, to the view that violent conflict is beneficial, it is clear that we must always be mindful of the misuse of this powerful—and so easily misinterpreted—theory (Burke, 1985, p. 262–267).

The problem for us today is that our technological prowess has reached such a level that we can commit acts of violence that have effects that far exceed anything even the most powerful animal can achieve. In our ancestral past, an individual in a fit of rage might have killed a few individuals with a club or an axe; now a person with a firearm can easily kill dozens. A single act of organized violence in the preindustrial past might have resulted in the death of an entire family or tribe, or more recently the destruction of a city; now with nuclear weapons the whole planet can be rendered uninhabitable. This is the problem of possessing behavioral inclinations that were evolved for a world that was very different from the one in which we now live. Our capacity to deploy the fruits of our intelligence to generate higher material standards of living has far outrun our evolutionarily derived behavioral inclinations. To put it bluntly, we were not evolved to live in the world we only recently created. This is the underlying problem that rests beneath all the conflicts we live with today and is a direct consequence of the rapid pace of change.

We are arguably in a transitional period now as we try to more effectively use money and markets to secure and distribute resources, and so limit our use of force to acquire them. However, in the past, violence was one of the important types of behavior our ancestors used to get what they needed to ensure their survival and the survival of their children. The tendency to engage in violent behavior is still with us because sufficient time has not passed for it to be selected out. So we have to be taught to restrain and channel our aggressive impulses. Remember, too, that the ability to learn new behaviors, and then change the way we interact with our environment, is also an evolutionarily derived characteristic.

Nevertheless, it is this incompatibility between our old behavioral repertoire, and our present capabilities that drives home the need to understand the basis of our current behavior. And this is most definitely the case with matters relating to gender.

REFERENCES

Bronowski, J. (1972). *The ascent of man.* Boston: Little, Brown. pp. 364–367.

Burke, J. (1978). *Connections.* Boston: Little, Brown. pp. 8–12.

Burke, J. (1985). *The day the universe changed.* Boston: Little, Brown.

Calder, N. (1979). *Einstein's universe.* New York: Greenwich House.

Cameron, R. (1989). *A concise economic history of the world.* New York: Oxford University Press. pp. 20–43.

Cantor, N. (1993). *The civilization of the middle ages.* New York: HarperCollins pp. 289–372.

Clark, S. R. L. (1994). "Ancient philosophy." *The oxford history of western philosophy.* Kenny, A. ed. Oxford: Oxford University Press. p. 31.

Darwin, C. (1859). *On the origin of species.* London: John Murray.

Dennett, D. C. (1995). *Darwin's dangerous idea: evolution and the meanings of life.* New York: Simon & Schuster.

Diamond, J. (1997). *Guns, germs, and steel: the fates of human societies.* New York: W. W. Norton.

The Economist, "The brewing storm." Vol. 399, no. 8739. June 25, 2011. pp. 31–32.

Fausto-Sterling, A. (1985). *Myths of gender: biological theories about women and men.* New York: Basic Books.

Ferguson, N. (2006). *The war of the worlds: twentieth-century conflict and the descent of the west.* New York: The Penguin Press.

Fukuyama, F. (2011). *The origins of political order: from prehuman times to the french revolution.* New York: Farrar, Straus and Giroux.

Gould, S. J. (1989). *Wonderful life: the burgess shale and the nature of history.* New York: W. W. Norton. p. 126.

Greenwood, J. D. (2009). *A conceptual history of psychology.* New York: McGraw Hill.

Harman, P. M. (1998). *The natural philosophy of james clerk maxwell,* Cambridge: Cambridge University Press, p. 6.

Kagan, J. (2012). "Psychology's missing contexts." *The Chronicle of Higher Education.* April 8, 2012.

L'Hermite-Leclercq, P. (1992). "The feudal order." Klapisch-Zuber, C. ed. *A history of women: silences of the middle ages.* Vol. 2. Cambridge: Belknap Harvard. pp. 213–220.

Malthus, T. R. (1798). *Essay on the principle of population.* London: J. Johnson.

Maybury-Lewis, D. (1992). *Millennium: tribal wisdom and the modern world.* New York: The Viking Press.

Meeks, W. A. (1993). *The origins of christian morality: the first two centuries.* New Haven: Yale University Press. pp. 52–65.

Nasar, S. (2011). *Grand pursuit: the story of economic genius.* New York: Simon & Schuster. pp. xii–xiii.

Palmer, J. A. & Palmer, L. K. (2002). *Evolutionary psychology: the ultimate origins of human behavior.* Boston: Allyn & Bacon. pp. 16–23.

Pinker, S. (1994). *The language instinct.* New York: Harper Perennial.

Plato. *The Republic.*

Spade, P. V. (1994). "Medieval philosophy." Anthony Kenny, ed. *The oxford history of western philosophy.* Oxford: Oxford University Press. p. 88–92.

Stringer, C. & Andrews, P. (2012). *The complete world of human evolution.* London: Thames and Hudson.

Veyne, P. (1987). "The roman empire: marriage." Aries, P. & Duby, G. general eds., Veyne, P. ed. Goldhammer, A. trans. Vol 1. *A history of private life: from pagan rome to byzantium.* Cambridge: Belknap Harvard. p. 33–49.

Wood, M. (1992). *Legacy: the search for ancient cultures.* New York: Sterling. p. 20.

Name   Date

1. Though we live with twenty-first century technologies and attitudes, why do the ways people behaved in the past still intrude into our relationships?

2. What is meant by the "old ways of knowing" versus more modern ways of understanding the world?

3. In the past, did people marry for the same reasons as they do today? What changes have come to the nature of marriage?

4. What makes it difficult to effectively ban same-sex marriage?

5. What two ways of understanding the world did Thomas Aquinas reconcile? Why was this important?

6. What is an operational definition?

7. Why is it important to be aware of social constructions in research?

8. How do the biological essentialist, epigenetic, and social constructivist views differ on the question of the objective reality of the world?

9. What is reification?

10. What is meant by the statement "correlation does not indicate causation"?

11. What is evolution?

12. What is evolutionary psychology?

4

Chapter 4

The Nature of Change

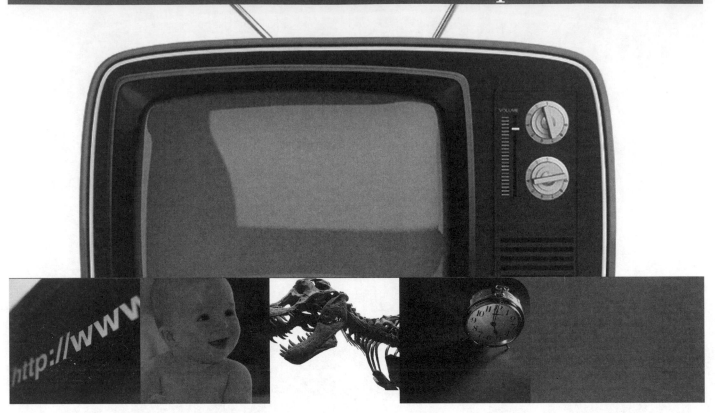

4

We humans have this curious tendency to feel that the most recent fashion trend, the latest clothes, or the current "look" is somehow the best, is in some way perfect. Of course, we only have to look back in time to see the ridiculousness of this view. Bell bottoms the height of fashion—give me a break! Simulated wood grain on the side of a car—you must be joking! Yet there will come a day when the "must-have" clothes and accessories you regard as essential to be seen in public will look absolutely silly to future generations—even to your older self. The smartphone you can't live without will likely be a technological dinosaur someday. The car you covet now will no doubt look old fashioned when you're older—if we even have cars in the future.

FIGURE 4-1. Fashions change.

In other words, today's awesome "must-have" item will trigger tomorrow's derisive snigger. (My first cell phone back in 1993 was bigger than a shoe and weighed two pounds—and all it did was make phone calls!) Your parents have probably heard you laugh at a high school picture of them: "Oh my god, what are you wearing, Dad?" "You drove that, Mom!" And someday your son or daughter may react the same way to a picture of you they find languishing in some corner of social media—if it still exists.

Which begs such questions as: Is there ever an end to development? Is there a level beyond which things cannot be enhanced?

There is nothing definitive about fashion. It is completely subjective and is, consequently, a social construction. Today's "cutting edge" will inevitably be out of date some time in the future. Things change. Tastes change.

Change is very much a part of life. You were once a helpless baby, a toddler, a young child, a grade school-aged individual, and a teenager… and through all these transitions in your development your sense of self was altered. Well, I certainly hope it has. That you are able to read these words and comprehend their meaning means you learned to read and developed the capacity to understand concepts. Very likely you have the expectation that in the future you will know more than you do now. The fact that you are attending college implies that you are open to the possibilities of growth and further development.

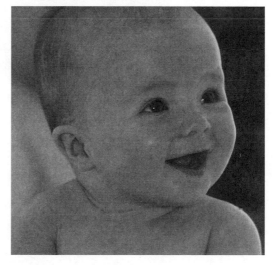

FIGURE 4-2. Each life is a journey with a beginning…

But I'm sure few individuals have the expectation that they will ever possess "perfect" knowledge or "ultimate" wisdom sometime in their lifetime. No one enters college thinking they will learn the meaning of every word in the Oxford English Dictionary or know all the information contained in an encyclopedia.

So it is strange that many people conceive of evolution as a process whose goal is to generate the "perfect" living thing.

There are a lot of misconceptions about evolution and evolutionary processes.

. . . .

"Any sufficiently advanced technology is indistinguishable from magic."

No finer words were ever written to characterize the late 20th and early 21st centuries. The statement is Clarke's Third Law and was first presented in May 1967 in a lecture given by the futurist, Arthur C. Clarke (1972), concerning technology and its effects. I have always suspected that the current fascination with wizards, vampires, and zombies—which all have magical elements in them—have, at least in part, their origin in our declining understanding of the technology that structures our lives.

FIGURE 4-3. In the minds of many people, it has almost magical properties.

For example, consider the smartphone. Inside that handheld slab of plastic and metal are micro-electronic devices that can store and process vast amounts of digitized information into a format (images and sound) that you can interact with. The hardware and the software that reside in that machine, not to mention the vast unseen cyber-infrastructure that supports its functions, are incomprehensible to the average user. The sheer complexity of the computerized world in which we live is staggering. And as Sir Arthur so eloquently put it, all the manifestations of cyberspace are certainly advanced enough to appear to be motivated by magical forces.

And that's the trick, isn't it? Many of the things that are integral parts of our lives today appear to be so complex, so powerful, so other-worldly, that we throw our hands in the air and resign ourselves to mystified incomprehension.

Think about the global economy. The 24/7 flow of goods and services, enormous sums of money moving electronically around the world, the leveraging of assets to bewildering levels of valuation, the fantastically complex derivatives market that generates heady profits seemingly out of thin air... and much, much more. It all feels dazzlingly beyond our intellectual capacity to grasp.

It all seems like magic.

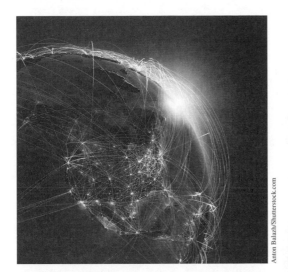

FIGURE 4-4. What unseen forces do you think shape your life?

Unseen forces shaping the landscape of our lives, lurking out there in the mist… that's what it feels like to many people. Certainly the Internet and the global economy have intimations of the supernatural.

Yet if you make a concerted effort, you can understand the workings of smartphones and high finance. If you major in Computer Science or Economics, these elements of the post-modern world lose their mystery. It's not magic. They can be understood and used to your advantage. The trick is whether you want to make the effort to learn to "use" these systems, or give up and allow yourself to be "used" by them. And the first step toward taking back some control of your destiny is to understand some of the fundamental elements that order the world in which we live.

Change is one of those elements and is a consistent part of our lives these days. Figuring out what to major in is no easy task when the requirements of the job market morph and alter with startling speed. Today's "must-have" degree may lead to lifelong personal prosperity or to tomorrow's unemployment line. Indeed, during your working life you will likely have many different kinds of jobs which means you will have to constantly re-educate yourself over the decades.

FIGURE 4-5. Is a degree a "must have"?

One of the key concepts that we humans have developed to understand change is evolution. Like the workings of the global economy in which the notion of "buying low" and "selling high," of the interaction of supply and demand, have been elaborated into a monstrously complex array of principles and practices, evolution is actually a simple concept that has grown to encompass nearly everything.

Unfortunately, a lot of misconceptions surround this way of understanding change (Buss, 2012). Like the view that many people have of the technology that is such a part of contemporary life, elements of magic are attributed to evolutionary processes. For example, it is commonly believed that evolution is somehow a conscious process: that plants, animals, and people "will" themselves to adapt to the environment. As noted in the previous chapter, this is absolutely false. Another belief is that the goal of evolution is to create the "perfect" organism. Again, as noted previously, there is no truth in this view of evolution. Many people believe that some forms of life are superior to others. Nope. From an evolutionary point of view, such notions have no basis in fact.

This is where the contents of Chapter One in this book become important. Being able to discern what is a social construction and what is essentialist is vital in understanding evolutionary theory.

First off, evolutionary theory is itself a social construction derived from scientific observation with strict rules that are meant to describe the process by which change occurs. Charles Darwin, the originator of the modern theory of evolution, hoped that the mental model he developed about why plants and animals change over time accurately mirrored reality. This is why evolution is still referred to as a theory. It is not definitive—it is not the final word on the matter—and is itself subject to change. And indeed, it has been refined over the years. Very recently, the concept of "order for free" has been added to evolutionary theory (Kauffman, 1995) and very probably new refinements will come in the future. It's also possible that someday an even better theory of evolution will come into existence and Darwin's view of change may be relegated to the ash heap of outmoded things—like bell-bottom pants.

Secondly, it is important to understand that notions of "perfection" and of "superiority" are themselves social constructions. Perfection exists only in our minds. Nothing in the physical world is perfectly perfect. The notion of superiority is based upon human definitions and is therefore also a product of our thoughts (a social construction) and thus cannot be an essentialist thing. Bear in mind, because evolution is attempting to describe processes that are essentialist characteristics of the universe, social constructivist concepts like perfection and superiority can have no place in its theoretical structure.

Thirdly, evolution is not a supernatural force that guides the development of species. It is an entirely materialist approach to understanding change. There is no hidden mind with an agenda to fulfill pushing evolution along; it is completely mindless. There are no ideals that inform the direction of change. There is no unseen supernatural mechanism supporting it. Evolution is not concerned with progress toward more and more advanced forms of life. Indeed, progress itself is an idea, a social construction, which has only been around for a few centuries (Burke, 1985). The same can be said of the term "advanced." Humans, from the point of view offered by evolution, are just another product of the interaction of matter and energy over the four billion plus years of the Earth's existence (Sagan, 1980). We are not set apart from the rest of life on the planet from an evolutionary point of view. We are in no way a superior form of life from this perspective. (Indeed, what is to be made of an organism that destroys its own habitat?)

Adam Radosavljevic/Shutterstock.com

FIGURE 4-6. What concepts structure your worldview?

FIGURE 4-7. How do you perceive the world around you?

FIGURE 4-8. Have you ever considered how much time orders your life?

Now it is quite understandable why many view with disdain the theory of evolution. It seems to be a heartless way of looking at the world; it accords no special place for individuals and disregards many of the things we value. But remember we live in a world that is concerned with results—and despite whatever personal misgivings we may have about evolutionary science—it is so far the best model we have that explains the physical world in which we live.

2.

A view of one of the critical elements of evolution: time...

Time is not an easy thing to fully comprehend. It is not something that can be touched or tasted, seen or heard. Indeed, some physicists argue that it does not actually exist (Barbour, 1999). Yet we all know the saying "time is money," and are to varying degrees conscious of its passage in our daily lives. We acknowledge its role every time we celebrate our birthday or the arrival of a new year. Christmas, Thanksgiving, Halloween and many other holidays are all linked by their respective temporal "locations" as described by a kind of "map" of time, called a calendar. The recurring nature of our perception of time on Earth is evident by the cycling of the seasons: spring follows winter, and summer precedes autumn.

But when it comes to understanding the enormity of time, like when we're faced with the five million years that constitute the age of humankind, our minds are usually not quite up to the challenge. Why? When our own life experiences are measured in months, years and decades, really large spans of time are hard to imagine.

The reason I'm bringing the matter of the enormity of time up is because we have this tendency to think that the way we live today is the way people have always lived—which is very far from the truth. Your life is extraordinarily exceptional. Never in the history of humanity have the technologies you have access to, and the attitudes and values you possess, existed. The lifestyles and habits you take for granted were not available to people who lived in the past.

FIGURE 4-9. How is your life different from your grandparents' lives?

So how unique is our postmodern way of life?

Imagine for a moment if you could experience the entire history of humankind as a single person's life. In other words, what would it be like to proportionally compress five million years into a century of living? What would that person experience over the course of her life?

Try this mental exercise: You are Milly Millennium. You were born at the turn of the millennium, on the first moment of January 1, 2000. You lived exactly one hundred years and died on the first moment of January 1, 2100. Your life paralleled the five-million-year history of our kind. In other words, each day of the 36,525 days of your hundred-year life (100 years × 365 days + 25 leap days = 36,525) is equal to just under 137 years (36,525 × 136.9 years = 5,000,272.5 years).

Now imagine that you have to live as all your ancestors did over the course of your hundred-year life. For example, for most of human history people hunted and gathered their food on a daily basis (Diamond, 2012). So for most of your life as Milly Millennium you have to scratch a living from the Earth, searching constantly for fruits, nuts, and berries. If you're a guy, you have to risk life and limb every day, chasing after game with nothing more than a wooden spear or scavenging carcasses with stone knives for almost your entire life.

In essence, from our point of view, during nearly all your life you have to scratch a living,

foraging for food, while moving perpetually from place to place. You must find whatever shelter from the weather or fabricate one on a daily basis. It's a hard life.

FIGURE 4-10. The nomadic hunter-gatherer way of life has been with us for hundreds of thousands of years.

So when do things get better?

The practice of growing food and raising animals for their milk and meat has been around for about ten thousand years. If each day of your life is equal to a little less than 137 years of human history, you won't begin to experience an agricultural way of life until you are almost 99 years and 10 months old! Living with cities where you can go to trade and seek sanctuary does not come until you are in the last month of your hundred-year life. And we're *not* talking about civilization, as we know it today, with shopping malls and the Internet. Imagine a life of backbreaking work, tending little plots of land, trying to grow enough grain to feed your family using ox-drawn plows and digging sticks. The closest thing to a store is the gathering place by the shrine of the local god or goddess where people gather once in a while to barter what little surplus they might have.

Money won't come into existence for another seven thousand years after the advent of farming! Milly will be in the last month of her life when money begins to be used to buy things.

If you're longing to shop at a store to buy groceries, Milly will have to wait until she is 99 years, 11 months and 29 days old—two days away from death—before she can enter such an establishment.

FIGURE 4-11. For most of human history shopping did not exist.

Cars and airplanes won't exist until the 31st of December 2099, the last day of your hundred-year life. You'll be able to send your first email at around 8:30 pm that evening. In the last hour of your life, you can send a text message.

The United States exists on the last day and a half of your life. Women's rights and the feminist movement as we know them today are part of Milly's last day. Credit and debit cards, dishwashers, televisions, and microwave ovens, computers and cell phones are all developments that come in the final hours of your life.

From the first day of your life as Milly Millennium on January 1, 2000 to late October 2099, every day was spent walking from one place to another searching for food. The hunter-gatherer way of life is by far the dominant mode of existence for humanity. Only in the last seventy days of Milly's one hundred years of life is any discernible change in the essential ancestral pattern of daily life detectable. Everything is made by hand all the way up to the last two days of your life.

All Milly's long life she's done basically the same thing. Gathered food, had and raised children, observed the passing of the seasons, and struggled to find shelter against the elements. Her life condition on her first birthday and her ninety-ninth birthday were pretty much the same. The stone and bone tools were cruder on her first birthday than on her 99th birthday but they were still made of these same materials. Her standard of living changed very little over those years. Only in the last tiny fragment of her life has the world we know come into existence.

3.

So why is it important to get a feeling for the huge differences between our current way of life and the lifestyles our ancestors knew, as well as the enormous amount of time human prehistory spans?

· ·

FIGURE 4-12. Is it hard to teach an old dog new tricks?

You probably know the saying, "It's hard to teach an old dog new tricks." The implicit message is that an animal that has already lived beyond its early developmental period is less apt to acquire new behaviors easily. Also it suggests that older behaviors tend to persist making new ones more difficult to learn.

We humans are an extremely adaptable bunch. We can alter our way of doing things so that we can live in the heat of the Sahara or the cold of Antarctica; we can circle the Earth in the vacuum of space or travel in the depths of the seas.

FIGURE 4-13. For all our modernity we still have ancestral needs.

Yet despite our amazing behavioral plasticity, we still long for interpersonal contact. Most of us hate feeling lonely. Though it's bad for our health, we tend to love eating sweets as well as salty, fatty foods. Most people enjoy engaging in sexual behavior and many employ a variety of techniques and technologies to limit the reproductive consequences of such activity. Being uncomfortable with isolation, enjoying the consumption of sweet, salty, fatty foods, engaging in sexual behavior are all predispositions we inherited from our ancestors (Palmer, 2002).

Due to these tendencies, in the 21st century, we live with strange contrasts. We can send robot spacecraft into the depths of space but many people have difficulty controlling their weight. We can communicate with anyone on the planet yet many people feel isolated and lonely. We can develop incredibly complex systems like the vast electronic infrastructure that supports the Internet yet pornography constitutes a significant fraction of its content.

FIGURE 4-14. We live in a world of contrasts.

Why do these contrasts exist?

Remember Milly Millennium? For most of her life she lived as a hunter-gatherer, existing from day to day, relying upon the natural environment for all that she and her family needed for survival. For 36,524 of the 36,525 days of her life she never earned money on a regular basis. For 1,198 of the 1,200 months she lived she searched for edible wild plants while her male counterpart chased after animals that were desired for their meat and hides. The hunter-gatherer way of life made up more than 99 percent of her life experience. Only in the last tiny fraction of her life did city life exist, and money was used to purchase what she needed and wanted. Access to electronic communication systems came in the last moments of her life.

From the perspective offered by Milly's hundred-year life that mirrored the history and lifestyles of humankind over its five-million year existence, it becomes obvious that there hasn't been a lot of time for new behavioral predispositions to evolve. Think about it, after having lived as a hunter-gatherer for more than 99 percent of your life, the transition to the lifestyle of an urban-dwelling, job-holding, money-making, global consumer, would come as quite a jolt.

FIGURE 4-15. Have you ever considered the novelty of the post-modern way of life?

Consider all the difficulties that commonly plague individuals today: loneliness, stress in the workplace, obesity, handling finances, diabetes, anorexia, divorce, addictions to food, drugs, sex, gambling, then throw in more global matters that affect people like the economy, climate change, conflicts between nations, and it becomes clear that there are a lot of things we humans are not terribly good at dealing with.

A simple question arises: why is it so hard to live in the post-modern world?

All kinds of answers can be offered up in response to this question.

Perhaps the most direct way to address why we find contemporary life so difficult is simply that it's hard to "teach an old dog new tricks." In other words, we have a lot of baggage that we unknowingly carry with us. The accumulated adaptations of millions of years of living as hunter-gatherers are still with us, while the behavioral predispositions and adaptations for living in a world of money, markets, machines, and momentary social interaction have not had time to develop.

FIGURE 4-16. As a species, we are still learning to live in the present.

The one evolved characteristic we can fall back on is our capacity to learn new behaviors. We must do the hard work of *learning* to live in a setting that has existed for only a tiny part of our collective existence. (Remember Milly's life experience.) In other words, we've lived for such a short portion of human history in what can be termed "technological civilization" that we have not had the time needed to evolve adaptive responses to the new environment in which we live.

This is where the nature of evolution comes into play. We have the *capacity* to learn to live in the brave new world of the 21st century—in other words we have the predispositions necessary for educating ourselves—but it does not mean that we will inherently learn how to effectively live in the current context. We have to work at it.

FIGURE 4-17. We rely on our behavioral predisposition to learn to live in the present.

Consider for a moment if we had five million years of history living in the world we know today. Evolution would have selected for physiologies that can deal with high levels of dietary sugar, salt, and fat because individuals who weren't adversely affected by consuming such foods would have a reproductive advantage and so pass these characteristics on to their descendents. Our metabolisms would be suited for fast food. No one would suffer ill health from eating foods that didn't exist in the ancestral environment. No one would ever develop diabetes or become overweight. After five million years of living in a money economy, we would very likely possess behavioral tendencies to avoid economic downturns, to effortlessly handle our finances so that we never got into difficulties with debt and over-consumption. We'd have very probably developed behavioral predispositions to balance our need for social contact and for sexual expression so that we would never feel lonely or deprived. Our relationships would likely not be so stressful and unfulfilling.

If we had the benefit of five million years of biological, social, and psychological development derived from living in the world we know today, we would very probably be fairly well

adapted to its rigors and requirements. We'd likely seldom feel sad, stressed out, insecure, anxious, or be over- or underweight. (You can begin to understand why in the past people thought that our prehistoric ancestors lived in a world suited for them, that they lived in an Eden. It was because such ancestral people had the advantage of five million years of adaptations to the requirements of the natural world.)

FIGURE 4-18. Ever wonder why natural environments are so beautiful?

But we're never going to develop the adaptations needed to live comfortably in the post-modern world. Why? It changes so rapidly it is unlikely that we would have the opportunity to begin to develop adaptations to the new circumstance in which we find ourselves. Remember the briefness and the suddenness of the changes that came at the end of Milly's life?

4.

The nature of evolution…

Just to give you a flavor of how evolution works let's imagine you woke up this morning, turned to your boyfriend or girlfriend or partner, and randomly decided, "I've had enough of lectures, labs and exams. I want to do something practical. I want to learn how to farm, mill flour, and bake bread." Your life partner looked at you and said, "Yeah. I want to do that, too."

When you broadcast your intentions on social media you received a slew of responses like: "You'll never get a real job." "You'll never pay off your student loans." "You'll end up poor and destitute."

But you and your partner persevere and ignore their advice. Together you learn to live off the land and discover that your personal qualities match up nicely with this way of life. It's not glamorous. You and your partner don't become rich or famous, but you both eke out a living and feel good about what you've accomplished.

FIGURE 4-19. Do you have what it takes to live off the land?

Your social media friends shake their collective heads and tell you and your beloved, "You guys are nuts living like that."

Then one day the lights don't work. The Internet is gone. Cell service is inoperative. Walking to town with your usual load of bread to sell, you and your partner discover the entire

infrastructure of modern life has disappeared. A financial crash and a global cyber-attack have brought everything to a halt. War breaks out. The old system of global markets is completely disrupted.

Suddenly, you and your partner are among the most important people in the community because you know how to produce food. You know how to raise crops and mill the seed into flour to bake bread. (Ever wonder why the names "Miller" and "Baker" are so common? Millers and bakers prospered in the past and left a lot of descendents.) Now the social media friends who once looked down on you and your partner are begging for food, wondering how they can survive without the systems that once supported their lives. And you and your partner are doing just fine compared to most people, thank you very much.

What is the moral of this cautionary tale?

What may appear to be maladaptive today may be very adaptive tomorrow. Evolutionary change works in a similar way.

FIGURE 4-20. The dinosaurs were incredible creatures but they could not cope with changes that came 65 million years ago.

If you were a time-traveling zoologist who journeyed back more than 65 million years to when the dinosaurs dominated the Earth, you would probably marvel at the fantastic animals that walked, swam, and flew through the varying environments of the time (Palmer, D., 1999). Who would have ever thought that the tiny furry creatures—little critters the size mice—that scurried beneath their feet would ever amount to anything?

Then rapid change came (Alvarez, 1980). The environment was drastically altered and the characteristics the dinosaurs possessed became highly disadvantageous to their survival. Large bodies, with equally large appetites were not appropriate to the new surroundings. The dinosaurs disappeared. They became extinct.

Characteristics that once seemed so disadvantageous, like the small bodies of early mammals, were suddenly much better suited for the new conditions that had arrived. With the disappearance of the dinosaurs, mammals—the class of animals we belong to (Tudge, 2000)—could begin to occupy new niches in the environment.

FIGURE 4-21. The survival of genes is what counts

It's important to understand that the only thing that matters in evolution is the persistence of genes. In other words: survival. Our time-traveling zoologist's view of the magnificence of the dinosaurs is a social construction. Nature does not perceive the small bodies of ancient mammals as inferior to the large bodies of dinosaurs. The only thing that matters is the persistence of the genes of organisms (Dawkins, 1976). Before change came to terrestrial environments 65 million years ago, from the point of nature, tiny mammals were just as adapted to these setting as the enormous dinosaurs, because our little ancestors were able to eke out a living and multiply.

Sound familiar?

The decision to drop out of school, learn to raise crops, and bake bread was not planned because you and your partner foresaw that a global economic calamity was going to happen. You just happened to have the characteristics required to be a bread producer. At first these qualities did not seem advantageous. But uncertainty always exists and change can come at any time. When the infrastructure of global markets, money, and automation disappeared, these characteristics became highly advantageous. If conditions did not improve and being a miller remained an advantage, you and your partner might have more children than others. Your characteristics would persist.

The same could be said about the tiny ancient mammals that lived in the shadows of the huge dinosaurs. Their characteristics seemed unfavorable before change came. After the environment was altered by calamity 65 million years ago, seemingly disadvantageous qualities suddenly became highly advantageous.

FIGURE 4-22. Feeling lucky?

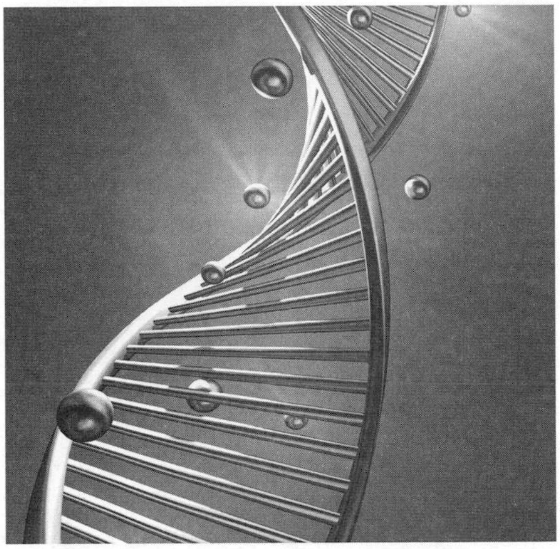

FIGURE 4-23. Random chance plays a big part in evolutionary theory.

The element of random chance, what we like to call luck (which is a social construction), is always at the root of evolutionary change. No one can predict, with any meaningful degree of accuracy, the future. Who would have ever thought the mouse-like creatures that shared the world with the dinosaurs would ever amount to anything? Yet their descendents—us—have reshaped the planet. Drop out of school to learn how to make bread? Are you kidding? But you never know what the future might bring…

There's a word for these kinds of events: serendipity. It refers to the "gift of finding valuable or agreeable things not sought for" (Merriam, 1971). What in the human mind seems accidental is very much a part of evolution.

Mutations occur in the DNA of animals and plants all the time. Most of the time these little changes in the genetic structure of organisms have little or no effect. Sometimes mutations cause illness and death. Mutations that adversely affect an individual's ability to live and reproduce disappear quickly because in the absence of offspring, he or she cannot pass these genetic traits on.

But once in a while a mutation *randomly* occurs that is serendipitously beneficial. Some time in the deep past a mutation happened in one of the species of little creatures that once ran between the feet of the dinosaurs. Perhaps the little change in its DNA made it better able to see in the dark or run faster or eat food others like it didn't consume. Individuals with these mutations prospered and left more descendents (remember the Millers) who all possessed the same alteration in their genes. Over millions of years these mutations accumulated until the little mouse-like creatures that looked so insignificant next to the dinosaurs became lions and tigers, squirrels and elephants, bats, bears, and people.

All these different animals descended from early mammals that somehow survived the catastrophe that took out the dinosaurs. They are all the result of random mutations.

FIGURE 4-24. Meaningful evolutionary change takes generations to occur.

FIGURE 4-25. It has what it takes to survive... for now.

The important thing to understand is that it takes many, many generations for small alterations to generate all the diversity that exists in the world today.

But how can an animal as elegant as a cougar, as graceful as a dolphin, as magnificent as a whale, as clever as humans, be the product of mindless, random chance changes in the DNA of ancestral creatures that lived long ago?

In human terms, the answer to this question is: if an organism does not have what it takes to survive and reproduce, it disappears. It goes extinct. If an organism possesses characteristics that allow it to survive, it is more likely to live long enough to reproduce. This is the reason a cougar appears, from our point of view, as an elegant predator, sleek and efficient, frightening in its power and stealth. (That we perceive the big cat as sleek and elegant is because we subjectively admire these qualities.) It has the characteristics needed to survive and reproduce.

Apply the same criterion to all the organisms of the Earth and a kind of pattern begins to emerge. Everything that is alive has traits that allow it to live and have offspring. Be it the seed that used the nutrients in the soil, energy from the sun, and water from the environment, to grow and become a tree that later produced fruit that contained seeds which held its DNA to produce another generation of trees, or the lion cub that consumed its mother's milk and later the meat it could catch so that it could grow to reproductive maturity and either sire or give birth to another generation of cubs, all things must run the gauntlet of survival in its environment and produce the next generation. Failure to follow this basic path results in extinction.

Remember, living things have no control over their evolutionary development. The occurrence of genetic mutations is entirely random. They are completely unpredictable. Plants and animals, fungi, bacteria and viruses, have no control over mutations. No living thing can "will" a change in its genetic makeup.

It is the environment that determines the fate of all mutations by mercilessly testing them. If the organism that has the mutation survives and reproduces, that mutation will persist in its offspring. If not, that mutation will disappear. It's much like a course in which the only grades that are awarded are either pass or fail. The criterion for "passing" is successful reproduction. "Failure" results when no future generation is produced.

FIGURE 4-26. In nature there are only two grades: "pass" or "fail."

The environment can be understood as a kind of filter that excludes maladaptive characteristics and only allows qualities that are adaptive—or that don't adversely affect the reproductive capabilities of an organism—into the future. So why doesn't evolution lead to a "perfect" organism?

5.

The element that disrupts the accumulation of seemingly advantageous mutations is change.

· ·

Probably one of the contributing reasons you consciously or unconsciously chose to take this course is that you want to improve your chances of having descendents. As we will see in following chapters, much of our behavior is motivated to one degree or another by the desire for offspring—for children. By furthering your understanding of the nature of being

intersex, female, and male, you may be better able to relate to others, function more effectively in the world of people and events, and so become more attractive to potential mates.

It may seem crass on one level to be so centrally motivated by the desire for descendents, but don't feel bad, you have these tendencies because you are directly related to individuals who successfully lived to maturity and had children. Your parents, your grandparents, your great grandparents and so on back through time, all had behavioral predispositions to keep the family line of descent going. Now it's your turn, and you should take advantage of every opportunity to improve your chances.

FIGURE 4-27. Will you add another link to your line of descent?

These are particularly challenging times in which to grow up, become a mature individual, and potentially have a family. Technologies are changing the nature of work, changing the way we interact, even altering the way we view ourselves (Ericksen, 2010). Volatile economic conditions are only adding to the uncertainty and instability that we all face. The strategies that your parents employed to make a living, get ahead, and nurture a family may no longer be effective or appropriate in the new economy.

Being nimble, being flexible, and being open to change are the keys to doing well in the 21st century, because the only constant is change.

And it is change that makes the evolution of an ultimate "perfect" organism impossible.

The dinosaurs were around for far longer, the better part of 200 million years (Tudge, 2000), than the mere five million years we humans have existed. Indeed, fully modern humans have only been around for about 400,000 years. Yet despite the passage of millions and millions of years during which evolutionary processes shaped the dinosaurs, these magnificent creatures are extinct. Yes, they were superbly adapted creatures—*but only for the environment in which they evolved*. But when that environment changed, those superb adaptations, which made them able to occupy so many environmental niches, were rendered maladaptive and obsolete. They disappeared.

All those random mutations that had been tested by the environment, which generated *Brontosaurus* and *Tyrannosaurus Rex*, were no longer suited when new conditions emerged 65 million years ago. The slow accumulation of countless advantageous mutations over millions of generations vanished when something fell from the sky and changed the climate.

Now we face a similar challenge. We humans are the product of the selective forces in our environment that endowed us with the characteristics we currently possess. Will these qualities that developed in a setting that was very different from the one we currently find ourselves in (remember Milly?) continue to be adaptive?

That so many people suffer from depression, loneliness, anxiety, obesity, addictions, and much more are signs that as a species we are struggling to cope. The maladies that plague our minds and bodies are warning indicators.

And here's the real challenge to living in the world that unfolds before us in the 21st century:

In the past, the natural environment shaped through evolution our bodies and our minds. Now our lives are ordered by the demands of the global economy. Its requirements differ from the original setting in which we developed. The global economy is concerned with efficiency and wealth generation, with the growth of markets and the effective use of capital and natural resources (Greider, 1997).

FIGURE 4-28. Are we as a species up to the challenge?

FIGURE 4-29. This is the new selective force that may shape our future.

In essence, we have created a new selective force that tests our ability to survive and reproduce. The socially constructed global economy is beginning to supersede the natural environment from which we evolved. Change as big as any meteor that struck the Earth and wiped out the dinosaurs 65 million years ago now confronts us. But unlike the dinosaurs we can see and feel the changes coming.

We are its cause.

So what does the new environment demand of us?

Efficiency. The global economy demands ever-increasing efficiency. Maximal return for minimal outlay is the underlying premise of the environment we now live in. Buy low, sell high. Squeeze every penny of profit from every activity. This is why despite the fact that the individual American worker is a hundred percent more efficient than he or she was only a generation ago, wages have not increased in any significant way for most people (Greider, 1997).

There is a model for efficiency. The machine.

FIGURE 4-30. Is this our new role model?

So does this mean that those of us who have the qualities needed to function like machines will prosper and reproduce in the future?

Perhaps. But unlike the dinosaurs, we are the authors of the change that is selecting for or against our characteristics. A social construction is shaping us plus it is altering the natural environment.

The speed with which change is occurring makes evolution through random mutation problematic. We don't have the time required for biological evolution to act upon our species. However, unlike the dinosaurs, we can use our evolved capacity to learn and acquire and develop new behaviors to deal with change. So, for example, instead of waiting for natural selection to evolve human physiologies that can cope with the ingestion of high levels of salt, sugar, and fat, we must consciously moderate our intake of certain foods through conscious effort. Similarly, we have the capacity to alter the economic system that now orders our lives.

Which begs the question: do we control our social constructions, or do our social constructions control us?

If we have endowed our social constructions with such power over our lives, then sooner or later the natural environment will act as a filter, either selecting for or against it. Perhaps then having the right stuff to be a Miller or a Baker may turn out to be a highly advantageous characteristic in the long run.

6.

Evolved potentialities and predispositions...

An interesting trend you might have observed recently is the growing practice of allowing pets on college campuses. Several universities now have dedicated dorms where students can live with their animals (Steinberg, 2010). Though a variety of pets share space with students, from birds to cats, dogs are particularly popular.

FIGURE 4-31. Dogs are predisposed to be fine companions.

FIGURE 4-32. Belonging to the pack is essential for survival.

Canine companions are especially suited for individuals who find the transition from living at home to living in a dormitory difficult. Dogs are extremely sensitive animals. They are keenly observant of the emotional state of their owners and if properly trained and socialized can do much to ease tension and bring comfort.

These abilities stem from the social nature of dogs. They're pack animals. In other words, in their ancestral past, they survived by living as a member of a group, much as our ancestors did.

You may have heard at one time or another, the terms "alpha female" or "alpha male" in reference to the social organization of dogs. They refer to the pair of animals in a pack that are perceived to be the dominant individuals in the group and often are the primary pair that reproduces. The fact that dogs, as a species, evolved in an environment in which they were members of a larger group, favored characteristics that enhanced their ability to live in such a way. Being aware of the emotional state of the alpha animals in the pack is essential. Possessing a mind that can encompass the pecking order of the group is also highly advantageous. Why? Dogs hunt cooperatively. Falling out of favor with the leaders of the group could doom an individual dog to isolation and starvation.

In many ways human groupings are similarly organized. Your parents are in many ways the alpha pair of the family from which you came. When you were growing up you were probably aware to some degree of the emotional state of your mother or father, stepmother or stepfather. You likely were consciously or unconsciously aware of the hierarchy of your family.

These parallel qualities make dogs extremely good pets because like you they have the behavioral predispositions to live in a socially organized environment. They were evolved to do so. The potential lies in every puppy to be a wonderful companion that, if properly trained and raised, can live in empathetic harmony with its owner all the years of its life.

FIGURE 4-33. Humans are social too.

FIGURE 4-34. Minds and bodies are shaped by evolution.

No matter how carefully you trained a goldfish or a turtle, you could never expect such animals to be as affectionate and loyal as a dog. The reason, of course, is because fish and reptiles were evolved to live in very different settings. Neither goldfish nor turtles are nurtured for an extended period of time in their early years by their parents. Neither evolved in highly organized social groupings. Consequently, natural selective forces did not favor adaptations that made goldfish and turtles social creatures. These animals do not possess the behavioral predispositions required to be faithful companions like dogs.

As much as evolution shapes bodies and behavioral predispositions through the selection of random mutations over time, it also shapes minds.

The fact that you can drive a car is not the direct result of evolution. Cars have only been around for a little over a hundred years. Sufficient time has not passed for "car-driving" adaptations to evolve. However, you have the characteristics necessary to operate a motor vehicle. In other words, you have the required evolved physical, perceptual, behavioral and intellectual predispositions that together make it possible for you to travel streets and highways at high velocities.

We are related to animals that are highly adept at moving through three-dimensional space. The common ancestor of chimpanzees, bonobos, and us was a capable tree-climber. Like our ancestral relatives, we have grasping hands that can effectively manipulate objects. We have stereoscopic vision that allows us to accurately judge the location and distance of objects. We are active beings who are predisposed to travel great distances to get what we need and desire. We have an intellect that allows us to understand complex relationships, which we can apply to learning to operate machinery.

FIGURE 4-35. We have the predispositions to drive a car but learning is still central.

FIGURE 4-36. Our ancestral predispositions still shape its use.

These are some of the evolved characteristics that make it possible for us to drive cars. Evolution did not "intend" motor vehicle operation. But because of our predisposition for learning entirely novel behaviors, we are able to effectively coordinate these characteristics into the complex activity of navigating through three-dimensional space in a two-ton machine at relatively high rates of speed.

Similarly, the social environment in which intersex, female, and male individuals live changes all the time. For example, evolution did not "intend" for us to use social networking in order to make friends, interact with people who have similar interests, and potentially find mates. But our inborn tendency to engage in behavior that in some way enhances the chances of getting our genes into the next generation shapes our use of such technology. Think about it; for all the high-minded hopes of computer technology expanding the sphere of our knowledge, of forging closer ties between communities and nations, of bringing people closer, it is used principally for chit-chat, selling goods and services, gambling, gaming, and disseminating pornography. This is not meant to be a criticism of the medium, but it does illustrate the power of the predispositions that tend to shape our behavior.

7.

Needs and wants...

We live in a world in which there is a lot of data out there, but not a lot of interpretation of all that information. Type in a question on a search engine and all kinds of references and links appear. You could easily become utterly lost in the mountains of raw data that can be summoned up by simply hitting "enter." You've probably scanned through page after page of "stuff" wondering, what does it all mean?

Your field of study, your major, is a reflection of your interest in a specific area of knowledge and expertise. During the course of your undergraduate studies, you will hopefully assimilate vast amounts of information, write papers and take exams that will potentially help prepare you for your life after college.

FIGURE 4-37. The study of gender is basically about learning to live with people.

FIGURE 4-38. You were born with needs.

The study of gender is at the most basic level about learning to live in a world of people. It is about interacting as a gendered individual with others who identify themselves through a gender category. In many respects, it is among the most fundamental courses you will ever take because it directly relates to some of the essential aspects of being a living person: getting along with others, maybe finding a partner, potentially having children, and raising them to healthy maturity.

There's a lot of information associated with gender, but discerning the meaning—dare I say—finding the "wisdom" that informs the field is often elusive.

So, I'll be blunt.

One of the keys to understanding human gender behavior is being able to distinguish between what you *need* and what you *want*.

You are born with what you need. You learn what you want.

Your need for food, shelter, nurture, love, and care was with you the moment the DNA from your mother and father recombined to create the unique individual that is you. These characteristic needs are common to all humans wherever they live, and most important, whenever they lived. These requirements are essentialist because they are determined by your nature and are the product of at least five million years of evolution.

Every child needs to be properly fed and protected from the elements, but it is the nurturing care from adults that is such an essential need that often goes unacknowledged today. We know from studies of orphaned babies who receive adequate food and shelter but inadequate social interaction that they often fail to thrive and die. Those that survive to adulthood are unable to form ties with others. We know from primate animal studies that if given a choice between a mother who provides nutrition, or a mother who offers comfort and warmth, young monkeys will choose the latter (Blum, 2011). That young children are often left to stare at a television for substantial periods of time indicates that needs are going unrecognized and unfulfilled.

And this is the basic conundrum of post-modern life. So many of our essentialist human needs are being ignored due to the social constructions of the post-modern world. For example, parents have to work in order to provide for the material needs of their children. The socially constructed economic system requires it. However, time away from family means that the social needs of the young are often neglected. Youngsters frequently do not receive the face-to-face nurture they are evolved to require for their growth and development.

as physically and emotionally demanding. It does not conform well to the requirements of an economically inspired setting. As a result, parents are put in a difficult position. Either they put in the time to properly socialize their children and forego career opportunities, or they must essentially entrust someone else to undertake the task of childrearing (nannies or daycare workers), or they use an electronic surrogate to occupy their children's attention (television and computers). The last option is, in the short-term, the most economically efficient (the cheapest and most convenient) but is a poor substitute for what children actually need.

FIGURE 4-39. The demands of family and work weigh on many people.

FIGURE 4-40. The most efficient childrearing option?

If you have ever been frustrated or irritated by the way people inappropriately interact with you, then you may have experienced the consequences of young children not receiving the social interaction they need. If you have ever felt that social networking does not provide the connectedness to others you desire, then you are experiencing the effects of needs that are going unfulfilled. Feelings of chronic loneliness are a consequence of unmet needs.

Remember, the socially constructed economic system is concerned with efficiency. Proper childcare is time consuming as well

However, it is important to emphasize that television and computers are not the problem. It is how they are used in the context of childrearing that is problematic.

Indeed, think about your own behavior: how many times have you distracted yourself from unpleasant feelings by surfing channels or sites? This is where "wants" come into our lives.

It may have started when you were having a bad day and someone older gave you some money and said, "Buy yourself something nice." Or a commercial sent the message that you are entitled to some happiness or comfort after a long slog at work or at school. Over time you learned that your need for relief from stress, anxiety, fatigue, and much more could seem to be achieved by getting what you were taught to want.

FIGURE 4-41. Have you ever bought something to feel good?

Wants have their origins in culture, not in biological essentialist elements. In other words, no one is born wanting a fancy car or a shopping spree. (Indeed, any parent will tell you small children find shopping tiresome and unpleasant. Hence the demand for play-centers in shopping malls.) Wants are taught to us and are socially constructed.

It is easy to distinguish between needs and wants by asking yourself how our ancestors would react to something we think is essential to our lives. The desire for love and affection is certainly a need since in the present and the past individuals longed for both. A motorcycle is definitely a want since such a machine did not exist for most of human history. A large array of footwear is certainly a want.

Arguably a motorcycle or lots of shoes could be regarded as a need for some individuals, such a vehicle may be needed to get to work cheaply, a diversity of sandals, shoes and boots may be required to maintain a person's position in the social hierarchy. But remember, regular work for regular wages and apparel-determined pecking orders are social constructions. They are relatively new social innovations. No child was ever born with an innate need for a motorcycle or a collection of shoes.

The problem with wants is that they can severely distort the perceptions and behavior of individuals. The lust for possessions can be ruinous. They can easily distract us from the most essential parts of our lives. The number of people who have compromised their physical and emotional health, their relationships, and their standing in the community is probably beyond count.

Again our evolutionary history can come to our aid. We have at least five million years of accumulated adaptations to deal with what we inherently need. Our needs have been tested through the filter of natural selection. Most of the things we want have little or no history behind them. Sufficient time has not passed for wants to be tested.

So are our wants always problematic? Not at all, the trick is to use our evolved predisposition for rational thought and learning. Examine the consequences of wants and decide whether they enhance your life or detract from the real happiness you need.

REFERENCES

Alvarez, L. W., Alvarez, W., Asaro, F., Michel, H. V. (1980). "Extraterrestrial cause for the cretaceous-tertiary extinction." *Science* 208 (4448): 1095–1108.

Barbour, J. (2000). *The end of time: the next revolution in physics*. New York: Oxford University Press.

Blum, D. (2011). *Love at goon park: Harry Harlow and the science of affection*. New York: Basic Books.

Burke, J. (1985). *The day the universe changed*. Boston: Little, Brown and Company. pp. 239–240.

Buss, D. (2012). *Evolutionary psychology: the new science of the mind, 4th ed*. Boston: Allyn & Bacon. p. 17–18.

Clarke, A. C. (1972). *Report on planet three and other speculations*. New York: Signet, New American Library. p. 130.

Dawkins, R. (1976). *The selfish gene*. Oxford: Oxford University Press.

Diamond, J. (2012). *The world until yesterday: what can we learn from traditional societies*. New York: Viking Press. p. 7.

Ericksen, L. & Shimazu, M. (2010). *Nations of one: the emerging psychology of the 21st century*. Xlibris.

Greider, W. (1997). *One world, ready or not: the manic logic of global capitalism*. New York: Touchstone Books.

Kauffman, S. (1995). *At home in the universe: the search for the laws of self-organization and complexity*. Oxford: Oxford University Press.

Merriam-Webster (1971). *Webster's seventh new collegiate dictionary*. Springfield, MA: G. & C. Merriam Co. p. 791

Palmer, D. ed. (1999) *The Simon & Shuster encyclopedia of dinosaurs & prehistoric creatures*. New York: Simon & Schuster.

Palmer, J. A. & Palmer, L. K. (2002). *Evolutionary psychology: the ultimate origins of human behavior*. Boston: Allyn & Bacon. pp. 244–270.

Sagan, C. (1980). *Cosmos*. New York: Random House. p. 338.

Steinberg, J. "Colleges extend the welcome mat to students' pets." http://www.nytimes.com/2010/06/06/education/06pets.html?=0&pagewanted

Tudge, C. (2000). *The variety of life: a survey and a celebration of all the creatures that have ever lived*. Oxford: Oxford University Press. pp. 433–514.

Name   Date

1. Explain why fashion is a social construction.

2. What is the meaning of Clarke's Third Law? Besides computer technology and the global
    economy, what other things seem so incomprehensible that they appear to be motivated
    by magic?

3. What makes the theory of evolution a social construction? According to the text, why is it
    a theory?

4. Why is it incorrect to think of evolution as a perfect-seeking process?

5. What point does the exercise of compressing five million years into the hundred-year lifespan
    of a single individual make?

6. According to the text, why do so many people have such a hard time living in the post-modern world?

7. According to the text, why can a characteristic that seems disadvantageous one moment be highly advantageous the next? How does serendipity fit in?

8. Why is it animals do not have any control over their evolution?

9. From where do the behavioral predispositions that make dogs good companions come?

10. From an evolutionary psychological point of view, how do "needs" differ from "wants"?

Chapter 5

FOUNDING MYTHS AND FOUNDATIONAL VIEWS OF GENDER

1.

What is myth?
. . . .

In today's technological world we tend to dismiss myths as irrelevant parts of our historical past. Indeed, the term "myth" is commonly used to designate something as untrue. For example, among those individuals who maintain that premenstrual syndrome is a social construction, the phrase "the myth of PMS" might be used to illustrate their position on the matter (see Chapter 6).

But myths are much more than fanciful stories about heroes and gods and goddesses. An important insight into the nature of myths came from a Greek philosopher who lived more than two centuries before the birth of Christ. His name was Euhemerus and he is known to be the first person to suggest that the gods and goddesses who make up the pantheon of deities celebrated in Greek tradition were in fact not divine beings. He argued that stories about Zeus and Apollo, and all the rest, were actually derived from tales about real men and women who achieved something of social significance. In order to canonize the lessons their acts might impart, they were elevated to the status of godhood (Harris, 2013). This process can be perceived as a way of preserving historical information at a time when most people were illiterate. By transforming factual accounts into the stuff of legend, the crucial elements of some past event could become part of the cultural tradition of a people.

We can glimpse an aspect of this process when we consider the almost reverent view many people have of outstanding athletes. The life stories of tennis stars and football players, hockey and baseball legends ring with an almost divine tone, particularly in accounts about their dedication to personal excellence.

2.

The purpose and function of myth.
. . . .

That myths are common to all the cultures of the world indicates that it serves a vital purpose in the social structure of all human groups. Beyond creating a storytelling vehicle through which important individuals and events are retained in the collective memory of a people, myths also personify ideas and concepts. For example, Venus was the goddess of love for the ancient Greeks and Romans. Thor is the god of thunder in the pre-Christian Scandinavian mythic tradition. For the ancient Sumerians, Enki was the god of wisdom (Bently, 1995). These mythic personifications of natural and psychological elements helped pre-modern people comprehend the forces that shaped their lives. The ache of unrequited love, the fearsome power of an approaching storm, and the ability to perceive deep-seated truths were all brought into focus by meditating on Venus, Thor, and Enki, respectively.

The noted 20th-century scholar of mythology, Joseph Campbell (1988, p. 31), maintained that myth has four vital functions:

The first he termed the mythic function. Mythology opens the mind of the individual to the wonder of the Universe, and to the wonder of the self. Awe is the emotion that resonates through this first function of myth. It makes the surrounding environment a place of transcendent mystery.

The second is the cosmological function. Myth informs the individual of his or her place in the grand scheme of existence and the nature of the Universe that encompasses everything. Science has its origins in the cosmological function of myth.

The third is the sociologic function. Myth serves to support and validate the structure of the society within which intersex, male, and female individuals live. It can be seen in the collective beliefs we share and that we accept as social norms. These are the social constructions we regard as basic to our way of life and form our notion of what is right and wrong.

The fourth function is the pedagogical. This is the function that is most important in the present. Myth must function to show us how to live as humans regardless of the conditions and circumstances that surround us.

Together these four functions mirror our collective concerns. They illustrate what matters to us. For example, the American Dream of self-determination, of being able to own a home and achieving some measure of material affluence through upward social mobility can be likened to a mythic outlook that to varying degrees orders the expectations of many individuals. Though few individuals actively consider their life choices through the lens of the American Dream, it nonetheless is an unconscious component of the way in which individuals view their cultural context.

The aspect of myths that has gotten out of hand more recently is the sociologic function. It is always important to apply the critique offered by social constructivism. Social norms are social constructions. As much as those in power might claim that such norms are a reflection of the natural (essentialist) order, it is important to remember that they are the product of human thought and feeling, therefore they are artificial creations. During the 1930s, for example, the Nazi regime in Germany put forward the view that certain races were inherently superior to others and that it was the duty of those on top to enslave or annihilate those below (Burke, 1985, p. 266). Under the guise of natural science, such a view was used to justify genocide. Sixty million people died in the Second World War that followed.

Myth is a powerful part of our collective psyches. It has been with us since the dawn of our species and will to varying degrees continue to be a part of our conscious and unconscious mental furniture for the foreseeable future. Every time you glance at a calendar or time stamp on your smartphone myths beckon to you. The days of the week are named for ancient mythic elements that ordered the lives of our ancestors—and which still order our perception of time to this day.

The sun and the moon are acknowledged in the first two days of the week: "Sun" day and "Moon" day. The one-armed Norse god of single combat, Tyr, is honored in "Tues" day. The theme of war is perpetuated in the French, Italian, and Spanish names for Tuesday, *mardi, martedi,* and *martes,* which come from the Latin name of the god of war, Mars. Wednesday is named for Wodin (or Odin as we know him as the father of Thor). In other European languages with Latin origins, Wednesday is associated with the god Mercury, thus the name *mercredi, mercoledi* and *miercoles.* Thursday is "Thor's" day. Friday is named for the only female deity in the weekly pantheon, Freyja, the Nordic goddess of love. In Latin, Friday is associated with another goddess of love, Venus, so *vendredi, venerdi* and *viernes* are the French, Italian, and Spanish names for the last day of the workweek. Finally, Saturday is "Saturn's" day. The myths are well represented in your mental map of time (Boorstin, 1983).

3.

Are you aware of the ancient stories that influence our view of the genders?

· ·

REFLECTIONS OF THE PAST

In the stories of ancient Greece the gods often intervened in the destinies of men and women. The Greeks believed that the Furies, the female spirits of the underworld, sought out all who committed injustices and saw to their torments in hell. In the Norse legends of Scandinavia, gods like Thor and Odin fought epic battles against the forces of darkness, much as the ancient Vedic texts of India tell of the great battle between Indra and the dragon demon Vritra that ended with the creation of the land and the sea. In Mayan tradition women revered Ix Chel, the goddess of fertility and childbirth while among the people of the southern Pacific region, Hina's encounter with an eel brought the coconut to humanity (Bently, 1995; Campbell, 1988).

FIGURE 5-1. Tutankhamen (1341 BCE–1323 BCE) was one of the few kings worshiped as a god and honored with a cult-like following during his lifetime in ancient Egypt.

4.

Why are these old stories still relevant?

These tales are like mirrors held up to the cultures from which they originate and reflect the concerns of the people of that society. Consequently, there are many ancient gods and goddesses found around the world concerned with fertility (Amon of Egypt, Ceres of Rome, and Daghdha of ancient Ireland, for example), with food (Inari of Japan, Rongo of the south Pacific, and Xipe Totec of the ancient Aztecs) and with warfare (Durga of India and Mars of Rome). There were deities associated with the forces of nature in the form of the sun (Ra of Egypt and Wi of the Lakota of North America) and the moon (Nanna of the Sumerians and Mama Kilya of the Inca), the wind (Aeolus of Greece) and the rain (Ilyap'a of the Inca). All these mythic entities personified the elements that influenced the lives of our ancestors (Bently, 1995; Campbell, 1988).

5.

How do myths inform our views of women and men?

Naturally, there are mythic tales concerned with man and woman. For the Dinka people of southern Sudan, Abuk was the first woman. She was responsible for bringing death and illness to humanity because her greed angered the high god. Among the Shona people of Zimbabwe, Mwetsi was the first man. The consequences of his actions brought drought, famine, and death to the land, which required his children to kill him in order to restore the world.

Myths are an expression of the worldview of the people who created them. It is interesting to consider the varying narratives that develop in different cultures. Among many of the early human cultures of the world, the sexes and sexuality were powerful components in the tales that emerged from this time.

6.

What do the earliest known stories tell us about men and women?

The earliest known story preserved in written form is the ancient Sumerian tale *The Epic of Gilgamesh*. It is concerned with the adventures of the King of Uruk—the first city (and indeed, Uruk was one of the first major human settlements; its ruins are located in what is now Iraq). His name is Gilgamesh. And like many tales of kingship, he is not a ruler with whom power sits well. He oppresses the people of Uruk. So, the gods send an uncivilized man named Enkidu to Uruk. He is still a "wild" creature. He is hair-covered and crude. However, a temple priestess named Shamhat invites Enkidu to have intercourse with her for seven days, and this transforms him into a civilized person. Later Enkidu befriends Gilgamesh and changes the king's behavior toward his people. When after many adventures Enkidu is killed, the story turns to Gilgamesh's quest for eternal life (Mitchell, 2004).

7.

What does this tale tell us about gender development today?

What is significant in the study of gender about this mythic Sumerian tale is the process of transitioning from a wild animal of nature to a civilized individual of the city. How fitting it is that the oldest know written tale in part addresses the lifestyle change from pre-agricultural nomadic ways to the new ways brought about by the innovation of civilization. In the mythic view of the Sumerians it was through woman, Shamhat, a priestess of the goddess Ishtar, that man is converted from a creature of the wild into a city dweller.

In the mythic tales of Scandinavia, Freyja is the goddess of fertility, who brings life to the

land and the sea. She is associated with sexual freedom and took many gods and humans as her lovers. Among the ancient pre-Christian people of Scandinavia her blessings were sought in marriage and during childbirth (Bently, 1995).

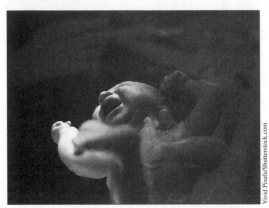

FIGURE 5-2. The ancient Scandinavians believed that the birth of a healthy baby was in part due to the blessings of the goddess Freyja.

Then there is the long-suffering Greek goddess Hera. Married to the ever-unfaithful king of the gods, Zeus, Hera ruled over the sanctity of marriage and was also associated with fertility and childbirth. Her children were Ares (or Mars in the Roman version), the god of war; Eileithyia, the goddess of childbirth; and Hebe, the goddess of youth (Hamilton, 1942; Bently, 1995).

FIGURE 5-3. Men and women have been arguing just like the gods of mythology since the dawn of our species.

These mythic stories informed the lives of the people that lived in the cultures of their origin and outlined the basic roles and natures of women and men, be they mortal individuals or high gods and goddesses.

 8.

What do myths mean to you?

. . . .

MYTHIC VIEWS

When people hear the word *myth* they make the association in their minds that stories of the Greek gods like Apollo and Aphrodite (she was the goddess of love and beauty whom the Romans called Venus, and whose name gives us the word *aphrodisiac*, which means to excite sexual desire) are just products of the imagination of the people who lived long ago. We tend to think that myths are purely fictional in their content and have no bearing on our lives. The term myth is sometimes used to suggest that a claim is an outright lie. However, from the psychoanalytic and the cultural anthropological perspectives, myths are much more than fairy tales, and they are certainly not untruths (Campbell, 1949).

FIGURE 5-4. The Legionnaire of the ancient Roman Empire left his personal fate in the hands of various gods.

9.

Consider the similarities between science and mythology...

. . . .

In many ways myths can be thought of as a subjective counterpart to the objective scientific approach to understanding the Universe. As we have seen in Chapter 3, science tells us who we are, from whence we come, and potentially, where we are headed, through the application of logic and reason and the careful study of reality using a variety of investigative methods. Myths can also tell us about our origins, our identity, and our destiny, and some might argue they do so more effectively than science does, but through a way of interpreting the world around us that predates science.

Like science, myth is based upon observations of the surrounding environment. But those observations are not subjected to rigorous examination, but are instead interpreted through the lens of cultural tradition; that is, they are inflected through the worldview that orders a particular society and expressed as a story. For the ancient Germanic peoples, thunder was the impact of Mjölnir, Thor's hammer. For the ancient Egyptians, the stars were spread across the body of the sky goddess, Nut. Chaos, in one version of ancient Greek tradition, sprang from Chronos (time), and from Chaos everything in the physical world appeared (Bently, 1995).

FIGURE 5-5. The Scandinavians believed that when Thor threw Mjölnir—his hammer—it meant that the thunderstorm that followed was capable of leveling mountains.

10.

The old views still offer insights into scientific inquiry.

Though in the light of contemporary thought many of these beliefs may appear quaint and perhaps even childish, they often contain important insights that continue to structure our knowledge even today. For example, the importance of time as a dimensional element that structures the Universe, and is an important aspect of Einstein's relativity theory, can

be traced back to the philosophical and mythic thought of the Greeks (Bently, 1995, p. 47; Calder, 1979). Another essential Greek mythic concept, chaos, is a fundamental element at the leading edge of research as diverse as climate change to information science (Gleick, 1988).

Myths are products of the culture in which they developed. Like science, they offer a way of making sense of phenomena as varied as the sky above, the earth below, and everything in between. Myth structures the world for an individual or for a people much as science does. The physical and behavioral sciences offer us a view of ourselves as biologically evolved, culturally shaped individuals who live in a globalized economy in which technologically driven change requires us to continuously update our knowledge of everything. Myths offered our ancestors and offer us views of ourselves that are older, more stable, and more enduring. For the antique Greeks they lived in a world (a Cosmos) where order was, in part, not based upon impersonal physical forces but upon the whim of various gods and goddesses. It helped them to cope with, and find meaning amid, the seemingly random turns of events that brought fortune or disaster. What we call their mythic worldview offered truths to them that were emotionally felt as well as intellectually assimilated (Campbell, 1949).

11.

Myths helped to explain the natural world for our ancestors and also structured their moral beliefs.

Myths, being cultural creations, also encapsulate the moral outlook, notions of right and wrong, of the people for whom they are held as important. There is often what might be called a pedagogical (or learning) element to mythic tales; in other words, myths offer important life lessons and teach individuals about what is regarded as normal within the prevailing cultural context or what may impart a cautionary message (Campbell, 1988, p. 4, 55). For example, Freud reinterpreted the mythological story of Oedipus Rex, the ancient Greek tragedy of the man who kills his father and marries his mother, and that warns of the hazards of incest, to illustrate our ancestor's understanding of the internal identity developmental conflict that young males undergo as they mature (Freud, 1955). The story of Antigone, the daughter of Oedipus and his mother Jocasta, tells the tale of a woman so bound by duty that her life is not her own. In many ways Freud was prefiguring certain aspects of feminist thinking by using the imagery inherent in Antigone to illustrate the burden of living solely according to the directives of others (Kaschak, 1993). Psychoanalysts like Freud, and particularly his colleague, Carl Jung, understood that mythic tales address universal themes that are part of the human experience of all people, irrespective of their cultural context. Like the psychological theories of human development that help us to make sense of the seeming chaos of personal existence, the myths act to bring structure and impart meaning.

©Hayden-McNeil, LLC

FIGURE 5 6. Carl Gustav Jung (1875–1961) was a Swiss psychiatrist and the founder of analytical psychology. An archetype, according to Jung, is a universally understood symbol. Archetypes appear in myths and stories in all cultures and help guide our behavior.

ONCE UPON A TIME...

All of us have narratives we tell ourselves. It may be partly based upon the raw facts of our lives—when and where we were born—it may also be a selective account about the events that were significant to us, the people and places that affected us. It tells a tale that describes our sense of who we are, of what we are about, and what is important to us. What might be called personal myths coalesce into stories that become part of an autobiography that are integral to our identity.

12.

Stories help us make sense of our lives.

In a sense, every narrative begins with "once upon a time" from works of lavishly embroidered fantasy to painstakingly documented records of fact, and is an invitation to adopt another frame of reference, another perspective from which to view the world. And though the nature of the stories we tell ourselves may vary greatly, there is always an element of truth in all of them. For if a story does not hold at least a kernel of truthfulness, it is meaningless and will never be relevant to anyone. Such a tale would be quickly forgotten, lost to memory like any poorly composed episode of a TV series.

13.

What myths surround gender?

There are many myths that surround gender, but there is an over-riding theme that I have noted among many of them that runs something like this:

Once upon a time, all lived in peace and harmony. Then change came from the act of a man or a woman and conflict spread. People realized that there were things that made them different from each other. And man found himself in conflict with other men, and woman found herself in conflict with other women. And woman found herself in conflict with nature, and man found himself in conflict with nature. And woman and man found themselves in conflict with each other. And what had once been a paradise was lost.

FIGURE 5-7. Fortunately, most myths are preserved in books, and lately, even in movies.

In psychology there is a term for a story that everyone is familiar with, for a tale that resonates in the past and in the present—and will very likely be meaningful even in the future. Such stories and images are called *archetypes*. The concept of the archetype was identified and articulated by Carl Jung, who maintained that there is a collective memory and a collective consciousness we all share. These memories are not of specific recollections, but are of images and themes we all recognize because they are part of the human psyche (Campbell, 1971). So that when we see a movie like *Star Wars*, though the setting and characters are unique, the story itself is very familiar. The struggle between the forces of light and the forces of darkness, the search for the missing parent that is actually the quest for personal identity, the presence of a wise old mentor who provides guidance and spiritual awareness, the great battle in which the hero or heroine faces death—these are all archetypes that were formed over uncounted millennia and reflect the psychological experiences of our ancestors. Without the archetypes that echo from the

deep past through our unconscious and emerge as consciousness, stories like *Star Wars* would be little more than the depiction of a bunch of stuff that happened.

FIGURE 5-8. The archetype of the nurturing mother: the Madonna with child.

The reason the story of the woman or man suddenly finding him or herself in conflict with other women and men, with nature, and with each other, resonances within us is because it is a tale as old as our kind. Yet it is given new vitality because we live at time in which the individual has become the primary focus of our culture (Ericksen et al., 2010). One inflection of this mythic theme is of the ill-fated romance. Whether it is a tragedy like *Romeo and Juliet* or your own personal account of the relationship that did not work out, it is very much at the heart of the Western conception of gender and of the roles of men and women. The needs and desires of the individual are often in conflict with circumstances and even with our own natures. And this is one of many important themes that inform the Western cultural tradition of gender.

FIGURE 5-9. An image of a modern-day love story that hopefully will not end as tragically as Shakespeare's *Romeo and Juliet*.

WESTERN RELIGION'S VIEW

For many individuals, religion is an important spiritual source of knowledge about the world, of man and woman's place in it, and of the relationship between the self and all that lies beyond the self. Like science, religion also informs us of who we are, from whence we come, and where we are headed. The nature of faith connects the individual to powers and to a structure of knowledge that far transcend the concrete world of the here and now, and it, too, presents a view of the genders.

If you think about it, the narrative motif of man and woman finding themselves in conflict with nature, society, with each other, and even with God is also found in the story of Genesis, the first book of the Old Testament of the Bible, a text that is central to the Western worldview. In addition to the founding conception of the original humans living in harmony with their surroundings in the Garden of Eden (Genesis 2:9), the account accurately foreshadows the

path that we humans have taken. For it was the act of eating of the fruit of knowledge, and therefore aspiring to the power of the divine (Genesis 3:5), that signals the dawn of human intellectual awareness of the world in the cognitive-based sense that we use today. This act, taken literally and metaphorically, demarks an important developmental watershed in human psychical evolution, for it can be argued that this was the point at which concepts of man and woman superseded the biological essentialist view of female and male differences as just aspects of our reproductive physiology. For it was the change in consciousness, of the formation of an awareness of self and of the consequences that sprang from it, that initiated the awareness of the struggle for existence. The examples given in Genesis of continual toil in the fields for man and the pains of childbirth for woman (Genesis 3:16–19) were the fundamental signs that marked this change.

FIGURE 5-10. An illustration of holy writing.

In other words, our ancestors who lived in pre-agricultural societies, who lived in the wild spaces of the Earth, simply lived with and gave no thought to the physical differences between males and females (Genesis 2:25). Each gender had its own circle of concerns. Each made a vital contribution to the survival of the family or the tribe. Each could not long survive without the other, and a kind of elemental equality emerged from the inherent naturalistic quality of the nomadic hunter-gatherer way of life.

14.

Think about how the old pre-agricultural ways of life differ from ways of living that exist today.

Only when we humans developed agriculture and civilization in the form of cities and systems of government, when complex monotheistic religions that encompassed ethical and moral issues, and power concentrated in the hands of the few did the familiar realm of debate over the rights of the individual, and of women and men, first begin. The transition from the old ways that extend deep into our long prehistoric past, to the rise of the first settlements and the advent of settled life is, according to scholars, the underlying history that runs beneath the teachings of the Bible (Bronowski, 1973). It recounts the formation of the first cities, the first organized struggles for religious, ethnic, and national identity. And for much of the last several thousand years it has exerted a profound influence over male/female relations in the Judeo-Christian West. Particularly in the last two thousand years, first with the rise of Christianity out of Judaism through the teachings of Christ, the formation of Roman Catholicism, the Protestant Reformation, and most recently in the deeply personal nature of contemporary religious belief, faith-based doctrines about the genders continue to shape our views of women and men.

15.

Remember the worldview of social constructivism from Chapter One?

The social construction that formed the context that we have until recently lived with has been largely male dominated. The role of women in the West, as established by the Judeo-Christian faith that informs it, has been greatly circumscribed by the principle examples of Eve—who is interpreted by many to be the initiator of the fall and the expulsion from Eden—and, among Christians, of Mary, the chaste virgin mother of Jesus. These two women became powerful role models in the Western conception of the nature of the female. The role of males in the West was greatly influenced by the view of divinity as God the Father and of God the Son, who together with the Holy Spirit, form the trinity.

Religion is an essential source from which our conception of the genders in the West originates.

FIGURE 5-11. A blossoming apple tree: the tree of knowledge in the Garden of Eden.

THE BROADER MYTHIC CONTEXT

Another prevailing story that informs our view of the world and that tends to support the male accent on power and control in Western civilization is the theme of conflict not only between man and woman, but also between in-group and out-group. Violent conflict between the forces of good (the in-group to which an individual belongs) and the forces of evil (the out-group that is perceived as the enemy) is a recurring pattern not only in the mythic imagination, but also in the hard reality of human history.

16.

What is the persistent theme of human conflict?

We are still living with the unfolding consequences of the cultural innovation our ancestors undertook roughly five hundred generations ago: the shift from a hunter-gatherer nomadic way of living off the land to a settled agricultural lifestyle with the accompanying rise of civilization. It can be argued that we humans are even now working through all the changes that sprang from that social transformation. And we have gained much by letting go of a way of life that had existed for millions of years and adopting one that provides us with a material standard of living our ancient ancestors could never have imagined.

A lot has changed, but certain aspects of our past still persist. One thing that has seemingly remained a constant throughout the history of humanity is war (Morris, 2010). Whether it is between tribes fighting over hunting rights or between superpowers vying for global domination, conflicts have been a recurring human activity. At the root of nearly every war is competition for scarce resources. In the past it was usually fought for control of territory, which was essentially a fight over food and water, and it could also be over labor and reproductive opportunities, as when one group sought to conquer or enslave another group of people. Today, wars can still be fought over these old resources, though new ones like control of energy and economic systems (which

means that such conflict is still over resources) now tend to be the goal. But irrespective of the period in human history, conflict has been a persistent activity.

FIGURE 5-12. Protection of our national interests still remains a priority.

This accent on violence has tended to emphasize the male component of most human cultures. Protection of the in-group and the expansion of its interests are arguably an innate part of our worldview. And for better and worse these aspects of human cultural and biological existence have tended to make all societies oriented toward, to varying degrees, the matter of violent competition for resources. Since males are typically the biologically (essentialism) and culturally (social constructivism) assigned gender that engages in violent behavior, this orientation has tended to favor the priorities of the male over the female.

The social constructivist view would no doubt maintain that war is a product of male socialization and is an effort by this subset of humanity to use violent conflict to maintain its power. However, the prevalence of violent conflict over resources in animals as varied as insects, reptiles, and many mammals would indicate that such competition is inherently part of nature. And though we may wish to believe that we have somehow transcended this aspect of our biological nature (though we are trying to do so through the global use of money and markets—instead of war—as a means to control the distribution of resources), we have yet to achieve this goal. There is also the simple fact that throughout history the vast majority of males did not want to go to war. Given a choice no man wants to risk life and limb and follow a course of action that may lead to premature death. (Though as we will see in the following chapters males have evolved a predisposition for taking risks that for some makes the prospect of participating in war an acceptable gamble.) These elements suggest that war is not a strategic activity designed specifically to foster male dominance.

17.

History is a nightmare of violence...

The formative centuries of all civilizations are marred by violent conflict. The ancient Greeks worshipped their god of war, Ares, just as the ancient Romans worshipped Mars, because hostilities were a persistent feature of their lives (Bently, 1995, p. 24, 129). The ancient Chinese fought for centuries for control of their territory and eventually built several "great walls"—some of which were among the greatest engineering projects of the premodern world—in an effort to keep their enemies out (Morris, 2010, p. 279, 442). War raged across Europe throughout the centuries that followed the fall of the Roman Empire as nations tried to secure their borders and resources. Even the United States was born in the fires of revolutionary war. It would seem that history is telling us that the effort to achieve order is always marked by struggle and conflict. And this pattern has tended to emphasize the male aspects of humanity, for better or worse.

FIGURE 5-13. The word *civilization* is sometimes simply defined as "living in cities," and the remains of a few stately buildings are evidence of living conditions from long ago and the struggle to maintain those ways of life.

18.

Have we humans changed much since the dawn of civilization?

From a larger historical perspective, human civilization is still in its early developmental stages. Only in the last two hundred years have global markets come into existence that act to mediate violence as a means to secure the resources needed for the continuity of life. That women are now able to assert their right to overt political, social, and economic power is an indication that we are transitioning from a mode of existence in which violent conflict was the only means to win resources to one in which non-violent acquisition is becoming the norm. In the time scales of human history this change is occurring with incredible swiftness, though from our point of view it is happening with agonizing slowness. Wars are still fought, but as the cost of engaging in such activity grows ever more unsustainable, we humans may finally come to a developmental tipping point in which war becomes simply too expensive and therefore passes from our behavioral repertoire. Perhaps then the priority given to the needs of war and defense may be eased and a truly equitable balance achieved between the sexes. Then our collective myths of violent conflict may truly become a thing of our past.

FIGURE 5-14. By any measure, wars are becoming too costly for us to conduct.

Let us look now beyond the tales we crafted from the recesses of our psyche to cope with the realities of human existence and consider the unfolding processes that shaped males and females through the long prehistory of our kind.

But just one last note about mythic and religious images and how they still affect our outlook: the next time you see a smartphone, or a computer, or any other device made by Apple, ask yourself whose bite out of the apple is represented in the company's logo.*

_____
* Eve.

A VIEW OF THE DEEP PAST

The sky above was a deep penetrating blue as a harsh cold wind blew across the open expanse of grassland. The sun was at the horizon, casting rays of golden light. There were times now when the piercing hoarse voice of the wind did not cease for day upon day. The old one knew what the voice of the wind sang of, as it whipped her hair about her face. She could vividly remember her grandmother's warning of the terrible cold that would always follow when the song of the wind went long.

She stood at the edge of the camp that her kin had made the evening before. The small children stood huddled around the central fire that was being fed the last of the sticks that had been gathered by the girls. The young mothers were feeding their babies. The men were readying themselves for the hunt. Everyone looked tired and hungry, for the game animals had grown scarce. It was not a good time to go without meat, the old woman thought to herself.

As she turned her gaze to the south she saw her long dead sister's son running toward her out of the immensity of open wind-tossed grass. He waved his spear and as he drew nearer his cries could be heard.

"A herd of mammoth on the move!" he roared.

She turned to relay this message to the men, but they had already heard the call. Hurriedly they grasped their spears, then bent low to touch the earth with their free hand and rub a dab of soil onto their face, and then they took to their feet running as quickly as they could to the south. As the men left, the women called blessings upon them for success in the hunt.

One of the younger men paused when he came to the old woman. She smiled at her grandson—how like her daughter he was in face, though he had his father's eyes—and said, "Be as the great cat, son-of-my-daughter." And he nodded reverently at her words and then took to his heels running hard to catch up with the hunting party.

A small child came to stand next to the old woman. She reached up to grasp her grandmother's hand and asked, "Will they kill today?"

The old woman looked to the nodding grasses as a strong gust swept by and she replied, "Yes, they may. And we might eat well today and in the days to come, but there are difficult times ahead for us, granddaughter. The season of fruit and nut are long gone and there will be less and less to eat."

Then she turned around and bade her dead son's daughter to look to the north. A line of mountain summits entirely covered in dazzlingly white glaciers stood just beyond the curve of the horizon.

"See, little one," said the old woman, "the ice pursues us, and soon it will overtake us with the first snow. Hopefully, we will be able to wait out the long cold in the caves to the west, and there you and the other women will be able to tend the hearth fire through the darkened days and hard nights."

The girl looked intently at the northern mountains as she tightened her grasp of her grandmother's hand. The wind blew her hair back and away from her face.

"Remember, when the wind sings long through day and night, the season of cold that follows will be unforgiving," the woman intoned.

"When the wind sings long through day and night," the child echoed.

As terrible as the Great Recession that began in the last quarter of 2007 was to so many people, it would have counted as a non-event compared to the arrival of periods of intense climatic cooling that our ancestors experienced tens and hundreds of thousands of years ago. According to the geological record, the Earth went through several periods of global climate change in the past two hundred thousand years that resulted in the widespread advance of glacial ice over much of the land (Smith, 1981). Many of the plants that our hunting and gathering ancestors relied upon for food no doubt became scarce during these long, multi-generational stretches of winter-like conditions. Much as the native people of the Arctic regions, like the Inuit of northern Canada and Greenland, once lived on a diet based largely on meat, our ancient ice age ancestors relied more and more on the hunt for sustenance (Fagan, 2010).

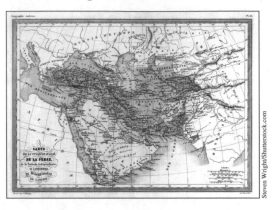

FIGURE 5-15. Antique 1870 map of the Middle East. Iraq is in the center of the map. It was between the Tigris and Euphrates Rivers that civilization was born.

Only in the last fifteen thousand years or so has the climate become more temperate and mild. Over millennia the struggles of the ice age peoples to survive amid freezing drought came to an end and the beginning of a new way of life began. Some archaeologists make the claim that it was this change in global conditions that sparked the development of civilization roughly ten thousand years ago in Mesopotamia, between the rivers Tigris and Euphrates (in what is currently Iraq), and in Egypt along the Nile River (Morris, 2010, pp. 85–89). For it was in the area that we now call the Middle East, and a little later in India, China, and in the Americas, that the systematic practice of intentionally growing plants for consumption—agriculture—became the primary means by which people secured the nutrition necessary for survival.

19.

Have you ever wondered what it would be like to hang out with your ancestors of five hundred generations ago?

. . . .

The way of life we take for granted, of consuming plants and animals that were grown, bred, raised, and harvested or slaughtered by farmers solely for our use, has only existed for a short period of time. Ten thousand years is only roughly five hundred generations—which as noted in the previous chapter is hardly any time at all from the view of evolution through selection of random mutations.

The seedbed for the origins of our views of males and females comes from a time when conditions were quite unlike the one in which we currently live. The world as seen through the eyes of an old woman who lived more than ten thousand years ago near the end of the Pleistocene epoch (the period of intense glacial cold that preceded the Holocene, the epoch in which we currently live) is not far removed from our own in terms of evolutionary time scales. From a genetic point of view, she was just as fully modern as any person alive today. She could, from an evolutionary biological point of view, be you!

From the evolutionary psychological perspective, we can for a moment put aside all the contemporary arguments of the respective gender roles of women and men, of men oppressing women or women controlling men, by looking into our ancestral past. By examining how the people we are descended from lived, we can begin to understand the origins of gender roles and how these roles have evolved in response to changes in the environment.

FIGURE 5-16. Anthropologists study bones and can from remains like this ascertain how people lived a long time ago.

20.

Be aware of the difference between prejudice and discrimination. Prejudice is a negative attitude held toward a person or a specific group. Discrimination is the resulting behavior an individual exhibits that results from the prejudice.

. . . .

PUTTING ASIDE PREJUDICES

A central problem with using our forebearers' way of life as a starting point for understanding gender issues, however, is that we tend to look condescendingly upon our "primitive caveman" ancestors. The stereotype that great-great-great grandpa was a club-wielding dullard who dragged women by their hair, whose speech was a series of grunts, and who liked to eat meat raw is a prejudice that all too often colors our judgment of humans who lived before the advent of civilization. It is an image that has become the default reference used to characterize males in general when their behavior is less than creditable in our own time. Sadly, it is also at the heart of many prejudiced views of individuals who are regarded as members of out-groups and is the basis of many discriminatory acts.

We need to discard our condescending views of our forebears and view them as finely adapted beings, well suited to the rigors of the environment in which they lived. They were not shambling fools. Their bodies and minds were shaped by millions of years of life in a variety of natural landscapes.

21.

Try to walk in your ancestors' footsteps.

· ·

We would do well to take a page from cultural anthropology. This discipline is concerned with all of humanity, not just the individual or groups of individuals (which are the respective centers of focus for psychology and sociology), and the cultures that arise as specific responses to the environments that humans inhabit. In cultural anthropology researchers try to adopt an objective, non-judgmental view of the ways in which people live. This means putting aside our culturally constructed notions of political correctness, of progressive or conservative, of sexist or liberated, of primitive or developed, and use our human capacity to "stand in someone else's shoes" to appreciate the various ways humans have adapted to their surroundings. This approach to understanding collective human existence offers the researcher the opportunity to gain deep insights into different cultures and experience different views of the Universe.

FIGURE 5-17. What would your world be like if it were suddenly unplugged?

So imagine what it would be like if you woke up one morning and discovered that a massive computer network breakdown had occurred. All the cellphone lines were dead, all the credit and banking systems were wiped clean of their records, all the electricity and Internet connections were gone, all the systems of food, water, and energy distribution had collapsed. How would you get in touch with anyone? How would you buy anything? How would you find anything to eat? Loot a store? And if you did find food, how would you keep it from spoiling if there was no power to run a refrigerator? How would you cook it? Do you know how to start a fire without technologies like matches and lighters? Where would you go to get clean drinking water? Would you even recognize clean water when you saw it?

22.

Imagination as well as intelligence is required to do social science well and develop an understanding of how context shapes behavior.

· ·

Now imagine a world without cities and factories, ports and airports, roads and sewers, homes and stores, farms and businesses. Think of what it would be like to live before the first city—or tiny village—existed. Imagine walking for hour after hour, never seeing a man made structure, a sign, or even a path in the ground, just to find water. No metal objects, no plastic wrappers, no glass, no paper, no concrete, no money, get your mind around this vastly altered environment and you can begin to see through our ancestors' eyes. Indeed, you need to stand not in their shoes, but in their bare feet.

23.

Can you imagine surviving without money?

· ·

If you lived as our prehistoric forefathers and mothers did your priorities would be totally transformed. Worrying about money and credit worthiness was utterly unknown to our ancestors. Looking forward to a night out with friends, texting and tweeting, surfing sites or channels, being entertained by anything more than a person telling a story, was inconceivable. The notion of work for pay did not exist in the prehistoric past.

Perhaps the greatest personally felt difference between the way we live today and the way our hunter-gatherer ancestors lived is the relationship we have with material things— our stuff. When people live off the land, that is, eat whatever wild fruits and vegetables are available and hunt whatever animals are present, but do not yet have the technology

to raise crops or livestock, it does not take long for all the edible material in a given area to be consumed. Consequently, it is necessary to move on to a place that has not been depleted of food. In other words, our hunter-gatherer ancestors were nomads. They built no permanent structures in which to live not because they were intellectually incapable or lazy but because there was no point in settling in a single place. They always had to be on the move.

All the stuff that we regard as essentials—all the clothes, shoes, beds, chairs, tables, china, utensils, pots, pans, not to mention computers, cars, and homes—would have been impossible to lug around, much less maintain, in the prehistory of our species. We can value ownership of things because we live settled lives. Nomadic people have to travel light. They got what they needed from their environment and when they were done with it, they abandoned it. In a sense they were the original litterbugs, except that everything they discarded was biodegradable (Morris, 2010, p. 88). Attachment to possessions simply was not practical or practicable.

FIGURE 5-18. An Inuit individual can eke out a living in what we would regard as a sparse environment.

Living in the wild, competing with other animals for food and water, as well as with other groups of humans also trying to eke an existence off the land, focused our ancestors' priorities. What mattered to them were people they could count on, individuals to whom they were attached through kinship, friendship, or some other form of alliance. Fellow human beings were the most important elements in their lives. Whether female or male, young or old, each individual had a role and a place in hunter-gatherer societies.

Loners were doomed in prehistory.

It is common to view our ancestors' way of life as primitive and to judge them as less sophisticated and intelligent than we, but is this really a fair assessment? They had a deep knowledge of their surroundings. They knew which plants were edible and which were toxic. The behavior of the animals they hunted, they knew intimately. The smallest details of the rhythms of nature, the turning of the seasons, the cycles of weather, the appearance of life, and the occurrence of death were well known to our prehistoric forebears. How well would we do in their environment? How well would we do in our own world if the artificial infrastructure that supports our lives disappeared? How many of us could generate our own electricity, fabricate our own clothes—much less cook a meal—entirely from scratch?

24.

How long do you think you would survive living as a member of a hunter-gatherer tribal grouping?

. . . .

That our hunter-gatherer ancestors would from our point of view score poorly against socially constructed measures of propriety, refinement, and correctness is not a sign of their inadequacy, but an indication of our inability to see beyond our own prejudices.

THE OLD WAYS

It is very instructive to sit in the back of a lecture hall. As I waited to be introduced to give a talk about how advertisers use evolutionary psychological findings to shape their

ad campaigns, I watched easily more than half of the students in the packed hall staring intently at their various devices. Most were texting; their heads tilted downward, shoulders twitching ever so slightly in rhythm to the movement of their thumbs across the touch screen. Some were interactively gaming and a few were shopping and tweeting. The rest were either napping or listening attentively to the lecturer prepping the class for the presentation.

FIGURE 5-19. Could you live without cell service?

Mobile communications devices and their supporting networks illustrate a powerful aspect of our collective humanity. We like to be in touch with others.

"In touch" is actually a very appropriate way of describing our desire for "contact." Among our primate relatives, physical contact is an important part of maintaining group bonds. When chimpanzees are at ease, individuals will often pair up and spend extended periods of time grooming each other's fur. They will remove parasites and dry flakes of skin, loose hair and bits of debris caught in their coats. The individual being groomed will sit very still in what appears to be a state of blissful calm while he or she is being picked and probed and cleaned. Primatologists have noted that this behavior strengthens ties between the individuals involved (Dunbar, 1996, p. 1–2).

25.

Did you know we humans are social animals?

. . . .

For social animals, group cohesion is vital for survival. In our prehistory we humans, like our primate relatives, were utterly dependent upon those individuals we regarded as members of our immediate in-group—family, friends and trusted allies—for survival. Compared to the predators that our ancestors competed with for sustenance, we lacked the powerful claws, sharp teeth, keen senses, and swiftness of stride that so characterized animals like the big cats that once dominated the Pleistocene landscape. We made up for these deficiencies by pooling our energies and capabilities (Dunbar, 1996, p. 17–19). Like many animals that suffer predation, we set up warning systems in which individuals took turns so that at least one group member was always on guard, ready to warn the whole tribe if danger threatened.

FIGURE 5-20. Finding edible plants was a time-consuming task.

Before the development of agriculture, hunter-gathering people had to cover large areas of territory to find edible plants and game animals. Again cooperation and group togetherness were vital to the successful execution of either task. The hunt required skillful coordination to track, pursue, and kill particularly large animals like bison and mammoth, both of which were apparently mega-fauna favorites among our ancient kin. Yet as spectacular as a mammoth at mealtime was in prehistory, much of the calories consumed long ago came from vegetable matter. Here again the laborious task of picking, digging, and gathering berries, tubers, nuts and various greens that were and still remain the main part of a balanced human diet required the coordinated effort of many hands (Buss, 2012, p. 80–85).

This is the reason a loner in prehistory was doomed. Such an individual, who could not be relied upon to contribute to the well-being of the family or tribe, would be considered an outsider and would be hard pressed to continually watch for predators, let alone successfully hunt or gather enough to eat.

The hunter-gatherer way of life tends to select for those individuals whose characteristics are conducive to the maintenance of group cohesion. In the uncompromising conditions of prehistory, individuals who were disposed not to be active members of a group were less likely to reproduce and so left fewer or no descendents who shared this behavioral predisposition. Over many hundreds of thousands of generations the attributes favored by group living would very likely be widespread among those populations engaged in such a way of life.

26.

How do you maintain your ties with friends and loved ones?

Now the problem with grooming as a method of maintaining ties with other individuals is that it requires great concentration on the part of the groomer, and stillness by the groomed, over extended lengths of time. Though we humans still enjoy being "in touch" through physical contact (note the continued popularity of massage), according to some evolutionary psychologists we developed a variation of intimate grooming time: gossip (Dunbar, 1996). Rather than pick at each other's skin and fur, we shared our little observations, our speculations about others, our thoughts and anxieties, our confidences, with another person to further the bonds of familiarity and trust. Think about your own experiences and very likely you can remember the glow of that feeling of belonging when someone close to you took you into his or her confidence and shared something special, something unknown to everyone else. Or recall the simple pleasure of being able to unburden yourself of guilt and anxiety, confess your misgivings and peccadilloes.

There is a reason the feeling of belonging is so comforting, so positive to you and to me. We are all the descendents of the people who lived as hunter-gatherers—people whose characteristics were shaped by an environment and by circumstances that demanded that they stick together and cooperate against all manner of adversities. Through famine, flood, drought, epidemic, and deadly competition with other groups, our ancestors managed to survive and pass on their genes to successive generations. We are the beneficiaries of their efforts and of the selective forces that favored their behavioral predispositions.

FIGURE 5-21. Contemporary women talking and gossiping.

Among our ancestors, this innovation—gossip in place of grooming—made it possible for them to engage in pursuits like foraging for food plants, caring for babies and children, preparing food, and many other activities while simultaneously strengthening ties with others members of their in-group. It could be argued that multi-tasking began long ago when the shift from staying in touch through physical contact gave way to being connected by conversation. The other great benefit that came with gossip was the exercising of that fantastically powerful cognitive facility we house in our brains. For gossip can be much more than the mere trading of personal snippets of information. As we all know, it can be used to shape the outlook and attitudes of those around us. Gossip can be so cunningly delivered, so cleverly clouded in implication and innuendo that the behavior of whole communities can be altered. It is a tool—potentially more powerful than any device of wood, metal, or some high tech material—through which an adept wielder can gain power and influence. Indeed, there are evolutionary psychologists who make the claim that it was intimate conversation between individuals and the manipulations that were contrived by the shaping of feelings and attitudes by such discourse that was one of the important selective forces that favored the intelligence we now possess (Miller, 2000).

27.

Think about your own behavior: do you gossip while talking or texting?

The subtle play for power through gossip can be conceived of as a kind of mental arms race. Say one group of individuals (let's call them the "manipulators") develops the intellectual faculties to effectively trick other individuals who are not so clever (let's call them non-manipulators) through gossip and innuendo. The manipulators get the not-so-clever non-manipulators to do things that benefit them (the manipulators) to the detriment of the non-manipulators. Perhaps the manipulators trick the non-manipulators into trading their food for something of lesser value. If allowed to continue over time, the advantages the manipulators gain over the non-manipulators could facilitate greater reproduction for them, and thus make the manipulators more and more common over many generations among most of the general population.

As the smarts required to effectively manipulate others becomes common through inheritance, descendents who possess the manipulative intellectual faculties may be able to evolve—or better yet, learn—cognitive strategies for countering the manipulative abilities of those around them who are also good manipulators. This puts pressure on those individuals who continue to try to manipulate others to develop more clever methods, which in turn puts pressure on the rest to develop

more effective countermeasures. And so the upward spiral of measure and countermeasure begins. An ever-escalating battle of wits would result.

This is an over-simplification, but it is not hard to see the trend that results. A kind of mental arms race is initiated. Living in a social environment in which manipulative individuals are seeking to exploit others generates selective forces that favor minds that can analyze and develop mental models (sound familiar?) of the desires, methods and motivations of other individuals to counter potential exploitative behavior. In order to keep up with the increasing complexity of social manipulations that gossip facilitates, individuals would have to hone their social and analytical skills to ever increasing degrees of sharpness. This arrangement, in which a person must always work ever harder just to keep up with the demands of the social environment, is at the heart of the concept of the "Red Queen hypothesis" (Ridley, 1993).

In Lewis Carroll's (1871) *Through the Looking Glass*, the Red Queen tells Alice (the main character of Carroll's more famous *Alice's Adventures in Wonderland*) that in order to stay in place, she must run as fast as she can. Some evolutionary psychologists argue our cognitive faculties developed in this context. In order to survive among other clever humans, our ancestors had to develop their intellects to keep pace with the ever-increasing sophistication of social interactions. As manipulators became more adept at manipulating, the rest had to develop the faculties required to counter their manipulations. The consequences for our ancestors—and if you think about it, even for us—of not keeping up with the trend for ever more complex and nuanced social interaction could be disastrous.

SPECIALIZATION AND THE ORIGINS OF GENDER ROLES

If you have ever looked through a listing of doctors in a major city's phonebook (or scrolled through a similar listing on your smartphone) you have no doubt noticed the enormous number of specializations that are represented. There is a specialist for nearly every kind of ailment and for every organ system of the human body. There are physicians who concentrate just on the illnesses of babies and children, or on those of the very old. There are specialists concerned with illnesses that originate from the smallest biological components of our being, our DNA. There are psychiatrists, psychologists, and psychotherapists who treat every kind of mental or behavioral disorder. Every nuance of our minds and bodies has been parsed down to its critical parts and become the domain of individuals who have made the study and treatment of these critical components their life's work.

28.

Why is specialization necessary?

Specialization is a consequence of the stupendous enormity of knowledge and expertise we collectively possess. No one individual could ever encompass all that is known about the human body and the psyche that is expressed by the brain, let alone master and administer all the different curative procedures that result from this mass of information. And it is not only in the field of medicine that specialization has become the norm. Check out any departmental directory at any university and you will find listings for scholars who have devoted their careers to very particular areas of study within a larger discipline. Like the specialist who knows the biomolecular details of arteriosclerosis (hardening of the arteries), there are engineers who are intimate with the strength of seemingly mundane materials like concrete, as well as cultural anthropologists and historians who have studied the subtleties of pre-Columbian Mayan religion.

Nevertheless, though it may seem that specialization is a recent innovation and is the result of the explosion of data that has accumulated

in the modern era, the tendency to specialize has been with us since the origins of our kind. In the pre-agricultural past, the circumstances in which our ancient forebears lived dictated a very specific division of labor. In other words, the survival and biological requirements of the time determined the roles to which men and women were bound.

29.

Remember the biological essentialist, social constructivist, and nature via nurture perspectives?

The reason there is so much debate about whether our behavior arises from inborn genetic factors (the essentialist view), or whether they are the result of learning (the social constructivist view), or the interplay of genes and environment (the epigenetic, or nature via nature view) stems at least in part from our long childhoods. Like all mammals, our young require care after birth. Indeed, the term *mammal*—which is the class of animals to which we belong—is a reference to mammary glands, which all female mammals possess, and the provision of mother's milk for the nourishment of the young. For unlike many non-mammalian animals like turtles and most insects whose offspring are on their own at birth—hence all their behavior must be innate since they have no opportunity to learn from parents—the offspring of all creatures belonging to the class of vertebrates called mammals need significant amounts of care over an extended period after their emergence from their mothers' wombs (Tudge, 2000). However, what sets us apart from the rest of the mammals is the extreme length of our maturational period.

Part of the reason human childhood is so long is because of the relative physical immaturity of our young when they are born. The organ that sets us apart from most other animals is an incredible liability at birth. Our brains—and the heads that house them—would be too big to pass through the birth canal if we physically matured beyond the approximately nine-month period of pregnancy (Hrdy, 1999). Before the relatively recent technologies that made cesarean sections (c-sections) safe for mother and child, childbirth has throughout human history been one of the principal causes of death among women of childbearing age.

FIGURE 5-22. Bear cubs only stay with their mother for two years.

Being born immature means that every child needs intensive attention and care during the early years of its life. While bear cubs are already being chased away by their mother so that they will live on their own by their second summer of life, human babies are still learning the basics of moving about and certainly cannot fend for themselves at age two.

The other aspect of our development that necessitates a long childhood is the amount of cultural knowledge each individual must learn and assimilate in order to be a member of a family, a tribe, a community, or more recently, a nation. It is this long learning period that predisposes many to believe that all, or nearly all, of our behavior is learned (the social constructivist view). The evolutionary psychological view argues, for example, that each of us during childhood was stimulated by the language or languages being spoken to us to acquire speech through our inborn capacity to pick up verbal communication. Similarly, we developed our innate capacity to interpret the

world around us through our senses as well as coordinate our motor skills so that we could affect our environment.

FIGURE 5-23. Human children need at least 18 years of specialized training to fit into our society.

It is this subtle distinction between cognition and behavior that springs entirely from the process of learning—which is the social constructivist position—and the position that we are born with certain predispositions like speech development, and that through interaction with the environment (nature via nurture) we develop characteristic behavioral attributes, that is at the heart of the social constructivist versus epigenetic debate. Nevertheless, learning the intricacies of human culture, from how to play with peers to how to engage in the most important of life's rituals, all take years and years. And indeed, it has been argued, as human culture becomes more and more complex our "childhood," which now extends into adolescence, will grow ever longer and longer (Ericksen et al., 2010).

30.

Why was the cost of raising children so high for our ancestors?

The cost to hunter-gatherer parents to raise their children was enormous compared to the investment other animals put into their offspring. But the benefit derived from the effort can be seen all around us. For better or worse, we are the inheritors of advances that came from among a variety of social and environmental elements, including uncounted generations of parental care that produced individuals who made possible the rise of agriculture, the formation of cities and of civilization, and all the knowledge that supports every aspect of our daily lives, and that affords us standards of living that no other form of life on the planet enjoys.

And when we consider the ancient specialization of gender roles that underwrote human development, it is vital that we put aside the social constructs that so condition our present-day view of such roles. We have to remember that our prehistoric ancestors did not have access to the power or the resources that we take for granted. Biological, not economic or sociopolitical, requirements dictated their lives. Adequate food, drinkable water, shelter from the extremes of weather and climate, security from predators, and most critically, the continuation of our kind were the primal elements that ordered our ancestors' life priorities. It is important to remember that our present-day notions of gender equity and fairness, of political correctness, are products of our circumstances, not theirs.

The essential point is this: from the perspective of the economically ordered way of life we live with today, childrearing is not a well-paid activity, which suggests that it is not a productive enterprise. Yet from the context of the long-term survival of our species (and even ironically of economic growth), few things are more vital.

31.

How did our ancestors divide labor among themselves to ensure the survival of the group?

For our hunter-gatherer ancestors, labor was divided between adult males and females. For the most part women provided the intensive care and interaction that children require. Lactating women provided the breast milk needed by newborns and that very young children require before being weaned onto solid foods. During the early years of childhood, women were the primary cultural instructors of the young (Hrdy, 2000). Women also gathered the nuts, berries, roots and other vegetable matter that constituted the bulk of the calories consumed (Buss, 2012, p. 84–85). Men hunted and contributed the animal protein portion of the ancient human diet. They also provided security against predators and other groups of humans (Buss, 2012, p. 80–83).

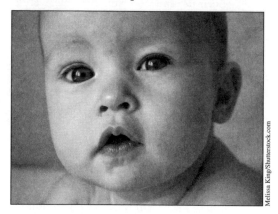

Melissa King/Shutterstock.com

FIGURE 5-24. This baby has a lot to learn in order to become a productive member of society.

For female children, learning the "ways of women," of identifying and gathering the right plants, of birth and of nurturing the young, were central to their formative development. For male children, learning the "ways of men," of initiation into the hunt, learning to protect their in-group of family and tribe, were the formative themes of their lives.

32.

Do the old divisions of labor by gender still echo in contemporary society?

· ·

This was the ancient division of labor, the elemental specialization of the genders that echoes from the past and into the present, and that sparks so much debate today because of the ways in which it still affects our behavior. For millions of years, through ice ages and periods of mild inter-glacial climate, over a span of human existence that constitutes over ninety-nine percent of our species' total time on Earth, this pattern of specialization was the norm. Whether we like it or not, it still influences our outlook and behavior as gendered individuals. Like our evolved predisposition to stay in touch with others through grooming, then through gossip, and most recently through technology-mediated communication devices, the old ways still inform our characteristic ways of living.

However, I wish to emphatically point out that we no longer live in the same context as our prehistoric kin. The old responses to the demands of the environment are no longer necessarily adaptive. Consequently, the old roles of man, the hunter, and woman, the gatherer and caregiver, are no longer necessarily suited for the new world that unfolds before us with the introduction of every new innovation.

Nevertheless, it is only by understanding how ancient humans lived that we can develop an understanding of where many of our attitudes about gender came from, but at the same time, we must always keep in mind that we live in a very rapidly changing world. Gender must, therefore, also be viewed as an aspect of our personal identity that is shaped by the alterations going on in our surrounding social and cultural—and technological—context.

We humans have come very far very fast. For millions of years human gender roles were determined by the biological dictates of survival. Then in the last tiny fraction of our species' history, a whole new world bloomed with incredible swiftness. A product of the intellect that was born on the savannas of prehistory, civilization transformed us. The old biological essentialism that ordered the lives of our ancestors was reshaped and inflected by new ideas, new lifestyles, new social constructions that generated an epigenetic hybrid world in which ancient urges like staying in touch is facilitated by global networks and nano-electronics.

Biological essentialism, social constructivism, and nature via nurture—each has its place in the developmental scheme of human gender identity.

TO SEE THE WORLD THROUGH THE EYES OF OTHERS

Still holding her granddaughter's tiny hand, she watched until the hunting party had disappeared into the distance. The wind quickened again and she shivered. Her granddaughter looked up into her face and she could see that the child was hungry but did not complain, for it was the way of their tribe to be stoic in times of want. She reached into a pouch she had tied to her side and felt the small handful of nuts she had been saving and drew one out.

"Here," she said to the child as she placed it by the tiny lips.

The little girl thanked the old woman, said a short prayer, then took the nut into her mouth and carefully chewed it. She closed her eyes as she savored its flavor.

Together the old woman and the young girl walked back to the camp where the women were readying themselves to begin the day's foraging. Infants were being wrapped and tied to their mothers' stomachs, the young boys and girls were standing about, waiting to commence their customary search for food.

One of the other grandmothers, Ria, holding onto the hand of a child who still walked uncertainly upon his feet, came to the old woman, as the women and children of the tribe began their slow trek to where it was remembered that edible roots had been found twelve moon-turns before.

"Mima, may we walk together and talk of many things?" she asked.

"You wish to talk of pairing your son's son to one of my granddaughters?" the old woman replied quickly, as she gestured for her granddaughter to join the other children, for she knew that Ria had become angry because the newborn of her grandson did not look like him and she thought that his mate had been with another man.

Ria grunted and said tersely as they walked side by side, "Yes, my grandson needs a new partner."

Mima was silent for a time, "Give the child a chance to grow, he may yet prove to be his father's son."

The other woman replied quickly, "I grow old, Mima, I cannot wait through many more passages of the moon to know—I want my grandson to be paired with your granddaughter, Jovna—for they would make a better match."

This is her true intent, thought the old woman, for Jovna was the daughter and only child of the current leader of the tribe and so would better position her grandson in line to possibly succeed him. She mused over this.

"You hesitate," accused Ria.

Mima did not reply but remained silent to hear what argument Ria would use to plead her grandson's case.

"Did not my grandson make many kills in the hunt, did he not share meat with your grandchildren during the last winter?" Ria declared flatly.

The old woman sighed, and listened for a time to the song of the wind rather than the recitation of the debt Ria thought was owed to her grandson.

The men had been running hard, spears in hand, through the morning and much of the afternoon yet they did not push themselves to their physical limit, for they must keep some reserve for the killing. The mammoth were moving toward the south, the men knew that with the wind blowing from the north they would have to stealthily overtake the herd on its flanks and then turn if they were to have surprise on their side. Otherwise the mammoth would smell their approach. Though no one spoke of this, all knew this was how it was to be done from many hunts together.

Mima's daughter's son had good stamina, so the older hunters signaled him to run ahead and reconnoiter the movement of the lead animals of the mammoth herd. He nodded and redoubled his stride, running through the tall grass, the wind at his back.

Soon he saw to his right the laggards of the herd, the young and the old of the beasts. He turned his path slightly to his left to be sure that his scent would go undetected. Then he abruptly stopped and lay low in the grass.

Another party of hunters was approaching from the east. He watched the hunters as they made ready to charge the herd.

How ugly these hunters are, he thought to himself, how crudely their spears are shaped, how clumsily they move as they begin to stalk the mammoth. Their women and children are probably stunted in growth because they are not good hunters, he speculated.

"We can take them in a fight," he whispered to himself, then turned and ran low in the grass back toward his comrades.

Though many millennia separate us from our hunting and gathering ancestors, cooperation and competition are still familiar to us. We may no longer wander the grass-covered plains of ice age landscapes any more in search of food, but the way of life still marks our bodies and our minds.

33.

Who is better at multi-tasking, men or women?

. . . .

There are variations in male and female physi-ologies and in our behavioral inclinations that can be traced to the division of labor inherent in the hunter-gatherer way of life. In the office environment of the twenty-first century, for example, a premium is placed on the ability to multi-task. Research has shown that generally women are better at simultaneously engaging in communication in a variety of media while executing other unrelated tasks (Chancellor, 2002). This is not to say that males cannot develop this skill, but by and large, women are more adept at multi-tasking. Conversely, when it comes to focusing sustained attention upon a particular task or problem, males are generally more inclined to employ this approach.

34.

Interpretations of male and female behavior...

. . . .

From an evolutionary psychological perspec-tive, these tendencies are among many others that are the result of present-day circumstances impressing upon ancient evolved predisposi-tions. In other words, an epigenetic effect is oc-curring: the old ways that differentiated males and females still act as nudges in our behavioral repertoire. The multi-tasking competencies of women are a result of predispositions inher-ited from ancestral women being transposed from the old context of gathering food, caring for the young, and maintaining ties through conversation that are suited to the current interactive cyber-office setting. This is why women are better at multi-tasking than men (Gray, 2010). Likewise, the tendency to stick doggedly to a single task while being oblivious to consideration of peripheral events, which

many males are inclined to do, is a throwback to the hunt. From the biological essentialist and the epigenetic view, natural selection fa-vored these predispositions in the past and so we still possess these tendencies in the present. But it also important to note, that we have the capacity to learn to harness these tendencies productively in our current environment.

To get a feel for our ancestral past imping-ing on our present-day lives, consider the difficulty many of us have with maintaining a healthy weight. Obesity is a real problem in the twenty-first century. More and more people are suffering real health issues, from diabetes to heart disease, from organ failure to cancer, all because of excessive weight. Many might ask, how is it that evolution has not eliminated this condition? Shouldn't natural selective forces have gotten rid of our tendency to retain so much fat?

Our struggle with weight can be traced, ac-cording to evolutionary biologists, to the way our ancestors lived (Palmer et al., 2002). Hunting and gathering does not ensure a steady supply of food. A great kill of bison or a great find of wild potatoes might occur only once a month or even less frequently during the winter. Feast or famine, as we would call it, was the norm during all of human prehistory. These conditions would tend to favor those individuals who had metabolisms that stored extra calories in their bodies as fat (since there was no other way to store surplus food) so that they could get through lean times. Another characteristic that would tend to be favored is a preference for fatty, salty, and sugary foods, since these are quickly converted into fat stores in the body. People who possessed these tendencies would then be more likely to successfully reproduce, since they could survive through lean times and so pass on this characteristics way of storing excess calories to their offspring. Over countless generations these characteristics became common among all human populations. Even after the develop-ment of agriculture and the rise of civilization, feast and famine were common features of life for the vast majority of people throughout the world, despite the more consistent food supply that resulted, making these fat-depositing tendencies adaptive up to almost the present day.

Then in the decades after the middle of the twentieth century, technological gains and increasing standards of living combined to give us things like fast food and high-calorie snacks that included everything from premade cookies and candy to chips. Our old evolved taste for a feast of barbequed bison and starchy root vegetables predisposed us to savor a greasy hamburger with deep-fried salty fries and a sugar-laced soft drink or fat-filled milkshake, only now we could eat like this three times a day instead of once a month. Suddenly the old adaptations that got our ancestors through lean times were no longer advantageous—in fact, these old survival characteristics were killing us.

Dieting is problematic because of our old ways of living. When you go on a diet and take in fewer calories, you are recreating the conditions our ancestors knew as starvation. Your metabolism, like theirs, grows sluggish in order to slow the loss of fat reserves. This is why dieting takes so frustratingly long. As you lose weight you are re-enacting the long torturous process our ancestors experienced of going without for an extended period of time, which in the ancestral environment was a life-threatening event. Finally, when you have lost the desired weight, you treat yourself to some long craved-for food. To your evolutionarily programmed physiology, this is the day the famine ends when the hunters finally make a major kill of mammoth or reindeer or antelope, or the gatherers find a field of ripe wild strawberries or figs, and your body's craving for nutrition is sated. But once those calories start coming in again, your body goes into fat-storage mode with a vengeance, and before you know it, you've not only gained back all the old weight, you've put on some extra.

Our struggle to maintain a healthy body weight, from an evolutionary point of view, is a consequence of the recent bounty of easily available tasty food coupled to the old realities of persistent feast and famine. Throw in the fact that we no longer lead nomadic lives in which walking for long distances were an everyday occurrence, along with the sedentary nature of high technological "work," and the perfect set of circumstances are established to create a population suffering from chronic obesity.

The problem stems once again from the rapidity of the pace of change. We have lived with fast food and snacks for only a fraction of a century, while famine has been with us for millions of years. Once again, not enough time has passed for natural selection to favor physiologies that do not respond to continual access to high-calorie food by turning the excess into fat. The process of selection is taking place. Consider the differential rates of reproduction for obese individuals of childbearing age, but it takes many, many generations for evolutionary forces to significantly alter a species.

To put it bluntly, we were not evolved to live as we do today.

35.

A new way of understanding contemporary problems...

What is the best way to deal with obesity? This is the evolutionary conundrum; the very traits that helped to ensure our survival in the past are a threat to our survival in the present. However, we do not have to wait for natural selection to change our physiologies and our behavior. We have the capacity to learn. This means accepting our evolutionarily derived physiological response to feast and famine and consciously altering our behavior on a permanent basis—what we call a lifestyle change. Constant appropriate exercise that mimics the physical activity of our ancestors—and for which our bodies were shaped by evolution to undertake—along with a diet that parallels the ancestral one in which calories from animal fat were scarce, consumed in amounts that even out the feast and famine cycle, would do much to achieve the goal of a healthy body weight. But it is the conscious application of our cognitive powers to overcome our ancestral cravings and behavioral predispositions that is essential. We live in a completely different environment from the one in which we developed as a species, and we need to recognize the consequences that spring from this change and make adjustments to suit.

Our old evolved traits certainly make their presence felt in our waistlines, and similarly, they also lurk just beneath the surface of nearly every other aspect of our lives. Many of the stereotypical roles associated with being male or female have their origins in our deep pre-agricultural past. The old division of labor is recalled from the past when we fallback on the view of men as breadwinners and women as caregivers, because it was once the primary pattern of human existence. The problem is that, like our evolved dietary and metabolic predispositions, the old ways are no longer suitable or even necessarily adaptive, in the world we now inhabit, and we are slow—sometimes even reluctant—to catch on to this fact.

THE PAST NUDGES US ALONG

Why do the differences that characterize male and female humans exist? Since women and men are both human, why, when the physical characteristics of populations of each are averaged out, are there differences in size, in weight, in the percentage of body mass that is fat or muscle? Are the differences in the way females and males behave caused entirely by the way we were raised when we were young? Or does our ancestral past still manifest itself in the way we behave?

In the world we live in today, females and males can each function equally well. So why do gender differences exist?

In Chapter 2, the prenatal genetic and hormonal influences that nudged each of us toward male or female or intersex were discussed. Now we will examine some of the ways in which our evolved prenatal development is expressed within our personal natures as gendered individuals.

The overarching structure that offers insight into general gender differences is again the context within which our human nature developed, the long hunter-gatherer period of our collective past. In other words, the physical and psychological demands of the hunter-gatherer way of life shaped our bodies and our minds, and from the evolutionary perspective, underlies the differences that characterize the sexes and the genders. We humans are like any other animal on the planet; we are shaped by our environment.

When you look in the mirror in the morning and regard the image of your reflection, you are not likely to think of yourself as being shaped by the lifestyles of your forebears. However, you might notice that you have your father's eyes or your mother's nose. Turning to gaze at one side of your face, you might perceive that at certain angles you bear a slight resemblance to your aunt or your uncle, perhaps one of your grandparents. Maybe your temperament or personality is similar to another member of your extended family. And like these subtle echoes of your bloodline that show you are part of a long line of descent, so too are there murmurs of a deeper past that we all share. All those millions of years of hunting and gathering have left their mark on us.

36.

To understand women and men, we must look to the past.

. . . .

Consider then that women, being the gathers of various edible plants, would be under selective pressure to develop predispositions that suited them for this task. Those women who were better gatherers would very likely find more food, and would therefore consume more calories, and be healthier than women who did not have the predispositions that made them better gatherers. These good gatherers would then be more likely to have more children and be better able to provide for their nutritional requirements. The long-term result would be that these women would have more descendants than those who did not have these tendencies. Over many generations, the prevalence of good gathering tendencies might become common among women.

Meanwhile males, as the hunting part of the ancestral human populace, would be under selective pressure to develop characteristics that predisposed them to be good hunters. Those men who possessed traits that made them better hunters would have more meat to eat and to share (with no way to store food in the ancestral environment much less efficiently transport it, hoarding would be pointless). This might make them more attractive to females as mates. Consequently, they would be more likely to have more offspring and so pass these traits on to future generations. In time, these good hunter qualities might become common among most males since they would be more likely to be descended from these individuals.

And indeed, there are differences between men and women that can be attributed to the old division of labor. For example, in tests of spatial abilities, in which subjects are shown an array of objects and then later asked to recall the location of a specific object in that array, women tend to do better than men (Buss, 2012, pp. 85–86). In an effort to recreate a naturalistic setting typical of the hunter-gatherer environment, subjects are asked to located specific plants amid other types, a highly advantageous perceptual adaptation for those engaged in gathering activities, and here again women tend to do better. It was noted that women in general are also more likely to use features in their surroundings like trees and other fixed landmarks to determine their location and to give directions, thus showing that women are more adept at remembering the features of their surroundings. This is another trait conducive to the gathering mode of food collection. Males, on the other hand, are more likely to do well on tests that measure the ability to mentally imagine an object as seen from other perspectives. The ability to rotate an image in the mind would be suited to the needs of a hunter who must be able to accurately perceive and interpret the movements of prey animals from any position and determine the trajectory of a projectile like a spear. Men are usually better at finding their way through unfamiliar landscapes and are thus more likely to use conceptual directions like those found on a compass, since they cannot call upon remembered reference points in novel settings (Buss, 2012, pp. 86–87).

Beyond the perceptual predispositions suited to the demands of hunting and gathering, there are also physical adaptations. Males usually have more upper body strength and have proportionally longer forearms than females, both adaptations conducive to the launching of projectiles like stones and spears (Buss, 2012, p. 82). That men are more predisposed to throw overhand while women throw underhand (compare a women's softball game to a men's baseball game and you will see this adaptation in the respective pitchers' throw in action), is another physical manifestation of the hunt.

Men have proportionally more internal surface area in their lungs than women, making it possible for them to more quickly enrich their blood with oxygen in preparation for physical exertion (Glucksman, 1981). Women, on the other hand, have a more efficient physiology, which means that they can over the long haul do more work using less energy. In essence, female physiologies are better suited for long-term efforts—adaptive qualities conducive to gathering—while the hunt has inclined men to better performance in relatively shorter-term bursts of effort.

37.

How did the ancestral environment affect prenatal development and pregnancy?

· ·

However, the most significant physiological/perceptual differences between males and females result from the ability that most distinguishes the sexes—those characteristics associated with pregnancy and childbirth. Females developed very important reproductive adaptations in the ancestral environment that helped ensure the healthy prenatal development of their children.

Low-level amounts of toxic substances are retained in many plants as an adaptation to dissuade animals from consuming them. We perceive these toxins as tastes that are unpleasant to varying degrees when we bite into foods like raw broccoli or celery. They are bitter. Toxins are also present in spoiled food and are the product of microbial organisms' metabolic activity. Again we are able to detect these toxins through taste and smell. Our inborn reaction of disgust when we smell toxic or rotten food is an adaptation that was developed long, long ago, and protects us from consuming life-threatening substances (Buss, 2012, p. 75–76). However, among women during the critical first third of the roughly nine-month period of pregnancy, when an embryo is going through crucial phases of growth and organ development, many become extremely sensitive to the smell and taste of various kinds of foods. Commonly referred to as morning sickness, this heightened sensitivity effectively

protects the embryo by preventing mothers from eating anything that may adversely affect it (Buss, 2012, p. 77–78). For it is during these first weeks of life that any disruption in normal growth and development can have long-term and far-reaching consequences for the child. Toxic compounds, bacteria, viruses, and parasites can all produce abnormalities that can prove debilitating and deadly to an embryo.

Nearly all women report feeling repelled by the smell of certain foods some time during the early months of their pregnancy. More than half of all pregnant women report vomiting in response to nauseating food—some even if they have done nothing more than smelled it. Generally the foods perceived as most revolting are those that have the greatest likelihood of potential toxicity: meat, alcohol, and vegetables. Animal flesh can be home to vast quantities of living bacteria, fungus, and parasites. Even if the meat is thoroughly cooked, a process that usually kills all such pathogens, the products of their metabolism—their waste—will still remain within the meat and may even in tiny amounts prove toxic to the child. Alcohol—and remember this next time you have a beer, a glass of wine, or any spirit-based drink—is, to be blunt, the crap that yeast produces. Vegetables and fruit-based drinks like coffee, tea, cocoa, and juice all have the potential to contain toxins that plants retain to make them unpalatable to animals that might eat them.

This tendency to be repelled by foods that could harm the developing child is a significant evolved defense. Women who do not react negatively to potentially toxic material in the environment are three times more likely to have spontaneous abortions (miscarriages) than women who experience aversion to such things (Buss, 2012, p. 77–78). This suggests that by being insensitive to potential biochemical hazards, those women who do not develop morning sickness are more likely to ingest toxins and microorganisms that adversely affect the developing child which then causes miscarriage.

Once again, it is abundantly clear that these are evolved physiological and behavioral traits specific to women that greatly enhanced the survival prospects of our kind. The vast majority of women are descended from females who possessed this evolved characteristic and so genetically inherited this quality. So powerfully beneficial from any evolutionary point of view is this selective ability to detect and avoid—even at the risk of starvation in the ancestral environment—foods that could do harm to the mother and the child during the early months of pregnancy.

Men are repelled by the smell and taste of toxic substances, too, but tend not to react with the same degree of disgust as women. Indeed, testing has shown that even when a woman is not pregnant she is still far more likely to react with disgust to the smell of toxic, rotten, or foul things in the environment (Buss, 2012, p. 76).

The setting within which our kind evolved was not one in which developed world systems, like indoor plumbing, sewage treatment, waste disposal, water treatment, and personal hygiene, existed. For nearly all of human history clean water came from the sky in the form of rain and snow, and collected in lakes, rivers, streams, and glaciers. Solid human waste was at best buried. The practices of proper personal hygiene we view as normal were unknown to our ancestors—indeed, even after the rise of civilization, approximately ten thousand years ago, it was not until the nineteenth century that sewage removal systems that we would regard as acceptable first came into existence (Burke, 1985, p. 234). As a result, before we developed the knowledge and public health policies to protect our health, we had to evolve behaviors and physiological responses like morning sickness, an aversion to foul smells, and a dislike of certain foods to minimize exposure to toxins and pathogens. This is why no matter where you might travel in the world, everyone tends to react the same way to the odor of decay, to the stench of sewage, and the stink of unhygienic practices. And among women this revulsion is usually more pronounced due to the critical nature of prenatal embryonic development and the vital need to limit their exposure to substances that could prove toxic to themselves and their offspring.

These are some of the basic behavioral and physiological characteristics that our ancestral ways of life imposed upon our nature. Without these evolved predispositions we would very likely not be here today.

SUGGESTED DOCUMENTARY FOR CHAPTER 5:

Joseph Campbell: The Power of Myth with Bill Moyers. 2001. Athena Videos.

REFERENCES

Bently, P., general ed. (1995). *The dictionary of world myth*. New York: Facts on File.

Boostin, D.J. (1983) *The discoverers: a history of man's search to know his world and himself*. New York: Vintage. New York. p. 15.

Bronowski, J. (1972). *The ascent of man*. Boston: Little, Brown. p. 60.

Burke, J. (1985). *The day the universe changed*. Boston: Little, Brown. p. 234.

Buss, D. (2012). *Evolutionary psychology: the new science of the mind*. Boston: Allyn & Bacon.

Calder, N. (1979). *Einstein's universe*. New York: Greenwich House.

Campbell, J. (1949). *The hero with a thousand faces*. New York: Pantheon Books.

Campbell, J. ed. (1971). *The portable jung*. New York: Penguin Books, pp. 59–69.

Campell, J. with Moyers, B. (1988). *The power of myth*. New York: Doubleday.

Carrol, Lewis. (1871). *Through the looking glass*. New York; Barnes and Noble Classics.

Chancellor, H. (2002). *Science of the Sexes: Growing up* [DVD]. United States: Windfall Films.

Dunbar, R. (1196). *Grooming, gossip, and the evolution of language*. London: Faber and Faber.

Ericksen, L. & Shimazu, M. (2010). *Nations of one: the emerging psychology of the 21st century*. Xlibris Press.

Fagan, B. (2010). *Cro-magnon: how the ice age gave birth to the first modern humans*. New York: Bloomsbury Press. pp. 197–217.

Freud, S. (1955). T*he interpretation of dreams*. New York Basic Books. pp. 278–282.

Gleick, J. (1988). *Chaos: making a new science*. New York: Penguin.

Glucksman, A. (1981) *Sexual dimorphism in human and mammalian biology and pathology*. Academic Press, pp. 66–75.

Gray, R. "Scientists prove that women are better at multitasking than men." *The Telegraph*. 17 July 2010.

Hamilton, E. (1942). *Mythology*. Boston: Little, Brown.

Hrdy, S. B. (1999). *Mother nature: a history of mothers, infants, and natural selection*. New York: Pantheon.

Kaschack, E. (1993). *Engendered lives*. New York: Basic Books.

Miller, G. R. (2000). *The mating mind: how sexual choice shaped the evolution of human nature*. New York: Doubleday.

Mitchell, S., (2004). *Gilgamesh: a new english version*. New York: Free Press.

Morris, I. (2010). *Why the west rules—for now: the patterns of history, and what they reveal about the future*. New York: Farrar, Straus & Grioux.

Paler, J. A. & Palmer, L. K. (2002). *Evolutionary psychology: the ultimate origins of human behavior*. Boston: Allyn & Bacon. pp. 245–248.

Ridley, M. (1993). *The red queen: sex and the evolution of human nature*. New York: MacMillan Publishing.

Smith, D. G. (1981). *The cambridge encyclopedia of earth sciences*. New York: Crown Publishing/Cambridge University Press. pp. 300–302.

Tudge, C. (2000). *The variety of life: a survey and a celebration of all the creatures that have ever lived*. Oxford: Oxford University Press. pp. 443–460.

Name   Date

1. What are myths, and why are they important to the study of gender?

2. How are myths similar to science? How do they differ?

3. What is an archetype?

4. How does religion affect our view of women and men?

5. How did war contribute to the formation of male roles?

6. Why is it important to put aside our prejudices when we examine the way our ancient ancestors lived?

7. How was the world of our ancestors different from our own?

8. What was the most important thing in the lives of our ancestors?

9. Why was the change from grooming to gossip significant in the development of our species?

10. What are some of the adaptations to the ancestral environment that still affect our lives today?

11. What is meant by the "Red Queen" hypothesis?

12. How was labor divided between men and women in the distant past?

6

Chapter 6

PERSONAL FRAMES OF REFERENCE: THE EXPERIENCE OF BEING FEMALE, THE EXPERIENCE OF BEING MALE, THE EXPERIENCE OF BEING INTERSEX

6

1.

If you are female, have you ever wondered what it *feels* like to be male? If you are male, have you ever wondered what it *feels* like to be female? If you are intersex, have you ever wondered what it *feels* like to be female or male? If you are either male or female, have you ever wondered what it *feels* like to be an intersex individual?

. . . .

There is a basic truth that underlies nearly all arguments between individuals, and it is articulated when someone declares, "You don't understand!" Though we are all human, being a particular gender is one among many things that foster differences in our experiences and perceptions. This makes it difficult for a male to understand the world as a female experiences it. Likewise, women find it hard to see the world as men see it, and for an intersex person, both male and female perspectives may be difficult to understand, and most males and females are unlikely to know how an intersex individual experiences the world. And the sad truth is that unless some new technology is developed that allows us to transpose our consciousness onto another person's mind, we shall never have the deep experience of perceiving the world through the eyes of others. Despite the fact that most of us can to varying degrees empathize with others—that is, relate to another person's emotions and thoughts—we cannot know exactly what another person is going through. We are never directly connected to anyone else—we have to infer the thoughts and feelings of others through indirect means. Visible behavior, affect, verbal statements, subtleties of expression—these are the things we learn to interpret to guess at what is going on "inside" others. Some of us are quite good at reading these signals and can discern the smallest details of feeling and intention, but no matter how adept we may become, we can never know with complete certainty the experiences of others.

2.

Is PMS real?

. . . .

There is, for example, much debate about whether or not PMS is real. Is premenstrual syndrome a real, hormone-based physiological event that affects women in the days before they begin their menstrual period, or is it something that has been socially constructed (Rodin, 1992)? Very likely when you read the first sentence of this paragraph, you had a very definite reaction to this statement. Yet according to research done to determine a connection between symptoms of backache, bloating, general discomfort, swelling of the breasts, tension and irritability, changes in sleep patterns, sexual behavior, and work habits to specific hormonal changes in women, no relationship was found (Hsiao et al., 2004). The absence of an apparent connection between hormone changes and PMS makes diagnosis problematic. It would seem to suggest that there is no objective way of diagnosing the onset of the syndrome. Nevertheless, for many women PMS is a real, even debilitating, condition. How can PMS not be real?

FIGURE 6-1. A woman seeking inner peace by doing yoga.

The question of the authenticity of PMS illustrates the essential problem of trying to truly know what others are experiencing. Even with the methods that science makes available to us, we cannot know about PMS with complete objective clarity. Yet most of us would be more than willing to attest to its existence.

3.

Have you ever tried to imagine seeing the world from a completely different point of view?

Another factor that makes "seeing the world through the eyes of others" difficult is the amount of variability among individuals. Here again PMS is instructive. There is considerable variation in the personal experience of premenstrual syndrome. Some women report no changes in their physiology or their mindset, while at the other extreme, there are women who report nearly or completely incapacitating symptoms. On the other hand, a woman may not even be aware of changes brought on by

PMS, yet other females, males, and intersex individuals interacting with her might notice changes in her physiology, behavior, or temperament, attributable to this condition.

4.

What is your personal view about PMS? Do you think it is real? Do you think it is a shared social construction?

The point of all this is that it is not an easy task to try to make generalizations about how respective genders experience aspects of personal existence. The subjective nature of our personal self and the highly individualistic ways in which we understand and interact with our surroundings makes any broad description challenging. Nevertheless, it is important to acknowledge that our sex and gender do affect our worldviews, while at the same time, remembering that there is no right way, or better way, to perceive the Universe. We each have our personal frames of reference, shaped by our life experiences, our culture, and our biology. In other words, nature via nurture, social constructivism, and biological essentialism all come together to form the structure of our gender perspective on life. The unique interaction of these multi-faceted elements contributes to our respective worldviews, yet there are broad commonalities that can be described.

FIGURE 6-2. Do you think the worldview of an African-American woman is different from the worldviews of individuals from different backgrounds?

WOMAN'S VIEW

FIGURE 6-3. The moon is the ancient mythic symbol of woman.

We humans are biological beings, but we are not strictly limited by the dictates of our biology. Our capacity to innovate and develop the potential abilities and characteristics our genes impart upon us (this is the epigenetic view) means that we can far surpass the limitations of our inherent biology. Nonetheless, we must not lose sight of the fact that our biology (the essentialist aspect) forms the foundation from which further development builds upon. Our cultural context (the social constructivist part) provides us with the information and social guidance, which can come from family, educational institutions, the church, and other groups, to shape the potentialities of mind and body toward goals of our own choosing.

It is against this developmental background that we examine the broad outlines of the feminine worldview.

The moon has long been a symbol for woman (Bently, 1995, p. 198; Ronnberg, 2010, p. 26–30). Change is inherently part of the experience of being female. For as the moon goes through its phases, waxing and waning through successive days and nights, so the hormonal rhythm that functions in accord with the processes of reproduction is a part of every healthy woman's life. The cycle of rising and falling hormones during the fertile years that facilitate the release of an ovum (egg cell), its passage through the Fallopian tube where it may be fertilized, the preparation of the uterus for possible implantation of the ovum, and absent the arrival of a fertilized egg, the elimination of the prepared lining of the uterus with the menstrual flow, thus re-initiating the cycle, are regular roughly monthly events (Barrington, et al., 2012, p. 136). The degree to which individual women are affected by this recurring succession of physiological and hormonal fluctuations varies greatly. Some women accommodate it with little effort, while others find it a highly disruptive aspect of their lives. Nevertheless, it forms what could be called the short phase rhythm of a woman's life.

5.

Did you know that a woman's menstrual cycle coincides with the moon's cycle of 28 days?

. . . .

There is a longer-term phase transition that also informs the nature of woman. There is first the passage, at puberty, from childhood into sexual maturity with the beginning of menarche (the initiation of the menstrual cycle), then the next phase of many years of childbearing fertility, which is followed by the phase marked by the onset of menopause that marks the cessation of regular menstruation and the end of the possibility of having children (Barrington, et al., 2012, p. 139, 472), and finally, post-menopause, what some anthropologists call the alloparent period (Hrdy, 1999, p. 274–279). This last phase is the time during which a woman may invest her energies and resources into the care and well-being of her children's children.

FIGURE 6-4. Four generations of women.

These are the short cycles and long phases of a woman's life from a biological perspective. However, in the world we live in, these biological phases are not strict determiners of any individual woman's life. She may or may not decide to participate in the process of pairing up with a mate. She may or may not choose to have children. Today it is not unusual for a woman who has a child to be a single parent, or to be in a relationship with another individual other than the biological father. She may or may not choose to actively participate in their upbringing. She can choose to use any of a variety of methods to control her fertility. With the occurrence of menopause, she may experience profound changes in her physiology and her psychology. However, there are women who report few changes during this transition. Some women choose to undertake hormonal therapies that counter or moderate the changes menopause brings. If she has had children and they have children of their own, she may or may not choose to invest her time, energy, and resources to assist in their upbringing. In other words, there is an enormous amount of variability in the personal choices that individual women can now bring to the biological nature of their lives. Recent technological innovations like the birth control pill, other types of contraception, hormone replacement therapies, surrogate mothers (women who are paid or volunteer to carry a pregnancy to term for another woman), *in vitro* fertilization (when an egg is fertilized outside the body), and many other therapies have greatly added to the number of options available to women alive today.

6.

Is having children an essential part of a woman's identity?

. . . .

Many women claim that the impulse to have children, to participate in the long chain of reproduction that ensures the continuity of our species, is an important part of their lives and of their personal identity. Though women can and do choose to turn their energies to activities that are not related to having children, most women respond at some time during their lives to the natural processes that so structure their physiology, and have children.

7.

The only constant in a woman's life is change.

· ·

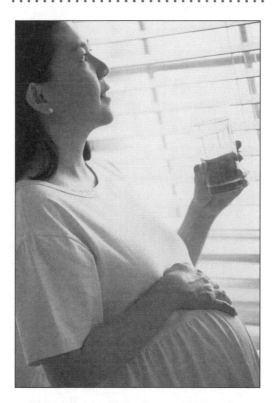

FIGURE 6-5. Pregnancy and childbirth are life-changing events.

Change is very much at the center of a woman's worldview. There is change in her social status that comes with menarche and the end of childhood, physical changes that follow the fluctuation of hormones on a monthly basis, social and psychological changes when pairing with a mate, physiological changes that come with pregnancy and then when the child is born. There are many changes that come with raising a child. There are changes in a woman's relationship with those around her when she becomes a mother. The nature of her relationship with her son or daughter changes as the child passes from infancy into childhood then into adolescence and then adulthood. There are profound physiological changes

that arrive with the onset of menopause. Then there are the post-menopausal years that, with contemporary life expectancy, can last three or more decades.

Now that we live in a time of constant rapid social and technological innovation, women have in many ways an innate advantage over men because of their familiarity with change. The evolutionary forces that shaped the characteristics of the female aspect of the human species coincidentally also made women more adept at coping with, and responding to, the demands and requirements of a changing world.

MAN'S VIEW

FIGURE 6-6. The sun is the ancient mythic symbol for man.

If the moon through its phases is the metaphor for woman, then the image for man is the constant sun (Bently, 1995, p. 198; Ronnberg, 2010, p. 22–25), for males have few major biologically determined phases in their lives. There is the onset of puberty and the physical changes that signal the transition to physical maturity, like the appearance of facial and body hair, the lowering pitch of the voice, the behavioral agitation, and increased interest in sex and risk-taking behavior that accompanies increases in testosterone that males experience (Barrington, et al., 2012, p. 135). But these changes are minor compared to what women experience. There is no clear, unambiguous male counterpart to menarche that indicates the arrival of reproductive maturity. There is also great variability among males in the degree to which these signs of approaching maturity manifest themselves. Males typically reach their physical peak in their early twenties (Zastrow, 2009) and then they slowly and steadily decline through the remaining years—and in modern times, many decades—of their lives.

8.

After puberty men can father children throughout their lives.

FIGURE 6-7. Older fathers are not uncommon these days.

Men, like women, may or may not choose to participate in the process of pairing up and having children, and they may or may not choose to actively participate in the upbringing of their offspring. There are some men who, like their single-parent female counterparts, raise children on their own. Some men choose to use contraception to control their fertility. However, there is no menopause-like event in the biological lives of males. Their sperm count declines as they age, but there is no point when sperm production ceases altogether. Similarly, males have no short-term fluctuations in their hormone levels. One day is much the same as the next. Males experience neither monthly cyclical hormonal changes nor profound

longer phase physiological changes like those women experience with pregnancy, childbirth and child rearing, and the later cessation of menstruation with menopause. Healthy, fertile men can become fathers pretty much until they die (Stringer, 2011, p. 224).

9.

There are few, if any, rites of passage into manhood for males today.

In contrast to women, men have few developmental signposts in their development. In hunter-gatherer societies, boys are usually taken away from their mothers to be raised by men in order to teach them the ways of the hunt from about six years of age. This does not coincide with any significant physical change beyond the fact that it is at about six years of age that most children, both male and female, have probably achieved a degree of physical growth and manual dexterity, along with the cognitive capacity, in which training for the tasks associated with hunting and gathering is possible. In the Jewish religious cultural tradition, boys undergo the *bar mitzvah* on their thirteenth birthday to mark the attainment of self-responsibility and manhood. (Girls have their *bat mitzvah* at age twelve, thus signaling self-responsibility and womanhood a year earlier than males.) In the United States, aside from far less significant socially constructed events like driver's licensing, high school and college graduation, the attainment of voting age at eighteen, and the legal right to consume alcoholic beverages at twenty-one, there are no fixed meaningful biologically determined, essentialist milestones in a male's life. In contemporary Western culture, aside from mandatory basic education, the individual male is pretty much left to personally choose if and when he will participate in any of these cultural activities. Even military service, which every able-bodied male was once required to undertake, is now entirely a personal choice in the U.S.

FIGURE 6-8. Getting a driver's license is often seen as a rite of passage for both men and women. It means that you are mature enough to follow the rules of the road. Being old enough to drink is another socially constructed rite of passage.

10.

Males have a different view about children and child rearing than women.

The physiological nature of the male generates a worldview that is unvaryingly constant compared to that of the female. The biological impulse to have children varies significantly among males, as does the desire to invest resources and energy in his offspring, should he have any. While women have a limited period in their life in which they can have children between menarche and menopause and experience significant physiological changes on a monthly basis that are part of their reproductive life, men do not experience any such boundaries after puberty in their chances to have children, nor any cyclical hormonal changes related to childbearing. Also, it is important to understand that males are not intimately aware of childbearing because they themselves have—from a strictly biological point of view—a very limited role in the process. At the very minimum he may contribute

nothing more than half of a child's DNA. This is not to say that it is at all appropriate for a male to be so indifferent to his offspring and to his mate, but from a purely biological referent his part in the birth and upbringing of a child may be quite minimal (Buss, 2012, p. 206–208).

FIGURE 6-9. Some fathers invest a lot of their energy, time, and resources into the upbringing of their children.

11.

In traditional cultures, birth control and abortion are strictly "women's business."

In many traditional pre-agricultural cultures there are distinct borders that divide the concerns of women from the concerns of men. The biological nature that distinguishes male from female, in which one must invest so much more of herself into the bearing, feeding, and nurture of children, while the other need invest much less of himself into their conception and upbringing, gives women great power and authority over her respective area of activity. For example, today in the West there is much heated debate and controversy over matters of abortion and contraception. The largely male-dominated political arena is rife with argument and counterargument. However, from the point of view of individuals who live in traditional pre-agricultural societies, much as our ancestors did, such debate does not quite make sense. Reproduction is strictly the province of women. Biology determines the sphere of power and control. Males in such societies typically regard matters related to childbearing as outside their sphere of influence. Our ancestors would probably view the present-day rancor and acrimony over reproductive issues as bizarre. They would probably wonder why males are concerned with matters that are clearly in the realm of womanpower.

12.

Who tends to be better suited to live in a rapidly changing world, women or men?

. . . .

As much as we would like to believe we are in complete control of our lives, biology plays a big part in the way we view ourselves and the world around us. Biological essentialism rests at the foundation of our perceptions. It is difficult for a male to imagine living as a female, just as it is for a woman to conceive of living as a man. Our biology does to a very large extent structure our worldviews. Women tend to be better suited for living amid a changing world because the very nature of their biology teaches and predisposes them to live with constant change and transformation. For men, constancy characterizes their worldview.

FIGURE 6-10. A solar eclipse, which results from the alignment of the sun and the moon, can be used as the symbol for intersex individuals.

INTERSEX VIEW

If the mythic image of the moon characterizes woman and the sun is the symbol for man, then the solar eclipse—that astronomical event when the moon passes in front of the sun and appears as one with it—is perhaps apt for the intersex individual. For it is in that alignment of moon and sun that a unique light is cast upon the world and a condition in which the stars are visible in the daytime sky occurs.

13.

Try to see the world through the eyes of an intersex individual.

. . . .

Just as it is hard for a woman to see the world as a man does and vice versa, it is even more difficult for both males and females to conceive of the world through the eyes of an intersex person. So much of our fundamental identity is biologically shaped (essentialism) and then interpreted through the lens of culture (social constructivism and epigenetics). For all cultures assign roles to females and males that to varying degrees define their respective identities, as well as their function and behavior in a given societal context. For the intersex individual living in the West, there is little or no formal acknowledgment of being intersexed. In the United States, male and female are listed as the only categories to which an individual can be identified in official documents like driver's licenses and passports. Unlike countries like Australia and India that recognize intersex as a category, there is no formal legal status for being intersexed in most countries. Indeed, it is not unusual for people to be unaware of the fact that there are more than two sexes.

This lack of recognition—even of acknowledgment—puts the intersexed individual in a kind of socially constructed "no-man's land." Labels like "weird" or "queer," which are typically references to sexual orientation—which is not the same as sex and gender—reflect the lack of awareness about being intersexed in the general population.

FIGURE 6-11. Though we are all part of nature and all belong to the same species, loneliness can still be a feature of our lives.

14.

A summary of parts of Chapter 2.
· ·

As noted in Chapter 2, the prenatal formation of intersex is a variation in gender development that has many sources. Intersex can have its origin in genes, in hormonal exposure, to the fusion of multiple genes or the interplay of multiple genotypes. The variations among intersex individuals are considerable. Some intersex individuals are genetically one sex but in terms of their body configuration they are another sex. There are intersex persons whose visible physique possesses characteristics of both male and female. There are some whose internal organs are indicative of both female and male but appear externally to be one or other sex. And perhaps the most difficult aspect of identifying with being intersexed in a particular way is the unique subjective experience of living and experiencing the world as an individual who is neither male nor female that each intersex person feels.

15.

Do you feel empowered or penalized by your gender? What happens when you remove that perception from your consciousness?
· ·

If you are a male or a female, take a step back from your own life experiences, try to adopt an objective viewer's point of view, and think for a moment about how much your place among your friends, family, and co-workers is shaped by your gender and your potential for having children. Think about how you as a daughter or son are viewed by your parents, how you as a brother or sister are regarded by your siblings, how you as a nephew or niece are recognized by your aunts and uncles, or as a granddaughter or grandson by your grandparents. Consider how easily you fit into their sense of who you are and what you are like because of your gender. If you are female, think about your relationship with your girlfriends and even your male friends. If you are male, consider your ties with your buds and even your female friends. Think about your hopes of meeting the right guy or girl, about family and perhaps having children, or if you are in a relationship, how your spouse or partner views you. Think about the job you ideally want and how you might be able to advance your position in that occupation, and how your gender might be an asset or a liability.

Now take away all the gender references that define you.

Bam! It all falls away.

You are adrift. This is what it is like not to belong to either of the conventionally recognized female or male biological and socially constructed categories.

It is unknown exactly what percentage of the population is born intersex. For reasons of privacy, doctors do not disclose how many gender assignment operations they do to children to make external genitalia appear in conformance with conventional expectations of male or female. Indeed, there are many individuals who do not know they are intersexed. And among those who do know that they are intersex, many choose to conceal their sex and strive to appear "gender appropriate." The great disservice done to intersexed individuals has its source in the rigidness and pervasiveness of sex roles and stereotypes, those social constructions that place limitations on all individuals, but which most profoundly excludes those for whom no meaningful status is afforded.

FIGURE 6-12. How would your perceptions change if you discovered that this man was actually an intersex individual?

16.

Nature favors diversity.

The worldview of the intersex individual varies greatly. Nature favors diversity, for it is out of variation that biological evolution springs. Diversity is also necessary for cultures if they are to flourish amid change—particularly the rapid change we are now experiencing. I seriously doubt that we can afford to dismiss the unique perspective of intersex individuals.

All individuals have an inherent right to live in accord with their feelings, thoughts, beliefs—and most certainly their biology.

THE BROAD THEME OF HUMAN LIFE

If you had to pick a single piece of music that would be the theme song of your life, which one would you choose? What kind of song would it be? What would be its message?

FIGURE 6-13. Which song is the soundtrack of your life?

And in a deep sense the theme of gender can be heard in every love song and ballad, from the ancient poems of romance and longing to tomorrow's chart-topping download. Gender's theme is as old as humanity and as new as now.

The reason gender exists—the reason there are males, females, and intersex individuals—can be traced back to the first earthly forms of life that swapped genes and mixed their genotypes together to create a completely unique individual. As discussed in the second chapter, this way of reproducing was highly advantageous to the resulting offspring and to the long-term survival of sexually reproducing organisms. But there were enormous consequences that came with this reproductive method. And this is where theme songs come to play a role in our lives. Since we humans do not clone ourselves, the need to participate in the long song of producing, nurturing, and preparing offspring to take their place in the line of human descent—in order to maintain that multi-million year long music of our kind—is a significant part of our lives.

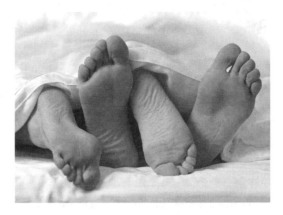

FIGURE 6-14. It is only natural to long to love and be loved.

17.

We all long to love and be loved by someone special.

The predisposition, the deep inclination, to pair up with another person, whether for a lifetime or for an evening, is a result of our ancestry and our evolutionarily derived reproductive nature. At the genetic level, we as individuals cannot continue our kind alone by ourselves. We are not cloners. We each carry only half of the genetic endowment that our potential offspring require. For an egg to be fertilized, its DNA must be paired with the DNA carried in a sperm. If you think of the egg as the lyrics and the sperm as the melody, each of us is only half of the genetic song of life.

That the act of engaging in sexual activity is a significant part in the lives of most individuals is inevitable due to the very mechanism of biological survival that has served life on Earth so well. Without sex, none of us would be here. But there is more to our essential biological nature than having sex to reproduce, just as there is more to reproducing than just having babies. Sex is also an important part of the way in which the genders interact and communicate.

And as a result, it is in the intricate dance of attraction and selecting a partner that gender matters become so intensely important to most individuals.

WORLDVIEWS SHAPED BY OUR NATURES: AS GUARDIANS OF THE FUTURE, WHAT DO WOMEN WANT?

The question that continually hovers in the minds of many males and whose answer seems forever to elude them is, what do women want?

If ever there was a clear indication of how difficult it is for individuals of one gender to see the world through the eyes of another gender, it is the matter of what each wants in a mate. Again, it is important to remember that evolutionary psychology can only offer a broad view—an over-arching simplified outline. The particulars of culture and circumstance provide the details to the outline and greatly influence what it is women want. There are also the unique tastes and personal preferences that inform each individual's choice.

18.

To see the world from another perspective is as much an emotional experience as it is an intellectual one.

A note to the guys: If you really want to know what women want, you have to make a sincere effort to see the world from another point of view—and more—you have to try to *feel* the consequences of millions of years of biological evolution that forms the foundation of the female perspective on mate selection inflected through the particulars of culture and personal preference.

Though most of us feel that we are not living our lives from moment to moment trying to figure out how to ensure the continuation of our kind and pass our genes into the future, it nevertheless forms the background music of our existence. When we meet new people there is a part of us that is evaluating the characteristics of each individual. We may be clearly conscious of this mental activity or not but it is, nonetheless, part of our evolved nature (Buss, 2012, p. 108–109).

19.

Who selects whom?

First off, more often than not, women do the choosing of mates (Trivers, 1972). Though there are cultures (social constructs) in which women are forced into marriages by their parents or other family members, through most of human history and certainly in contemporary Western cultures, women are the ones who usually do the choosing. Second, for the purpose of having children, women tend to be extremely selective about their mates, far more choosy than men (Palmer et al., 2002, p. 112). Why? Think about it, guys: if you had to pick one person with whom to pair your genes, then deal with the potential short-term and long-term physical, social, and psychological requirements of the resulting relationship as well as the consequences of nine months of pregnancy for each child, then commit yourself to the physical, financial, and psychological cost of twenty plus years of intense child rearing, while keeping in mind that you have a limited window of opportunity between menarche and menopause to have children, wouldn't you be choosy? In the past, our ancestors did not have access to the supporting infrastructures of food, energy, and goods production and distribution that we take for granted. So raising children alone for our forebears was not an approach to child rearing that was likely to result in reproductive success. This makes choosing a good partner who has suitable genes, positive behavioral tendencies, and access to resources, clear imperatives for a woman.

20.

Women and mate selection: what is important to females?

Jason Stitt/Shutterstock.com

FIGURE 6-15. There is no book of instruction about selecting a partner, so how do women go about choosing a mate?

For women—and remember, this is an evolutionary psychological generalization that may or may not accurately describe any particular individual at a particular time in her life—two essential criteria tend to structure the basis for evaluation of potential mates. One is the predisposition to consider the suitability of an individual in terms of his physical characteristics, which are cues about his genetic traits. The other is the tendency to evaluate the behavioral/mental suitability, which is also indicative of his genes as well as the effects of the nurture via nature he received during his life, and that includes consideration of his access to resources, of an individual (Buss, 2012, p. 109–137). The former is biological and the latter is epigenetic (if we define the behavior qualities of an individual as the interaction of nurture via nature).

Unlike the 1997 movie *Gattaca*, set in a future in which Uma Thurman's character could check out what she thought was Ethan Hawke's character's DNA (though he had been using Jude Law's character's genome),

women, at least for now, have to use cues that are visible to evaluate genetic suitability. And there is an important point that needs to be made here: women are not seeking the "best" genes with which to pair their DNA; they are seeking the best match for their DNA.

Now you might be asking yourself how we evaluate a potential mate's genetic characteristics and consider them with reference to our own genes, especially since we cannot see a person's DNA. This is where the evolved characteristics of our minds step in. There are subtle physical characteristics like facial symmetry—to what degree does the left side of an individual's face precisely mirror the right side (Buss, 2012, p. 122–123)—and even the relative proportions of the fingers of the hand—ring fingers that are longer than index fingers are signs of prenatal exposure to testosterone—that women consciously, but more often unconsciously, perceive that are indicative of the general developmental health and genetic character of an individual male (Manning, 2010). Over countless generations those women who were good at selecting suitable mates were more likely to successfully reproduce, bear healthy children, and raise them to maturity. Those women who were not good at selecting suitable mates probably did not leave behind a lot of offspring. This would suggest that all women tend to be the descendents of women who were good judges of males for the purposes of mate selection in the context of the ancestral environment in which this ability evolved and developed. Consciously—but far more frequently, unconsciously—individual women can perceive which potential mate would be most suited for her genetic characteristics and for the task of raising the child or children that might result.

This is arguably the mysterious part of catching a glimpse of the one you are intended to be with, in the midst of a bustling gathering, and knowing instantly that it is meant to be, seen through the lens of evolutionary processes. The act of falling in love, of finding your "other half," is this evolved system of mate selection in action. It may well be that the intense feeling of "that's the person I should be with" is this ability to evaluate a potential mate signaling the suitability of a particular person.

21.

Trust your nose: there are also important clues that can be smelled out.

· ·

FIGURE 6-16. It is no easy task to select the right mate.

A note here for the girls: There are many ways in which cues about a male's characteristics are perceived. As noted above, facial symmetry and hand shape are two visual cues, but some of the most important signals are perceived through smell. And here is a very significant gender difference: as noted earlier, females have a much better sense of smell than men. For it is through smell that a woman can perceive many of the physiological qualities of a male. One component, among many, that a woman can discern about males through smell indicates the nature of what is called his "major

histological complex" (Hrdy, 1999, p. 193). This refers to his immune system, the bodily defenses that greatly contribute to resistance to disease. Women are predisposed not to be attracted to men whose smell betrays an immune system that is similar to hers. First, because this might be a sign that he is too closely related to her, and second, because it is better for her potential children to have as varied an immune system as possible to ward off disease, since they would inherit characteristics of both her and her mate's immunological systems (which shows that it is not the "best" genes that are favored, but the genes that are best matched to her genes).

22.

Do females consciously select mates?

· ·

Now you may be thinking, how can a girl be aware of something like that when choosing a mate? Remember, this is not a conscious selection process. This is another of those inclinations that is programmed into us and has come down to us from our deep ancestral past. Part of being a woman is having the sensory sensitivity and the ability to unconsciously make these determinations about potential mates. Natural selection endowed women with this power simply because in the past, those women who did not possess this capacity to smell and react to the major histological system of males, among other things, were more likely to have children who were either too inbred (remember in our ancestral past we tended to live in small tribal groups, and a woman may not have consciously been aware to what degree she was related to a potential mate) or who lacked good immune systems. Over countless generations this ability made a difference by favoring women with the capacity to sniff out good genes. Consequently, all the women from whom you are descended very likely had sound noses.

23.

Birth control pills and the ability to smell a good man...

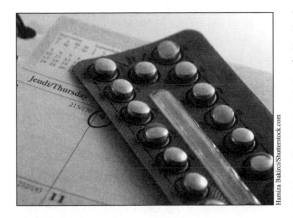

FIGURE 6-17. Perceptions of potential mates are affected by the use of birth control.

A cautionary note for girls: It has been observed by researchers that a woman's perceptions of potential mates are affected by the use of birth control pills because of the hormonal ingredients of these contraceptives (Weaver, 2012, p. 8). Please note, I am not advocating any position on the use of oral contraception use—that is entirely a personal decision. However, it would seem to suggest that the ancient evolutionarily derived sensing systems that women possess could be impaired by its use. As a result, according to researchers, the use of a non-hormone based contraceptive method while selecting a potential mate might yield better choices.

24.

Information everyone can use...

Now guys, there is something that you can take away from this, too. When a relationship does not develop with a girl for seemingly no apparent reason, it may be possible that she is responding to ancient evolved sensory perceptions that are subtly telling her that this was not a good genetic match (Honeycutt & Cantrill, 2001). This is something she feels and so she may not be able to use cognitive references to explain her preference. You may be thinking, "but I had no intention of having children with her." But you need to understand that you are seeing the world of interpersonal relationships from a male point of view in which your potential investment in intended or unintended offspring can vary significantly. From a female point of view, the consequences of developing a relationship that could have intentional or unintentional long-term multi-generational effects for her, for any potential children, and may have far-reaching outcomes for many more individuals, is no trivial matter. Indeed, though there is no objective way to make a determination with any certainty, the relationship that fell through may have been "the bullet" both you, and the girl you were interested in, dodged.

25.

Unfortunately, rejection is a part of mate selection.

FIGURE 6-18. A man and a woman in a relationship...will it last?

The sting of rejection is something no one, irrespective of gender, enjoys. However, in the complex dance of human interpersonal relationships there is far more going on than meets the eye—or the nose. Trusting in our evolved sensibilities about mate selection is no easy thing, but keep in mind, it has served our species well for a long time. Without these behavioral tendencies, you might not exist (Schmitt, 2005).

So what is it from an evolutionary psychological perspective that women are seeking in a potential mate?

Guys, be aware—remember there are two broad categories of mate selection. One is genetic. The other is behavioral. Most of the time they tend to be combined in a woman's outlook. But sometimes they are not. In the environment in which our ancestors evolved, this tended to nudge the approach to mate selection along three different paths.

26.

What are the broad behavioral paths that mate selection tends to follow?

. . . .

One, find a partner who combines suitable genetic/physical characteristics and nurturing behavioral tendencies (which includes access to resources or possible future access to resources, and the willingness to share those resources) that will likely ensure the well-being of potential children and the family that would result. Settle into a committed relationship with this individual, have children, then raise them to maturity, and perhaps assist in the care of grandchildren.

Two, if the two broad criteria of goal one cannot be found in a single individual, select an individual with the most apt genes, have children with him, and if he proves over time unsuitable to the task of raising and nurturing them, try to make the best of it or move on. If the latter is chosen, try to find another partner as described in mate selection goal

one or, if this is not possible, two. However, if a mate still cannot be found who combines either categories, move on to mate selection goal three.

Three, and this is the least likely of mates to find, select an individual with the behavioral characteristics and access or potential access to resources suited to raising already existing children and perhaps have additional children with him.

There is one other important quality in any potential mate that also figures into selection criteria: adaptability. Remember a woman's life is marked by change. Change comes in short cycles and longer phase transitions, and the history of any long-term relationship will feature passage through these episodic periods. Adaptability may not be selected for from the onset of a relationship, but in the long run it is one of the key attributes in a partner that will ensure stability (Buss, 1995).

27.

Is mate selection really this cold and calculating?

. . . .

Again, it is important to emphasize that this is a vast simplification of evolutionarily derived mate selection strategy. It is arguably an extremely unromantic and coldly unsympathetic view. Most women would never consciously pursue such a strategic approach to mate selection. However, if these three approaches were applied broadly to most conventional male/female relationships that we in the West commonly recognize, very likely they would cover the vast majority of such relationships. The particulars of any given relationship between individuals can vary enormously and are significantly shaped by circumstance and by culture, but beneath the details and specific complexities, when it comes to mate selection for the purposes of reproduction, these are the essential tendencies.

In simple terms, what evolution and the environment have predisposed women to want in a partner are those characteristics that contribute to her well-being and the well-being of the potential offspring that might result from the union (Gangestad & Simpson, 2000). In prehistory this meant being a good hunter, being a person she could rely upon to help and protect her, and to protect and help raise the children. If he had status and power among the other members of the family and tribe, this was felt to be a positive because it would improve her status and the status of any possible offspring, thus improving everyone's chances for survival. Being faithful to her was important because if he began to devote his attention and resources to another mate, this might affect the survival status of their children as well as herself (Geary, 1998).

28.

What other complications are there in mate selection?

. . . .

FIGURE 6-19. Are long-term relationships a thing of the past?

The complexities of twenty-first century female/male interaction have added greatly to the already multi-faceted character of mate selection. The rapid rate of change and the short-lived nature of everything from occupations to relationships have put enormous pressure on women—and men. Seeking security in an insecure setting where few things can be counted on to last makes mate selection highly problematic. Nevertheless, essential criteria that come from the past can still be inflected onto the present. Desirable men in the past tended to be males who understood the nature of the times, were emotionally mature enough and intelligent enough to know how to respond effectively to change, and had the energy and resourcefulness to take advantage of the opportunities that presented themselves. His behavior and personality did not detract from the survival of his mate and his children (Schmitt, 2007).

And in many ways, these qualities are still desirable today.

Contemporary economic conditions and the technologies that now support our lives are also offering women another set of options—ones that did not exist in the past. The single mother may well be the wave of the future. As more and more of the sphere of our personal needs enter the fee-for-service realm, we are on the threshold of a brave new world in which everything is basically for sale. There are women now who hire other women to have their children for them. They select a man's genes from a sperm bank, have her egg fertilized then implanted in a surrogate, and after the child is born, hire professional caregivers and educators to raise the child to supposedly optimal maturity. All that is required is money (Turkington & Alper, 2001). Of course there is enormous emotional attachment to the child, but in many respects, maternal investment is literally counted in dollars and cents. Paternal investment in such an arrangement can amount to nothing more than a half-strand of DNA.

Is this our future? Possibly. But very likely the process will not be a smooth one if we choose to follow this path because the ancient predispositions that were born on an African savanna long ago will not disappear over night. There are unforeseen consequences that we have yet to work out.

29.

Do all women adhere to her evolutionarily derived predispositions?

FIGURE 6-20. Some women consciously elect not to follow the old evolutionarily derived predispositions.

It may appear from a contemporary perspective that too much emphasis is placed on reproduction and child rearing in these explanations of why and what women want. After all, not every woman wants to have children. Not every man wants children either. But remember that we are all descended from individuals who lived with far less access to resources than we do today, and their priorities were strictly focused on personal survival and the continuity of their family lineage. This generated a distinct mindset that we inherited from them and which still predisposes us to view interpersonal relationships in the light of their priorities—not ours—even if our personal goals and desires differ greatly from theirs.

If you think about all the women who are our ancestors, you can begin to perceive how they invested their lives to a degree that we can hardly imagine today to ensure our existence. This is why woman can be characterized as the guardian of the future.

WORLDVIEWS SHAPED BY OUR NATURES: AS CITIZENS OF THE PRESENT, WHAT DO MEN WANT?

The Western cultural tradition is based upon the idea of free will. We like to believe we are completely in control of our lives. Freedom is deemed an essential good that must be maintained and broadened as much as possible. Though less often emphasized, we also believe that an individual must be responsible for his or her behavior and live with the consequences that follow. We want to be able to choose our own destinies, make choices for ourselves, and select our paths through life.

FIGURE 6-21. Some people consciously plan what they want out of life.

30.

Do you believe in free will?

. . . .

The debate over free will and whether we really exercise our purported ability to choose is not new. Long arguments have raged in theological, philosophical, and psychological forums for centuries (Kenny, 1994). Books have been written, sermons have been read, and symposia have been assembled to argue the various sides of this issue. To adequately summarize all the positions that have been taken would itself be a daunting task.

The following is not a definitive activity that brings a final resolution to the issue of free will, but try this little exercise: imagine your perfect partner, your perfect mate. Imagine what this individual looks like, sounds like, feels like, smells like, and how this person behaves toward you. Consider all the qualities that would make this person distinct—and more desirable—from all the other people in the world. Imagine that this person interacts with you exactly the way you would like. This is your perfect significant other. Every quality, every characteristic, every action, every expression of emotion, every preference is to your liking. Think about all the things that make this person perfect in your eyes, your heart, and your mind. Get in touch with the feelings you would have about such an individual.

Now, imagine an individual who embodies the exact opposite of the idealized person. Keep in mind that this individual is in every way the anti-version of the ideal. Freeze that image in your mind. Now ask yourself, could you find a way to feel attracted to this person?

31.

What do men look for in a mate?

. . . .

According to research, when people are asked what they find attractive in other people, the answers do not really vary much. In a nutshell, we are all inclined to be attracted to individuals who appear healthy, intelligent, and socially well adjusted (Palmer et al., 2002, p. 113). Of course, the exact details of how we perceive an individual to be in good health and possessed of smarts and social skills can vary somewhat according to the social conventions of the place, time, and cultural context in which we live, but by and large, healthy humans are attracted to other healthy humans. Another way of looking at it is that we tend to evaluate the fitness and attractiveness of others using culturally defined criteria (social constructivism) but the essential qualities that we are evaluating are biologically determined (essentialism) (Buss, 2012, p. 153–154).

From an evolutionary perspective, this makes perfect sense. For during the process of mate selection, no one intentionally pairs up with another person to produce defective, unhealthy children or to end up in a miserable relationship. Once again our preferences can be attributed to the predispositions that we inherited from our forebears. So, in a sense we do not have a completely variable range of mate preference. After all, could you bring yourself to feel attracted to the imagined opposite version of your ideal partner?

When it comes to mate selection, the basic, fundamental criteria from which we view others are not infinitely variable. It would be difficult to will yourself to be attracted to someone who possesses all the qualities you deplore. This would suggest that there are at the very least limits to the range of choices that you would be willing to entertain when exercising your freedom to choose.

Sometimes when I give a lecture before a large gathering of people, to warm up the audience, I pose the following questions: How many women here find wealthy men attractive? Some women laugh as nearly every female in the room raises her hand. Then I ask: How many men are attracted to beautiful women? Nearly every male in the room raises his hand.

32.

Why are males so concerned with appearance when selecting a mate?

FIGURE 6-22. Among males, health and attractiveness go hand in hand.

A note to the girls: If you really want to make sense of male behavior, you have to adopt their worldview. Understand that like the female priorities that tend to order mate selection, millions of years of evolutionary forces have shaped the predispositions of males. Their criteria for picking mates are based upon the circumstances that informed the male outlook over the long history of our species. And like the plea to guys about trying to *feel* what women experience, it would help to attempt to feel what men experience to gain some insight into their outlook.

A general note: There is a lot of controversy that surrounds the issue of male behavior, and like the behavior of all people in the world,

there is a considerable amount of observable variation. Remember that once again evolutionary psychology can only offer a broad outline of male behavior and of the underlying forces that motivate it. And it should be noted, too, that the explanations offered by any perspective view of human behavior, whether it is essentialist, social constructivist, or epigenetic, does not justify any mode of human activity. However, from nature's point of view there are only those traits that tend to result in the continuance of any particular species and those that do not. Remember, ethical judgments are ultimately social constructions, and may deny us the opportunity to gain important insights.

For men, survival is a gamble.

FIGURE 6-23. Survival is a high-risk undertaking for men.

Women also faced the possibility of early death and the prospect of leaving behind no descendents, but males confronted longer odds than their female counterparts in the past.

In the ancestral environment, compared to gathering edible plant material, the hunt was a much more dangerous, high-risk undertaking. Tracking, pursuing, and killing large animals could easily result in injury or death (Fagan, 2010). Yet men engaged in this activity because the rewards were significant. The hunt provided not only food in the form of rich animal protein and fat, but also skins and fur for clothing, as well as bone, tusks, and antlers that could be fashioned into implements like needles, and frames for tents. But more important than the nutritional and raw material gains, women tended to reward men for their hunting prowess and risk-taking (Buss, 2012, p. 83).

33.

Why do men play the role of the "good provider"?

· ·

In the context of the hunter-gatherer social environment, good hunters were good providers. They literally brought home the bacon. This tended to make them more attractive to women. Thus such males were more likely to be selected as mates and so have the opportunity to pass their traits on to future generations. Some of the characteristics that made for a good hunter, however, are the very ones that cause problems for males today.

FIGURE 6-24. Imagine trying to survive under such conditions.

A good hunter of the last ice ages needed to be aggressive when the most potent weapon he had to bring down a mammoth or a bison was a spear. He was inclined to fix his attention very intensely on the matter at hand and disregarding everything not relevant to the kill. Being distracted by sentiments was not conducive to success—or survival—while engaged in risky tasks like facing down packs of wolves or another group of humans that were

also interested in the remains of the animals he killed. Thus aggression facilitated the ambition to be a good hunter—a quality that had its rewards (Buss, 2012, p. 118–119).

In other words, life for our ancestral fathers was quite unlike our own, and the predispositions that were favored by the women in their lives and by the environment in which they lived would not have made them popular in most contemporary social settings. Yet these behavioral predispositions were appropriate for the circumstances in which they evolved. Over thousands and thousands of generations, the demands of life on the windswept savannas of the past honed and shaped theses traits, just as the characteristics that made our ancestral mothers efficient gatherers and caregivers were selectively favored.

34.

Can a man ever be certain that a child is his?

· ·

Now you may recall back in the second chapter that it was the inherent immobility and the relative enormity of the egg cell compared to the tiny and mobile sperm cell that is at the heart of the biological difference between males and females. One of the significant outcomes of this arrangement is that a woman always knows who is her son or daughter because the ovum (the fertilized egg) develops in her womb. But a man can never be completely certain if a child is his (Hrdy, 1999, p. 227). Today through blood tests we can determine paternity, but remember that male behavioral inclinations developed long before such technology existed. This has significant consequences for males.

A note to girls: Put yourself in our ancestral male's place. You wake up every morning hoping that maybe today you will bring down a really big animal, then everyone in the family and tribe will have enough to eat to live for another week, and you will be recognized as a good hunter—but you may also be trampled to death by an angry mammoth, or killed by a pack of wolves, or assaulted by members of another tribe attempting to steal your catch. Death is an ever-present companion. You can let fear cripple you or you can stoically stare it in the face and do the best you can. Either way, it is not a way of life that would favor sensitivity or thoughtfulness. But there is another tendency that springs from constantly risking death.

35.

Rolling the dice when it comes to selecting mates…

Men prefer young, physically attractive women because these qualities tend to indicate fertility, and with the strong possibility that today's gamble with death might turn up snake-eyes (a reference to rolling the dice and getting two 1s, which is the lowest possible score and a losing roll, hence the reference to the beady eyes of a snake), from an evolutionary point of view it would be adaptive for a male to take advantage of every opportunity to mate and have children in order to get his genes into the next generation. Favoring older, less attractive, and potentially less fertile females under such circumstances would decrease the likelihood of reproductive success (Buss, 2012, p. 142). This, combined with the inability of ancestral males to know with certainty if a child was his, produced the predisposition to seek out as many mating opportunities as possible and to be less invested in any given relationship than his female partners. After all, if he could never be certain any resulting child were really his, the possibility always existed that he was devoting his energy and resources to raise another man's son or daughter. In prehistory, men who did not have these behavioral tendencies probably did not leave behind as many descendents as those who did.

Granted there is again an element of over-simplification here, but it illustrates that a calculation of reproductive risk that our predecessors of each sex unconsciously evaluated in prehistory influenced their respective strategies. The answers they derived from the calculus of their differing biological natures coupled with the demands of their ancient gender roles produced predispositions that are still with us today.

Does this justify inappropriate and destructive behavior that spring from these inherited traits today? No, it does not. We all have the capacity to bend our inborn characteristics and live according to the requirements of the times. However, the insight offered by the history of our species sheds light on male and female behavioral predispositions and helps us to understand why these echoes from the past still nudge us in certain directions.

Our ancient forefathers lived with death dogging their heels all the time. They had to live in the moment, as citizens of the present.

WORLDVIEWS SHAPED BY OUR NATURES: AS UNRECOGNIZED HUMANS, WHAT DO INTERSEX INDIVIDUALS WANT?

Amid all this discussion of mate selection and all these evolutionary predispositions acting on individuals, you might wonder, what about love? What about companionship and friendship? What about the simple pleasure of being with someone else and just enjoying each other's presence, and all that stuff about attraction and offspring and preferences can go to—you know—that place where it is always hot and the sun never shines!

I hear you.

FIGURE 6-25. Friends enjoying each other's company.

36.

When are we, as a species, going to grow past our old programming bequeathed to us by our ancient predecessors?

In a sense this is the deep message of all the great religions. To transcend—to go beyond the physical and behavioral structures that inform our worldview and that we carry in our DNA and minds like so much musty old baggage—has been the goal of many of the wise individuals of the past. This is why people who are very spiritually inclined often talk about letting go of power and money and belongings, because these are the culturally designated (social constructivist view) things that we use in our society to evaluate the personal fitness, intelligence, and social adjustment of individuals. By letting go of the things that are used to judge the qualities of others, the person who wishes to move beyond the evolved worldview that our ancestors developed long ago, is taking the first step toward a new way of living.

37.

Considering how many people are alive today, are our old predispositions still appropriate?

There are more than seven billion of us on the planet now, with another two billion to be added by the middle of this century. Do we really need to be so focused on having babies and getting our genes into the future? Do we need to be so discriminating in our mate selection along lines of gene traits, behavioral inclinations, and resource access anymore? Must we judge people by their appearance?

The answer is very definitely, no. But it is difficult for us to let go of our collective past.

We live in a paradoxical situation in which our evolved behavioral tendencies run counter to our survival needs. Remember the problem we have with controlling our weight in an environment in which cheap, high-calorie, low-nutrition food is widely available? This is just one of many instances in which our evolved responses to the environment do not mesh well with the actual circumstances in which we now live. But we still tend to hold onto the old ways. We still tend to make judgments about the suitability of other people based upon ancient criteria.

Robnroll/Shutterstock.com

FIGURE 6-26. What would our ancestors think of our high-tech world?

We weren't evolved for the high tech world that we have made for ourselves, and the confusion that many feel living in the midst of this rapidly changing context, that is the hallmark of the twenty-first century, is caused by this mismatch (Wells, 2010). However, to transcend the old program that we inherited from our ancestors requires that we do the hard work of creating a new one. And this has to be done in the midst of multitudes of people who are completely committed to the old ways.

38.

Is it time we all grew up?

In many respects, the inclinations and predispositions that we got from our Pleistocene predecessors, like classifying people into in-groups or out-groups, of evaluating males principally in terms of their access to resources, of men

judging women by their physical appearance, of ignoring individuals who do not fit into categories of male or female, are out of date. They are anachronisms. And though they are no longer entirely suited for the new world unfolding before us, the old ways are easy to fall back upon. They form a kind of default way of living that served our ancestors well, but that now requires revision.

However, it takes time for new behavioral patterns to develop—and far longer for these new ways to become "second nature"—to be part of our inherited behavioral tendencies. Hard work must be done to form new conventions and norms—and it takes a long time for people to learn them, perhaps accept them, and maybe incorporate them into the personal worldviews of the general populace.

Ultimately, the problem is that too much change is happening too fast for too many people. All the heated debate surrounding the so-called "culture wars" in the West, about matters like abortion, same-sex marriage, environmental policy, and many other highly divisive issues, come from the disparity that exists between the old worldviews and the requirements of living in new circumstances. A kind of general backlash against the new ways that emerge from postmodernity is occurring.

As a result, many people are holding steadfastly to the older evolved perspectives on the roles of women and men, among other things, at the very time when others are trying to transcend them.

39.

Can you imagine being an intersex individual in today's world?

This is the context in which the intersex individual lives. In many ways, the ancient priorities our species places on reproduction makes the intersex person invisible. Those individuals who do not participate in the dance of procreation tend to be marginalized and excluded because they do not fit into the overarching context that forms the basic structure of most people's outlook. Think about your own experience—there is a good chance that many of the people you know are not aware of a gender outside of male or female.

Nonetheless, intersex individuals are human beings, as human as any other person. They have the same evolved need for fellowship and companionship, for inclusion in family, in a larger circle of friends, and in community-based social groupings as any other gendered individual. We all want to love and be loved.

It can be argued that the issue of same-sex marriage and the recognition that individuals of varied sexual orientation are demanding for equal rights are a direct challenge to the cultural inflections of our ancient evolved behavioral predispositions. In the new cultural context that is emerging out of the social and technological innovations that shape our world, individuals who are not defined by the traditional reproductive pattern of male/female relationships are attempting to transcend our collective past.

This, too, is the essential message of the various feminist movements as well (Thébaud, 1994). Males and females need to recognize how the ancestral predispositions that chain us to old ways of interacting limit personal growth and development. The old ways lock us into roles and outlooks that prevent individuals from realizing their full potential. We need to change with the times and circumstances.

A new world is unfolding in front of us. Are we going to continue to limit ourselves to the old ways?

· ·

FIGURE 6-27. Many paths beckon.

On the other hand, many find the pace of social, economic, and technological change threatening. The prospect of having to constantly adapt to new ways of doing things, to new ways of thinking, of having to assimilate new values, morals, and ethics is unnerving and disorienting. Some would claim it is simply wrong. Consequently, many long to return to a time and a way of life when all things were stable and known, when constant change was not a feature of daily life.

For some, change cannot come fast enough; for others, it is happening far too quickly. For the intersex person there are alternative paths from which to choose. Some individuals decide to bend to prevailing norms and adopt the expected appearance and behavior of one traditional gender or another. Others will seek acceptance and recognition of their personal conception of their intersex identity. For many it is an ongoing process of learning and self-discovery that leads hopefully toward full awareness and complete acceptance of their unique character.

REFERENCES

Barrington, E. & Stamm, J. (2012). *Image of Health*. Plymouth, MI: Hayden-McNeil Publishing.

Bently, P. (1995). *The dictionary of world myth*. New York: Facts on File.

Buss, D. (1995). "Evolutionary psychology: a new paradigm for psychological science." *American Scientist*, 82, 238–249.

Buss, D. (2012). *Evolutionary psychology: the new science of the mind*. Boston: Allyn & Bacon.

Fagan, B. (2010). *Cro-magnon: how the ice age gave birth to the first modern humans*. New York: Bloomsberry Press.

Gangestad, S. W. & Simpson, J. A. (2000). "The evolution of human mating: trade-offs and strategic pluralism." *Behavioral and Brain Sciences*, 23, 573–587.

Geary, D.C. (1998). *Male, female: the evolution of human sex differences*. Washington, DC: American Psychological Association.

Haiso, C. C., Liu, C. Y. & Hsiao, M. C. (2004). "No correlation of depression and anxiety to plasma estrogen and progesterone levels in patients with premenstrual dysphoric disorder." *Psychiatry and Clinical Neurosciences*, 58, 593–599.

Honeycutt, J. M. & Cantrill, J. G. (2001). *Cognition, communication, and romantic relationships*. Mahwah, NJ: Lawrence Erlbaum Associates.

Hrdy, S. B. (1999). *Mother nature: a history of mothers, infants, and natural selection*. New York: Pantheon.

Kenny, A. (1994). *The oxford history of western philosophy*. Oxford: Oxford University Press. pp. 62–63, 72–73, 105, 155–156,165–166.

Manning, John. (2012). "Finger length and digit ratio hand news." Fingerlengthdigitratio.wordpress.com

Palmer, J. A. & Palmer, L. K. (2002). *Evolutionary psychology: the ultimate origins of human behavior*. Boston, Allyn & Bacon.

Rodin, M. (1992). "The social construction of premenstrual syndrome." *Social Science & Medicine*. July 1992. Vol. 35. pp. 49–56.

Ronnberg, A., Ed. in Chief. (2010). *The book of symbols*. Cologne, Germany: Taschen.

Schmitt, D.P. (2005). "Sociosexuality from argentina to zimbabwe. A 48-nation study of sex, culture, and strategies of human mating." *Behavioral and Brain Sciences*, 28, 247–311.

Schmitt, D.P. (2007). "Sexual strategies across sexual orientations: how personality traits and culture relate to sociosexuality among gays, lesbians, bisexuals, and heterosexuals." *Journal of Psychology and Human Sexuality*, 18, 183–214.

Stringer, C. & Andrews, P. (2011). *The complete world of human evolution*. New York: Thames & Hudson.

Thébaud, F., ed. (1994) *A history of women: volume five: toward a cultural identity in the twentieth century*. Cambridge: Belknap Harvard.

Triver, R. (1972). "Parental investment and sexual selection." *Sexual selection and the descent of man*. New York: Aldine de Gruyter. pp. 136–179.

Turkington, C., & Alper, M. M. (2001). *The encyclopedia of fertility and infertility.* New York: Facts on File.

Weaver, J. (2012). "The problem with the pill." *Scientific American Mind.* Vol. 23, No. 1, March/April 2012. p. 8.

Wells, S. (2010). *Pandora's seed: the unforeseen cost of civilization.* New York: Random House.

Zastrow, C., Kirst-Ashman, K. K. (2009) *Understanding human behavior and the social environment.* New York: Brooks Cole. p. 411.

Name   Date

1. Why do some claim that PMS is not real? What do you think?

2. What important insights can be gained by trying to see the world through another person's eyes?

3. What are the short-term cycles and the long-term phase transitions of a woman's life? And why is the moon the symbol of woman?

4. Why are women better able to deal with change?

5. What is the nature of the male lifespan? And why is the sun the symbol of man?

6.   Why is the worldview of the intersex person so different from females and males?

7.   Why can women be characterized as "guardians of the future"?

8.   What do women find attractive in men? From an evolutionary view, why do women find these characteristics attractive? What do males find attractive in females? From an evolutionary view, why do they find these characteristics attractive?

9.   Why can men be characterized as "citizens of the present"?

10. Why are our old evolved predispositions no longer well suited for the world we currently live in, and how do these inclinations affect intersex individuals?

Chapter 7

GENDER AND POWER

Chapter 7

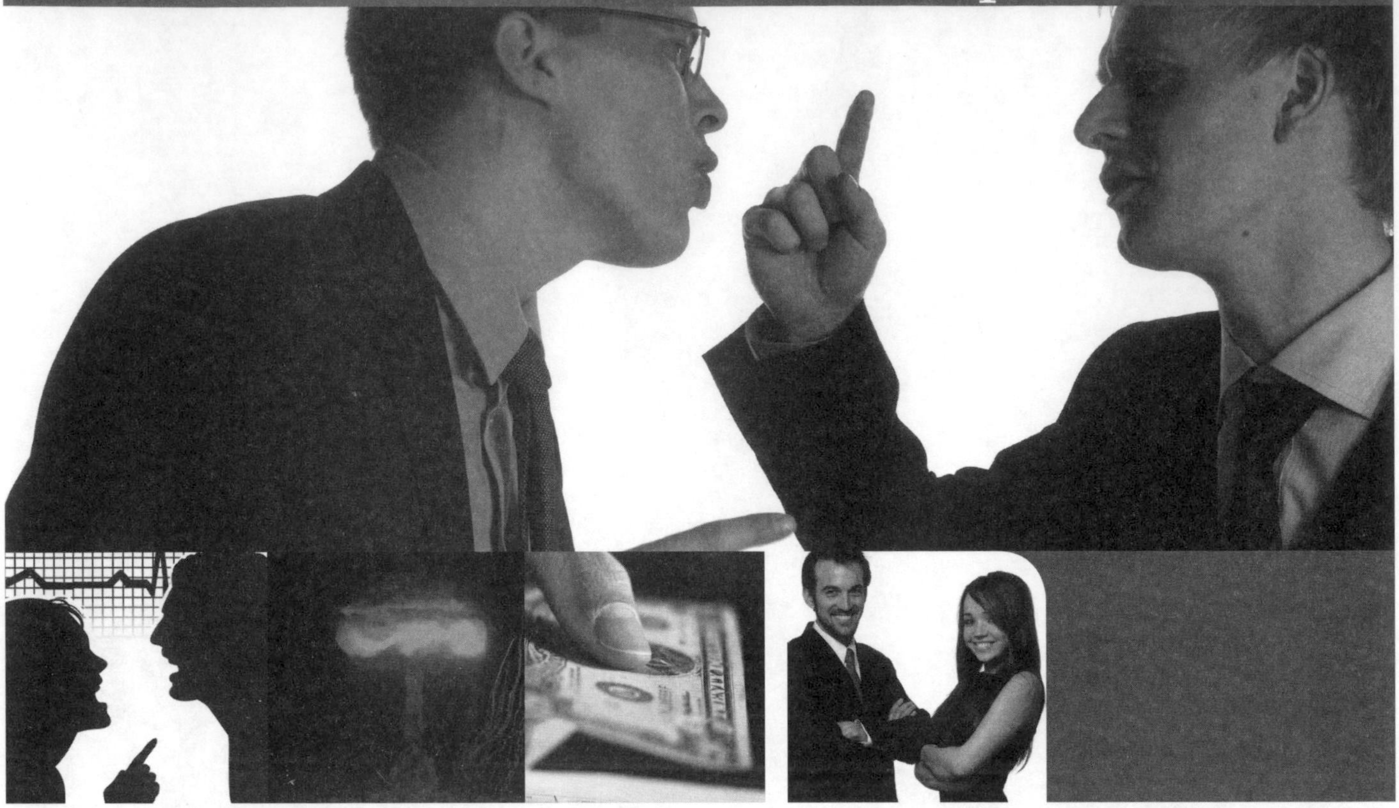

POWER

Standing at the edge of millions of years of patient sculpting by wind and water in the bright north Arizona sunshine, you can feel the power of nature when you look out across the Grand Canyon. The rich earthen hues that color that enormous stone monument to time and to the forces of nature delight the eye. The wind that issues from the canyon whispers a song so old that it predates the birth of our species. The landscape that extends outward as you stand in its midst hints of the slumbering energy that rests within the Earth, and renders, by comparison, the activities of humanity a mere vanity.

FIGURE 7-1. Beauty and power brought together in one sweeping view.

 1.

Have you ever considered the varying types of power that have shaped the world and your life?

· ·

But you do not have to travel to the American southwest to catch a glimpse of the power of nature. The sun that brings the dawn every morning is a star whose diameter is more than a hundred times greater than the Earth's. It is a huge sphere of roiling hydrogen, helium, and other trace elements in which thermonuclear reactions are releasing prodigious amounts of energy into the surrounding vacuum of space by fusing lighter elements into heavier ones. Though light travels at 186,000 miles per second, the sun is so distant from the Earth that it takes eight minutes for light leaving its surface to make the journey to us. Yet despite its distance from us (93 million miles), it provides heat and daylight, it drives the weather cycles, it is the primary source of energy for nearly all life on the planet (Mitton, 1977). Ancient humans worshipped and revered the sun, and though they did not have the insights that science offers us, they knew that their lives were tied to that great sphere in the sky.

FIGURE 7-2. The sun powers much of the life on Earth.

To see the material effects of an even greater source of power than the sun, you need only look at your own hand. The oxygen and carbon and calcium atoms, as well as other trace elements that comprise the molecules that constitute the skin tissue, blood vessels, bones, and muscles of your body were made long ago, before even the sun and the Earth existed. Much of the matter that you are made of was born when a huge star that would have made our sun look like a jack-o-lantern glowing in a late October evening exploded. In the inferno of that unimaginably huge explosion, the heavy atoms, like the calcium in your bones and the iron in your blood, were synthesized. The sun and the Earth and all the other planets of the solar system—and you and me—are made of the recycled bits of that colossal supernova explosion that occurred more than five billion years ago (Sagan, 1980).

We come from the stars.

FIGURE 7-3. A new solar system is forming out of the remains of an ancient star. The sun, the Earth, the planets, and you and me are made of the atoms left over from a star that exploded long ago.

2.

Consider the significance of the power we command…

. . . .

That is power on a scale that far surpasses anything we humans can muster. There is consolation in the knowledge that no matter how terribly and destructively any one of us, or any group of us, behaves, all the power that we can summon cannot affect a single star in the heavens. The power-obsessed among us may gain the means to influence whole nations, even change the destinies of billions of people, but they cannot alter a single twinkling point of light in the night sky.

FIGURE 7-4. Our power cannot begin to affect the heavens.

3.

What lengths would you go to acquire power over others?

. . . .

Power. It is a thing that we humans are infinitely fascinated by and many are willing to do almost anything for.

It is a subject that is seldom directly addressed in books about gender. Instead the issue is usually discussed in terms of the roles that define males and females, and how the hierarchy of power compels both to conform to their respective positions, in which women are typically cast as passive and men as dominant. And in the assessment of power relationships between the genders, the assertion is usually made that males have access to most, if not all, of it, and that this resource is used principally to control and oppress the other genders. This is the standard socially constructed view that tends to order our understanding of power and the genders. But as we shall see, there is more to this matter than meets the eye.

FIGURE 7-5. Power. We are fascinated by it.

FIGURE 7-6. The economic health of the world is the socially constructed reference to power most people accept today.

Power is more than the simple ability to assert our will onto others and get what we want. It has many forms and can be wielded in many ways. Its effects can be felt immediately or its reach can span millennia. It can be used to create and to destroy. Its goals can be as direct as the acquisition of food, shelter, or the opportunity to reproduce, or as subtle as the shaping of feelings and attitudes. Power can be as personal as the requests that issue from our lips or as indifferent to our existence as a tsunami bearing down upon a coastal community. Power can be the expression of physical might, or it can be the product of knowledge and insight.

Power is an issue that can be viewed through several perspectives.

From a social constructivist view, power is what we collectively say it is. In the twenty-first century, most people would probably identify the economic system we live within as the main referent to power. And for all its faults and virtues, whether we like it or not, it defines and structures our lives. It touches nearly every aspect of our daily existence and affects our interactions with other people.

4.

Does power seem like a force for good or ill in your mind?

. . . .

THE NATURE OF POWER

Science is neither good nor evil. The knowledge that makes it possible to produce energy from the splitting of atoms in order to provide electricity to heat and light our homes, to cook our meals, and keep our food cold to prevent it from spoiling is the same knowledge that was used to fabricate the atomic bombs that leveled the cities of Hiroshima and Nagasaki at the end of the Second World War in August of 1945 (Bronowski, 1972). What we choose to do with our knowledge reflects our priorities, our values, and our character. In other words, tools as rudimentary as plows and arrows, or technologies as sophisticated as cellphones and nuclear weapons, may come from the application of knowledge, but by itself science is not inherently positive or negative. Only when we humans exert our will and apply our knowledge to achieve particular goals do ethical judgments of right and wrong arise.

FIGURE 7-7. We give power its character.

As a concept, power is a similar matter. By itself it is neither good nor evil. How we choose to exercise the power we possess, or have access to, determines its character. How power is inflected through the choices we make imparts a particular quality to it.

The ability to influence, the capacity to order, the authority to shape, the might to control, and the strength to govern our life course as well as affect the destinies of others—these are the customary ways we tend to think about power. To project our will on to other individuals, to make them do what we want, and to get what we want—these are the goals that typically inform our understanding of power. Consequently, within the context of the relationship between the genders, much emphasis is placed on power and its effects. Yet there is little discussion about power in terms of its origins within human social systems, and how men and women distinctively wield it.

What is the social constructivist view of power and its relationship to the genders?

The contemporary social constructivist view is that power is not fairly or evenly distributed between the genders, and those who have power do everything they can to maintain their hold on it. From the current social constructivist view, the power imbalance between the genders is the root cause of many of the problems and conflicts that exist between men and women. The remedy that is put forward is usually one in which power is properly redistributed, thus empowering those with less power. The resulting equality, according to this view, would do much to put matters right (Thebaud, 1994).

FIGURE 7-8. Balance of power…who has the upper hand?

6.

What are the essentialist and epigenetic views of power and its relationship to the genders?

. . . .

The biological essentialist and nature via nurture frames of reference do not directly address the issue of power. The nature of power among humans—how it originated, how it is understood, and how it is used—has its origin in the ancestral environment in which we evolved and is reflected in our culture. It is a sociological phenomenon, and consequently, is not a purely psychological or genetic characteristic. However, it can be inferred, from the structure of the essentialist and the epigenetic ways of understanding human development, that power in its present distribution among the genders can be traced to historical and evolutionary trends. This would suggest that insight into traditional power relationships might be gained by examining the circumstances in which our species evolved.

FIGURE 7-9. The past may be a portal to insights about our nature.

However, once again it is important to emphasize that the conditions under which our kind developed its behavioral predispositions are not the same as those with which we currently live. There is no inherent guarantee that old inclinations are necessarily adaptive in a

world that differs markedly from the setting in which they formed. As we have seen in previous chapters, it is the mismatch between behavioral tendencies born in the ancestral environment and the new requirements of living in the rapidly changing postmodern world of the twenty-first century that is at the center of many of our problems. This means that essentialist and epigenetic views should not and cannot be used to rationalize or justify what may now be deemed the improper use of power.

When it comes to the specific application of power, it is important to point out that enormous variation exists among individuals in the way they acquire, maintain, and use power. The old approaches to power that we inherited from our ancestors are also shaped and inflected by the social situation in which we currently live and by our present surroundings. However, as we shall see, irrespective of the contrasts that arise from these differences, the ultimate goal of the personal exercise of power today is still one our distant forebears would recognize.

7.

How should we be mindful about the use of power?

. . . .

A CAUTIONARY NOTE
All power corrupts.

The abusive use of power is a common feature of human history and was, no doubt, a regular part of our species' prehistory as well. From the smallest omission of truth to wholesale genocide, the scale of the inappropriate use of power is wide indeed. And the curious thing about power is that the smallest infraction or the grossest outrage can have equally devastating and far-reaching consequences. How many "little white lies" have launched wars?

FIGURE 7-10. How many conflicts have their roots in little distortions of the truth?

The problem with discussions about power is that it is easy to twist any argument to imply the justification of nearly any act. The pages of history are littered with accounts of individuals and nations rationalizing their behavior to justify the pursuit of self-interest at the expense of others. We humans have a strong tendency to use our intellectual faculties to fabricate seemingly sound reasons to exercise power in order to achieve less than worthy goals (Shire, 1960)—a behavioral tendency that is probably common to every human culture, at every time—which implies that a frank examination of power is not an easy thing to accomplish.

FIGURE 7-11. How many nations of the world have not rationalized their behavior?

Nevertheless, an important distinction needs to be made. As noted earlier, power by itself is neither good nor evil. How individuals choose to wield power determines how we judge its application, and these judgments are based upon contemporary cultural norms (social constructions) that are commonly shared. We need to adopt a perspective that transcends current social agendas that seek to blame and stigmatize individuals or groups of individuals for the abuses of the past, and try to consider this matter with the interests of all people—indeed, all life—as central.

There is an additional element to be considered as well: what may seem like the blatant misuse of power from one point of view may appear entirely appropriate and just from another. Once again, frames of reference need to be considered and taken into account in any discussion of power and its uses.

8.

What is the current social constructivist view of power and the genders?

With respect to gender relations, the deep problem is that there are significant differences in the relationship that males and females have with power. Much of the writing and research done on power and gender proceed from the view that males tend to be the dominant partner in most relationships, and that men are more likely to be concerned with power and status. The resulting consequence of this perspective of the existing imbalance of power is that women are viewed as the victims of male domination. The larger implication is that the entire superstructure of Western civilization, and indeed of many other cultures, including those in East Asia, the Indian subcontinent, Africa, and South and Central America, can be generally characterized as male oriented and male dominated. And though there are indications that the apparent power imbalance that exists between the genders is declining in some parts of the world, according to this view, there remains a significant empowerment gap that favors males to the detriment of females.

FIGURE 7-12. The struggle for power between men and women is ongoing.

The selective killing of female newborns in China, the occurrence of "honor killings" in Indian and Pakistani cultures in which a husband or father murders or severely injures a wife or a daughter for some perceived act of disrespect, the widespread use of rape as an act of war in the conflicts that occur among African nations and that has long been a part of human conflict, the terrible practice of female genital mutilation in parts of Africa, and the long standing wage disparity in which women are paid substantially less than men that occurs in all countries are just some of the manifestations of unequal access to power. A complete list of the acts of violence and other crimes that are the product of inequality between the genders would be encyclopedic in length.

But it should be noted that men are also victims of the power inequalities that exist in any given society. Approximately twenty-five million men, most of whom were forced into military duty, lost their lives in just the second of the last century's two world wars. Among all the conflicts that have been waged over human history, the tally of males killed in action

is probably in the billions. Men are also raped and sexually assaulted, but because either the social conventions of the culture do not recognize male rape or because being a victim of rape is so threatening to men they choose not to report it, this injustice goes largely unacknowledged. Male genital mutilation has been a common act of violence as well. Wages among males have never been equitable either. The disparity between top earners and the vast majority of workers in the United States is only growing worse with time.

There is no denying that human history—and undoubtedly, prehistory—is rife with injustice. The cost to women, to intersex individuals, to children of all genders—and to men as well, is staggering. The loss to our species and to all human cultures is immeasurable. The number of lives that have been extinguished or ruined by the blind acceptance of the power structures that have informed the relationships between women and men, and between individuals in general, is beyond count. The need to remedy this problem is very real.

9.

We need to view power as more than brute force.

The first steps in attempting to change this sorry state of affairs is surely to develop an objective awareness of the essential nature of power, to understand its uses, the goals to which it is applied, and to gain some insight into the perceptions of those who wield it. Power and gender are complex matters. There is much more to power relationships than the brutish view of "me got stick, you do what I tell, or you get hit." Power comes in many forms and can be projected in many ways. It can be exercised with forthright directness or with barely perceivable subtlety. It can be used to achieve any number of short-term and long-term goals, and no gender has ever had complete control of it.

Songquan Deng/Shutterstock.com

FIGURE 7-13. Power can take many forms.

As you may be able to deduce, and as we will see, from an evolutionary frame of reference there is really only one measure of power within the context of Earthly life. From this vantage point, one gender very definitely is more in tune with the long-term requirements for survival.

10.

Which gender do you think is the most powerful from an evolutionary point of view?

· ·

But a problem persists. It is difficult to put aside our personal experiences and feelings when attempting to analytically examine the nature of power. Our preconceived views tend to severely color our personal perceptions on the matter. In addition, social constructivist views of power tend to dominate our interpretation of its character. We are inclined to allow the social context that informs our lives to wholly shape our thoughts and feeling. Consequently, many people are apt to be more receptive to claims about how males obsessively wield power to their advantage, to the detriment of all others, rather than to consider the distinctive ways each gender attempts to use power for its own ends and purposes. The

knowledge that whole classes of people have been systematically oppressed and exploited is ever present. And rightly so, but the socially constructed frames of reference of oppressors and the oppressed make it hard to attempt a more objective understanding of power.

Once again, we need to try to take a step back from the conventions that tend to order our view of the topic and how it affects gender identities and attempt to take in a broader view. Perhaps only then we can develop fresh insights and find ways to truly empower individuals irrespective of their gender. Then we can perhaps better understand the imbalances that have existed for so long, and create a more equitable world for all people.

FIGURE 7-14. We need to adopt a step back from our conventional views of issues…

THE INNOVATION OF MONEY

11.

Our most recent social construction of power: money.

· ·

Money—how many times have you heard couples get into arguments about it? If there is one thing that causes more disagreements in contemporary relationships than any other single issue, it is money. Why is that? Why do males and females so often find money such a contentious matter? Why are so many divorces at least in part motivated by an inability of couples to come to some compromise over money? Perhaps your parents split up over money. Maybe you can recall raging arguments, heated accusations, and tearful demands. Perhaps you have had your own struggles getting a person in your life to see eye-to-eye with you about matters related to expenses and finances.

FIGURE 7-15. Money: ever thought about how it shapes your life?

To get some insight into why the genders often disagree about money matters, it is important to understand what money is in the first place, how it affects us, and has changed the way we interact with each other.

12.

Have you ever asked yourself what money really is, or have you always just taken it for granted?

. . . .

The next time you hold a coin or a paper bill in your hand, or pull out your debit or credit card, or execute a banking transaction over

the Internet, or use some e-commerce transfer system like Paypal, you might want to whisper a "thank you" to an unknown individual who lived thousands of years ago, who saved your life (particularly if you are male). Saved your life? Absolutely.

FIGURE 7-16. Money touches nearly every part of our lives.

More than all the doctors and scientists who have found cures for disease, more than all the political leaders who resolved conflicts peacefully, the person who invented money did more than anyone else to save human lives by reducing the incidence of violence (Ferguson, 2008). As much as we may find earning money, dealing with paying bills, and buying things we need that seem to always be going up in price tedious, the creation of money a few thousand years ago fundamentally revolutionized human life. What money altered were the old ways in which humans had acquired what they needed and wanted for millions of years.

Before the foundation of the first cities, the rise of the first civilizations, the development of agriculture, and the creation of money, which all began roughly ten thousand years ago, our nomadic hunting and gathering ancestors simply took what they wanted and needed. To use our current way of thinking about such matters, their transacted exchanges that were unequal. Our forebears took from the environment food, water, and other resources they required without immediately compensating their surroundings beyond perhaps thanking the gods they worshipped. In other words, they did not pay for what they acquired from the land. The hunters hunted and the gatherers gathered. Their efforts were rewarded not with dollars and cents but with game to bring back to the family or the tribe, or with vegetables for the next meal. The edible animal or the pile of fruits, nuts, and berries were not purchased with paper money or an electronic transfer of funds. Our ancestors sought, grabbed, and consumed.

Now as much as this may seem like an idyllic way of life—there were no concerns about having or earning money, no taxes to pay, no worries about unemployment, no thoughts about showing up to work on time—there were some elements that we would find difficult to accept.

FIGURE 7-17. What would our ancestors have thought about the conveniences we take for granted?

First off, the effort our ancestors put into getting their next meal was not always productive. Sometimes the hunt and the vegetable search came up empty. How many of us would put up with going to the supermarket, paying our money, and coming home with nothing?

Second, our ancestors could never save for a rainy day, as we would say. They lived with constant insecurity. While we can reliably look

forward to time off, to the weekend, perhaps to vacation time—maybe even retirement—our forebears never knew with any degree of certainty when food would become scarce, when the hunt would fail or the gathering go poorly. They could dry some foods and put away some nuts for later consumption, but because they never settled in one place for long, they could never store enough provisions to get them through lean times. This is the great advantage of being paid for your labor with money. It can be carried about easily (or put away in a bank or investment) and does not go bad (though inflation can affect its value negatively), which makes saving it over long periods of time feasible, and it can be used anytime to get what you need or want. Without money, our ancestors never knew when they could relax or when they would have to make a desperate effort to get something to eat.

FIGURE 7-18. Have you ever considered all the things money protects you from?

Third (and this is the reason the invention of money has saved your life) because our ancestors were accustomed to taking what they wanted from the land, they also tended to treat other groups of humans in much the same way. We know from studying present day hunter-gatherer societies that in the absence of money and trade, raiding is the means by which one group got what they wanted from another group (Ferguson, 2008, p. 18).

No doubt the equitable exchange of goods—what we commonly call barter—did on occasion happen in prehistoric times. A deerskin for a stone axe head, some nuts and berries for a spear shaft—but the problem was that nomadic people tended not to carry a lot of tradable goods around with them. There was also the problem that economists call coincidence of wants: an individual with something to trade may not encounter anyone who had something that individual desired and would be willing to accept in kind (Smith, 1776, 2003). (You have experienced an aspect of this problem when you've entered a shop and walked out without buying anything: that store had nothing you were willing to trade your money for.) This means that the fair and peaceful exchange of goods was not a common feature of our ancestors' lives.

FIGURE 7-19. All this would be impossible without money.

There are serious consequences that arise from the rarity of barter and the nonexistence of a medium of exchange (money). Like chimpanzees that attack other groups of chimps in order to gain access to resources (food) or to mating opportunities (females), our forefathers took through violence and intimidation what they wanted from other humans. What we call theft and robbery were normal features of prehistoric human life, and so was the violence that tended to accompany such acts.

13.

Have you ever wondered how money shapes our attitudes and values?

· ·

You can begin to appreciate why, when we first started to use money and markets with the rise of the first civilizations, the commandment "thou shall not steal," which seems so obvious to us, must have been like something out of the blue to people adopting the then new settled way of life. Such a rule had to have the force of divine directive behind it when taking things from others by force had been the norm for so long.

FIGURE 7-20. "Thou shall not steal" is the 8th Commandment.

But for our pre-agricultural, prehistoric forefathers, planning a raid on another group of people, or planning a defense against a possible raid from another group of males, was a fact of life. Large percentages of males died of violence that resulted from such activity (Ferguson, 2008, p. 18). In many ways, it can be argued that raiding is just another form of hunting. Tracking the movements of another group of people, determining what resources they might possess that would make a raid worthwhile, assessing their vulnerability to attack, gauging the likelihood of a successful raiding effort, and then executing the raid parallel the hunt and utilize much the same killing skills. Indeed, a raid in which things like an already butchered slab of fresh mammoth meat, skins and pelts, stone tools, and fertile females might be gained would be much more profitable and rewarding than a similar expenditure of energy invested in bringing down an angry mammoth.

However, the cost to the raiders was often quite high. Many were injured or killed in such a grab for resources and reproductive opportunities. But remember, as we learned in Chapter 6, men are predisposed to be gamblers. (Though we might react with horror and disgust at the notion of stealing women and children, remember that until fairly recently, slavery was deemed an acceptable institution. Sadly, it was only very recently that the social construction that slavery is unacceptable became widely accepted—a few centuries ago. Whether we like it or not, many of the civilizations from ancient Babylon, to Rome, to America were, at least in part, built on slavery.) The rewards that male members of a tribe received for the gains acquired through raiding from female members of their family or tribe were substantial. A male who was perceived to be a bold, successful raider was viewed as a good provider. Thus he was seen as an attractive male by females and would be more likely to successfully reproduce. This in turn created the incentive for continued raiding. It would not be far off the mark probably to venture the guess that at least some women—even today—find the Indiana Jones/swashbuckling/corporate raider type attractive.

FIGURE 7-21. Corporate raiders are often perceived as "good providers."

But the payoff, nevertheless, of adopting less life-threatening ways of securing the necessities as well as the luxuries of life made the innovation of money and markets very appealing. Besides avoiding the violence that is inherent to taking resources by force, the use of money also gets around some of the limitations that raiding shares with simple barter. What if the group being plundered does not have what is desired? And as much as ancient males might have liked taking fertile females, these captives also required resources to feed and shelter if they were to bear children, which put even more pressure on the raiders. Nevertheless, only very recently have the convergence of innovations that include trade, commerce, money, and markets—plus the ethical and legal systems to support these institutions—developed. What we would recognize as shopping has only existed for about three hundred years (Burke, 1985), a tiny miniscule of the total amount of time our species has existed.

14.

How did the raiding way of life affect our ancient forebears as well as us?

But until the advent of the settled agrarian lifestyle—in which surpluses of grain and livestock could be saved for trade, the rise of civilizations in which marketplaces could be established, and the widespread agreement to accept money as a medium of exchange to facilitate transactions—taking by force what was needed and wanted was a simple reality of life for most of the humans who have ever lived.

This element of ancestral life probably contributed as much to the differences between males and females, as the differing physical requirements of hunting and gathering did. Men are much more predisposed to engage in violent behavior than women because the rewards of taking resources from others, or defending against an attack by other males who sought to take what they wanted, reinforced this characteristic inclination.

The restrictions that having children and caring for them placed upon our ancestral fore mothers made it highly unlikely that they would be in any way inclined to have any part of raiding behavior, except to enjoy the spoils their men folk brought back. Indeed, the argument could be made that the general abhorrence of violence that most women feel is evolutionarily derived from the long-running kill-grab-and-run "economies" of pre-agricultural human existence.

FIGURE 7-22. The ancestral requirements of childcare do not predispose women to engage in violent behavior.

That we tend to divide people into in-groups or out-groups to this day indicates the ancestral importance of knowing whether an individual was a potential ally or an enemy. In the past when raiding was common, misclassifying a person could be the difference between life and death. In the present, however, this predisposition, like the male tendency to engage in violent behavior, often creates unnecessary and inappropriate tensions between individuals and groups. Once again the setting in which we now live makes the old evolved predispositions dysfunctional.

The habit of taking things without equitable compensation, though, is still with us. People still try to get something for nothing all the time. Even nations attempt to use this old method of acquiring resources. We call them wars.

When that unknown individual thousands of years ago said something like, "Take this seashell that is a token for a sack of nuts that I have back at my farm so that I can have your rack of lamb now" (until we develop a time machine we can never know the exact nature of the first transaction), our world was changed forever. That man or woman found a way to make power easy to carry, resistant to decay, and amenable to what we would call trade.

FIGURE 7-23. The first money transaction changed our world forever.

15.

But we still have problems related to money…

MONEY AND FEMALES AND MALES

"Her closets are so stuffed full of shoes and clothes she could go for years without ever wearing the same outfit! Every month the credit card statements look like a page out of a telephone book, listing all the places she has shopped for stuff she hardly ever uses!"

"That motorcycle of his is like a drain that we pour all our money down! It makes a lot of noise! It raises our insurance rates! It only seats two and we can't even get the groceries home with it! He can only ride it when the weather is good and there's no way I'm ever letting the kids ride with him on it!"

Sound familiar?

Why do men and women tend to have such divergent views about the use of money? Why do they often disagree about the priorities they place on economic and financial matters? Can evolutionary psychology shed any light on something that has only recently entered the lives of humans?

It is not unusual for people to chalk up the ways women and men use their financial resources to gender differences, and they are right to do so.

A VIEW OF FEMALE POWER

From an evolutionary perspective, women are the more powerful of the genders.

Though males tend to run corporations, lead armies, preside over governments, conduct global commerce, and seek to rule over the destinies of countless individuals in families and communities, they are ultimately playing only a supporting role in a larger drama. From the point of view of the continuity of the species, all the efforts that men undertake are motivated by the underlying effort to contribute their genes into future generations of offspring. At the most fundamental biological level, all the things that males tend to do are designed to signal to potential mates that they should be selected to participate in the grand play of reproduction. To put it bluntly, males are predisposed, from the time they are boys to the last day they are old men, to try to impress girls—and females sometimes reward them for this inclination.

FIGURE 7-24. Most men want to participate in the grand play of life.

16.

What is the nature of womanpower?

. . . .

From the essential reference point of the survival of our species, womanpower—the ability to bring new life into the world, to sustain and nurture it—is the most potent force on the planet. All the manifestations of male power, creative and destructive, are meaningless in the long run without the power that females literally and figuratively bring to life.

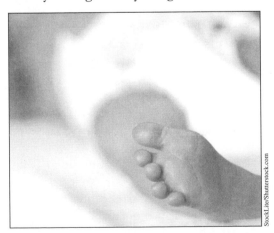

FIGURE 7-25. The ability to bring new life into the world is, from an evolutionary point of view, the greatest power.

17.

How are women competitive, and why?

. . . .

Though females control and mediate all the principal roles in the great play of life, this does not mean that competition is not a part of their lives. Women are very competitive—they have to be, because the resources they value like all desired resources are not available in unlimited quantities.

In Chapter 6, the criteria by which females evaluate men were discussed. Now it is time to consider how women attract the men they select.

Pay attention guys, you need to be aware of this. It is true that females are more adept at collaborating with each other and maintaining ties with each other (Fisher, 1999). Women are better at forming and furthering the interpersonal grooming behavior we call gossip discussed in Chapter 5. They are more likely to form alliances with other women in order to ease the burden of childcare (Hrdy, 1999). Yet despite these tendencies to engage in cooperative behavior, females are also very competitive with each other when it comes to getting the mate they have selected.

FIGURE 7-26. Competitors? You bet.

This is why those closets tend to be full of clothes and shoes. Women are fully aware of what men find attractive, and the multi-billion dollar apparel, footwear, accessory, cosmetics, fragrance, and hygiene industries are material manifestations of this fact (Saad, 2011). And though males are notorious for not noticing the specific lengths to which women maintain their place in the hierarchy of attractiveness (clothes, hairstyles, make-up application, etc.), they nonetheless consciously or non-consciously appraise the females they encounter.

As much as men are accused of being hierarchical, women are just as prone to developing a pecking order. But rather than being openly competitive as males are inclined to do in the hunt or in the boardroom, females use their appearance both to attract the mate, or mates, they have selected, and to signal to the other females in the vicinity her relative power to attract (Buss, 2012, p. 170).

 18.

What is covert power?

In other words, guys, just because girls do not overtly muscle their way to the top does not mean they are not competitive. What might be called covert power—the ability to persuade, seduce, intimidate, manipulate, shape perceptions and subtly direct behavior is the realm of womanpower. This is not to say that women cannot or do not wield the kind of overt power that men are more inclined to use, it is just that like the power of innuendo, rumor, and implication discussed in reference to gossip in the fifth chapter, covert power is no less a force that is wielded to influence people and outcomes than overt forms of power.

FIGURE 7-27. She could influence the destinies of millions.

History is usually a chronicle of overt power. Wars, revolutions, political upheavals are more easily interpreted and understood through tangible acts and overt statements. But how many conflicts were nudged along by gossip and innuendo? How many acts of courage and heroism were motivated by the hope that a desired potential mate would appreciate such an effort? That history does not record assertions of covert power does not mean that its use is any less important than the overt forms of power that men tend to use.

 19.

Perhaps the most powerful woman who has ever lived is a person you are probably unaware of.

Have you ever heard of a woman named Livia? She lived two thousand years ago and was arguably the most powerful woman of the ancient Western world. She stood at the head of no armies, she commanded no fleets of ships, and she conquered no territories, yet she indirectly shaped the empire that has informed Western civilization for two millennia. Livia was the second wife of Augustus Caesar, the first emperor of the Roman Empire, and through the subtle application of covert power, she set in motion events that ensured the continuity of Roman power over what was then the known world for more than four hundred years (Barrett, 2002). That is twice as long as the current age of the United States. If ever there were a "mother of imperial Western civilization," she would figure highly as such a maternal force.

consequences. This is something males, who are more apt to use overt power, are often slow to realize. How many women have influenced the course of human history through the use of covert power? No one can ever know, but the old saying, "there is a great woman behind every great man," is certainly an acknowledgement of our cultural awareness of the covert power of the feminine.

FIGURE 7-28. As impressive as the Colosseum may be, very likely not one stone of it would have been assembled were it not for the political continuity Livia established.

FIGURE 7-29. How many "great men" were actually made great by the "great women" in their lives?

20.

The advantages and disadvantages of covert power.

But because she did not use the kind of easily observable forms of overt power, like commanding forces in war or making epic speeches in the halls of government, she is only familiar to historians. The disadvantage of covert power is that the person wielding it is unlikely to receive recognition for the accomplishments that result from its use. On the other hand, the great advantage of covert power is that its inherently subtle nature makes it possible for the person wielding it to avoid all responsibility for negative outcomes, or for any adverse fallout that might result from unintended

21.

Some objections about the issue of the use and limitations of covert power.

Of the objections that are often given voice to the issue of covert power, the most common is that though women have access to this way of influencing events and individuals, they are nonetheless still not able to directly affect their own destinies in many cultures. For example, it is pointed out that many women are often forced to marry against their will, that many lead lives of poverty and destitution and have little access to power. And this is very certainly true; much of the world's population through most of human history, and even today, live with terrible material want and has little control over their lives. But this is not limited to just women—all genders have lived and continue to live under conditions that have deprived them of their human rights.

Rape is also at issue in any discussion of overt and covert power. Various claims have been made about its role in the evolutionary development of our kind (Buss, 2012, p. 336–341), and enormous controversy surrounds these positions. However, the violation of an individual is never justifiable. That consideration of the violent circumstances in which we evolved shows why it has remained a feature of human life lends insight, but it does not validate it anymore than the equally spurious notion that murder is acceptable because it had its place in the ancestral environment. It is always important to remember that we live in a world quite unlike our ancestral one.

However, there is an important gender insight about the matter of the personal rights of women that needs to be considered. According to cultural research conducted into acts committed on women that deprive them of their well-being and dignity, it is often not males who are behind these practices or uphold them, but elderly high-status females who (often covertly) impose these practices on younger women. In traditional Chinese culture, for example, it was older women who enforced the painful and disfiguring custom of binding a young girl's feet, so that as she grew her feet would remain small. The mutilation of female genitals is also done at the behest of older, high-status women (Pratto, 1996). And behind many arranged marriages the machinations of mothers and potential mothers-in-laws have been evident throughout history.

FIGURE 7-30. Men and women have known poverty throughout human history.

The historical record, because it focuses on those with overt power, creates the impression that all men are powerful. This is certainly not the case. The vast majority of males were not kings or emperors, religious or military leaders. Until very recently most of them were hunters or humble peasant farmers scratching out a living, struggling to keep body and soul together, while supporting their families at standards of living we would regard as unacceptably low (Nasar, 2011). From antiquity to the present day, males form the vast majority of the rank and file of armies that tend to face the most hazardous of conditions and suffer the greatest number of fatalities. The view that all males are great masters of overt power is a misreading of history.

Similarly, to dismiss covert power as somehow inferior to overt power is a cultural convention (social construction) that springs from our perceptions. One is plainly apparent, while the other is frequently hardly perceptible. From the hunter who pursued a prized game animal to the very limits of his endurance to impress a potential mate, to the hedge fund manager who works in a state of continuous frenzied exhaustion seven days a week, sixteen hours a day to provide the material standards of living his wife and children have come to expect, it is clear that there is much more to power between the genders than meets the eye.

22.

What about male power?

. . . .

SOME INSIGHTS INTO MALE POWER

As revolting as the male fixation on looks may be to many women, it is important to understand that the underlying reason men are attracted to pretty girls is not culturally constructed. Males are prewired to find certain physical characteristics attractive because these features are indicative of fertility, just as women are prewired to find men who have access to resources (the current manifestations of which we call wealth and power rather than hunting prowess) attractive because such mates are more likely to be able to provide for the material well-being of offspring, thus better ensuring their survival.

Imagine for a moment a guy and a gal who lived on the windswept savanna of the last ice age. Let us suppose that neither of them possessed any innate predispositions (no biological essentialist characteristics) to be non-consciously aware of indicators of reproductive health and of access to resources respectively. Let us say they belong to a cult (a social construction) that taught its followers to find the ability to meditate attractive. How long do you think a cultural system like this, much less a population of men and women who lived without conscious or non-conscious regard for reproductive issues, survive? How many children do you think they would produce and nurture to maturity? Not many, if meditation was more important that mating.

FIGURE 7-31. We are all descended from women and men who reproduced successfully.

Remember, we are all descended from individuals who reproduced successfully despite incredible difficulties and very long odds. We are the benefactors and the inheritors of their predispositions to get their genes into future generations while making sure that the children who composed those future generations survived into maturity. Our negative view of aspects of male and female mate selection is a result of the attitudes and values (social constructions) that have come with the new world we have only very recently created for ourselves.

(Does this mean that the old ways we still use to choose mates should be thrown into the trash heap of history—or prehistory? That is a very complicated matter that will be addressed in Chapter 12.)

Likewise, much of the disagreement that couples have with each other about resource utilization stems from the fact that financial instruments like money and credit are so new to human experience that we have yet to evolve behavioral adaptations appropriate to it. In other words, while females can discern through smell some of a male's genetic and immunological characteristics and men can non-consciously assess a woman's fertility by her appearance, we have not evolved the ability to look at individuals and accurately discern their financial health. Nor have we developed the innate ability to manage money efficiently and effectively.

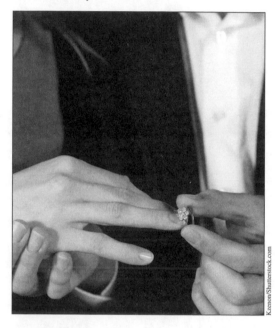

FIGURE 7-32. An engagement ring is more than just a piece of jewelry.

This is why men tend to purchase what their mates often regard as ostentatious, unnecessary, and often ridiculous items—like motorcycles. The problem for males living in a world in which pillaging and plundering are no longer acceptable, and monetary transactions are now the norm, is that money is largely invisible. Waving wads of cash around is a dangerous activity—the old habits of taking desirable items by force has a tendency to be reawakened by such showy displays—so males usually seek other ways of making potential mates aware of their access to resources. For example, most males show a certain reluctance to settle for a cheap, safe, reliable mode of conveyance, an inclination the manufacturers are more than happy to accommodate. They tend to desire

vehicles that announce to potential mates their wealth, vigor, and (relative) youth: hence the inherent appeal of vehicles like sports cars and yes, motorcycles.

Even if a male is in a committed long-term relationship, his inborn behavioral predispositions still manifest themselves and are inflected through culturally constructed tastes and attitudes. His claim that the motorcycle is purely for his enjoyment of the open road may be perfectly sincere on a conscious level; it is just that the old inclinations born on a windswept savanna long ago still substantially shape his choices and his behavior. Combined with the tendency of some females to acknowledge his display of resources, the ownership of items like motorcycles is made very compelling to many males.

From an evolutionary perspective, power is not an end in itself for males. It is the means by which he can either force potential mates to perpetuate his genes into the future, or more frequently, to make himself appear to be a good, reliable provider to potential mates. If you think about it, the degree to which most males are willing to work to secure access to resources and the extent to which they may risk their health and life to attract the attention and favor of females is a proof of the power that women embody in the grand scheme of life.

FIGURE 7-33. There is much more behind these symbols of power than meets the eye.

23.

Why are men often more reckless with money than women?

Listen up, girls. That money and power are merely the means to an end for men is an important insight women need to understand. Men are more apt to be cavalier about resources, more reckless with their spending, because financial security for males is not, from an evolutionary point of view, the ultimate goal. The fact that males cannot make babies means that they must either force or persuade females to allow them to contribute their genes into future generations. Forcing women to have their children only works when males have a monopoly on power—a condition in the ancestral environment that they very definitely did not have and certainly do not possess today. Consequently, males will go to great lengths to demonstrate to females their worth. The problem is that even after they are in a committed relationship, the tendency to "show off" does not disappear. The inclination to gamble in the great game of reproduction is deeply ingrained in the male psyche.

FIGURE 7-34. The tendency to "show off" never fades.

24.

Our evolutionarily derived predispositions have been bent to consumption.

The extent to which we are all inclined to want notoriety and wealth is based on our ancestral predispositions to seek those things that enhance the likelihood that we will genetically perpetuate ourselves by ensuring the generation of healthy viable offspring (or by producing lots of offspring thus increasing the odds that some will survive to maturity and reproduce). The problem is that the differences in the particular ways that females and males pursue this goal tend to cause a lot of tension and antagonism between individual men and women. The old ways that males and females evolved to achieve the continuance of our kind are deeply and subtly part of our mental software. It was shaped by circumstances that we have largely left behind us in the money- and market-based world of the twenty-first century. Consequently, we often find ourselves at odds with our old inclinations and our current cultural setting—and this is felt most intensely very often when we are dealing with those closest to us.

Should women stop excessively consuming those goods and services that are non-consciously motivated by their evolved inclination to announce their relative reproductive ability to potential mates and to maintain their position in their hierarchy? Should men stop obsessively trying to make potential mates aware of their access to resources by making their relative wealth visible? And this begs the question, why do we use our financial resources in ways that—from a purely evolutionary perspective should be placed on reproduction and child rearing—do not really contribute to the achievement of long-term goals? After all, spending money on things like closets full of clothes and shoes and buying and maintaining motorcycles do not directly help our offspring.

THE POWER OF THE AD

25.

Seduction in the cause of consumption...

· ·

Look around you. Look at the images that continually appear and disappear at the edge of your vision every time you are on the web. Look at the logos that are on clothes, on electronic devices, on cars, on the packaging of the food you eat. Look at the ads that are on billboards, that flicker by on the edge of television programs, or that you might see on a bit of litter lying in the street. All around you, every moment of your waking life, images beckon for your attention. On the handle of your toothbrush, on the label at the collar of a shirt, on a box of cereal, in the middle of the steering wheel of your car, on the back of your smartphone, logos momentarily come into your field of vision.

FIGURE 7-35. What shoe doesn't have a logo on it these days?

Psychology is a field of study that has many practical applications: counseling, psychotherapy, childcare, personal development, education, health care—but by far its most penetrating, widespread use is found in advertising. Understanding how our minds work is as vital to the mental health professional as it is to the advertising executive.

The purpose of advertising is to get you to buy stuff. To part with money you currently have or may have in the future, and purchase some good or service that you feel that you should or must possess, is the ultimate aim of advertising. And because we live in a society in which more than two-thirds of the entire multi-trillion dollar U.S. economy is based on consumption (*The Economist*, 2011)—the buying of goods and services—advertising is an indispensible part of the socioeconomic infrastructure that supports our lives. For no matter what line of work you undertake, whether it is at the throbbing heart of commerce or on the periphery of economic activity, either directly or indirectly, advertising affects you as a consumer, as a seller, as a citizen, and as a woman, man, or intersex individual.

We do not customarily think of advertising as a force in our lives. Ads do not have the power to force us to buy a particular car or vote for a certain candidate. They do not intimidate us into eating at certain restaurants or attend particular sporting events. Advertising is based upon seduction. It is a type of covert power. It whispers to us that if we buy that line of clothing we will appear more attractive, more culturally in-step, and perhaps, more powerful. It beckons to us to order that pizza to satisfy our midnight cravings, promises to make us feel better about ourselves if we purchase that type of home, this brand of toothpaste, or use that Internet service provider. Advertising pitches images that suggest elegance and prestige, comfort and convenience. Its message often implies that others will envy us, look up to us, and regard us with respect—even awe— if we purchase this product or use this service.

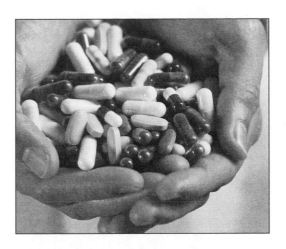

FIGURE 7-36. Some accuse advertisers of promoting unhealthy lifestyles.

There is a lot of criticism of the advertising industry for its role in promoting everything from excessive, financially destructive spending by consumers to purportedly endorsing idealized images of male and female beauty that compel many people, particularly the young, to feel discontent about their personal appearance, thus adversely affecting their self esteem. Many feel that advertisers are saturating the environment with so much ad material that we are perceptually drowning in an ocean of media images that dull our senses and numb our minds. Others point out that advertising inappropriately uses sex to hock products, and creates an unhealthy view of women as well as men, and human sexuality in the process. The glorification of consumption has been overdone and has contributed to financial downturns (the so-called Great Recession that began in 2008 had its origins in excessive consumption using risky financial instruments in the housing market) and the view that only money matters, argue many critics (Klein, 1999).

Why do advertisers promote goods and services in a manner that many commentators maintain does so much damage?

26.

What shapes advertising?

There is a kind of natural selective process that shapes advertising. An ad that effectively conveys its message to potential customers results in the sale of the product. An ad that is not effective results in few or no sales. Over time, manufacturers or service providers can see quite clearly which ad works and which ad does not. Those ads that are effective will persist and those ads that do not will disappear, much as species that are adapted to their environment continue to exist and those that are not well adapted go extinct. This is what determines the content of advertising—what shapes the images that are used to get people to buy goods and services. Unfortunately, in an economic setting in which profit is of paramount importance, an ad firm that does not strive to shape advertising according to what works but upon message that we might regard as pro-social would very likely disappear very quickly. The companies that hire ad firms are operating in a competitive environment in which considerations of profit come before much else.

FIGURE 7-37. Does everything have to be measured by profits?

This does not justify the content of advertising (that there are no cigarette commercials on television anymore, for example, indicates that in the United States, we are willing to legislate certain limits on advertising), but as long as the profit motive structures human behavior, selective forces will largely govern what we see in commercials and on billboards. In other words, there is no conspiracy out there to promote what might be deemed inappropriate messages in advertising; market forces are the shapers of ad content.

Why then do often negative images and messages have such appeal? Why do ads that many claim endorse unhealthy behaviors and attitudes, and that seemingly endorse inappropriate views of men and women, work with potential customers?

27.

The application of evolutionary psychology onto advertising.

Advertising operates on the premise that an ad should transmit its appeal to buy a particular good or service to as many people as possible in the most cost-effective manner. To achieve this goal, the underlying message of an ad has to be crafted in such a way that it connects with as broad a segment of the potential customer base as can be reached.

Consider the following ad descriptions for a white shirt and blue jeans, and ask yourself which would more likely get you to buy the items:

A photograph of a white shirt and blue jeans on a gray background with the caption "Made of cotton, available in a variety of sizes, reasonably priced."

A photograph of an attractive woman wearing a white shirt and blue jeans kissing an attractive man wearing a white shirt and blue jeans in a romantic setting at sunset with the caption, "Swept off your feet..."

Which ad would be more effective? Which ad would capture your attention?

FIGURE 7-38. Are we being seduced by advertising?

From an evolutionary psychological perspective, the second ad would be more effective—and result in more sales of white shirts and blue jeans—because it touches something within our minds that all of us have in common. The ad portrays an image that we can all relate to on an emotional level. The implication of the message contained in the ad is that the products being pitched can be associated with romance. And the great advantage of selling products in this manner is that the motivating force to buy these products does not have to be stirred up within the potential buyer—the ad is based upon emotions that we are already primed to feel and, most significantly, that have contributed to reproductive success in the past and in the present.

Most advertising plays on emotions that have been selected for by natural selection (Saad, 2011). Our desire to pair up with another individual and our tendency to want prestige and recognition (something that social media attempts to deliver in a manner our ancestors could never have imagined), are predispositions that helped to promote reproductive success. Advertisers inflect these behavioral inclinations in new directions with the implied promise that by consuming any particular good or service, your chances of appearing attractive to potential mates are in some way or another ultimately enhanced.

The commercial sphere that envelops us essentially whispers to our ancient savanna-structured psyche that if we buy certain products, our chances for reproductive success will be enhanced. By consuming goods and services we will be perceived as beautiful, healthy, high status, intelligent individuals worthy of participating in the long chain of descent that ensures the perpetuation of our species. We may not be conscious of it, but this is in many ways the highest praise that any of us can possibly receive.

The problem is that the act of excessively consuming goods and services may so adversely affect our control of the relatively new, socially constructed signifier of power—money—that our reproductive abilities may be severely impaired.

A CHANGING WORLD

FIGURE 7-39. Adapting to a world so unlike the one our species evolved in is no small challenge.

The kind of power we personally possess today is far beyond anything our ancestors knew. Indeed, at the press of a button or the tap of a touch screen we can summon up forces and capabilities that even kings and queens who lived only a century ago could not have

imagined. We can buy products from the other side of the world at will. We can communicate instantly with nearly anyone on the planet who has access to the right technology. We can travel thousands of miles at hundreds of miles an hour through the air—something our ancestors believed only the gods could do. And the fruits of our power can be counted in the more than seven billion people that now inhabit the Earth, in the billions of barrels of oil we consume every year, in the vast cities and the sprawling suburbs that cover the land. It can also be counted in the number of economic downturns, recessions, and depressions that have plagued human history over the past half millennia, and that have sometimes sparked worldwide conflicts (Chancellor, 1999). Science and technology have taken us to a place our forebears could never have imagined. The power we possess is enormous, yet the mindset, the motivations, and the priorities that order our behavioral tendencies are older than the oldest human ruins that hearkens back to technologies that were based upon little more than the application of muscle power to stones and animal bones.

In an economy in which consumption fuels a large fraction of the overall financial operation of the nation and where evolutionarily derived behavioral predispositions are manipulated to further commercial interests, individual men and women find themselves in a brave new world. The old ways that were shaped over millions of years and over countless generations are being tested by social and technological innovations that emerge with startling rapidity. The power relationships that once informed the way the genders interacted are growing more and more out of step. The world has changed too much for the old ways to be relevant anymore. New power relationships are needed.

We face change on a scale that is probably unprecedented in the long history of our kind, and money and power are at the leading edge of our personal struggle to cope.

REFERENCES

Barrett, A. A. (2002). *Livia: the first lady of imperial rome.* New Haven: Yale University Press.

Bronowski, J. (1972). *Science and human values.* New York: Perennial Library.

Burke, J. (1985). *The day the universe changed.* Boston: Little, Brown. p. 163–193.

Buss, D. (2012). *Evolutionary psychology: the new science of the mind.* 4th ed. Boston: Allyn & Bacon.

Chancellor, E. (1999). *Devil take the hindmost: a history of financial speculation.* New York: Farrar, Sraus & Giroux.

The Economist (2011). *Pocket World in Figures.* London: Profile Books. p. 236.

Ferguson, N. (2008). *The ascent of money: a financial history of the world.* New York: The Penguin Press.

Fisher, H. (1999). *The first sex: the natural talents of women and how they are changing the world.* New York: Random House. pp. 29–56.

Hrdy, S. B. (1999). *Mother nature: a history of mother, infant, and natural selection.* New York: Pantheon. pp. 119–381.

Klein, N. (1999). *No logo: money, marketing, and the growing anti-corporate movement.* New York: Picador.

Mitton, S. ed. (1977). *The cambridge encyclopedia of astronomy.* New York: Crown Publishing.

Nasar, S. (2011). *Grand pursuit: the story of economic genius.* New York: Simon and Schuster. p. xii.

Pratto, F. (1996). "Sexual politics: the gender gap in the bedroom, the cupboard, and the cabinet." Buss, D. M. & Malamuth, N. M., eds. *Sex, power, conflict: evolutionary and feminist perspectives.* New York: Oxford University Press. p. 204.

Saad, G. (2011). *The consuming instinct: what juicy burgers, ferraris, pornography, and gift giving reveal bout human nature.* New York: Prometheus Books.

Sagan, C. (1980). *Cosmos.* New York: Random House. pp. 218–243.

Shire, W. L. (1960). *The rise and fall of the third reich: a history of nazi germany.* New York: Simon & Schuster.

Smith, Adam (1776, 2003). *The wealth of nations. New York: Bantam.* Book 1, Ch. 4. pp. 33–42.

Thebaud, F. (1994). *A history of women: toward a cultural identity in the twentieth century.* Cambridge: Belknap Harvard.

Name   Date

1. Within the context of how the genders interact, what is power?

2. From the contemporary social constructivist view, what is the balance of power between males and females?

3. Why is it important to look to our past to understand the power relationships between females and males today?

4. Can knowledge gained from our understanding of our past be used to justify our present uses and abuses of power? Explain.

5. Why do females and males have different views on the use of money?

6. How did money and markets make our ancestors' lives less violent?

7. How do men characteristically use power?

8. How do women characteristically use power?

9. What is the difference between what are termed "overt" power and "covert" power?

10. How does advertising use our evolutionarily derived predispositions to get us to consume products?

Chapter 8

GENDER AND SEX AND SEXUALITY

THE ELABORATION OF SEX

We humans have this interesting tendency to build and expand upon the features of our lives that matter to us. We make them much more complex. Think about how something as simple as play has been elaborated into the Olympic games or the NFL. Similarly, we have gone from throwing sticks and stones at each other to building and maintaining forces that can annihilate any enemy and turn the planet into a wasteland. The elemental act of eating is more than the ingestion of nutrition. It is part of our social lives. It has been incorporated into religious rituals. It has resulted in the creation of an enormous industrial infrastructure concerned with production, processing, and distribution, and has become an organizing force in our lives by structuring our day around meals, breaks, and snacks.

FIGURE 8-1. Ever notice how complex football is? Yet it's just an elaboration of play behavior.

1.

Do you think most people think of sex as just a way to reproduce?

. . . .

So perhaps it is not surprising that sex has become more than just a reproductive activity for males, females, and intersex individuals. While most animals have specific periods during the year when they are sexually receptive, timed to ensure that the resulting offspring are born when conditions are conducive for development and survival (Ehrlich et al., 1988), mature humans are sexually active all year round. This adaptation makes it possible for us to transform a principally biological function into one amenable to social constructions far removed from the mere transfer of genetic material from one sex to another.

FIGURE 8-2. There are many feelings associated with sex.

Sex is used to create emotional bonds between individuals. Sex is used to divide individuals. Sex is used make others jealous. Sex is used to relieve tension. Sex is used to cause tension. Sex is used to enhance self-esteem. Sex is used to humiliate. Sex is used to signal status. Sex is used to communicate. Sex is used as a means to express personal preferences. Sex is used to act out fantasies. Sex is used for profit. Sex is used to empower and to remove power. Sex is used to control. Sex is used to liberate. Sex is used to enslave. Sex is used to create and destroy. Sex is used as an expression of love or as an act of hate. All the manifestations of sex are evocations of our personalities, the good, the bad, the beautiful, and the ugly, and everything in between. Sex is a projection of our personal natures; it reveals our character. And in the deepest sense this is why we tend to be so hung up about it. An individual's attitude toward sex—indeed, a society's attitude toward sex—says a lot about that individual or that society. There is a certain psychological vulnerability that comes with delving into matters related to sexuality. People often feel uncomfortable because sex is one of the few things in our lives from which our true selves emerge, when the public, socially acceptable, politically correct mask that we hide behind is removed. If we do not fully accept the characteristics of the person that lives behind that mask then sex can be a very threatening subject because it forces us to confront our innermost selves.

FIGURE 8-3. What "shoulds" are attached to sex and sexuality in your life?

Beyond the personal psychological aspects that surround sexuality, sex is also imbued with all kinds of socially constructed features. The "shoulds" that surround sex are many and varied. Religious authorities proclaim what is and is not appropriate. Political leaders attempt to

control it through legislation. Social commentators try to shape public opinion. The medical community has its view of human sexuality, as do all the behavioral sciences. Parents, educators, the entertainment industry, the media, law enforcement, even the military, corporations, and businesses have their respective positions on matters related to sex.

 2.

Do you think sexual harassment is declining or increasing in the workplace?

For example, sexual harassment is currently a hot-button topic in the workplace, in the courts, and in corporate boardrooms. The right of individuals to live free of the coercive effects of the press of sex on their lives is a struggle that is long-fought. The effort required to make all people aware of the abusive use of sexuality is considerable and requires the creation of a social consciousness that apparently takes a lot of time to develop. Indeed, half the battle seems to be to make individuals aware that certain expressions of sexuality are threatening, and that these acts impinge upon the sense of safety and dignity vital to psychological—and physical—well-being.

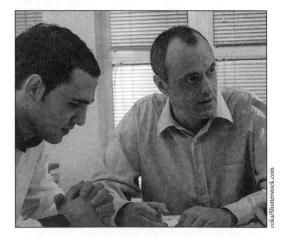

FIGURE 8-4. Appropriate contact needs to be part of our social awareness.

At the heart of the issue of sexual harassment is the unwanted and unprovoked imposition of personal power onto another individual. It is this connection between sex and power that makes this type of harassment so egregious, and that make victims feel as though they are little more than objects to be used and exploited by those who feel they have the right and the power to project their desires in such a manner. From the point of view of victims of sexual harassment, this type of interaction recalls the inherent master/slave relationship, in which one has control over the other and takes advantage of the imbalance of power in a sexual manner.

This dynamic of pairing sex and power in the workplace, and in other settings, has become so common that corporate policy and government legislation have been promulgated with great vigor to counter it. Sexual harassment is formally defined as a *quid pro quo* arrangement in which those with power in the workplace, employers or supervisors, demand sex as compensation for employment, for positive evaluation, or for advancement within the firm. Sexual harassment is also present if in the work environment sexually abusive or offensive situations arise. The harassing behavior is frequently directed at individuals because of their gender (Fitzgerald et al., 1997). Yet despite the efforts at education, the lawsuits continue to pour in as the incidence of this misuse of personal power and this particular manifestation of human sexuality persist.

How did it come to this? How did something so fundamental to life and its continuance get so entwined with matters of power, in culture wars, in arguments about what is appropriate and inappropriate, lawful and unlawful? How did something so fundamental to the interaction of the genders and that has been a part of that interaction for millions of years become so complex?

3.

What is your gut feeling about sex?

FIGURE 8-5. Matters relating to sex and sexuality can cause a variety of emotions to emerge.

To honestly address sex and sexuality, you have to first ask yourself a basic question. In your heart of hearts, do you perceive sex as a part of the natural processes of life or do you perceive it as separate from the biological world? The answer to this question indicates whether you lean toward a view of sex and sexuality that is mainly biological essentialist or social constructivist. There are no right or wrong answers to these questions; it is just that the outlook that results from examining your feelings about the natural world tends to influence your view of sex. Indeed, you may feel that sex is part of both worlds, the natural and the "unnatural," in which case the nature via nurture, or epigenetic, view may lend insight.

PERSPECTIVES ON SEX: SOCIAL CONSTRUCTIVISM

In Chapter Three, Aristotle's logic-based approach to discovering the truth was discussed. This way of interpreting the world around us was, in its time, revolutionary. Logic generated a new way of thinking and offered a view of reality that could not be ascertained through the old ways that informed our ancient ancestors' thoughts and feelings. However, the effort to comprehend the Universe did not end with his work. The understanding of the physical world that came with Aristotle's philosophical methodology was superseded in the seventeenth century by Isaac Newton's work on gravity and calculus that resulted in the formation of a deterministic clockwork conception of the world (Feingold, 2004). Then in the twentieth century, Einstein's theory of relativity, along with the development of quantum mechanics, made Newton's view obsolete, bringing to us an awareness of a probabilistic, relativistic Universe in which certainty is an illusion (Herbert, 1985). In the future, new findings will no doubt yield theories that result in completely new conceptions of the nature of reality.

FIGURE 8-6. We live in a dynamic changing world: at the intersection of the past and the future.

We humans are not static unchanging entities. As new insights become part of our general knowledge, our worldview changes in response. In Aristotle's time the Earth was the center of the Universe; the sun, the moon, and the planets lay on concentric crystal spheres that encompassed the sky. In the sixteenth century a new conception of the Universe developed in which the Earth and all the planets circled a central sun. Today we know that the solar system we live in is but one of billions scattered across the Milky Way galaxy, which is itself one of unknown hundreds of billions of galaxies in an expanding Universe that extends across an expanse infinitely greater than the one Aristotle imagined.

Nevertheless, the Earth that lay beneath Aristotle's feet is still the same one that lies beneath ours. What has changed is the context in which it exists.

The same is true with sex. Our conception of sex is very much a product of "knowledge" we get from our cultural context (Ryan et al, 2010, pp. 46–60). Whether we think of sex as good or evil, pleasurable or painful, as something we can do casually or only in very specific circumstances, are social constructions. Like the Earth beneath Aristotle's feet and our own, sex as a biological act was the same for our ancient ancestors as it is for us. What has changed is the context from which we view sex and our own sexuality.

FIGURE 8-7. What we know informs our view of many things.

4.

Does your view of sex differ from your parents' view of sex?

· ·

There have been periods in the past when sex was viewed very differently. As noted in an earlier chapter, in the ancient Sumerian tale *The Epic of Gilgamesh*, sex was seen as a civilizing force in human life. In the story it was a priestess who initiated the wild man into the ways of civilization through sex (Mitchell, 2004). In ancient Rome, sex was simply a fact of life. Male and female prostitution was legal and sanctioned by religious authorities. The male head of a Roman family could have sex with almost anyone (family member or slave except for male relatives) in the household at anytime (Everitt, 2007). No one batted an eyelash; this was the accepted norm. At other times in history, sex was thought of as a dangerous irrational force that must be controlled (Milio et al., 2009). In Europe, during the Middle Ages, new attitudes and values developed that made certain sexual contact immoral and illegal. Many of these medieval standards still persist into our own time as debate continues to rage over matters like sex education, contraception, and same-sex marriage.

FIGURE 8-8. Our conception of the world changes all the time.

Things change. People change. Their conception of the world changes too. And their views of something as central to life as sex changes in kind.

So is there one "right" way of thinking about sex? Is there a definitive way of examining it? If we accept that each culture's social construction of sex is valid within that culture, then no, there is no one right way of looking at sex. Even within the United States there are many different conceptions of sex and sexuality. This is reflected in the fact that in some states, same-sex marriage is legal. In other states, marriage can only legally occur between a man and a woman. The arguments for one position, and against another, come thick and fast.

The way social constructivism is applied to matters relating to sex and sexuality has tended to be limited by its own context in this situation. Since our conventional understanding of sex tends to be largely culturally determined, we tend to be locked in to the views that are predominant in the culture that informs us. As a result, either we can simply go with the "insider view" as individuals who adhere to the norms that surround us, or we can be cultural "outsiders" who look past these norms. But bear in mind, outsiders can point out all kinds of inconsistencies and hypocrisies that exist in a given culture, like the double standard that surrounds male and female sexual behavior that labels guys and girls who are promiscuous "studs" and "sluts" respectively, but there is nothing that requires social constructions to be logical or fair. The response "that's just the way it is" is essentially valid *within* the context of a society's norms.

FIGURE 8-9. Do you see things from the point of view of an "insider" or an "outsider"?

5.

Do you view sex as an "insider" or an "outsider"?

. . . .

The way the social constructivist critique of sex is used often leads to little more than claims about the motivations of those who shape the attitudes, values and laws that constrain human sexuality along certain lines. For example, why do we tell teenagers that they should not have sex until they are older? To answer this question, psychological, social, political, religious, moral, and legal arguments are put forward as explanations, but more often than not, these responses are not based upon objective factors that would be applicable to every culture. Typically, the reasons are based upon social conventions that are widely accepted in that culture: teenagers are not emotionally mature enough for sex; unwanted pregnancies may occur which would disrupt a teenager's education; their children have poor outcomes (Strayhorn, 2009). However, though these are valid reasons within our social context, there is no absolute reason that dictates that teenagers should not have sex that would be appropriate in every human culture.

FIGURE 8-10. What does being a teenager mean?

First off, the concept of "teenager" is itself a Western social construction that came into existence a little over a hundred years ago (Savage, 2007). Before this time, no one between the ages of thirteen and nineteen were referred to as teenagers (Metcalf, 2012). Second of all, in the past girls in some Western countries could marry when they were as young as twelve years of age (Robertson, 2010), which obviously indicates that teenaged sex was regarded as completely appropriate (at least for married females) through much of history. Thirdly, for nearly all of the millions of years that humans have existed, ancestral individuals who lived to sexual maturity (most of whom had lived through more than thirteen orbits around the sun or through more than fifty-two seasons—which is another way of indicating that these individuals were what we call "teenagers") were likely to be sexually active. In view of how short life spans were for our prehistoric ancestors, if males and females did not reproduce shortly after reaching sexual maturity, we would probably have gone extinct.

And though I am not advocating for sexual activity for individuals who are legally regarded as minors (another social construction), it is clear that the inclination to prohibit sex among teenagers is a recent social innovation, not a ban that has some objective basis in biology. What is derived from such a discussion is not a definitive explanation of sexual behavior. Further examination of the issue would reveal the social conventions that support the claim that teenagers should be prohibited from having sex until they are adults, not some objective reasoning that could be applied to every human culture. What is really brought to light is the rationale upon which a culture bases its view of sex and sexuality. Which is fine; we should be fully aware of the accepted norms of the cultural context that informs our lives. But at the same time we should always remember that these norms are limited to the culture from which they originate and might not be applicable outside of this context.

However, if we are interested in developing a deeper understanding of sex that goes beyond the "that's just the way it is" view of social constructivism, we need to take a step back and adopt a broader perspective.

FIGURE 8-11. How many people do you think feel trapped by "that's just the way it is" statements?

PERSPECTIVES ON SEX: THE HISTORY OF OUR BIOLOGY AND THE BIOLOGY OF OUR HISTORY

 6.

What does the biological frame of reference tell us about sex and human sexuality?

· ·

It is important to understand that with reference to these matters, biology can only tell us about our past and our present. It is not a deterministic system that argues that the future is indelibly shaped by what has gone before. Rather, the past predisposes us to behave in certain ways but we are not slaves to it. Indeed, if biology really were as essentialist as critics claim, evolution would not be possible.

But even beyond the social constructivist critique of biology there is another aspect of the natural sciences that makes many people reluctant to entertain the view that arises from it.

Science tends to humble us.

The more that science reveals about the Universe around us, the more mundane our place within it appears. We once thought we lived on a planet that was the center of all things. We once thought we were a special form of Earthly life. We once thought our mental faculties were unique.

The scientific discipline that most contributed to the demise of our vaunted place in the grand scheme of things is, no doubt, biology and, in particular, evolutionary science.

 7.

Why is the history of biology full of argument and debate?

· ·

The reason evolution is unacceptable to many people is not because it is difficult to understand; it is because the worldview that springs from it does not sit well with their conception of humanity and its place in the grand scheme of things. According to the Judeo-Christian religion that forms much of the foundation of Western culture, humankind was made in God's image. In the hierarchy revealed by faith, we are beneath God and above all the animals. The angels serve God and humanity.

FIGURE 8-12. Faith offers a different view of our place in the Universe than science does.

FIGURE 8-13. According to evolutionary biology, we share a common ancestor with this animal.

Our place in the grand scheme of things that emerges from evolutionary biology is quite different. Genetic research indicates that our DNA and the DNA of our closest primate relatives, the chimpanzees and the bonobos, are almost identical. There is a more than ninety-eight percent match (Diamond, 1992). The fossil evidence that paleontologists have gleaned combined with the genetic match indicates that we share a common ancestor with these primates. About five and a half million years ago the chimpanzees, bonobos, and we humans had the same forebear and then our lines parted ways (Stringer et al., 2012). Some of the descendants of that common ancestor because us. Some descendants became the chimpanzees and the bonobos.

If we look back in time a few million years more, we discover that we have a common ancestor with the gorilla as well as with other apes that are now extinct. Run the clock backward even further and it becomes apparent that the orangutan is a relative (Diamond, 1992). Delving into the past more deeply, we find that we share a common ancestor with all the primates, from the gibbons and the baboons, to all the various monkeys and the lemurs. A still deeper leap into the past finds that the tree shrew and the bats are our next closest currently living kin. Still further back and our next line of common ancestral mammals are revealed to be the squirrels, the hares, and the cats. Back even further in time and we find that we are related to all the mammals, from the kangaroo, the bears, the whales, and even to the elephants. Back hundreds of millions of years ago we can find a common ancestor that we share with the reptiles, from the crocodiles to the dinosaurs (Tudge, 2000). Eventually, we can find around 600 million years ago the ancestor that links us with all the other animals that have every lived (Gould, 1989). And if you follow this process back still further, 3.7 billion years into the past, there is an ancestor that we share that connects us to all living things on the planet (Buss, 2012), from the tree casting a cooling shadow on you on a summer's day, to the mushroom on your pizza, to the bacteria that dwell in the soil and in your gut that help you digest lunch, to the viruses that give you a head cold.

What are the implications of our relatedness to all living things?

· ·

We share a common ancestor with all living things, which means that everything that is alive is related to us. And while we might still be inclined to think that we are somehow "better" than all the "lower" forms of life that live in ways we find demeaning, like the flies that buzz about a rotting pile of garbage, evolutionary biology offers a different view (Gould, 1977). What matters in biology is whether any given species possesses characteristics that are adaptive for the environment in which it lives that enable it to reproduce and continue to survive. So from this perspective, the fact that many species of insects have been around for far longer than we humans indicates that this is not a type of creature that should be dismissed as inferior. We may apply our socially constructed views on a fly that lays its eggs in Rover's poop and derive a feeling of superiority over that insect, but from a biological frame of reference, that bug is just as evolved, just as adapted to its environment as you and me. From the point of view of biology, the socially constructed hierarchy that says we human are at the top of the evolutionary pecking order is just another chauvinism. Like the old-fashioned notion that one sex or gender is better than another, it is a belief based on outdated conventions.

Science humbles us.

FIGURE 8-14. We are related to all the life of this planet.

Biology offers a view of our species that differs significantly from the one that our culture presents. We are just another kind of ape in the biological scheme of things (Ryan et al., 2010, p. 1). Our bodies do not differ greatly from those of chimpanzees and bonobos—and why should they? Our genes are almost identical.* The few millions of years that separate us from our ape cousins is a trivial length of time compared to the 3.7 billion-year-old history of life on Earth.

It is also humbling to realize that only in the last tiny fraction of the history of our species have we lived in ways that differ significantly from our primate relatives. Ten thousand years of city life out of five and a half million as hunter-gatherers does not constitute even a hundredth of one percent of the total time our kind has existed.

---

* If you think about it, if our biology were truly different from all the other animals of the world, what would we be able to eat? The reason the nutrients found in chicken or beef—or cauliflower and carrots for that matter—are nutritious is because all these living things have the same chemical compounds in their flesh as we do. If a being from another planet with a physiology based on different chemicals—say silicon or germanium, for example—arrived on Earth, eating its carcass would probably not be a good idea.

When we consider biological issues like sex and sexuality from the essentialist reference, it is clear we are not unique. Sex is a touchy subject for many people because it viscerally reminds us of our ancestral connection to animals we are accustomed to regarding as somehow beneath us. It reminds us of our earthy biological nature. Though we may elaborate sex into all sorts of rituals and ascribe all kinds of connotations and meanings to it, when we put aside all the social constructions we attach to it, sex is something we have in common with many other forms of life.

SEX AND THE GENDERS
No. Don't do that.

 9.

Why do we put so many restrictions on sex?

. . . .

How often have you heard those words? When you were growing up, how many times did someone tell you not to do something that seemed perfectly natural and harmless? How many times were you lectured about the hazards of doing this or that, punished for doing something that you thought was no big deal? Very likely your childhood memories are peppered with recollections of sternly stated instructions, not so subtle directives, and lots of fairy tale-like reasons for suppressing this impulse or that whim. Fear and guilt were used to get you to behave in a manner that was deemed appropriate.

Why is that? Why do we have to be told how to behave? Why aren't we born with all the desires and drives that are suited to our surroundings? With millions of years of evolution behind us, why aren't we born with the right behavioral tendencies already programmed into us?

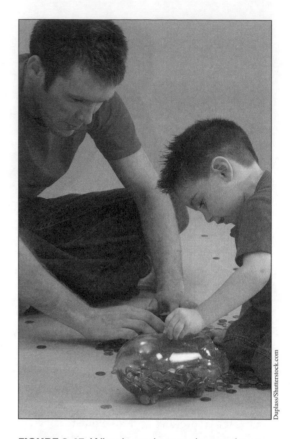

FIGURE 8-15. Why do we have to be taught so much when we are young?

Well, the right stuff is already programmed into our brains; the problem is that the setting in which we live has changed. We live in a social environment that is radically different from the one for which our program of behavioral predispositions was developed (Wells, 2010). It is rather like we grew up in a culture in which ordering cooked infant cow at a restaurant was perfectly acceptable—no one gave it a second thought—but we now find ourselves living among folks for whom such tastes are appalling.

And if there is one aspect of our natural born selves that is most firmly channeled and controlled, it is our sexuality.

Don't do that. Don't touch that. Don't think that. No, no, no, no, no.

Sex is fundamental to life. Without it, you would not exist to read these words. None of us would be here. Surely we don't need to be taught about something that is as basic to life as eating and sleeping? And in a sense we do not need to be taught terribly much about sex. Left to themselves, children explore their bodies and develop an awareness of their own sexuality (Larsson et al., 2002). At puberty, physical maturation occurs and the ancient inclination to engage in sex begins to really nudge our behavior along toward the achievement of this goal.

SO WHAT'S THE PROBLEM?

We humans are social beings. We do not live solitary lives like adult bears, only get together with other members of our species once in awhile to have sex in order to reproduce. All kinds of contacts occur between individuals all the time, and an important product of this social interaction is culture. In many ways culture is the common social glue that binds us. The language we use to communicate with each other, the formal and informal customs we use to guide our behavior, the general outlook we have about the world, are part of the collective social construction we share. If a person were to walk up to you dressed in unfamiliar clothing, speaking a language that was unintelligible while standing so close to you that the tip of his nose was almost touching yours, you would probably regard this individual (first, as a potential threat) as someone not acquainted with the norms that inform your life.

Well, in a sense, when it comes to the sexuality we inherited from our hunter-gatherer ancestors, some of us are like that person speaking a foreign language, dressed in strange clothes, and standing too close for comfort. The inborn sexual predispositions that roughly half the population of humanity tends to express is more suited for circumstances that existed in the past. While roughly half of our kind is more apt to express sexual behavioral predispositions that tend to be more in tune with, and shaped by, conditions that have more recently developed.

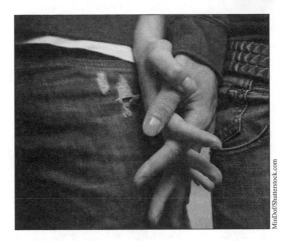

FIGURE 8-16. Who is more in tune with the present? Who is more in tune with the past?

10.

Would you care to venture a guess which gender is more inclined to behave in a manner more suited to the past and which to current circumstances?

· ·

Sex and sexuality are aspects of our lives where biological essentialist, social constructivist, and epigenetic (nature via nurture) forces converge to generate many of the conflicts that divide females and males today. In this arena of human life, perhaps more than any other, the incompatibility between the way our ancestors lived and the way we live now makes itself felt. Sex has its origins in the most basic of all biological impulses, to have children and raise them to maturity. Yet at the same time, the specific conditions in which reproduction takes place must be taken into account because this element very much affects the success or failure of having and raising children. However, these two components that underlie reproductive behavior, biology and social context, unevenly influence sex and sexuality in men and women. This is one of the key areas where significant differences between the reproductive genders exist and which drives many of the powerful tensions that make contemporary relationships so difficult for men and women.

The epigenetic element of our sexual behavior is evident in the tortuous way men and women struggle to deal with the different ways each gender responds to the desire for sex and the realities of the environment (nature via nurture). The consequences of the conflict that result from the different ways females and males behave are part of nearly everyone's life today. The high incidence of divorce, single parent families, children who shuttle between the various households of their parents, grandparents, and step-parents and live in a state of constant insecurity, the decline of marriage, child abuse and neglect, all have their origin in the different epigenetic responses to biology and to context that shape the sexual behavior of women and men.

FIGURE 8-17. It is not easy being a child in a rapidly changing world.

The basic problem is this: female reproductive behavior is very flexible and tends to be very sensitive to the conditions in which it occurs, while male reproductive behavior is less flexible and has not been as sensitive to the specific context in which it occurs (Ryan et al., 2010, pp. 272–276). As we will see this subtle difference has profound effects.

ARE WE NATURALLY FAITHFUL?

 11.

Do you think we are naturally prone to be sexually faithful to one person?

. . . .

We want very much to believe that our Western view of sex and sexuality is natural. We tell ourselves over and over that the "normal" way men and women tend to get together is in lifelong pair bonds. In other words, that males and females are predisposed to have sex with only one person—their spouse—their entire lives. That this arrangement, which we call monogamy, is the one right way that humans mate, according to the social construction that is widely accepted in our culture.

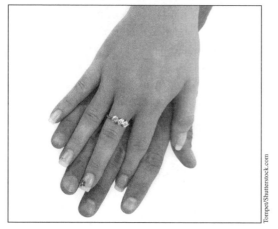

FIGURE 8-18. Are we naturally faithful?

But wait. Some people object, monogamy is not a social construction; it is a biological essentialist fact of life. We are biologically predisposed to form monogamous ties.

Is this really true?

There are cultures in which extramarital affairs (non-monogamous sexual relationships) is a crime punishable by death. In some cultures couples caught engaging in sex with someone other than their spouses are gruesomely executed. In some cultures, a man who discovers that his wife is unfaithful is obligated as a matter of honor to kill her. The last of the Ten Commandments of the Judeo-Christian faith includes a prohibition on coveting thy neighbor's wife. In contemporary American culture we may wink at extramarital affairs, but we voice formal disapproval of such activity. Such activity can ruin the reputations and careers of individuals in public life. Yet despite the penalties and moral condemnation, people engage in non-monogamous sexual relations all the time. Is the tendency to be polygamous—having sexual relationships with more than one person—merely an aberrant form of behavior?

The socially constructed view of sex and sexuality that informs our lives tends to lean in this direction. The husband who "cheats" on his wife may very shortly be facing divorce proceedings. The girl who is sexually promiscuous is derided as a "whore." But are we biologically inclined to be monogamous?

12.

What does biology tell us about monogamy?

. . . .

Among the class of animals that includes *Homo sapiens*, the mammals, ninety percent are polygynous, that is, one male mates with several females (Roughgarden, 2009, p. 54). So, non-monogamous relationships are common in nature. Indeed, monogamy is the exception not the prevailing norm among mammals and other sexually reproducing animals. Among humans, significant percentages of men and women report having had more than one sexual partner during their lives. And perhaps most telling of all is the roughly fifty percent divorce rate that surely indicates that we are not predisposed to mate exclusively with just one person. This would certainly suggest that we are not naturally inclined to be monogamous.

FIGURE 8-19. If we were naturally monogamous, would we need marriage laws?

Think about it: if monogamy were an evolved predisposition (biological essentialism) that ordered our sexual behavior would rules, morals and laws, as well as punishments (which are all social constructions), have to exist to enforce it? No culture ever created rules and laws designed to force people to eat or drink. If we humans are truly apt to be monogamous, moral conventions, rules and laws supporting it are unnecessary. We would simply conform to this norm without a second thought.

But we do not easily conform to this socially constructed norm. What, then, is our real sexual nature?

THE FACTS OF LIFE

In Greek mythology there is a story about an argument that Zeus, the king of the gods, had with his wife, Hera. They were arguing about who enjoyed sex more. Zeus maintained that women got more pleasure from sex, while Hera said that it was men who did. To break the stalemate, they asked a person who had been magically transformed into a woman and then later a man to address the matter. The answer did not please Hera and she took this individual's sight in her rage. Women get far more pleasure (nine times more than men according to the Greek tale) from sex (Ryan et al., 2010, p. 39–40).

And indeed, the Greeks knew a thing or two about sex, for scientific research into the male and female sex response does support the view that women are inherently able to enjoy sex more than men. To understand why this is so, we need to understand the fundamentals of the human sexual response.

13.

What do research findings indicate about human sexuality?

· ·

William H. Masters and Virginia E. Johnson (1966) did perhaps the most important research into the physiology of human sexual behavior in the middle of the previous century. Over the course of their twelve-year study they studied the sexual behavior of 382 women and 312 men. Their observations of over ten thousand repetitions of sexual activity showed that there are four phases in the human sexual response (Klein et al., 2007, p. 394).

The first is the *excitement phase*. This occurs when sexually arousing stimuli is sensed. For both men and women the heart rate accelerates accompanied by increased blood flow to the genitals. This condition known as vasocongestion occurs when the blood vessels in the genital area dilate (expand) and fill from the increased blood volume. For males the penis becomes enlarged and erect as a result of vasocongestion, and for females the blood vessels in the clitoris and labia dilate. The clitoris enlarges, the labia swells, and fluid begins to seep through the walls of the vagina in order to lubricate it to facilitate intercourse while the vagina itself expands. During this phase, for both females and males myotonia—the rhythmic contraction of the muscles—causes the nipples to harden.

This state of arousal continues until it reaches what it referred to as the *plateau phase*. During this period, both males and females are in a heightened state of sexual arousal as a result of continued sexual stimulation. Breathing,

pulse rate, and blood pressure are at increased levels, thus generating the tension that is the precursor to orgasm.

Orgasm is the next phase of the human sexual response. For females, the involuntary rhythmic muscle contractions of myotonia occur at roughly eight-tenths of a second intervals during orgasm and is felt as a sensation that spreads from the clitoris across the entire pelvic region of the body. Three or four consecutive contractions characterize a mild orgasm, while a strong orgasm may comprise as many as a dozen consecutive myotonic muscle contractions. For males, orgasm is a two-stage occurrence. In the first stage the male senses the contraction of the vas deferens, the seminal vesicles and the prostate gland. Myotonic muscle contractions force seminal fluids, which is composed of sperm and the supporting fluid to transport it, into the urethra. During the second stage of male orgasm, the penis and the urethra experience myotonia in an eight-tenths of a second contraction, thus expelling the semen out of the urethra. Males experience this ejaculation of seminal fluid as the culminating event of orgasm.

Following the orgasm phase, the *resolution phase* results in muscle relaxation, lowering heart and respiratory rates, and a return to a non-aroused state. For males, at this point a period known as the refractory period arrives, during which males usually cannot be re-aroused to orgasm again for a significant length of time. The refractory period varies among men from a few minutes to as much as twenty-four hours. However, for women, the resolution phase is not followed by a refractory period. Females can immediately have successive orgasms after having had an orgasm.

Indeed, women do not always follow the four-phase progression of the human sexual response. Some women do not experience separate plateau and orgasmic phases but instead go straight to a sustained series of orgasms. Some women go from excitement to the plateau phase then onto the resolution phase without an orgasm (Klein et al., 2007, p. 394–396).

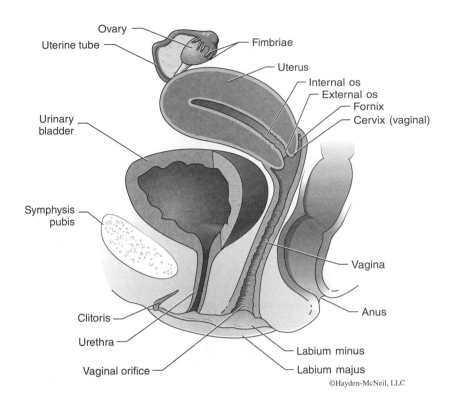

FIGURE 8-20. Female genital anatomy.

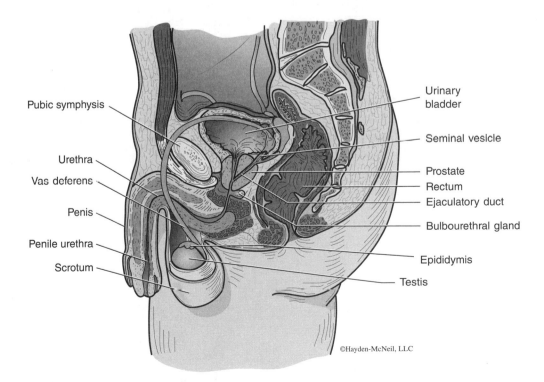

FIGURE 8-21. Male genital anatomy.

It is important to note that the human sexual response also occurs during masturbation for both females and males. This is important because it reveals that the female orgasm, which was once thought to come in two varieties, one induced by the stimulation of the clitoris and the other through vaginal stimulation, has in reality only one source. The clitoris is the organ responsible for orgasm in the female human sexual response. Though it was once thought that vaginal orgasms existed (and were thought to be superior to clitoral orgasms), research has definitively revealed the role of the clitoris. This belief in the existence of multiple types of orgasm (and of the superiority of one kind over the other) in females is probably connected to the socially constructed view among some groups of individuals that masturbation is somehow unhealthy and unsuitable, since female masturbation usually involves the direct stimulation of the clitoris. Thus the erroneous claim that clitoral orgasms were inferior to vaginal ones. (Orgasm occurs during vaginal intercourse because the movement of the penis in the vagina causes the skin tissue around the clitoris to rub against it, which causes the stimulation needed to induce orgasm. However, it should also be noted that some women report that they can experience orgasm without direct clitoral stimulation. In other words, contact with parts of the body not directly connected to the clitoris can induce orgasm. There have even been self-reported cases of women "thinking" themselves to an orgasm. Nonetheless, in all cases the physical sensation of orgasm itself initially originates at the clitoris [Hyde et al., 2000].) From a biological and physiological standpoint, there is nothing dangerous or abnormal about masturbation (Bancroft, 2004). Indeed, from these perspectives, it is a perfectly normal expression of human sexuality and is an effective way of lowering sexual tension in the individual man or woman.

Nevertheless, there is a tendency among many people to believe that women enjoy sex less than men, and the attitude that masturbation is wrong persists in many Western cultural settings and among many groups of individuals. This is why the social constructivist aspects of matters relating to gender, and particularly sexuality, must always be considered.

SOCIALLY CONSTRUCTED SEXUALITY

What do these findings mean to us?

Despite the fact that Masters and Johnson's extensive study of the human sexual response clearly shows that females have the physiological and neurological capacity to enjoy sex much more than males (perhaps the Greeks myth was accurate in its claim that women enjoy sex nine times more than men), why do males seem to be the gender that pursues sexual gratification more intensely than women? Why have there been periods in the past, such as in Western countries during the nineteenth century, when female interest in sex was thought to be much lower than it is now? Why do the socially constructed range of categories from "prude" to "slut" exist to characterize the spectrum of female sexuality while males are invariably thought of as "horny"?

FIGURE 8-22. Why does the expression of human sexuality differ between men and women?

15.

How do these social constructions affect our outlook on sex?

· ·

The answer to these questions can be discerned from a fundamental difference between men and women that can be gleaned from the way in which each gender approaches matters relating to contemporary issues.

One of the reasons this book is structured along social constructivist, biological essentialist, and epigenetic perspectives is because the first two orientations are themselves expressions of the outlook from which each of the reproductive genders tend to view the world. For example, feminist claims about gender relations tend to emphasize social constructivist views of human behavior, while the biological essentialist view is usually associated with a more male-oriented worldview. (The epigenetic view is a relatively recent effort to bring together the unique insights of social constructivism and biological essentialism together.)

Consequently, feminists have justly advocated for women's rights through legal, moral, and political arguments that clearly illustrate the inappropriate and unjustifiable oppression of individuals based upon sex and gender. And rightly so, for within the social context within which we currently live, discrimination based upon sex and gender, as with race and ethnicity, is wholly unacceptable. The human rights that form the foundation of Western civilization necessitate the recognition of women—and indeed of all individuals—as equal.

Those individuals who are not sensitive to, or who oppose, the demands for gender equality have tended to use (or misuse) biological essentialist arguments. For example, the January 14, 2005 statement that Larry Summers, then the president of Harvard University, made about the lack of women in the highest ranks of science and engineering being attributable in part to the intrinsic qualities of females, is an

example of the use of the biological essentialist perspective to support a his claim (Ceci et al., 2007). Indeed, the misuse of essentialism has a long history. Aristotle made the claim in the *Politics* (Book 1) more than two thousand years ago that certain groups of humans were "natural" slaves, thus justifying the legal trade in human beings for the purposes of labor.

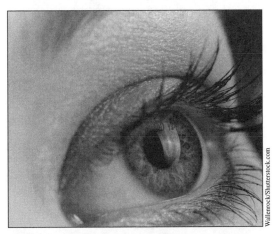

FIGURE 8-23. It is always important to consider the perspective from which a person views an issue.

However, this is not to say that biological essentialism is in itself an illegitimate way of understanding our species or any other form of life. We humans do have an inherent nature; we are after all the results of three and a half billion years of earthly biological evolution. Indeed, if you think about it deeply, social constructions are themselves a product of our biology.

But the important point to take away from this discussion is that the approaches, to resolving questions concerning the things that matter in our lives, that women and men use, is itself an expression of a basic difference between the genders. Women are more apt to view the world with a sensitive awareness of the details of the prevailing social context. Females tend to consciously and unconsciously perceive small changes in the conditions that surround them and adjust to these alterations. Consequently, social constructivism with its emphasis on the rapid-fire cultural responses to change tends to figure prominently. Men have a propensity to be less sensitive, even indifferent, to the fine particulars that characterize their surroundings. Consequently, males are more apt to fall back on biological generalizations rather than accommodate and appreciate the social ramifications that result from the specific conditions within which they live. Of course, there always exist a tremendous amount of variation among any given sample of individuals; perspective tendencies are not set in concrete.

FIGURE 8-24. Women are more apt to be aware of the prevailing social context.

16.

How do such tendencies affect sexual behavior?

These differences are most readily apparent in the way in which females and males express their sexuality (Ryan et al., 2010, pp. 272–276). Men are more likely to be invariable in their sexuality. A man will tend to want sex, pure and simple—biological essentialism in action. Women are more flexible in the expression of their sexuality and are more apt to tailor their sexuality in accordance with social conventions and the circumstances in which they live. A woman will tend to want sex, too—it is just that the expression of that desire is more likely to be formed and informed by the specific circumstances that surround her. In a nutshell, female sexuality is influenced more by social constructions than male sexuality. Male sexuality tends to conform to biological influences.

WHAT DO WOMEN *REALLY* WANT?

This question has confused and perplexed men for at least ten thousand years.

From a male point of view so many questions seem to hang in the air, keeping them in a state of anxious uncertainty: does she want me to regard her with respect and defer to her wishes, or does she want me to take charge? Does she want to initiate sexual contact, or does she want me to make the first move? How do I show a girl that I am attracted to her without being accused of sexually harassing her? How important is intimacy?

Invariably the question returns to, what do women really want?

FIGURE 8-25. For many males, females are a mystery.

There is evidence that the amount of sexual variability *among* women is greater than the amount of variability *between* men and women. You may have seen the cartoon-like image that is often used to characterize male and female sexuality: a simple on/off switch controls the male sexual response, while a fantastically complex array of dials, knobs, switches, and buttons controls the female sexual response.

But with this view of female sexuality, can anything meaningful be ascertained about what women really want?

17.

Is female sexuality merely a biological matter?

You have probably seen countless ads and commercials for medications designed to treat erectile dysfunction (a physiological condition in which the penis does not become sufficiently engorged with blood for sexual intercourse) in men. The basic effect of these medications is to increase blood flow to the genitals in order to facilitate penile erection. The more blood that engorges the penis, the more a male is apt to feel that he is able to perform in a sexually appropriate manner. Fix the biological/physiological impediment and all is well. It

is a rather straightforward biologically deterministic remedy for this particular dysfunction (Goldstein et al., 1998).

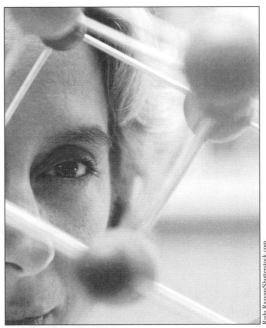

FIGURE 8-26. Is sexual fulfillment simply a matter of chemistry?

For years pharmaceutical companies have sought a female version of this type of medication. Various reports indicate that a substantial fraction (perhaps up to three in ten) of women experience a lack of sexual desire. If female sexual desire was largely physiological based, as it is with males, therapies similar to those developed for male dysfunction should be effective. Based on the data revealed by Masters and Johnson's research on the human sexual response, it should be a simple matter of increasing the blood flow to the female genitals in order to facilitate the physiological events, the engorging of the labia and the clitoris, accompanied by the expansion of the vagina and its lubrication, required for sexual intercourse for women. Yet this treatment does not work in women (Bergner, 2009).

There is much more to the female sexual response, unlike the male sexual response, than the "flicking of a switch" to increase the blood supply to the genitals. In other words, for men the connection between physiological arousal and psychological desire is straightforward and direct. For females, the connection is not the same. Though the physiological responses that comes with increased blood flow to the genitals in women does occur with the use of erectile dysfunction medications, the corresponding increase of desire does not necessarily follow (Bergner, 2009).

The biological determinism of male sexuality is apparent in the effectiveness of those therapies that simply remedy problems through direct physiological intervention. The complexity of female sexuality emerges when such approaches are revealed to be ineffective in women.

18.

What do men and women really find arousing?

. . . .

Recent studies of gay men, straight men, lesbian women, and straight women have revealed important insights into the conscious and unconscious aspects of human sexuality. When lesbian and straight women, and gay and straight men are hooked up to devices that detect the flow of blood to their genitals (which is an indication of actual physiological arousal) while being asked to rate their conscious reaction to various erotic images and sounds, something very interesting occurs.

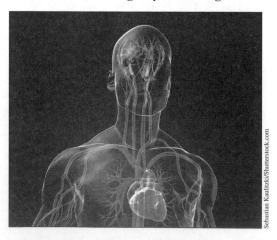

FIGURE 8-27. There's more to arousal than the flow of blood.

The physiological reactions of gay and straight men match their conscious reactions to erotic material. The blood flow to the genitals of gay men tends to increase when they are exposed to erotic stimuli involving males, and their conscious reaction to such stimuli tends to match their physiological reaction. Blood flow among gay men declines when exposed to erotic stimuli involving females, and they report that they are not aroused by such stimuli. Similarly, the genital blood flow tends to increases in straight men when they view erotic stimuli involving women, and their conscious reaction to such stimuli tends to correspond with their physical reaction. Conversely, their blood flow declines when they are exposed to erotic stimuli involving males, and they report that they are not aroused by such stimuli (Bergner, 2009).

The correspondence between physiology and conscious reaction found in males is not as clear in females. The blood flow to the genitals of lesbian women and straight women tended to increase when they were exposed to erotic stimuli involving males, females, and any combination of the genders. Yet lesbian women tended to only consciously report that they were aroused by erotic images of women, while straight women only tended to consciously report that they were aroused by erotic images of men (Bergner, 2009).

19.

What does this all mean?

. . . .

It could be argued that males, both straight and gay, are more inhibited about their sexuality, so that when they are exposed to arousing sexual stimuli that does not correspond with their sexual orientation, they react psychologically and physiologically with disinterest rather than arousal. More sophisticated scanning technologies used to image the brains of straight males while viewing arousing sexual images involving men showed the those parts of the brain associated with inhibition were not activated. Likewise, those parts of the brain involved with inhibition in gay men when viewing arousing sexual images involving women were not activated. This suggests that inhibition of the physiological aspects of the human sexual response is not a part of the lack of apparent interest that gay and straight men demonstrate when exposed to stimuli that does not correspond with their sexual orientation. It also implies that the male brain, whether straight or gay, is inherently wired for arousal along the matching sexual orientation of the individual (Bergner, 2009).

FIGURE 8-29. There are subtle yet significant differences between men and women.

FIGURE 8-28. Arousal is no simple thing for women.

Researchers put forward the view that unconsciously female sexuality is more generalized than male sexuality. Men are very targeted in their sexual interest, and their physiological response (increased genital blood flow) reflects the specificity of this tendency. On the other hand, women have a physiological response that encompasses a larger sphere of human sexual stimuli, but the arousal they consciously experience is very much shaped by the context that informs their view of their sexuality.

It may be that women simply have more control of their sexuality than men. There are many reports of women adopting a lesbian sexual orientation in one segment of their lives and then assuming a heterosexual (straight) sexual orientation in another. The recent controversy that lesbian actress Cynthia Nixon sparked when she claimed that her sexual orientation was a matter of personal choice (Witchel, 2012) might be a reflection of this feminine characteristic. The direct, biologically deterministic nature of male sexuality may explain why gay men are more apt to claim that they are inherently homosexual and that no amount of conditioning can alter their sexual orientation.

From an evolutionary psychological perspective, the variable nature of female sexuality, the conscious and unconscious sensitivity women have to the surrounding social context, and the ability to shape the qualities of feminine sexuality in response to prevailing conditions, are highly advantageous. In the ancestral environment, when humans did not have the resources and the capabilities to ignore the vagaries of change, the ability to tailor sexuality to the specific needs of the moment and ensure successful reproductive outcomes would have been a powerful adaptation.

What do women want? The reason there is no definitive answer to this question is because women's conscious desires tend to be largely determined not by fixed biological drives but by changeable socially constructed ones.

DIFFERING HUMAN SEXUAL RESPONSES

20.

What does it mean that male and female sexual responses are so different?

You might have noticed that according to Masters and Johnson's research the nature of the female orgasm is quite different from the male orgasm. After reaching orgasm males then enter a refractory period that makes continued sexual intercourse unlikely. For most men, once ejaculation occurs, they are done. Females, however, have a different human sexual response. Women can reach orgasm and then continue to engage in sexual contact and potentially reach orgasm over and over again. In other words, males tend to be quick to excitement, to reach the plateau phase, reach orgasm, and then transition into the resolution phase with its long refractory period. The pattern of the female sexual response proceeds at a different pace. Women are more apt to take longer to enter the excitement phase, then to reach the plateau phase, and can then sustain continued sexual intercourse for much longer than males and achieve multiple orgasms. It is also important to remember that females are not limited to the four-phase sexual response pattern and at least some women report that they can transition from excitement to orgasm without passing though the intermediate plateau phase, or transition from excitement to resolution without the plateau and orgasm phases (Klein et al., 2007).

In terms of pace, the hare and the tortoise imagery of the differences between the female and male human sexual responses appear to be an apt one. In fact, the tortoise does not necessarily have to follow the path of the race course and has the option to take short cuts.

FIGURE 8-30. Tortoise and hare?

Considering how important sexual contact is both to maintaining relationships between individuals as well as it is to reproduction, why does this mismatch exist between men and women? How did this enormous disparity come into existence?

The answer lies, once again, in our past, for the human sexual response is part of the evolved set of behavioral characteristics we inherited from our ancient ancestors. The slow to arouse but multiple orgasmic nature of the female sexual response and the quick to arouse and quick to orgasm nature of the male sexual response are echoes from our evolutionary past.

FEMALE SEXUALITY AND CIVILIZATION

The weekend after the initial public offering of Facebook shares on the Nasdaq stock exchange, the founder of the social networking site, Mark Zuckerberg married his long-time girlfriend. It was interesting to note the number of editorial comments found in various media that came after these two events that included best wishes and the hope that Zuckerberg and his new wife had signed a pre-nuptial agreement.

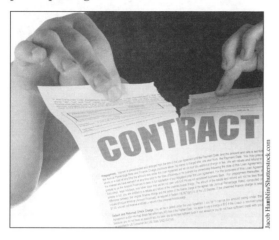

FIGURE 8-31. What does the existence of pre-nuptial agreements say about our relationships?

Such an agreement is essentially a premarital contract that details the division of property in the event of divorce. The importance of this sort of binding agreement between two individuals, entered into before they are even married, is a reflection of our cultural view of marriage and the priority we place on wealth and its preservation. This legal instrument also shows that we view marriage as an impermanent and inherently unreliable relationship, and those individuals with substantial financial resources should undertake formal measures to protect their finances in the likely event it fails. But what is relevant about the pre-nuptial agreement for our understanding of the difference between the male and female sexual response is what its indicates about the way we seek security.

21.

How we have changed…

In the twenty-first century we have nearly completely "monetized" personal security. We buy insurance for our car, for the home we rent or own, for medical and dental care, and even insure our lives against injury and death. Some people insure their pets and take out policies to cover their recreational activities as well. People invest in all kinds of financial instruments from retirement funds, 401k plans, mutual funds, to simple savings accounts to save for the future and to have a reserve against the possibility of tough times. Though no one really likes to pay taxes, we are in essence supporting all manner of government-provided programs from law enforcement, to national defense, to consumer protection, to social security, and much more, all of which are meant to contribute to our health and safety. Banks, various federal agencies, the stock market, the bond market, commodities markets, derivative trading, credit default swaps, and many more exotic ways of making and managing money exist to facilitate our financial well-being. All these entities came to be a part of the world in which we live because money has become, for us, the means by which we maintain our personal security.

FIGURE 8-32. In your mind, how important is money?

It is easy to forget that this vast money-based infrastructure has not been around for even one percent of the history of our species. Indeed, money itself has existed for only a few thousand years (Howgego, 1995). For almost all of our ancestors, personal security came not from using money but from belonging to a close-knit family and to a larger community of allied individuals. Rather than buying food and shelter, paying for protection from raiders and predators, childcare, and all the other things needed for survival, our forebears shared their food, their labor, and their skills and knowledge with kin and with members of their in-group in order to maintain their personal well-being (Maybury-Lewis, 1992).

For our nomadic hunter-gatherer ancestors, the best insurance policy against hard times was strong, enduring bonds to other individuals. If you have ever felt the emotional distress that comes with being lonely and insecure, it is because you are descended from individuals who longed to live within cohesive families and tribes. Our forebears knew that the only way they could survive in their world was by cooperating with those close to them. The loneliness and alienation so common to contemporary personal experience comes from our powerful inborn psychological predisposition to want to feel encircled by people who accept us and love us, whose positive regard for us, comes not from our net financial worth but because we are our parents' daughter or son, because we belong. This is the ancestral social context that made—and still makes—humans feel safe and secure. All children want to live in the warm glow of family, to be part of a solid, reliable social unit that loves and cares for them. And this is what has disappeared for an increasing number of young people today, as families are fractured and shattered by the seismic forces of social and technological change.

FIGURE 8-33. For most of human history, family has been essential to personal survival.

22.

How were relationships configured in the absence of money?

Without money and the institutions that arose from its use, our ancestors relied on each other for safety and security. The various relationship configurations that exist among humans reflect the environment in which they lived. For example, anthropologists claim that the practice of polyandry—the marriage of one woman to multiple men, usually brothers—is an adaptation that developed in response to farming land that was not particularly fertile and tended to produce low crop yields. This condition necessitated the pooling of the output of several men to support a single woman and her children. With polyandry, a wife customarily does not favor one husband over another to prevent jealous rivalries from developing, and because the children that are born of this pattern of marriage are at least nieces and nephews of her husbands, the sense of familial solidarity is maintained (Maybury-Lewis, 1992, p. 106–107).

FIGURE 8-34. Polyandry is an adaptation to harsh conditions.

As noted earlier, most mammals are polygynous. In this arrangement, one male mates with several females. Polygyny is a product of male competition. Among animals that are polygynous, such as gorillas, lions, and many other mammals, males fight other males for dominance and win the opportunity to mate with multiple females (Wright, 1994, p. 90). Among humans, there are societies in which the dominant male, through the exercise of the power he possesses within the culture that orders the social context in which he lives, is entitled to marry multiple females. The children that result from this marital configuration are at the very least half-brothers and half-sisters, thus supporting the relatedness of all family members.

FIGURE 8-35. Gorillas are among the animals that have polygynous relationships.

What is notable about polyandry and polygyny among humans is that they are both relationship arrangements that have their origin in settled ways of life. These patterns are determined by the setting in which they occur. Polyandry is apparently an adaptation to difficult agricultural conditions that necessitates the concentration of the meager output of several men to support themselves, their shared wife, and their shared children, while polygyny occurs in settings in which a male can monopolize the relatively plentiful resources of the surrounding environment to such a degree that he can effectively guard and support multiple wives and the children that issue from these relationships. The nomadic lifestyle that our hunter-gatherer ancestors enjoyed would never suit either familial arrangement. In the prehistoric environment one man could never hunt enough food and provide the defense against predators and raiders needed to support the polygynous configuration (Wright, 1994, p. 94). In the case of polyandry, while it would be difficult for a single woman to collect the plants needed to feed everyone (if such a family strictly maintained gender roles), the main impediment would be her inability to have enough children to maintain the familial lineage. Infant mortality is always a problem in setting where resources are scarce. If several men produced through one woman only a few children, it is likely that such a family arrangement would disappear in a generation or two. Childcare is also an enormously labor intensive activity. Women need help to feed and care for infants (Hrdy, 1999, p. 121). Remember our ancient foremothers could not hire nannies and babysitters. There were no stores from which to purchase baby formula, so mothers had to provide breast milk or their young would die of starvation. The requirements of childcare alone would make prehistoric polyandry exceedingly difficult to sustain.

23.

The ancestral family.

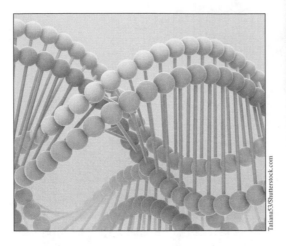

FIGURE 8-36. Our DNA is almost identical to the DNA of chimpanzees and bonobos.

Our ancestors lived like our primate relatives, the chimpanzee and the bonobo, in large communal groupings (Dunbar, 1996, p. 69). The fact that more than ninety-eight percent of our genes are identical with theirs and that we share a common ancestor about five million years ago means that we are not all that different. This living arrangement works by providing the numbers of individuals needed to maintain the labor force required to ensure the relative security of all members of the group.

That we can easily recall the faces and names of roughly one hundred and fifty individuals is an adaptation to the ancestral communal population that still remains part of our mental software and recalls the social context within which our forebears lived. This critical number of interconnected people, bonded by ties of family and friendship, provided for the well-being of individuals and sustained the successful reproduction, care, and upbringing of offspring. The division of labor that saw men going off to hunt as well as providing protection against raiders and predators, and women gathering the vegetable matter and providing the early childhood care so vital to the young, formed the non-monetized infrastructure that ensured the lives of our ancestors.

FIGURE 8-37. Can you remember the names and faces of 150 people?

In earlier chapters, the role of grooming and the development of gossip as a way to maintain group bonds was discussed. The innovation of intense one-on-one conversation offered our ancestors another form of contact through which interpersonal ties could be sustained and strengthened. Well, there is another very important way of maintaining group cohesion: sex (Ryan et al., 2010, p. 93).

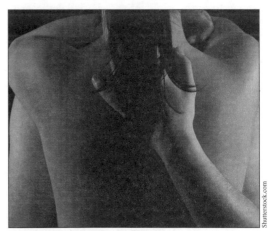

FIGURE 8-38. Group cohesion through sex?

Our primate relatives the bonobos are among the most peaceful of animals. They live in large groupings of related individuals similar to those our ancestors knew, and they use non-reproductive sex to relieve tension and to foster ties between each other. Female bonobos are known to rub their genitals against each other's as an apparent way of initiating bonds of friendship. Young and old engage in heterosexual and homosexual contact as a way to maintain group cohesion, and spend a significant amount of their non-foraging time involved in such activity (Ryan, 2010, p. 77–78).

Some evolutionary psychologists and primatologists claim that this social innovation, the use of sexual contact to preserve and sustain connections between individuals, has some important reproductive benefits. Male and female bonobos live in a highly cooperative social environment that creates a safe and supportive setting for young bonobos to grow and develop. The increased reproductive success that results from this arrangement benefits both males and females as well. Also, males who have frequent access to sex are less likely to be aggressive and violent, which creates calmer social conditions that are conducive to the safety and upbringing of the young (Ryan, 2010, p. 12).

The interesting consequence that emerges from a sexually supercharged social environment is that parenthood becomes generalized over the entire population of sexually active adults. A female may know which offspring are hers but a male can never be entirely certain under these circumstances. However, if all the male bonobos are to varying degrees related to each other, like the men involved in a polyandrous marriage, and have at one time or another had sexual contact with some or all the females, then there is a good chance that any particular youngster is at least a cousin, niece or nephew, son or daughter of any given male. This ambiguous parentage makes every young bonobo a potential blood relative of every male within the larger in-group and is thus more likely to be cared for by all adults.

24.

What this means for humans…

Among humans that currently live in pre-agricultural hunter-gatherer societies, there is in many of these groups the belief that sexual contact contributes to the development of a fetus. In other words, when a male has sex with a female he contributes his characteristics to the potential child that may form in her womb. Consequently, a woman will seek out a variety of males in order to acquire for her offspring as many of the positive characteristics of the men in her group as possible (Ryan et al., 2010, p. 91). The unintended result of this practice is that all the men with whom a woman has sex come to regard her child as being at least partially theirs. Spread over all the receptive women in the group, much like the bonobo arrangement, a kind of "fractional fatherhood" is generated that inclines all the men involved to support all the children in the community (Ryan et al., 2010, p. 102–103). In effect, these pre-agricultural societies are one big family and all the children in it are everyone's son or daughter.

FIGURE 8-39. How would fractional fatherhood affect family dynamics in a community of humans?

Without the monetized security that we enjoy being available to our hunter-gatherer ancestors, it made sense for them to pool the skills and aptitudes of all members of a given in-group, whether it is an extended family or tribe of related individuals, to provide for the well-being of everyone. The maintenance of group cohesion was thus vital; no one in these societies ever feels lonely and cut off from others. The use of conversation and copulation to achieve this end also had the benefit of spreading male investment into child rearing across the entire population of youngsters.

The contemporary view of interpersonal relationships that we have today, of marriage as a bond between one woman and one man, stands in marked contrast to the way our ancestors lived. You may have noticed as you read this section that it diverges somewhat from the standard view offered by evolutionary psychology, with its emphasis on the individual and the concern for getting his or her genes into the future. This illustrates how even a seemingly "objective" approach to understanding human behavior can be affected by social constructions. For we in the Western cultures tend to view behavior through the lens of the individual. We are after all the most individualistic of all human cultures. The focus is always on personal freedom and choice. However, in order to understand the gender differences inherent in the human sexual response, a perspective that more inclusively considers the needs of the group to which an individual belongs yields important insights.

FIGURE 8-40. One woman, one man, and their children: this is the convention we live with now.

The female sexual response, which differs considerably from the male version, may be an adaptation from a time when we all lived effectively as one large mating group. And the diverse ways the conscious expression of female sexuality manifests itself in the past and the present reveals the flexibility and the power of the feminine psyche.

A NEW SOCIALLY CONSTRUCTED SEXUALITY

From the perspective revealed by considering the sexual conventions and beliefs of humans who live in hunter-gatherer cultures and the mating behavior of our closest primate relatives, it is evident that our current ways of thinking about what we regard as "normal" human sexuality differs dramatically. Why then did we humans alter our sexual behavior so completely?

25.

Why did the configuration of the family change?

. . . .

The reason men are confused about what women really want is that the way females express their sexuality has changed enormously over the last ten thousand or so years. This is where the view that female sexuality is principally shaped by the particular social context in which women live, much more than male sexuality is affected, becomes glaringly apparent. In the ancestral environment, what we would today consider promiscuous sexual behavior was the norm (Ryan et al., 2010, p. 124–137). Very likely most of our ancient ancestors engaged in sexual contact with multiple partners all the time. The problem is that this behavioral predisposition still tends to persist in the male expression of sexuality, while the conscious expression of female sexuality has tended to change in response to new social conditions.

FIGURE 8-41. Farming and a settled way of life changed everything for our ancestors.

Those who study human sexuality's transformation argue that the crucial social innovations that initiated this alteration came ten thousand years ago with the establishment of a settled way of life, the advent of agriculture as a means to acquire year-round sustenance, and the creation of the concept of property (Ryan et al., 2010, p. 13–15). The cultural innovations of living in a fixed shelter rather than moving from place to place, growing food instead of hunting or foraging for it, and owning things, profoundly changed the expression of female sexuality. For when we humans stopped living off the land, we began to accumulate things that we now classify as assets, and with the passing of wealth from one generation to the next it became vital to be certain of a child's parentage. The old nomadic pre-agricultural hunter-gatherer practice of collective parenthood no longer worked in a property-owning cultural context. Parents wanted to be sure that children who were definitively their descents inherited their wealth and the social standing that went with it.

Very likely the concern for paternity began with the ruling classes that emerged with the foundation of the first cities and the emergence of the first civilizations, thus insuring that power remained in the family. So committed were the rulers of ancient Egypt to keeping royal authority in the family, for example, that pharaohs married their sisters or daughters, and only children born of such royal unions were potential heirs to the throne (Roberts, 1999). Until recently, European royalty seldom married "commoners," only other members of imperial families. Gradually, as living standards began to slowly rise, members of the lower socioeconomic strata also realized that by accumulating wealth over the generations their families' relative social standing could improve (Wood, 1994). Ownership of land, control of the productivity of the soil through access to water and to fertilizer, and the holding of whatever surpluses were realized after the harvest, all began to figure into the social constructions of early agriculturalist societies.

FIGURE 8-42. The Egyptians were very careful to keep royal power in the family.

26.

What were the consequences of this change brought on by ownership?

· ·

This required that men and women know with certainty the parentage of their children. Determining maternal ties was never a problem, but knowing clearly who fathered a child was perhaps the single greatest force that changed the nature of women's lives. The relative equality that women and men had known for millions of years as hunter-gatherers ended with property and inheritance. In this new context, female sexuality reconfigured to suit the requirements of settled life.

Monogamy was pronounced the "natural" order of things. Adultery was made a crime. Free, unrestrained expressions of female sexuality were condemned as immoral and depraved. Some cultures went so far as to surgically remove the clitoris from women's genitals in the belief that this procedure suppressed women's interest in sex. The practice of wearing clothes that completely concealed a woman's body in order to avoid inflaming the interest of other men became the norm in many societies. Women had to be accompanied at all times by a male relative when outside of the home. In this new context, rape became a crime against women and men because the paternity of any children that followed this event was cast into doubt. All these things and many more subtle and not so subtle attitudes and practices were incorporated into the religious, legal, ethical, and moral structures of many human cultures in order to simply ensure that a woman bore only her husband's children.

As more and more people assimilated the cultural doctrines that appeared from the need to ensure the lineage of children, we collectively forgot the ways our ancestors expressed their sexuality. Tales of Roman orgies and homosexual contact between men in ancient Greece were held up as evidence of a diseased and decadent past. When Westerners encountered pre-agricultural peoples, their sexual practices were frequently labeled abnormal, primitive, and animalistic.

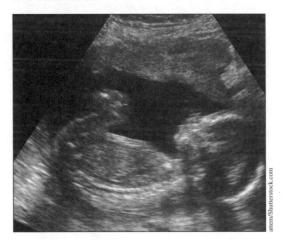

FIGURE 8-43. In our view of relationships, we tend to put a lot of priority on sex as a means to reproduce.

The view that sex was principally for reproduction, and that female sexual behavior had to be carefully monitored in order to ensure paternity, were born in the forge of civilization and a property-based economic system. It may well be that this fixation on the reproductive aspect of sexuality even contributed to the socially constructed view held by many people that homosexual contact was "unnatural" and wrong because it did not fit into the categories of acceptable sexual behavior demanded by this new arrangement.

This was the turning point at which our culture developed the view that sex and sexuality had to be controlled. With the increasing use of money and markets and other financial instruments to ensure the well-being of the individual, the need to maintain strong ties between group members began its ten millennia decline. Today the bonds we maintain are nowhere near as intense as those enjoyed by people who lived in face-to-face communities. We have insubstantial, fleeting ties with people over the Internet now and would never dream of relying upon them for our safety and well-being. Our personal security is now derived from money and the services that can be purchased with it. Today we are individuals in a globalized in-group of consumers in which our membership is purchased.

FIGURE 8-44. How deep are your ties with your online friends?

Women paid a huge price (notice how economic terms seep in) for civilization. They had to truncate their behavioral predispositions enormously such that their unconscious sexual reactions were entirely subsumed by their conscious capacity to shape and control the expression of these tendencies. The requirements of inheritance and the interests of personal power in a property-based cultural context have suppressed female sexuality and the inherent female sexual response.

And indeed, both men and women—and children too—have had to sacrifice much on the altar of civilization. Archaeologists have found by examining the remains of agricultural communities that the diet we acquired with the domestication of plants and animals has made us shorter, less fit, and less healthy than our hunter-gatherer ancestors (Palmer et al., 2002). Yes, until only recently, our average height was less than our pre-agricultural forebears. The incidence of infectious disease has also increased since the establishment of settled communities and cities. The divide between the wealthiest and the poorest of humanity has grown infinitely greater with civilization, with the billions of poor alive today living with standards of living much lower than those our hunter-gatherer ancestors knew. But perhaps most debilitating for us in the West is the pervasiveness of loneliness and alienation. Our children do not grow up amid close-knit communities where everyone cares for them. We tell our children to fear strangers who might kidnap or molest them. Our children grow up feeling that the world is a dangerous place. We don't know our neighbors, and the relationships we do have lean more toward competition than cooperation (Ericksen et al., 2010).

FIGURE 8-45. Do you ever feel lonely?

The imposition of the notion of monogamy as the "natural" human relationship pattern and the disconnect between the unconscious and the conscious aspects of female sexuality are two significant adaptations that came when we humans turned away from our ancestral way of life and adopted civilization.

PERSPECTIVES SHAPED BY CIVILIZATION

How has our thinking been changed by civilization?

Do you remember, in the first chapter, the discussion about male aggression and how the social constructivist view claimed that aggression is principally shaped by learning and reinforcement, while the biological essentialist view maintained that males are inherently aggressive? By examining how each of the genders changed in response to the challenge of adopting a settled way of life we can note the qualities of females and males, and discern why women are predisposed to think that aggression is a social construct—something learned—and men are predisposed to think that it is part of human nature. Female behavior tends to be shaped by learning and experience (social constructivism) because of the requirements imposed upon them by the relatively recent social conventions that have been adopted over the last ten thousand years. For example, she may be unconsciously aroused by a wider variety of sexual stimuli but her conscious awareness of what is arousing is apt to be more specific. (Indeed, some researchers claim that women are not consciously aroused so much by erotic stimuli involving men and women in general but actually aroused by types individuals irrespective of gender [Bergner, 2009].) Meanwhile male sexuality still tends to be shaped by their inherent nature (biological essentialism), thus what men find consciously and unconsciously arousing continues to correspondence with each other. These tendencies affect the view each gender has on matters like aggression and sexuality. And by extension, all behavioral issues are informed by these two distinct perspectives.

This basic difference between men and women can be perceived in other arenas of behavior as well. For example, disputes between couples often arise about financial matters. Though there is enormous variation in the specifics of the disagreement, there are certain commonalities that frequently appear. Note the way in which men and women perceive their spending. Women will tend to view expenditures, for example on apparel, with its emphasis on social context, as a desire to keep up with current trends and to maintain status in a given social setting. Men are apt to regard expenses, for example, on things like motorcycles and sports cars, as items that guys inherently enjoy—and require as an expression of their gender-specific nature. It's a "guy thing." The argument originates from the differing outlooks that order the worldview of the genders: sensitivity to current social conditions as opposed to the tendency to rely upon an essentialist foundation.

FIGURE 8-46. A "guy" thing?

The "boys will be boys" view that pervades discussions about male behavior reflects the essentialist view, while the controlling nature of the "good girl" designation reflects the social constructivist.

28.

How do these perspectives affect the matter of gender equality?

The struggle for gender equality can be understood as a raging argument in which the opposing camps have adopted different approaches to the matter, as though they were each speaking in different languages. And in a very real sense it is true, one is speaking in the language of social constructivism and the other biological essentialism. Women rightly get frustrated with men when the argument that is used to justify sexuality inequality is based upon the "that's just the way it is and will always be" biological essentialist rationale. For women have had to adopt socially constructed sexual behaviors for at least ten millennia and have had to accommodate their inherent human sexual response to a cultural setting for which it was not evolved. The natural question is "Why can't men do the same?" Males, on the other hand, have no conception of the magnitude of the sacrifices women have made, and so do not respond with an awareness of living within the boundaries of social constructions. This is the underlying issue that separates each of the genders, and shows why one gender cannot appreciate the viewpoint of the other.

The world is rapidly changing now. New context-driven social constructions are pressing upon both men and women—and I am confident, in the long run, women will tend to do better in this environment because they have ten thousand years of practice living with socially constructed norms imposed upon them. Men are only now beginning to catch on that holding onto biological essentialist behaviors may not be in their best interests as a new world unfolds before them.

THE SPECTRUM OF HUMAN SEXUALITY

29.

Lesbian, gay, and bisexual individuals…

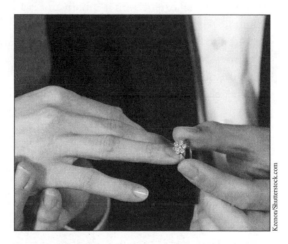

FIGURE 8-47. There is a lot of debate today about sexuality and relationships. Should marriage be defined by the sexuality of the people involved?

What about gay men and lesbian women, and bisexual individuals? Where do these individuals fit in the scheme of human sexual evolution?

Western views of male-male and female-female sexual orientations have tended to focus on the underlying forces that cause individuals to possess these characteristics. It also tends to proceed from the underlying assumption that heterosexuality is the default sexual orientation, and indeed, many people and groups maintain that it is the only correct one. There is much debate about whether homosexuality is a sexual orientation that males and females freely choose, or if it is an invariable part of individual sexuality. This approach to attempting to understand homosexuality, about whether free will has any part in sexual orientation, lends itself to the interpretation of homosexuality through social constructivist, biological essentialist, and epigenetic (nature via nature) perspectives.

It is interesting that no one ever studies why individuals are heterosexual, and whether or not individuals choose to be straight.

A large segment of the gay community maintains that sexual orientation is inborn and is an inherent part of a person's identity. Ironically, despite the fact heterosexual individuals claim that their own sexual orientation is something they are born with, the view that the male-female relationship pattern is the norm is so pervasive, that many in the straight population refuse to accept the notion that homosexuality is innate.

From a historical and biological perspective, there is much evidence to support the view that homosexuality are inherent orientations and not a matter of personal choice or socialization. For if sexual orientation were a matter of choice there should exist, in theory, populations of people in which no one is gay or, conversely, significant majorities who are homosexual. Studies of the incidence of homosexual orientation among various cultures reveal no such wide variation. Roughly less than ten percent of any given population of humans is always found to be gay (Brannon, 2008). There is apparently no group of humans that have no homosexually oriented individuals and none that are predominantly gay. All histories of human populations (for which we have reliable accounts) always have some mention of individuals who are homosexual. The consistency of the occurrence of female-female and male-male sexual contact suggests that it is a consistent feature of humanity.

The high degree of conscious or unconscious control that females have over the expression of their sexual orientation and the wide spectrum of female sexual response to a variety of sexual stimuli, as noted earlier in this chapter, also suggests that there is no fixed inherent human sexual orientation. For if women were truly always inherently heterosexual, the physiological reaction to non-heterosexual stimuli would not occur in females. And the high degree of correspondence that gay men exhibit between their conscious sexual arousal to stimulating sensory input depicting principally males to their unconscious physiological arousal to such stimuli, while showing no evidence of inhibition and no arousal to stimuli involving females, suggests that superficial choice does not determine sexual orientation in men.

Consequently, a lot of research into the "causes" of homosexuality have centered on genetic and hormonal elements. The effort to find a gene or genes that corresponds with the behavioral incidence of homosexuality has been going on for some time (though no similar research has ever gone into finding a "straight" gene). However, there are some problematic issues that arise from this approach. The likelihood that there is a specific gene that causes so complex a human characteristic as sexual orientation is highly unlikely. Sexuality is not like eye color or hair texture. It encompasses a large range of behaviors and outlooks, behavioral predispositions and tendencies that are not prone to be subject to the expression of a gene or an easily identifiable series of genes. We also know that genes are not static unchanging blueprints from which our bodies are built and programmed. Genes respond to environmental conditions—in other words, they are epigenetic in their operation—so to believe that that sexual orientation can be reified down to the presence or absence of specific genes is not likely to be a fruitful operational approach. There may be an array of genes that predispose individuals to a specific sexual orientation but they would still be subject to environmental influence (Palmer et al., 2002, p. 130). There is also the larger problem that we simply do not yet fully understand all the workings of our DNA. There are levels of complexity within its structure and operation that we have not even begun to glimpse let alone comprehend.

Indeed, studies of identical twins (people who are the result of a single zygote dividing into two individuals and who are therefore genetically identical) do not show a high degree of correspondence. Among identical twins, if one twin is non-heterosexual roughly twenty percent of the other is also non-heterosexual (Bailey et al., 2000). Though it is noted in such studies that the correspondence of sexual orientation within identical twins is higher among male twins than among female twins (which may imply once again that females inherently have more control over their sexuality than males).

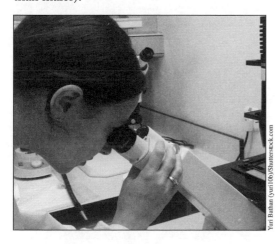

FIGURE 8-48. The search is on for the "cause" of non-heterosexual orientations.

The hormonal approach to accounting for the incidence of homosexual orientation among men and women has centered on prenatal exposure to androgens, specifically to testosterone. One of the key indicators that a fetus has been exposed to high levels of testosterone is the relative proportion of the ring and index fingers (Rahman, 2005). Among males the ring finger (the fourth finger starting from the thumb) tends to be longer than the index finger (finger next to the thumb). The longer the ring finger is in relation to the index finger, the higher the level of prenatal exposure to testosterone. It has been noted that lesbians (gay women) often have finger lengths more typical of straight men thus suggesting greater prenatal exposure to testosterone, while gay men are sometimes observed to have finger lengths that indicate lower prenatal exposure to testosterone. So there is some correlation between prenatal exposure as expressed by ringer finger and index finger lengths, but to proceed to the conclusion that prenatal testosterone exposure is the cause of homosexuality is premature.

There is also evidence that the stress placed upon a woman's body while carrying a male child (whose hormonal characteristics therefore differ from hers) increase the likelihood that if her next child is also a male, that child will be inclined to homosexuality (Bogaert, 2011). There is also anecdotal evidence that gay men often are the second born of consecutive male offspring. However, none of these correlations are definitive.

FIGURE 8-49. Social constructivists maintain that learning is central to sexual orientation.

There is also the social constructivist view that experience and learning are the main forces that shape individual characteristics. Some maintain that events in childhood shape homosexual orientation (Frisch, 2006). The problem with this perspective is that there is so much variability in the life experiences in any given population of individuals it is nearly impossible to tease out specific experiences that contribute to a particular sexual orientation. We know for example that children and adolescents do explore their sexuality and often engage in what can be termed homosexual activity. According to one survey thirty-seven percent of males and twenty-eight percent of females report that they have engaged in same-sex contact, yet such sexual experimentation has no correlation with adult sexual orientation (Kinsey et al., 1948, 1953).

30.

What does evolution tell us about homosexuality?

It is interesting to note that social constructivists and biological essentialists tend to object to evolutionary psychological views of human sexuality because non-reproductive sexual orientations do not readily fit into the scheme of getting our genes into the future. Here again the differences between views of survival that are based upon the individual versus those based upon group survival become apparent. The socially constructed individualist bias that emphasizes getting the genes of individuals into the future tends to put priority on those sexual behaviors that result in offspring. But as we have seen fostering a social setting that is conducive to the successful raising of healthy children is just as important as simply having babies. There is also the misinterpretation of evolution in the view that this process seeks perfection (in this case a population of individuals perfectly adapted to reproduction). Evolution is not a perfection-seeking process. Natural selection is about adaptability to the environment—and environments change all the time—which means that all adaptations are only provisional, temporary, states subject to constant alteration.

Jiri Hera/Shutterstock.com

FIGURE 8-50. Evolution is not a perfection seeking process.

From an evolutionary perspective, homosexuality could be a highly adaptive response to resource scarcity. For most of human history, times of food shortage were not uncommon. Consequently, it would be advantageous if not every individual were vigorously engaged in reproductive sex. Indeed, if a man or woman has a sister or brother who already has children, it might be more adaptive to invest in nieces and nephews that are already alive rather than to produce more cousins that would compete for resources (Buss, 2012, p. 160–161). Particularly in conditions of resource scarcity, non-reproductive aunts and uncles devoted to the care of their nieces and nephews might tip the balance in favor of survival. This is the evolutionary view of homosexuality's adaptive quality with a view to an individual getting his or her genes into the future through less direct means.

There is in science a principle called parsimony (Rosenstand, 2002). It is based on the notion that the simplest, most economical approach to understanding tends to be the most efficient and effective. The way our nomadic pre-agricultural hunter-gatherer ancestors lived, in which sex was used to maintain group cohesion, may offer just such a parsimonious approach to understanding lesbian, gay, and bisexual orientations.

Earlier in this chapter, the dynamic of generalizing paternity across all the males in a group created a group family condition in which all children were regarded as the potential offspring of all men. Females in such a setting would be inclined to mate with as many males whose characteristics she regarded as contributing to fit offspring as possible. This behavioral tendency created a less stressful, more relaxed social environment. It was also noted that among our closest primate relatives, the bonobos, sex was also used to support the integrity of the groups to which they belonged. The bonobos engaged in homosexual and heterosexual contact with all members of their collective social group in order to maintain

bonds of friendship and alliance much as the grooming effect of conversation supports ties among humans.

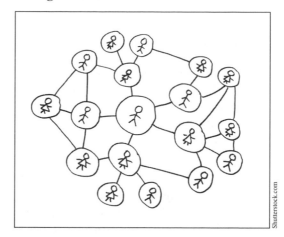

FIGURE 8-51. How differently we would view sex and sexuality if we thought about it in terms of the ties it creates between people…

If we remove the emphasis on sex as only a means to achieve reproduction and regard sexual activity as also a means to maintain ties between individuals (as it surely is in any relationship—straight or gay) then homosexuality does not stand out as such an aberration. In the ancestral past, before we got hung up about knowing with certainty the paternity of any given child, sex was just another way of keeping everyone invested in, and connected to, the group. In such a social environment there were bound to be some individuals who were more inclined to engage in male-female sexual contact and some who were more inclined to female-female sexual contact and some who more inclined to male-male sexual contact. What is being selected for from an evolutionary point of view is not reproductive success, but the maintenance of a social condition conducive for group survival and the raising of healthy children. In other words, because we humans have such long childhoods and require so much care to develop, merely having children does not constitute reproductive success. The existence of a stable, supportive social setting in which to raise children is just as important as making them. Consequently, those individuals who contributed to the cohesion of group members within their respective genders (homosexuals) were at least as important as those who maintained cohesion between genders (heterosexuals).

I cannot help but think that from this point of view, being gay or straight, from the reference of evolutionary history, is like having the inherent aptitude to be a musician or an artist, a doctor or a lawyer, a teacher or a firefighter. There may well be a specific genetic component that contributes to possessing the characteristics needed to be a musician or an artist, but it is the epigenetic (nature via nurture) effect that ultimately determines the expression of those inherent characteristics.

In other words, the simplest, most parsimonious, way of understanding homosexuality is not to account for its occurrence through genetic or hormonal or socializing elements, but to change the social context through which we view homosexuality. By simply removing the emphasis on reproduction we tend to place on sexual matters, and recognizing the role of sex in maintaining relationships, while accepting that in the past we lived in ways very different from those we current know, then being gay or lesbian or bisexual is merely an adaptation that successfully got our ancestors through the worst of times and the best of times.

Remember, nature favors diversity.

REFERENCES

Aristotle. *Politics*. Book 1.

Bailey, J. M., Bechtold, K. T. & Martin, N. G. (2000). "Genetic and environmental influences on sexual orientation and its correlates in an australian twin sample. *Journal of Perosnality and Social Psychology*. Vol. 78, pp. 524–536.

Bancroft, J. (2004) "Biological factors in human sexuality." *Journal of Sex Research*. Vol. 39. pp. 15–21.

Bergner, D. (2009, January). "What do women want?" *The New York Times*. Reprinted in *Human sexualities*. Hutchison, B. ed. (2012). New York: McGraw-Hill. pp. 39–45.

Bogaert, A. F. & Skorska, M., (2011 April). "Sexual orientation, fraternal birth order, and the maternal immune hypthesis: a review." *Frontiers in neuroendrocrinology*. Vol. 32 (2). pp. 247–254.

Brannon, L. (2008). *Gender: Psychological perspectives*, 5th ed. Boston: Pearson, Allyn & Bacon. p. 286.

Buss, D. (2012). *Evolutionary psychology: the new science of the mind*, 4th ed. Boston: Allyn & Bacon. pp. 19–20.

Ceci, S. J. & Williams, W. M. (2007). *Why aren't more women in science? Top researchers debate the evidence.* Washington D. C.: American Psychological Association.

Diamond, J. (1992). *The third chimpanzee.* New York: Harper Perennial. pp. 21–23.

Dunbar, R. (1996). *Grooming, gossip, and the evolution of language.* London: Faber & Faber Limited.

Ericksen, L. & Shimazu, M. (2010). *Nations of one: the emerging psychology of the 21st century.* Xlibris.

Erlich, P. R., Dobkin, D. S. & Wheye, D. (1988). "Breeding season." Retrieved from http://www.stanford.edu/group/stanford birds/text/essays/Breeding_Season.html

Enzensberger, H. M. (2000). "Forward." Anonymous. *A woman in berlin: eight weeks in the conquered city.* New York: Metropolitan Books. p. xi.

Everitt, A. (2007). *Augustus: the life of rome's first emperor.* New York: Random House. p. 47.

Feingold, M. (2004). *The newtonian moment: isaac Newton and the making of modern culture.* New York: The New York Public Library/Oxford University Press.

Fitzgerald, L. F., Swan, S. & Magley, V. J. (1997). "But is it really sexual harassment? Legal, behavioral, and psychological definitions of the workplace victimization of women. From O'Donohue, W. (ed.) *Sexual harassment: theory, research, and treatment.* Boston: Allyn and Bacon. pp. 5–28.

Frisch, M. & Hviid, A. (2006 October). "Childhood family correlates of heterosexual and homosexual marriages: a national cohort study of two million danes." *Archives of Sexual Behavior.* Vol. 35 (5). pp. 533–547.

Goldstein, I., Lue, T. F., Padma-Nathan, H., Rosen, R. C., Steers, W. D. & Wicker, P. A. (1998). "Oral sildenafil in the treatment of erectile dysfunction. *New England Journal of Medicine.* 338, pp. 1397–1404.

Gould, S. J. (1977). *Ever since darwin: reflections in natural history.* New York: W. W. Norton & Company.

Gould, S. J. (1989). *Wonderful life: the burgess shale and the nature of history.* pp. 321–323.

Herbert, N. (1985). *Quantum reality: beyond the new physics.* Garden City, New York: Anchor Press/Doubleday.

Howgego, C. (1995). *Ancient history from coins.* London: Routledge. p. 1.

Hrdy, S. B. (1999). *Mother nature: a history of mothers, infants, and natural selection.* New York: Pantheon.

Hyde, J. S. & DeLamater, J. D. (2000). *Understanding human sexuality.* (7th ed.) New York: McGraw-Hill.

Kinsey, A. C., Pomeroy, W. B. & Martin, C. E. (1948). *Sexual behavior in the human male.* Philadelphia: Saunders.

Kinsey, A. C., Pomeroy, W. B., Martin, C. E. & Gebhard, P. H. (1953). *Sexual behavior in the human female.* Philadelphia: Saunders.

Klein, S. B. & Thorne, B. M. (2007). *Biological psychology.* New York: Worth.

Larsson, I. B. & Svedin, C. G. (2002) "Sexual experiences in childhood: young adult's recollections." *Archives of Sexual Behavior.* Vol. 31. pp. 263-273.

Masters, W. & Johnson, V. (1966). *Human sexual response.* Boston: Little, Brown.

Maybury-Lewis, D. (1992). *Millennium: tribal wisdom and the modern world.* New York: Viking Press.

Metcalf, A. (2012, February 12). "Birth of the teenager." *Chronicle of Higher Education.* Retrieved from http://chronicle.com/blog/linguafranca/2012/2/28/birth-of-the-teenager/?sid=at&utm_source=at&utm_medium=en

Milio, J., Peltier, M. J., & Hufnail, M. (2009). *The history of sex.* [DVD] United States: History Channel.

Mitchell, S. (2004). *Gilgamesh: a new English version.* New York: Free Press.

Palmer, J. A. & Palmer, L. K. (2002). *Evolutionary psychology: the ultimate origins of human behavior.* Boston: Allyn & Bacon. p. 245.

Rahman, Q. (2005). "Fluctuating asymmetry, second to fourth finger length ratios and human sexual orientation." *Psychoneuro-endocrinology*. Vol. 30. pp. 382–391.

Roberts, J. M. (1999). *The illustrated history of the world*. Vol 1: prehistory and the first civilizations. New York: Oxford University Press. p. 123

Robertson, S. (2010). "Children and youth in history/age of consent laws." Chnm. gmu.edu. 2010-06-30.

Rosenstand, N. (2002). *The human condition: an introduction to philosophy of human nature*. Boston: McGraw Hill. p. 411.

Roughgarden, J. (2009). *Evolution's rainbow: diversity, gender, and sexuality in nature ad people*. Berkeley: University of California Press.

Ryan, C. & Jethá, C. (2010). *Sex at dawn: how we mate, why we stray, and what it means for modern relationships*. New York; Harper Perennial.

Savage, J. (2007). *Teenage: the prehistory of youth culture 1875–1945*. New York: Penguin.

Strayhorn, J. M. & Strayhorn, J. C. (2009). "Religiosity and teen birth rate in the united states." *Maclean's*. August 3, 2009. pp. 38–41.

Stringer, C. & Andrews, P. (2012) *The complete world of human evolution*. New York: Thames & Hudson. p. 12.

Tudge, C. (2000). *The variety of life: a survey and a celebration of all the creatures that have ever lived*. Oxford: Oxford University Press. pp. 181–513.

Wells, S. (2010). *Pandora's seed: the unforeseen cost of civilization*. New York: Random House.

Witchel, A. (2012, January 19). "Life after 'sex'." *New York Times Magazine*. Retrieved from http://www.nytimes.com/2012/01/22/magazine/cynthia-nixon-wit.html

Wood, M. (1994). *Legacy: the search for ancient cultures*. New York: Sterling. p. 197–198.

Wright, R. (1994). *The moral animal: why we are the way we are: the new science of evolutionary psychology*. New York: Vintage.

Name   Date

1. What are some of the things we humans use sex for?

2. What is sexual harassment?

3. Why is it important to be aware of the social context within which we consider sex?

4. What is the social construction of the "teenager" and what does it mean?

5. What is meant by "science tends to humble us"?

6.   How does female reproductive behavior differ from male reproductive behavior?

7.   From the social constructivist, biological essentialist, and epigenetic frames of reference, are we a monogamous species?

8.   How does the female sexual response differ from the male sexual response?

9.   How do men and women differ in their awareness of the details of their social setting and how does this affect their sexual behavior?

10. According to the text, why is the question "What do women want?" so difficult to answer?

11. How do polyandry and polygyny differ?

12. What is meant by "fractional fatherhood"?

13. Why is paternity so central to a settled way of life and the inheritance of assets?

14. How do social constructivism, biological essentialism, and epigenetics view lesbian, gay, and bisexual orientations?

15. What is parsimony in science?

9

Chapter 9

Gender and Children

Chapter 9

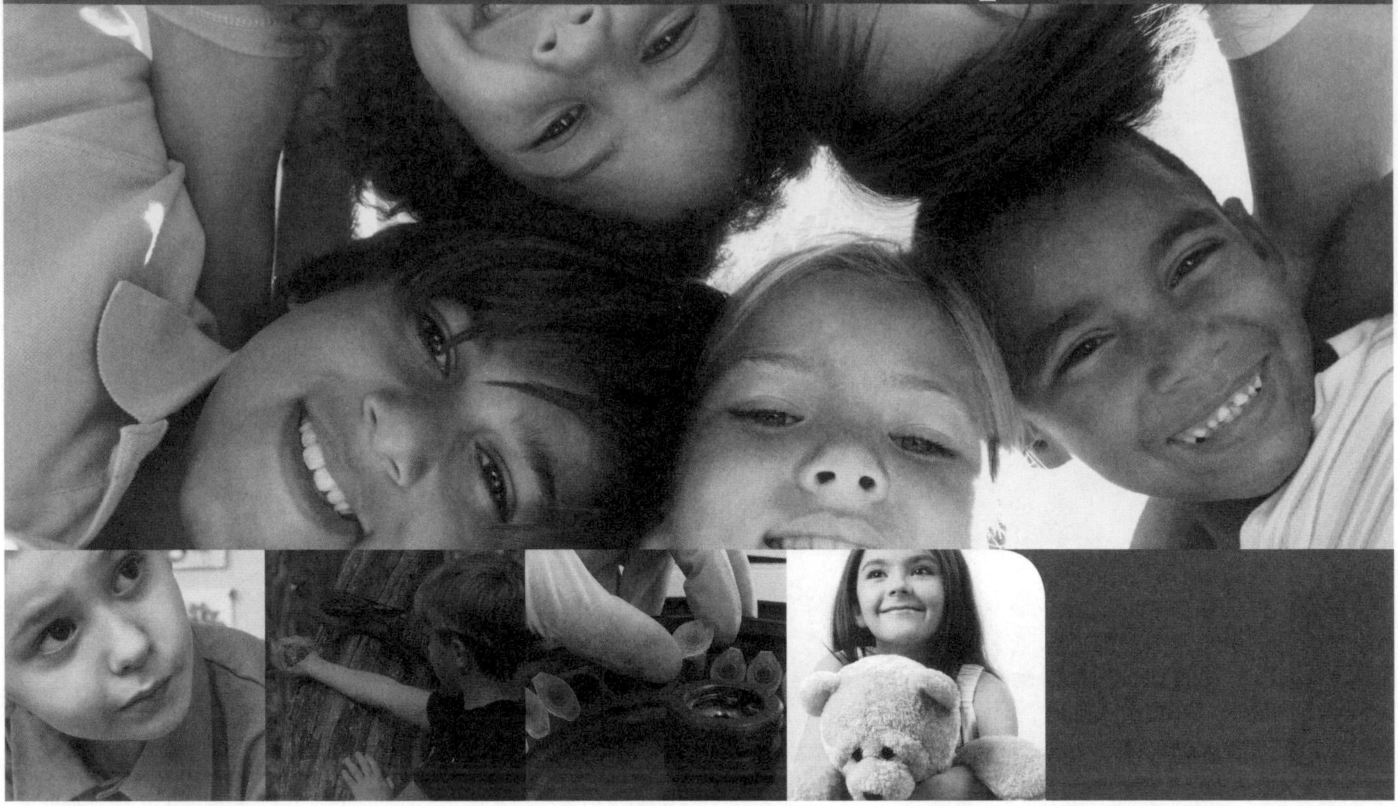

THE SOCIALLY CONSTRUCTED WORLD OF CHILDREN

The process that began approximately ten millennia ago, which took us from nomadic hunter-gatherers to what we are today, was not completed all at once. Over generations we humans used our inborn capacity to learn new behaviors, to develop and assimilate new attitudes and values, in order to conform to the requirements of the new lifestyle that came with a settled way of life. It was not an easy transition. The struggle to move beyond what we once condescendingly called our "primitive" and "savage" nature and attain the "perfection" of the civilized has been, from our personal point of view, a long one, though from an evolutionary perspective, this change has occurred with startling speed.

1.

What kind of world did we create when we left behind our ancestral way of life?

. . . .

FIGURE 9-1. What kind of world did we create when we "transcended" nature?

The goal of the path our ancestors set us on not so long ago in the history of our species was to transcend the limitations imposed upon our species by the environment and attempt to reshape the natural world according to our own designs. Whether to fashion a plow out of wood and metal, to fabricate a computer chip from minute traces of the most exotic of materials, or to utterly transform the biosphere, we humans embarked upon a unique voyage when we first sought to bend reality to our will.

But like the person who purchases a pair of shoes for its appearance without regard for the fit, we have made a world of labyrinthine complexity with an eye to what we *want*, with only secondary concern for what we *need*. This is crucial because out of this seemingly tiny difference we created a socially constructed setting that suited our image of ourselves without really knowing our own deep nature. And it is evident that in many ways, it was far easier for us to build a fabulous material environment than it was to reprogram the ancestral predispositions that still tend to order our psyches.

FIGURE 9-2. Looks or fit? Want or need?

The conflict that results from these two aspects of our lives—the contemporary social context and the ancient psychological evolved tendencies—can be found in many parts of our lives. From our struggles with obesity to the self-inflicted tumult of economic instability, our ancestral qualities do not smoothly and naturally interact with the new conditions we have created. And for gendered individuals the field of conflict is in the realm of interpersonal relationships. For we have put together a complex mix of competing behavioral tendencies and relationship configurations:

- The transition from *group* survival realized through cooperation and the sharing of resources to *individual* survival through an increasingly monetized system of competitive resource acquisition and management.

- The transition from polygamy that supported group cohesion to monogamy to keep resources in the family.

- The very recent transition from a two-parent union that supported a nuclear family unit (of mother, father and children) to a variety of reproductive configurations that include single parenthood, serial monogamy (marriage followed by divorce, followed by a new marriage followed by divorce), and informal monogamous relationships (living together and having children).

These transitions place enormous stress on females and males by imposing new socially constructed requirements that are in opposition to old emotional needs:

- The evolved emotional need to belong to a larger group of individuals goes unfulfilled resulting in chronic feelings of loneliness and alienation.

- The frustration of evolved sexual impulses to conform to the strict requirements of monogamy.

- The loss of trust between individuals in any relationship because of the awareness of the frustrated sexual desires all genders feel.

- The high levels of anxiety that come with unstable and uncertain relationships that result from high rates of divorce or from the inherently variable nature of legally informal "living together" arrangements.

- The sense of isolation that comes with the newer family structure of single parenthood.

FIGURE 9-4. Control seems to be a constant theme in our lives.

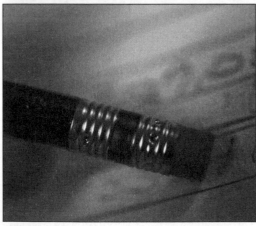

FIGURE 9-3. We have changed so much in the ledger of life.

Consequently, in order to accommodate these relationship requirements and emotional burdens, individuals tend to feel compelled in varying degrees to adopt:

- Rigid control of their sexuality as well as control over their surroundings (which includes the people in their lives).

- Other ways of fulfilling needs that are going unmet (such as habitually shopping for gratification, constantly seeking contact with others through electronic media, having extramarital sexual affairs, viewing pornography).

- Increasingly self-oriented views of personal security (not formally committing to interpersonal relationships through marriage or formally defining the boundaries of committed relationships through the use of legal instruments like pre-nuptial agreements).

All these elements that males and females struggle with, and attempt to accommodate into their lives, spring from the transition that began roughly ten thousand years ago. The more recent economic development of monetizing personal security and well-being has only greatly accelerated the process of change.

FIGURE 9-5. What kind of social environment have we created?

2.

What are some of the consequences of the social constructions that came with a settled way of life?

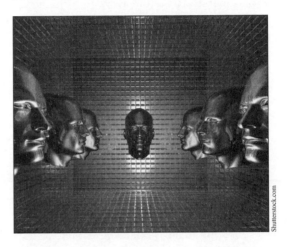

FIGURE 9-6. A new world?

Inadvertently and unintentionally, a very unwieldy, clumsy social dynamic that combines our ancient sexual behavioral predispositions with social constructions that tell us that monogamy is the natural relationship pattern between females and males joined to a monetized support system to ensure personal well-being has emerged. The messy result is a social environment in which many individuals are unfaithful to their spouse though they have been socialized to believe that they should be loyal, and the use of resources for personal gratification rather than shared needs, which produces a high divorce rate, declining rates of marriage, and the disintegration of the family. Generations of young people who have never known a stable family setting as a result of these converging social and cultural elements has become commonplace. The emphasis our cultural context has placed upon wealth and power, and the proper passing of these assets on to offspring whose parentage is beyond doubt, coupled with the view that all that is required for individuals to ensure their survival is access to money instead of membership in a well-connected family-oriented group, has required women to take firm control of their ancestral human sexuality and become extremely sensitive to the prevailing cultural context, while males have continued to rely more or less on the old ways that characterized male sexuality. This mismatch between a sensitively fine-tuned female sexuality and a relatively insensitive male sexuality has created enormous conflict between men and women in settings as diverse as the boardroom and the bedroom.

This is all the consequence of a world built on what we materially want rather than what we socially and emotionally need.

Nevertheless, though the convergence of these disparate elements has generated great difficulties for adult males, females, and intersex individuals, the problems these new socioeconomically derived arrangements have imposed upon the young are far more profound, and could have far-reaching unintended consequences.

THE LITTLEST LOSERS

Browse the shelves of the psychology section of any bookstore and you will find title after title devoted to getting relationships to work in a way acceptable to the potential reader. Check out the current affairs section and you will find some books about the break up of the nuclear family. What is missing among all these pages and pages of print that spout advice or hurl invective at one gender or another are titles concerned with the larger picture, with the well-being of those who very often have no voice in adult relationships, yet are the most important part of any civilization because they are its future. Few books ever give more than cursory coverage to the needs of children amid the tumult of the twenty-first century family.

FIGURE 9-7. The needs of children often go unconsidered.

You may have personally experienced the difficulty of living in, or coming from, a broken home. You may know the continuous trauma that many youngsters live with, of living in a state of chronic insecurity. As social and economic forces make the ties that bind families together grow more and more tenuous, it begs the larger question, has it always been like this?

In the previous chapter the mismatch between the female sexual response and the current social norms that govern human sexuality was discussed. From the psychological, physiological, and historical perspective, women have disproportionately had to develop new behavioral patterns in reaction to the social innovations that arrived roughly ten thousand years ago with the advent of settled life, agricultural, and the need to definitively know the paternity of her children. Males have also had to adapt to the new circumstances as well: until recently in the West, his allegiance to the state was called upon in times of war in the form of forced constriction, he was required to transition from hunter to laborer, and more recently, technology has made many of the strengths that favored men in the workplace redundant. But as much as the transformation from a nomadic hunter-gatherer way of life to the postmodern consumerist lifestyle has demanded much from both genders, the stresses placed upon children, on girls and boys, has also been significant.

3.

Let us consider the needs of children…

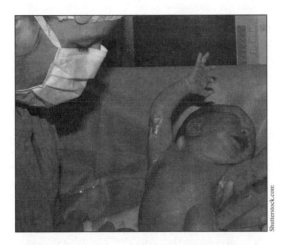

FIGURE 9-8. What does a newborn need?

If a newborn could tell its (the gender neutral pronoun "it" is used here intentionally, for if gender is a social construction, then before being socialized, a child is essentially without gender even if a child has a biological sex) parent or parents what it needs and wants, it would say, love. This is not based upon some romanticized vision of early childhood development; I mean this quite seriously. A vital element in a child's earliest days, weeks and months of life is "falling in love" with its caregiver (Lipscomb, 2004). All children require, as a part of their most basic humanity, the affirmation of their capacity to connect with other people. Each child is born with the innate desire to feel that it is cared for and cherished by someone in its life.

Research into the behavior of very small children, youngsters beneath the age of two, reveals that they inherently try to connect with the people in their surroundings. In an experiment in which a child sees an adult struggling to reach an object that the child can readily reach, the youngster will invariably attempt to assist the adult. This willingness and desire to cooperate with others is hardwired into the behavioral repertoire of the human infant, so strong is the innate predisposition to establish ties with others (Engel, 2009).

And if you think about it, such a characteristic is highly adaptive for a species that evolved as a social being, reliant on its relatives and allied tribal cohort for personal survival. When you look into the eyes of a small child, you can perceive the potential that rests in that tiny person for attachment, for the longing to be part of the dynamic give and take that is the hallmark of human relationships. Every healthy child wants to love and be loved, but for this inborn quality to attain its full appropriate form in an adult capable of enjoying the complete range of human interpersonal ties, the child cannot be ignored or made to feel that the people around it are indifferent to its needs. We are all born with the innate capacity to love, but for this aspect of our humanity to reach its full potential, it must be allowed to develop in the fertile grounds of childhood experience. Like the capacity to develop speech and the ability to accurately interpret sensory input from the senses, if a child is not afforded the opportunity to experience the warm psychological and physical embrace of supportive parents, family, and other people, that individual as an adult will never be able to completely participate in social interactions. We know that children who are not given enough appropriate love and care do not flourish, and many will simply die from this lack. Those that survive to physical maturity under such circumstances will never be able to develop the ability to engage in close interpersonal ties (Belsky, 2010). In other words, like our ability to develop native speech (that is, speak a language with fluency and without a non-native accent), which typically ends at about the age of thirteen, many of our innate psychological, social, and physical potentialities have a kind of expiration date (Pinker, 2002). If we humans don't get the care and attention we need when we are children, we will be emotionally, intellectually, and socially crippled for the rest of our adult lives.

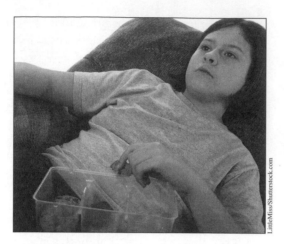

FIGURE 9-9. Our formative experiences affect our later development.

4.

What adjustments have children had to make in order to live in the social context we created ten thousand years ago?

· ·

In the ancestral setting, children lived in a rich social environment in which siblings, aunts, uncles, cousins, and grandparents, along with their mothers and—the hallmark of a group-family structured hunter-gatherer society—their many fathers, enriched their lives (Ryan et al., 2010). For all the material shortcomings that our ancestors may, from our point of view, have known, loneliness and alienation were not a part of children's lives. Pre-agricultural children may not have had video games and television, but what they did have were plenty of caregivers who saw to their physical and emotional needs. And like small children today, they had no notion of things like monetary assets and access to markets, but wanted most the comfort of living enfolded in the midst of many individuals who warmly engaged them in the intricate dance of love, family, and friendship and participated in the process by which each child became full-fledged complete human beings through appropriate face-to-face socialization. In the ancestral group-family setting, every child was potentially related to every one else, and consequently, no child was ever left behind; every child was an authentically esteemed member of the larger group.

In the space of ten millennia, the social environment children are born into has changed drastically. Gone is the ever-present extended family of aunts, uncles, cousins, and grandparents, now separated by geography and even cultural settings. With the increasing decline of intact families, siblings or half-siblings may be absent because any given youngster may be an only child, or because a brother or a sister might live in another household. Very often a child may enter the world with only one related caregiver, a single parent, and may receive over its childhood fleeting care from a variety of paid service providers (Belsky, 2010, p. 123). The community into which a child is now born supports its existence with little more than declining public funding for its education, and a law enforcement system mandated with maintaining minimum living standards through nearly non-existent monitoring and supervision.

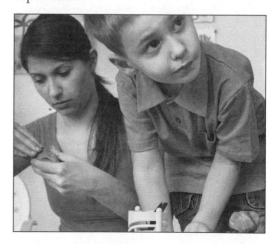

FIGURE 9-10. Daycare is a way of life for many children today.

Children have gone from a rich and varied social setting, in which to grow and develop, to a starkly empty social environment where too many youngsters live a substantial part of their lives bathed not in the warm glow of family and friends, but instead the cold flickering light of a television or a monitor.

CONTRASTING VIEWS OF CHILDHOOD

What is the social constructivist view of child development?

· ·

In the social constructivist frame of reference on human development, each of us is like a computer with no preloaded software. At birth everything works, the hardware is undeveloped and new and the memory is blank, and our genes offer nothing in the way of behavioral guidance. Aside from purely physiological functions like breathing and the ability to feed by suckling, a newborn child is like a new sponge waiting to absorb anything it encounters.

FIGURE 9-11. Mind like a sponge?

From this point of view, the origin of many of the problems that women and men encounter during their lives can be traced to specific events that occurred during childhood and adolescence. If an infant mind is a clean new sponge, then it must not come in contact with anything that will soil it. Anything that may adversely influence later behavior must be avoided. Only those things that foster desirable personality traits and conduct should be allowed to be present in a child's world.

In theory the emptiness of the infant mind should make it possible to "program" a child to be anything a parent wants it to be. Expose an infant to music and all the elements that comprise a complete musical education, throw in a lot of disciplined instruction, and the child can be raised to be a virtuoso performer. Expose a child to vice and dishonest behavior, and the youngster will become a criminal.

By extension, the social constructivist view on gender indicates that a child born male can be raised to play with dolls and act in a manner the prevailing culture designates as characteristically feminine, while a child born female can be socialized to play in a manner perceived as typically boyish. The larger meaning of the strict social constructivist perspective is that "male" and "female" are merely products of our social setting—artificial categories of behavior—that can be altered at will. The physical characteristics a child is born with are largely irrelevant to the future development of any child. In other words, males are not born to behave like men; they learn to behave in such a manner. Women are not naturally female; they are taught to be feminine.

FIGURE 9-12. From the social constructivist point of view, this girl was taught to cuddle with the stuffed bear.

What do the biological essentialist and epigenetic views of child development reveal?

· ·

The biological essentialist and nature via nurture frames of reference argue that infants are not born with empty, completely programmable minds. Like fresh-out-of-the-box computers, preloaded software is already present. Children may have sponge-like brains, ready to absorb whatever is in the environment, but the absorption qualities of their brains are predetermined. For example, it is unlikely that male children will play with dolls in the same way that female children are apt to do.

Boys are more inclined to take the doll apart while girls are more likely to nurture it. In general, female youngsters, with the exception of so-called tomboys (girls who prefer to play in a rough-and-tumble manner generally associated with boys), are more inclined to play in a cooperative manner with their same-gender age mates. Boys are more likely to engage in physically active, competitive play (Geary, 1998, p. 224–240). Nevertheless, there is enormous variation in any given population of youngsters. There are always children who seemingly do not conform to the stereotyped behavioral patterns of their particular sex and gender. From a biological essentialist and epigenetic perspective, this merely illustrates the degree of behavioral flexibility inherent to our species.

FIGURE 9-13. Generally, girls are afforded more behavioral flexibility than boys.

Nevertheless, from the epigenetic frame of reference, behavioral predispositions can be shaped to a large degree by the prevailing conditions that characterize the child's formative setting. As we have seen in the previous chapter, females are predisposed to greater sensitivity to their surroundings and are more apt to be able to tailor their behavior to suit. This is certainly the case when considering the range of traits that female young are capable of adopting. Girls can be competitive and aggressive, as is evident on the soccer fields of so many communities, while at the same time displaying typical culturally defined feminine behavioral tendencies. Indeed, girls are generally afforded much more behavioral variability than boys. The pressure on boys to be strong and autonomous from any early age in the West is often unrelenting as parents watch for any sign of "sissy" behavior in their sons, fearing that this may be an early indicator if homosexuality (Bering, 2012). But the point of the nature via nurture view is that innate qualities are merely elements within children that predispose them to certain behavioral tendencies, but does not rigidly predetermine behavior. For example, a male child who tends to act in an aggressive manner is not by nature destined to be a violent adult; rather, that aggression can be directed through nurture to more pro-social ends. His innate aggressive nature can manifest itself during adulthood not as fierceness, but perhaps as a dogged determination to achieve specific goals, which would be a positive quality in a physician or an emergency first responder.

7.

How do the three frames of reference contrast with each other?

· ·

The three frames of reference, social constructivist, biological essentialist, and epigenetic, from which we have considered sex and gender differences suggest very different developmental needs of children. Social constructivist views would argue that a high degree of control must be imposed upon the young, particularly during their early years, in order to ensure proper exposure to influences that will promote whatever developmental path parents desire for their offspring. The biological essentialist view would maintain that children are effectively preprogrammed to be male or female, and only extraordinary efforts at countering these tendencies will alter behavior. The nature via nurture view claims that experiences inflect through inborn characteristics to shape later behavior. Thus the acceptance of a child's

inherent nature is an important element, so that parents can at least nudge their child toward experiences that will foster positive inflections of innate characteristics.

So what do children really need? How should children be raised?

The disparity of views of child rearing that arise from these three perspectives requires that we consider the nature of boys and girls while always keeping in mind that there is always a lot of variation in any population of children.

FIGURE 9-14. Boys can be nurturing too. There is always variation in any group of individuals.

GIRLS AND BOYS

8.

What does the long childhood of human young indicate about our species?

· ·

It would seem that we humans have been tempting fate for much of the existence of our species. By having such long childhoods, the proportion of our effective lifespan that we can potentially reproduce is significantly lowered. While many animals are sexually mature for nearly all their lives, our hunter-gatherer ancestors were reproductively viable for only about two-thirds of their lives (if they lived into their fourth decade of life). This is no small price to pay in the high stakes endeavor of avoiding extinction. Yet our species devoted at least the first decade of life to growing up; it is even longer today, with adolescence now extending into the "thirty-something" age group and even for some into their forties (Settersten et al., 2010; Côté, 2000).

FIGURE 9-15. We live in an increasingly complex world where the past and the present interact in new ways.

The benefit of a long period of maturation is principally the formation of an individual who can function within a highly complex social organization that endows the human species with unique adaptive qualities and unprecedented power. During the long years of childhood, each youngster develops, among many other things, speech and assimilates a complete vocabulary of terms and concepts that make it possible to comprehend the thoughts, feelings, and intentions of others as well as communication the same to everyone. So adaptive is this facility to communicate that we are born with the innate ability to develop speech and to interpret the speech of others. All healthy children have the inborn capacity to be a competent speaker of any human language provided appropriate exposure and use occurs (Pinker, 1995). Within the structure of language there also resides the attitudes and

values of the group from which it springs. For example, though a statement like "it is important for parents to be invested in their child's development" is not about financial matters, the term "invested" reflects the cultural context in which we live and the priority it places on money. Thus through language and experience children also pick up the prevailing customs and norms that order the social interactions of the group to which they belong. In other words, children are born with the innate capacity to learn speech and to acquire the subtleties of the culture that informs the lives of their fellow group members.

FIGURE 9-16. There are slight inherent behavioral differences between boys and girls. But remember there are always variations.

It is interesting to note that there are slight differences in the language acquisition capabilities of children based upon sex. Girls are usually better at language than boys. Behaviorally this is reflected in the tendency among young girls to play in small groups, perhaps with as few as two or three individuals, in which conversation continually takes place. They are more apt to play indoors and engage in activities that require fine manual dexterity like drawing. Boys tend to play in larger groups and participate in physical activity, running and throwing objects, and roaming over a large area. Speech among boys often serves to establish a pecking order among the youngsters involved in play, while girls tend to converse in a manner that create ties between individuals (Helgeson, 2012, p. 222).

9.

What does our childhood behavioral predispositions say about our ancestral behavior?

. . . .

These patterns of play behavior very much recapitulate the ancestral sex differentiated behaviors of our forebears. The practice of gathering plant foods and the sharing of child care among several females, with its emphasis on fine motor skills and constant conversational contact between women and with infants and young children, are reflected still in the tendencies that young female children exhibit at play. The hunting behavior of males on the savannas of the ancestral environment are rehearsed in the play of young boys, with its focus on command and control among play group members, and the tendency to spread their activity over a large area.

Other adaptations to the old ways of life are evident in the characteristic way boys and girls develop. For example, boys grow more slowly than girls. Female children reach fifty percent of their full height when they are younger than their male counterparts, reach puberty at an earlier age, and stop growing earlier in life as well. This adaptation results in boys growing on average to a greater height and weight when they reach maturity, albeit on average two years later than females (Geary, 1998, p. 212). The result is that males require more time to reach physical maturity; however, it offers them the physical traits suited to the hazards of life as a hunter of, on average, larger stature and

musculature. For females earlier maturation offers, on average, roughly two extra years of reproductive potential, which in the ancestral environment could be crucial to the continuance of specific gene lines. (Perhaps this may also contribute to the age-related preference for younger women that males tend to favor in their mate choices.)

Specifically, during puberty young women's hips and pelvis widen while among young males, the shoulders widen. The one-and-a half to five-year length of male puberty facilitates the development of other physical characteristics that differentiate males and females. Larger hearts and more internal surface area in the lungs, which makes it possible to further oxygenate the blood that facilitates greater physical exertion, are some of the results. Females during puberty develop larger reserves of fat—an adaptation to the stresses of pregnancy and lactation—while boys are less apt to build up fat (Geary, 1998, p. 213). All these developmental adaptations prepared males and females for their respective ancestral behavioral roles.

That we still physically develop in tune to the demands of prehistoric ways of living is apparent in the area where females and males vary the most in term of their physical capabilities. The particular requirements of hunting apparently exerted significant selective forces in the past on males. More than ninety percent of boys, when they are four to seven years old, can throw objects farther and faster than their female age-mates. This difference is attributable not only to the way boys engage in play but also by their skeletal structure, and this ability persists all the way into adulthood (Geary, 1998, p. 213).

FIGURE 9-17. Throwing is a "throw-back" ability that reflects our ancestral behavior.

During the biological process of growing from a child to an adult, it makes sense that those evolved characteristics that were so essential to our ancestors' survival should manifest themselves during our own maturation. What can be discerned from the differences between male and female children is that during the process of growing up, the adaptations from the past still press upon personal development in ways that prepared us for many gender-specific activities that few of us engage in anymore with any regularity. After all, how many guys hunt animals for lunch everyday? How many girls gather wild nuts and fruits for dinner? That the most pronounced physical aptitude that males have over women is measured in the distance and speed of objects thrown illustrates the mismatch between the old adaptations and the new world we live in. After all, of what significance does throwing things have in the scheme of a high tech, money and market-oriented culture? This ability may have made the difference between life and death more than ten thousand years ago, but it does not count for terribly much now.

ANCESTRAL NEEDS, PRESENT DAY DEFICIENCIES

The problem with evolutionarily derived adaptations in a rapidly changing world is that they may no longer be appropriate in the unfolding setting children are developing within. Indeed, parents all too often discover that their own childhood experiences and lessons may no longer suit the current environment, as they seek assistance from their children to use their computers and navigate the Internet. But the sobering reality of the mismatch between what young females and males inherently need during their formative years, set in the context of the world in which they currently live, has produced many profound problems.

 10.

How does the world we currently live within affect the young?

One set of statistics serves as an indicator of the toll the difficulties adolescents face takes on them. From the middle of the twentieth century to its end, the rate at which the young commit suicide increased four-fold (Levine, 2006), with males in their early twenties dying at a rate six times greater than females (Helgeson, 2012, p. 533). Females are much more likely to think about suicide and attempt to kill themselves, but the rate at which they successfully terminate their lives is lower than males (Canetto et al., 1998).

FIGURE 9-18. The world we live in may not be designed for the needs of the young.

There are many ways that this data can be interpreted, but the stark reality is that the dysfunctional nature of the social setting in which the young develop is clearly making itself evident in the most extreme of ways. And it is not against a backdrop in which young males and females are suffering for want of food or shelter, for lack of educational opportunities or material things that these grim statistics arise. These deaths and attempted suicides are taking place in the quiet streets of suburbia as well as in the bustling avenues of urban settings, among the children of adults whose material well-being is incomparably higher than any our ancestors knew.

Another sign of the psychological distress of young females and males is found in the rate at which medications are prescribed for depression and other psychological disorders. The young are popping pills for everything from sleep disorders to ADHD, and a whole host of neuroses (Gibson, 2009). And yet when we look to populations of individuals who live in traditional societies, in ways that are more closely related to those our ancestors knew, the incidence of such psychological disorders is vanishingly small.

Since we humans embarked upon the project of shaping nature to our desires rather than adapting to its requirements, ten millennia ago, we have had a propensity to demand that the human nature of the young conform to the world we created to suit our desires. In essence, we proceeded from the social constructivist view that our psychologies are infinitely malleable and that through conditioning and training we could leave behind our ancestral ways of living altogether. We have reached the point in which the world we have made for ourselves is so different from the one in which we evolved that many individuals can no longer cope.

The lack of regard for what the young need is at the heart of the high levels of suicide and behavioral dysfunction.

FIGURE 9-19. The constant companions of the young today.

Consider the life of a typical young female today: she is the daughter of parents who very likely both have full-time jobs; perhaps she lives with one biological parent and a stepparent. Her morning begins with a mad dash to get ready for the day, then a ride to school, all the while texting, then hours of instruction interspersed with a few breaks in which to momentarily see friends, with a lunch break in the middle of the day. After class, it is off to after-school care or to soccer practice, or some other "enrichment" activity (Rosenfeld et al., 2000). Afterward there is dinner, sometimes at home, sometimes at a fast food restaurant on the way home; then there is homework or perhaps time to "veg" in front of the television or time to catch up on the entries friends have posted on social media. Then there are more texts to send to friends and sleep comes to dreams of texting, texting, and more texting….

For a young male, the day is much the same. The struggle to get up, the headlong rush to school, the buzz and hum of class, the fleeting interaction with others, the monotonous drone of lessons, the stifling regimentation, and the endless empty repetition. Then the after-school release into similarly structured activities, or the mental oblivion of homework, video games, social networking, and finally comes the late night re-entry into sleep. And so it goes.

11.

What are children missing in their lives today?

. . . .

What is so striking about the life patterns of the young today is the scarcity of relaxed unstructured social interaction, the kind of simple face-to-face time together in which thoughts, feelings, and experiences can be openly shared and pondered. Simply put, play has disappeared. Instead, there is always some task that needs to be done, some structured activity that must be undertaken, some distraction that must be dealt with, as though children are to always be steered away from the opportunity to just take it easy and be themselves. And the busy lives of their parents make many young individuals feel that they are in the way, that they are inconvenient aspects of grown-ups' lives that must not be allowed to intrude upon the demands of work or adult personal concerns. Many young males and females feel they are on their own, alone in the midst of people who do not care about them as individuals (Hersch, 1998).

We humans evolved in a setting in which close intimate contact was a constant part of our waking lives. Remember talking as a replacement for grooming as a way to maintain group cohesion and togetherness?

Among hunter-gatherers, after boys leave their mother's care around the age of six, the men of the tribe initiate them into the hunt. They spend much of the day learning by doing, by being out in the wild landscape with experienced males who teach them the ways of the animals, the tactics of stalking and killing, the methods of butchering and preparing the meat for consumption. Close bonds of trust and association are characteristic of men's groups. Young males are taught the rituals that bring success to the hunt, the spiritual practices that invite the prey animals to return to be caught again, and the acts of thanksgiving to the animal spirits that make life possible (Campbell,

1988, p. 71, 81). And in this process of being socialized into the community of men, the young males develop a lasting sense of identity. They undergo rites of passage that clearly elevate them into new positions of responsibility within their tribe. When they reach maturity they are taught sexuality and are allowed to have sexual experiences. Through it all, they always receive guidance and emotional support from the older men. They are never emotionally alone, never left adrift to find their own way through the trials of life.

FIGURE 9-20. In the ancestral environment, knowledge of the hunt was essential.

For young females in hunter-gatherer societies, the closeness of older women is an ever-present part of their lives. Their lives are a constant sequence of interactions with older women who instruct them in the intricacies of survival, of knowing which plants to collect and which to avoid, of the shared work of caring for the very young, of the subtleties of their own physiological development and the requirements of motherhood. Young girls develop a keen awareness of their surroundings, of the needs of their bodies, and out of this come a profound identification with the processes of birth, growth, and death—with the nature of life itself (Campbell, 1988, p. 83). Their rite of passage is signaled by the occurrence of their first menstruation. Through this event comes the recognition of their role in the propagation and continuity of human life. Their inherent sexuality is accepted as a virtuous, integral part of the process of life. And like their male counterparts, they are never left to feel that they are apart from the rest of their kind, never left to find their own way through unfamiliar territory.

FIGURE 9-21. In the ancestral past, the nurture of the young was an important part of women's lives.

12.

The current cultural context of the average young person...

Loneliness and alienation were not part of the ancestral way of life, while in the world we know today, they form the emotional background of far too many lives. Young males and females are seldom taught life lessons by respected members of their family or community. There is rarely a deep bond of trust between pupil and teacher. There is no meaningful initiation in adolescence or adulthood. Sexuality, in an academic setting, is formally taught in a cold, clinical manner—if it is taught at all—and is usually presented as a list of "should nots," while personal sexuality is discovered alone imbued with the aura of shame, guilt, fear, and uncertainty, while entertainment media portrays sexuality in the context of profit and power. Rites of passage are distilled down into clandestine use of drugs, getting a driver's license, having unsanctioned sex, graduating from high school and perhaps college. And through it all, the young male or female is tasked with finding a course through life with little or no help from anyone. Just do it.

CONSEQUENCES

13.

The price the individual pays in order to conform to the requirements of our time...

There is an important ideological undercurrent that pervades much of Western thought that has important consequences. The dominance of the social constructivist frame of reference that advocates the view that children are essentially lumps of clay that can be molded into what we deem fit, places the burden of living in a rapidly changing world squarely on the shoulders of the individual. There is ample evidence that dysfunction is growing more and more prevalent, and that much of what ails us, from fractured families to substance abuse, from a wide spectrum of psychological disorders to the decline of communities, have their origin in the mismatch between our evolved adaptations that served our forebears so well and the demands of a rapidly changing world. Though we know our circumstances are the source of so many of our troubles, we persist in trying to find remedies that require the individual to change. There is a refusal to accept the possibility that there are limits to the rate at which the human psyche can be made to adapt to and accommodate new circumstances. Though it took us millennia to make the shift from the old hunter-gatherer way of life to one structured around money and markets, we are now requiring the young and the old to make the jump to light-speed rates of change in the span of a single lifetime.

FIGURE 9-22. Change is happening at an ever-increasing pace.

This tendency to force the individual to conform can be readily perceived in the approach taken to effect cures. Chemical therapies for everything from on-demand sleep to depression, from fatigue to hyperactivity, are offered and even forced upon children. Rather than contemplating even slight modifications to the social environment, the default remedial methodology is inevitably one in which the child must be made to adapt to the conditions that are, more often than not, the cause of the dysfunction. Rather than making a concerted effort to meaningfully address the evolved needs of the young for stable family structures, for real companionship and reliable friendships, boys and girls are told they must be more resilient, more adaptable. The most damaging aspect of this approach is that instead of squarely acknowledging the deleterious effects of rapid change, blame is almost invariably focused on the child who cannot cope. He requires therapy. She needs treatment. The manic pace of socioeconomic and technological change is accepted and the human being is rejected.

The discipline of behavioral genetics now seeks to discover remedies not only for specific behaviors that are judged unacceptable, but cures for even points of view, attitudes, and political outlooks (Basken, 2012). The broader implication of such an approach to studying—and treating—individuals is that even our ways of viewing the world around us are subject to scrutiny with an eye for potential pathology lying in our opinions. Now we view unacceptable reactions to the postmodern world through the lens of genetics.

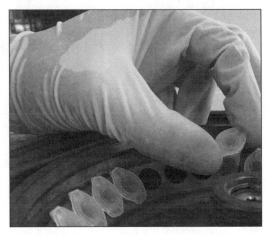

FIGURE 9-23. Will we try to manipulate our genes to control our thoughts next?

As discussed in the previous chapter, in view of the inherent tendency of males to be less sensitive to specific environmental conditions, and consequently, less likely to adopt new behaviors in response to change, it is perhaps no surprise that the young of this gender are currently experiencing grave difficulties. Young males increasingly are seen as unable to cope with the new world of work and relationships that is emerging from the confluence of technology and social innovation (Zimbardo et al., 2012). That it is young males who are more likely to take their own lives speaks to the growing disparity between the ability of this group to adapt and the demands change exacts on the individual. Though women still tend not to attain the summit of corporate power and are less likely to occupy academic positions in the sciences and engineering, the total proportion of female graduates from the universities of the world is now passing their male counterparts (Ceci et al., 2007). For indeed, knowledge—its acquisition and manipulation—is now the key element in the globalized economic environment that now structures our lives. And for many males, this shift is proving a difficult one to contend with, as the demand for the kinds of aptitudes that once served our species so well not so long ago become increasingly redundant, and decline with each passing day.

FIGURE 9-24. Is there anything natural about our world?

PERSPECTIVES

14.

Is the world we have created for ourselves good for us?

• •

It can be argued that a dispassionate evolutionary view should be used to when considering the struggles of the young, both males and females. The rapid pace of change that so characterizes the present can be understood as yet another selective force acting to differentiate between those individuals who possess suitable adaptations from those who do not. The logic of this process is that those who "have what it takes" will persist by passing these qualities on to future generations.

However, it is important to understand that the motivating force behind these selective forces is the product of human activity and human choices, not natural elements. It should also be noted that while some people are able to cope with the rapid rate of change, this ability does not come without cost to these individuals and to the children with whom they interact. Though ultimately survival is counted at the level of species, it is not enough just to simply reproduce successfully; there is also the matter of the general health of the species itself. For while individually we may be able to ensure our well-being through the monetized systems we have adopted and embraced, if sufficient priority is not placed on those fundamental psychosocial elements that are as essential as food and water to the young, then the likelihood the young will be able to thrive and flourish could be greatly compromised.

Yes, we humans are amazingly adaptive. Yes, children have an enormous capacity to acquire a huge range of behaviors and assimilate a vast amount of cultural information. However, these attributes are time sensitive. Children require the adults in their lives to provide the critical psychological and social nurture that hearken back to an earlier age to reach their full healthy human potential.

REFERENCES

Basken, P. (2012). Scientists look to genetics of behavior for answers to country's partisan divide. *The Chronicle of Higher Education.* June 11, 2012.

Belsky, J. (2010). *Experiencing the lifespan, 2nd ed.* New York: Worth Publishing. pp. 110–119.

Bering, J. (2012). "Is your child gay?" *Scientific American Mind.* 23, pp. 50–53.

Campbell, J. (1998). *The power of myth.* New York: Doubleday.

Canetto, S. S. & Sakinofsky, I. (1998) "The gender paradox in suicide." *Suicide and Life-Threatening Behavior.* Spring, Vol 28. pp. 1–23.

Ceci, S. J. & Williams, W. M., eds. (2007). *Why aren't more women in science: top researchers debate the evidence.* Washington, D. C.: American Psychological Association.

Côté, J. (2000). *Arrested adulthood: the changing nature of maturity and identity.* New York: New York University Press.

Engel, L. (2009). *The human spark.* [DVD]. United States: WNET.org Properties LLC.

Geary, D. C. (1998). *Male, female: the evolution of human sex differences.* Washington, D. C.: The American Psychological Association.

Gibson, G. (2009). *It takes a genome: how a clash between our genes and modern life is making us sick.* Upper Saddle River, New Jersey. pp. 99–120.

Helgeson, V. S. (2012). *Psychology of gender,* 4th ed. Boston: Pearson.

Hersch, P. (1998). *A tribe apart: a journey into the heart of American adolescence.* New York: Ballantine Books.

Levine, M. (2006). *The price of privilege: how parental pressure and material advantage are creating a generation of disconnected and unhappy kids.* New York: Harper.

Lipscomb, J. (2004). *Life's first feelings* [DVD]. United States: WGBH.

Pinker, S. (1995). *The language instinct: how the mind creates language.* New York: Perennial.

Pinker, S. (2002). *The blank slate: the modern denial of human nature.* New York: Viking.

Rosenfeld, A. & Wise, N. (2000). T*he overscheduled child: avoiding the hyper-parenting trap.* New York: St. Martin's Griffin.

Ryan, C. & Jethá, C. (2010). *Sex at dawn: how we mate, why we stray, and what it means for modern relationships.* New York: Harper Perennial. pp. 90–104.

Settersten, R. & Ray, B. E. (2010). *Not quite adults: why 20-somethings are choosing a slower path to adulthood, and why it's good for everyone.* New York: Bantam Books.

Zimbardo, P. & Duncan, N. (2012). The demise of guys: why boys are struggling and what we can do about it. TED Conferences, LLC.

Name

Date

1. What was the broad goal of adopting a settled way of life ten thousand years ago?

2. Why is it important to understand the distinction between what we want and what we need when considering the formation of the social constructions that order our world?

3. What are some of the key changes that came with a settled way of life?

4. What do children need and want most?

5. In what ways did ancestral childhood experiences differ from those that children experience today?

6. How does the social constructivist view of child development differ from the biological and epigenetic views of child development?

7. Why do we humans have such long childhoods?

8. Why are so many children suffering from depression, ADHD, sleep disorders, and other psychological problems these days?

9. What is the approach used to remedy these problems based upon?

10. Why are young males less likely to do well today?

Chapter 10

AN EPIGENETIC VIEW OF DEVELOPMENT AND ITS IMPACT ON GENDER

Chapter 10

1.

Is there one definitive way of understanding human development?

· ·

We need only remember that theories such as Darwin's, about the nature of change, are subject to alteration and modification. In science we are always testing the interpretations and conclusions of our collective research in an effort to delve ever closer to the truth. Our understanding of human development is no different. The best theories of the present may someday be relegated to the dustbin of obsolescence when better ones arise to replace them after being tested.

Erik Erikson's study of people who lived as our ancestors did revealed an innate pattern of development common to all humans that he detailed in his eight-stage theory of epigenetic development (1950). But it is important to note that his view of development is a social construction. Despite his efforts to be as objective as possible, his outlook is distinctively European. Born in 1902 in Germany, his epigenetic approach to human development is based upon the conflict between opposing elements in the human psyche. For example, in the first stage of life, trust versus mistrust is at the heart of the personal struggle for growth. This clash of opposites, of argument, and question and response, is very much in the tradition of Western philosophy and dates back to the ancient Greeks (Russell, 1945). Yet there are cultures in the world in which harmony not conflict is seen to be the underlying relationship between psychological elements. Add the fact that Erikson lived through the First and Second World Wars (1914–1918 and 1939–1945 respectively) plus his association with Freud who was very much concerned with internal psychological struggles and it is not difficult to understand why his perspective on personal development is so colored by conflict (Greenwood, 2009).

FIGURE 10-1. It is important to remember that Erikson's worldview was colored by two world wars.

Erikson's theory reflects the culture and the times in which he lived. So perhaps we can interpret his findings as being relevant to the context in which it originated. In other words, when people find themselves living in a culture of conflicting forces this is how development occurs. And this is certainly true for the setting in which we live today.

Thus the epigenetic (nature via nurture) character of his theory becomes apparent. The essentialist, inborn quality encoded in our genes expresses itself in a social context of conflicting elements in the manner described by Erikson's theory. If the social context of individual development were different (i.e., harmonizing rather than conflicting) then the interplay of genes and the environment would result in a different sequence of development. It's rather like our essentialist desire for power and status expressing itself in accordance with the context in which we live. Today's status-seeker in Western cultures might desire a big house and an expensive luxury car to show off her or his wealth, while a status-seeking male in the ancestral hunter-gatherer past might covet the hides of dangerous predatory animals to demonstrate his hunting prowess. The desire for status is still there but how it is expressed is epigenetically shaped by the surrounding context.

FIGURE 10-2. Practical mode of transport or status symbol?

2.

One way of considering the progression from birth to death...

Erikson perceived that there are eight stages through which we all seem to pass as we mature and age (1950). He proceeded from the view that during our long prehistory when we humans evolved as social beings, our psyches were shaped by the rigors of the hunter-gatherer way of life. From this interplay with the environment emerged a distinctive sequence of life-stages. It is an epigenetic process because it arises from the *interaction* of biological essentialist elements that are inherent in all of us, and the surrounding culturally constructed and environmental conditions that form the external world in which our forbears lived.

Indeed, it is the unique mix of ancestral behavioral predispositions and the current setting in which males, females, and intersex individuals live that makes personal development in the post-modern world so challenging.

FIGURE 10-3. Ancestral behaviors in a post-modern setting.

Erikson maintained that during the course of our lives we face important developmental milestones. At each there is a conflict between two extreme aspects of an important part of our lives—for example, trust versus mistrust—which shapes our personal nature. Successful resolution of these conflicts results in the formation of what he termed "virtues" that empower us, and further our ability to function well in the world of people and events, as well as appropriately transition from infancy to childhood to adulthood. Among these virtues were hope and love, wisdom and competence, and together with other attributes generate a foundation of personal strength that enabled our ancestors to face any challenge, be it climatic change, famine, migration, disease, conflict, and of course, death.

3.

Erikson's epigenetic stages of development.

· ·

This inborn process of development begins at infancy during the initial year of life. According to Erikson, a child's first developmental psychological stage is characterized by *Basic Trust versus Basic Mistrust*. How a child fundamentally perceives the world and—most important—the self, emerges out of this stage. It determines whether the youngster comes to view its surroundings as a safe, predictable, self-consistent place.

FIGURE 10-4. Do you perceive the world as a safe, predictable, self-consistent place?

During this stage parents, particularly the mother, play a vital role. The quality of the ties between the infant and mother imparts upon the child a sense of whether the larger world beyond the self is trustworthy. From this basic relationship between mother and baby comes the appreciation in the youngster of interconnectedness and relatedness that are a part of all interpersonal ties with others.

The virtue that springs from the resolution of this first stage of personal development, of *Trust versus Mistrust*, is *hope*. This indomitable quality has sustained humanity through every kind of adversity in the past and is an important component of personal strength that makes individuals resilient. Failure to resolve this first stage milestone results in feelings of hopelessness in the child that may pervade his or her entire life.

Ancestral ways of living in which constant face-to-face interaction between mother and infant was common did much to impart in the mind of the child the sense that he or she could trust his or her primary caregiver. Before the advent of regular work for regular wages, it was normal in the pre-modern past for women to devote a substantial amount of time to the upbringing of their children. Indeed, in such settings it was not unusual for a mother and child to be together all the time.

FIGURE 10-5. The bond between mother and child is crucial to the development of hope.

Consequently, the modern practice of daycare and baby-sitting along with separate sleeping accommodations for parents and infants, as well as the use of electronic media to entertain and distract the young, represent a significant departure from the old ways. Add the frequently unstable nature of contemporary family structures and it becomes clear why the positive resolution of the *Trust versus Mistrust* stage of development is not a forgone conclusion today.

From an Eriksonian epigenetic view of development, the feelings of hopelessness so commonly felt in the present may have their roots, at least in part, in the unsuccessful resolution of the earliest stage of personal development.

The virtue that may arise from the favorable resolution of the second life-stage is that sense of self-determination, of volition that we commonly refer to as will. From the age of one to about the fifth year of life, the child confronts the conflict of *Autonomy versus Shame and Doubt*. Here the youngster begins to test his or her ability to act upon his or her surroundings, and to receive feedback.

FIGURE 10-6. This child is on its way...

In the highly social environment our ancestors experienced, the young person developed a keen understanding of the effect of his or her actions. The reaction generated by those around the child did much to determine the outcome of this stage of development. It is during this second life-stage that gender-specific restrictions begin to enter into children's lives. Boys are often pressured to behave in a manner consistent with being male, while girls are generally given more latitude and allowed to be "tom-boys."

The obsession with the need to control outcomes so common in the post-modern world may have a negative impact on development. It is important for the child to feel that she or he has some degree of influence on his or her environment otherwise the sense of personal

volition, of self-will, may not fully form. The effort put forward by caregivers to ensure results they deem desirable may not always match those of the child. This conflict can do much to undermine the sense of autonomy that is such an integral part of individual will, thus adversely affecting the potential for a positive outcome of this stage.

FIGURE 10-7. Obsessive control can have a negative effect on development.

The meaning of a person's life often has its first intimations in play. Purpose, that sense of what our lives are for, comes in the third epigenetic life-stage. The essential conflict the individual faces is that of *Initiative versus Guilt*. Can the young person undertake something on her or his own without being told to initiate the task? Can she or he do it without feeling guilty? These are the basic matters that underlie the third developmental stage.

Again, the parental need to control the young in contemporary social settings is often problematic. All too often guilt is used to shape behavior. Excessive use can adversely affect the young individual by so inhibiting his or her own will to achieve specific ends that the child cannot function appropriately. In the present-day work environment, initiative is a particularly important quality to possess, which makes it vital that positive outcomes occur in this stage.

In the pre-modern world, unstructured play was a part of every child's development. And it is out of this seemingly goal-less activity that life goals arise. Remember, play is a product of at least five million years of evolution. It has a long track record and has proven to be a highly adaptive childhood activity.

FIGURE 10-8. Unstructured play is a vital part of childhood.

The fourth life-stage Erikson characterized is concerned with the conflict of *Industry versus Inferiority*. Between the ages of 6 to 11, individual children begin to perceive differences between themselves and others. During this time male children are likely to begin to engage in physical confrontations. Female children begin to learn to use soft power. These behavioral tendencies have their origin in our ancestral past. For it is around the age of six that young males in pre-modern cultures are separated from their female age mates and begin to be educated by older males.

In traditional cultures boys are taught to be hunters, while girls are schooled by their female relatives to learn the roles of mother and caregiver. The active nature of hunting requires young males to master their fear and to learn to use overt forms of power to kill prey animals. Young females acquire the skills needed to be effective gatherers of edible plants as well as nurturers of the very young. That male children tend to play with toys associated with the application of overt power (trucks and guns) while female children are more likely to gravitate toward dolls and stuffed animals reflects the innate behavioral predispositions that originated in the deep past of our species.

FIGURE 10-9. Learning has always been a part of human development.

The favorable outcome of the conflict between *Industry versus Inferiority* is a sense of *competence* in the young person. The feeling of being good at specific tasks is an important quality when living in a world in which constant change is an unvarying condition.

The fifth life-stage is concerned with a fundamental aspect of our ability to participate well in interpersonal relationships, for it deals with identity, that sense of who we are and how we see ourselves in relation to others. The conflict is characterized by Erikson as *Identity versus Role Confusion* and here again the role of parents and caregivers is of great significance. In the context of gender, the freedom parents give to the young to explore their own sense of personal identity, their sense of being a gendered individual, is pivotal. If this freedom is denied and the young person is forced to conform to expectations that run contrary to his or her own perceptions of personal gender then identity confusion will result. If given the leeway to discover his or her own identity, that individual will more likely achieve a positive resolution and achieve the virtue of *fidelity*.

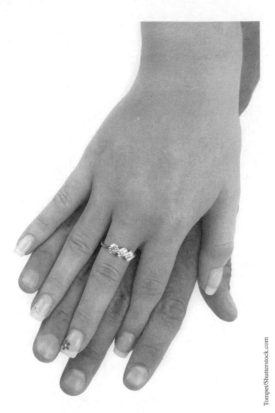

FIGURE 10-10. There is more to fidelity than not cheating.

We tend to think of fidelity as being faithful to the individual we're in a relationship with. Not cheating is part of the common way of perceiving fidelity. But it is also important to understand that being "true" to "who you are" is also a critical part of any interpersonal relationship. In order to authentically relate to another person, you have to know who you are and be comfortable with yourself. Not being clear about your gender identity would make any relationship problematic since gender is such a basic part of human interaction.

It should come as no surprise that *Identity versus Role Confusion* comes approximately between 12 to 19 years of age, at the turning point in our lives when we reach reproductive viability. Once again, the epigenetic nature of development is clear. For it is when our physiologies make the transition from childhood to adulthood, when we cross the biological Rubicon that makes pairing up with another

individual such an important part of our lives that we experience this conflict. The essentialist impulse to produce offspring is inflected through the socially constructed setting and epigenetically results in this conflict, which if resolved positively helps facilitate lasting relationships.

4.

The stages of adult development.

FIGURE 10-11. Love is the virtue of the first adult developmental stage.

Love is the virtue that may potentially result from the positive resolution of the next conflict according to Erikson's epigenetic developmental scheme. The underlying clash is characterized as *Intimacy versus Isolation*, and runs roughly from 18 to 35 years of age. This sixth stage of development is the first fully "adult" stage in our cultural context, and builds upon the successful resolution of the previous five stages.

It is important to note at this point the significance of infancy and childhood to the developing adult. In order to realize virtues like love and fidelity, the individual intersex, male, or female individual must have favorably resolved earlier conflicts. The virtues of hope, will, purpose, and competence are all prerequisites to later virtues. A child who never develops hope will likely never love in a completely healthy adult manner. Erikson's epigenetic theory of development starkly illustrates the primacy of a person's early life experience. Each successive stage builds upon previous ones, so that like a child who never learns to read will be unable to function in an office environment, a youngster deprived of appropriate nurture who never develops the virtue of purpose or competence will never be able to realize the capacity to live in a fully adult manner.

The challenge of the *Intimacy versus Isolation* stage of development to the individual is the formation of meaningful interpersonal ties. Intimacy—that quality of familiarity based on trust that makes long-lasting relationships possible—is tested during this time in a person's life. In the post-modern social environment, the prevalence of divorce, marital discord, and the impermanence of interpersonal ties all indicate that the positive resolution of the essential conflict of this life-stage is increasingly uncommon. Feelings of loneliness are a natural consequence of the failure to realize intimacy with others. Isolation is the result.

FIGURE 10-12. Intimacy is an important part of human bonds.

Love as a virtue needs to be understood not as something others give to you, but as a quality within the self that makes it possible for you to establish meaningful ties. Receiving love does not constitute an intimate relationship. It is the give-and-take of this emotion between individuals that facilitates lasting bonds.

Following the ancestral path of personal development, after reaching reproductive maturity the next task is the nurture of the young that comes with pairing-up. Care is the virtue that hopefully arises from the resolution of the seventh epigenetic life-stage. *Generativity versus Stagnation* is the name used to characterize this phase of life, which extends from a person's mid-30s to the mid-60s. The basic matter that informs this segment of a person's life is whether or not he or she is contributing to the next generation.

FIGURE 10-13. Care is a great virtue for a species that must invest so much in its young.

If a person has realized favorable outcomes in the six previous lifespan developmental stages, the intersex, female, or male individual will likely be in a stable interpersonal relationship. The impulse to contribute to the welfare of family, of those individuals to whom a person feels some connection, is the positive manifestation of the conflict between *Generativity versus Stagnation*. However, if any of the previous stages have not been successfully resolved, very likely nurturing behavior directed toward others will not result.

In many ways this stage can be thought of as a turning point in a person's life in which he or she becomes outwardly concerned to make the world a better place, or turns inwardly to dwell upon unresolved issues that continue to limit personal growth. If the individual has confronted earlier conflicts well then he or she will have the capacity to contribute to the well being of others. If he or she has not resolved earlier conflicts in a favorable manner then he or she will be caught in a cycle of stagnation in which the past will continue to inhibit personal development and so stymie outreach beyond the self.

The obsession with the self among older adults so common in today's social setting clearly indicates, from an Eriksonian perspective, the failure of so many to achieve positive outcomes in earlier stages of life. Once again, the conflict between the post-modern world and our ancestral needs is apparent.

FIGURE 10-14. Wisdom is the final virtue in Erikson's life-stage view of development.

The final outcome is becoming increasingly rare in the world in which we live: *wisdom.* The conflict is referred to as *Ego integrity versus Despair.* Running from the mid-60s to the end of a person's life, this is the time frame into which intersex, male, or female individuals look back over the span of their lives and perceive either achievement of meaningful accomplishments or failure to realize anything of merit. A sense of integrity, of personal honor, is derived from the former. Despair is the feeling that comes from the latter. The positive outcome that arises from the proper confrontation of this conflict is wisdom, that capacity to see beyond mere knowledge and perceive the essential meaning of life.

5.

A broader view of development...

From hope to wisdom, these are the component elements of the human psyche that make it possible for an individual female, male, or intersex person to navigate the rigors of growing from infancy with its requirements of physical development, to childhood with its emphasis on learning and maturation, to adulthood with its themes of love and childrearing, to late adulthood with its concern for the continuity of family and society. It is a path well trod by billions and billions of our ancestors. And as frightening as the final exit from life may seem at this point in your life, there is comfort in knowing that if you achieve the wisdom that is the hallmark of the last life-stage, you will have the integrity to face death well. Remember billions of others have journeyed on the same life-path. That we are predisposed to follow it shows that after five million years of human evolution it has so far proved adaptive.

The larger question is will it continue to serve us well in the world we are creating for ourselves in the 21st century?

FIGURE 10-15. What changes lie in our future?

REFERENCES

Erikson, E. (1950). *Childhood and Society*. New York: W. W. Norton.

Greenwood, J. D. (2009). *A conceptual history of psychology*. Boston: McGraw-Hill. p. 583.

Russell, B. (1945). *A history of western philosophy*. New York: Simon & Schuster. pp. 92–93.

Name   Date

1. Why is Erikson's view of human development regarded as epigenetic, yet the theory he put forward is a social construction? How did his own life experience shape his work?

2. The text describes how our innate longing for status is inflected through our circumstances, so that wanting a big house or an expensive car is the epigenetic expression of ancestral desires. Think of other examples of old desires being expressed in up-to-date ways.

3. According to Erikson, what shaped the eight stages of human development?

4. What do virtues do for us according to Erikson?

5. What is the first epigenetic conflict and what is the positive outcome? What is the negative outcome?

6. Why is face-to-face contact so important to infant development?

7. What is the favorable outcome in the second lifespan stage and why is it important? How can over-controlling caregivers thwart it?

8. What is the first adult stage? What is its positive outcome? Why is it important at this point in an adult's life?

9. What is the positive outcome of the last stage and why can it be elusive for many individuals? And why is it important that previous life-stages be properly resolved?

10. Do you think Erikson's developmental path will continue to be an adaptive characteristic in the future? Explain your answer.

11

Chapter 11

MAKING SENSE OF IT ALL

Chapter 11

You and me and every person you know, have known, and will ever know are a swirling mix of traits and characteristics. Our biological nature extends from the atoms that constitute the chemicals and compounds that make up our bodies, that form the genetic material that govern everything from the growth of our fingernails to our behavioral tendencies. Yet we are all very much beings of our times, in tune with the social norms and trends that spring from the dazzlingly rich interplay of billions of individuals spanning thousands of years that generates the social construction we call culture. And the inflection of all these elements, by the many facets of biology and social construction, propelled by the alchemy of chance and circumstance, produces the lives and life experiences that make each of us unique.

FIGURE 11-1. We are each unique individuals.

In the previous chapters we have considered, through the frames of references that offer insights into the nature of gender, matters as disparate as

- the way our biology shapes sex and gender

- how science makes the effort to objectively understand gender matters possible

- how the social constructions that inform our lives shape our gender identity

- the personal frames of reference that order our gender identity

- how gender influences the way we wield our personal power

- how our sexuality is shaped as much by the past as it is by the present

- gender and childhood

- personal development

1.

What meaningful things can we ascertain about gender issues?

Now comes the real challenge, attempting a synthesis—the bringing together—of these parts so that we see the "bigger picture" and perceive meaningful insights that we can apply to our daily lives. We can start with what is for many people the most vexing aspect of being a gendered individual—relationships.

FIGURE 11-2. Relationships can be a big part of our lives.

THE QUESTION OF FIDELITY AND THE DECLINE IN THE NATURE OF NURTURE

2.

How should our most important interpersonal relationships be ordered? What does the past indicate? What does the present demand?

· ·

We have painted ourselves into a corner.

The paint is the social construction that tells us that monogamy is the norm, that men and women should ideally be in lifelong relationships in which they have sex only with each other. We want to believe that monogamous relationships have been the norm for as long as our kind has existed.

FIGURE 11-3. Have we painted ourselves into a corner?

The floor upon which the paint has been applied is our evolved sexuality. And it is important to note that two different approaches to understanding human sexuality structure the evolutionary psychological view of what we are trying to achieve when we engage in sexual behavior. One is the individualistic concern for getting our own genes into the future. The other is the group-centered concern for getting our collective genes into the future.

The individualistic approach to survival offers a view of sexual selection in which females are concerned with finding the "right" guy who has suitable genes that complement her own and who has the right behavioral characteristics and access to resources that will ensure the welfare of the children they have together. The individualistic perspective on mate selection suggests that monogamy works so long as the male delivers the goods.

The group-centered approach to survival offers a view for a different strategy for mate selection. Rather than find one male with all the right characteristics and break off from the larger community to form a tiny two-person family unit, females behave in a manner that fosters community cohesion and ensures their place in a larger group of supportive individuals. By maintaining intimate ties with many males, the children produced in such a group-family would receive the care and support of several adults. The group-centered perspective on survival suggests that monogamy in the present would be hard to maintain, and penalizes offspring because they may not receive the support of the community.

Our prehistoric ancestors, as is the case with our primate relatives the chimpanzees and the bonobos, probably did not have the formal social construction we call marriage. The nature of the evolved human sexual response that females still possess suggests that the greater capacity for, and duration of, arousal and orgasm are adaptations to a group-family structured social order. However, the more recent socially constructed norms that we have adopted with the emergence of civilization and a settled way of life has tended to suppress female sexuality.

FIGURE 11-4. Control of the land was one of the key innovations that changed us.

From the point of view of access to resources, personal security, and the uncertainties that came with the nomadic hunter-gatherer way of life, group-family structures work by pooling the skills, talents, and abilities of the entire group or tribe to ensure the well-being of all. When we adopted agriculture and started to live in settlements, our ancestors no longer needed an extended group-oriented social structure for personal survival. A man and a woman, their extended family, and their children living amid primitive but developing markets, along with emerging systems of governance, could get all that was needed to maintain life. The demands of property ownership and of inheritance altered sexual behavior. Families had to be certain of the paternity (maternity is never in doubt) of their children, so women had to alter their ancestral sexual behavioral tendencies.

Beginning in the twentieth century a new twist was added to the already complex mix of ancient and contemporary forces that shaped our relationships. We monetized personal survival. Instead of relying upon a cohesive group of individuals or a stable marital relationship, an individual could ensure personal well-being through the use if universally accepted money

and sophisticated markets. By consuming goods and services provided by a variety of vendors, a lone man, woman, or intersex individual could obtain everything needed for life. From childcare to cleaning services, from meals to security, all that is required was the transfer of funds.

FIGURE 11-5. Money was another key innovation that altered our behavior.

This last alteration triggered a profound change in the way the genders wield power. The old incentives for cooperation between the individual and the group, which ordered the lives of our pre-agrarian ancestors, as well as the incentive for long-term cooperation between two individuals, which ordered the social construction of monogamous marriage, suddenly disappeared. The empowerment money and markets brought to intersex, male and female individuals made the old ways obsolete. A single parent could ensure personal genetic survival by having and raising a child or children alone (Ericksen et al., 2010).

3.

At the focus of an intense conflict between the past and the present...

Yet the learned, socially constructed conventions of the recent past that advocate monogamous marriage still echo in our conscious, while the ancient group-family urges still stir in our unconscious. The advent of a monetized individualized existence has removed the restraints that gave monogamy such power over our thinking and sexual behavior. From the point of view of resources, the lone individual is free and needs neither membership in a cohesive social group nor a spouse to survive and function in the twenty-first century.

But many of us still possess the conscious attitude that monogamous marriage is a laudable goal. Yet our unconscious still wants to participate in the vigorous sexual give-and-take of multiple relationships. The thin civilized coat of paint that covers our ancient predispositions forces many individuals into a corner in which a titanic struggle between the impulses of our ancestral sexual past and the relatively recent social norms of monogamy contend for control of personal behavior.

FIGURE 11-6. Frustration is a common feature of our lives.

In many ways, study of the deep past and the demanding present, through the insights of evolutionary psychology, reveal that Freud was right: we are a bunch of repressed females, males, and intersex individuals because of the social norms that run counter to our ancestral behavioral tendencies. And he was correct in his diagnosis that it is sex that rests at the center of the crush of competing elements that seek to control human behavior and which cause so much suffering and neuroses (Freud, 1989). But now, technological and socioeconomic innovations have converged with biology to annihilate the old restraints that once forced us to rigidly manage our urges and so terribly burdened us with guilt and fear.

4.

How are we to cope?

How, then, should couples deal with these fundamental changes that have remade the nature of interpersonal relationships?

Well, in a sense many individuals have already found *ad hoc* ways of navigating the new landscape of human sexual behavior. Consciously or unconsciously many people are choosing not to commit to long-term relationships. Some couples knowingly or unknowingly acknowledge the ancestral pattern of human sexuality and do not require sexual fidelity to be a part of their relationships, while some couples demand that each remain faithful to the other, and when this cannot be maintained, the relationship ends and each goes their separate ways to seek out new relationships in a process called serial monogamy (Ryan et al., p. 299). Intentionally or unintentionally, in some households parents blend their already existing children into new family configurations when they pair up with new partners who may themselves have children from previous relationships. The duration of the ties that form between individuals may be measured in days or decades. Yet the emotional, and even the financial, toll on individuals and their children remains unacceptably high. Apparently, we are muddling along trying to find some resolution to this difficulty.

FIGURE 11-7. What accommodations will this couple have to make in the course of their relationship?

5.

But what if you are committed to traditional monogamous ties?

Though there is a lot of variation among any population of individuals—and this is certainly true within the realm of human sexuality—it is important to understand that we are not descended from monogamous ancestors. Indeed, monogamous marriage is a label—an entirely artificial human cultural creation, a product of our socio-religious traditions. There is in nature no indication that such a prescription for lifelong pair bonding exists (Roughgarden, 2009). As noted earlier, the vast majority of the creatures most closely related to us, the mammals, are not monogamous.

As long as our socially constructed view of a meaningful relationship between two individuals encompasses sex and sexual fidelity, a profound conflict will exist. The evolved behavioral predispositions that were shaped over millions of years will always be at odds with doctrines of marriage that have existed for only a vanishingly small fraction of that time. To think that we can easily put aside behavioral tendencies that have proved adaptive in the past, and that have underwritten the survival of our species for so long, is at best a stretch.

At the start of the sort of relationship that may lead to marriage, the passionate physical love of intense sexual contact seems to burn with a fire that can never be extinguished. It may endure for some time, but eventually the frequency and intensity of such sexual expressions of love mellows—and if the relationship lasts, it moves into a new phase of deep attachment, commitment, and respect. This pattern of extreme passion changes over time, developing in some cases into a mutual connectedness that for some couples can last decades (Sternberg, 1986). The evolving nature of interpersonal relationships can be understood as an adaptation that tended toward monogamy and that helped ensure the survival of our kind.

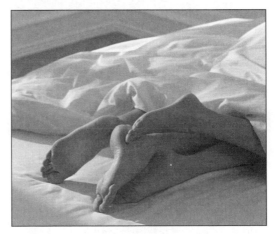

FIGURE 11-8. Sexual expressions of love mellow over time.

6.

How do our ancient predispositions affect our current sexual behavior?

· ·

The wild zeal of impassioned romantic love can be viewed not only as the chance meeting of two individuals who "click" but also as a manifestation of adaptive reproductive behaviors. We know from research that when women are ovulating, in other words, when their body is primed for reproduction, they are unconsciously more likely to seek out sexual contact (Saad, 2011). Thus a woman is more likely to dress in a provocative manner, more likely to be unconsciously receptive to the subtle biochemical signals of the men she encounters that informs her evolved sensibilities about their immune system, their genetic compatibility, and their general health. Remember, women do the choosing for they are the guardians of the future.

Men are gamblers, citizens of the present. To participate in the dance of life in the ancestral environment, they had to take whatever mating opportunity came their way. With the high mortality rates that existed in the past, if a man were the sort of person who could only commit to one woman this could prove disastrous for his personal line of descent. It may well be that this characteristic is not common among males, because individuals with this tendency in the deep past would probably not have left a lot of descendents.

And as much we tend to think that males are more likely to be unfaithful, research shows that after about three years in a committed relationship, females tend to start looking for new males to connect with in their surroundings (Fischer, 2008). But before we start applying our socially constructed judgments on men and women, perhaps we should ask why we tend to behave in this manner from an evolutionary perspective.

FIGURE 11-9. On the lookout after three years?

For our distant foremothers, three years was about the right amount of time to start looking for a new mate or mates. Assuming she had become pregnant three years earlier and had a child nine months later, her daughter or son would at this point be a little over two years old. In the ancient group-family social configuration her child would be regarded as a member of the tribe. No longer dependent on breast milk, her son or daughter would be receiving care and attention from her extended family of sisters, aunts, and grandmothers, as well as unrelated female friends. From a biological standpoint, for a woman, it was an opportune time to initiate the contacts that would result in the birth of another child.

This successful pattern of behavior, shaped over countless generations, still tends to appear in the behavioral inclinations of women today.

For our long ago forefathers, before the advent of a settled way of life that came with the rise of agriculture as a method of subsistence—before we owned stuff—the matter of definitively knowing the paternity of any given child would not be such an important matter. In a cultural setting in which belongings were few and resources were shared, it was probably functional for all men to feel that every child in the tribe was potentially theirs. From a biological point of view, men were still competing with each other to get their genes into the future; it is just that the competition took the form not of fistfights, battles for dominance, or competitive courtship.

7.

Another kind of competition.

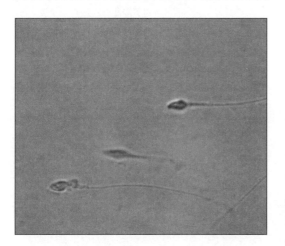

FIGURE 11-10. Competition not before sex but after?

Sperm competition occurs when more than one man's sperm is in the reproductive tract of a woman (Shackelford, 2010). In order to fully appreciate what sperm competition means we need to put aside our socially constructed preoccupation with monogamy and our notions of acceptable sexual behavior. In human prehistory this may have been one of the most important behavioral/biological innovations for our species' long-term survival. For it is through sperm competition that the genetic compatibility of potential mates can be truly tested, not by making inferences about a man's health and suitability through his appearance or smell, but by the biochemical gauntlet sperm must run in order to fertilize the egg itself.

Like salmon returning from the ocean to spawn, swimming up rivers and streams to reach the waters where they were born years before, sperm must also make an arduous journey. Mature salmon must leap up waterfalls, pass through columns of bears waiting to snatch them from the water, fishermen with their lines and nets poised, to achieve their goal. Only the healthiest and fittest make the trip. The female reproductive tract is surprisingly not an environment conducive for sperm. High levels of acidity, a long tortuous journey against the pull of gravity, and the woman's immune system all combine to weed out the less healthy sperm (Ryan et al., 2010, p. 264–265). The few that make it to the egg are like the few salmon that arrive after a hard-fought journey upstream: the ones with the most suitable characteristics.

FIGURE 11-11. Running the gauntlet, the drive to reproduce is fraught with adversity.

And this is not the only reproductive adaptation that promotes the selection of sperm. Males are also equipped to aid their reproductive cause. The penis is more than just a DNA injector. It is shaped in such a way that during intercourse it creates a suction effect that draws out any semen that is already present in a woman's vaginal tract (Shackelford, 2010). From an evolutionary perspective, this adaptation would be highly advantageous in the competitive vaginal environment, since it would tend to enhance the reproductive success of males who have this characteristic, thus making their male offspring more likely to possess it as well. Thus the common shape of human penises reflects the sperm competition of the past.

8.

What are the consequences of sperm competition?

I cannot help but wonder if this internalized competition between males that took place within females in the form of sperm racing to fertilize a hard to reach egg was the crucial element that promoted a more peaceful, less openly combative in-group social environment for our ancestors. Among animals in which polygyny (one male mates with many females) is the reproductive strategy, males must establish dominance through violent competition with other males. Think about bighorn sheep ramming their heads together or male gorillas fighting it out. While in a setting in which females choose from among the males they deem most attractive, such a need to establish dominance and control over a mating group is not required. Add to this a selective process that happens after sex, not before it, and the result is a population of males who do not have to fight among themselves—and if they are never entirely sure of the paternity of the children around them, will always be at least minimally supportive of all young. After all, we know from our own time that from among the adults in children's lives, step parents are the most likely to act in ways that are not beneficial to them (Hrdy, 1999). Remove the certainty of step-parenthood and the hazard to stepchildren might be largely alleviated.

FIGURE 11-12. Children need a safe, supportive social environment.

The reproductive strategy of sperm competition within females very likely created a calmer social environment—another plus for children. Our close primate relatives, the peaceable bonobos, also utilize sperm competition (Ryan et al., 2010, p. 65–66), and their offspring enjoy a supportive social setting, quite unlike the young of animals who live among males who openly compete for females. In extreme cases, for example among lions, if the dominant males lose their standing, their replacements will slaughter all the cubs the former males fathered, which brings all the females under their control into sexual receptivity, thus ensuring all future offspring are theirs (Pusey et al., 1994). Such an arrangement, which puts enormous selective pressures on dominant males, females, and their offspring, is not an efficient one from the point of view offered by our social conventions. It is a strategy we would certainly regard as unacceptable.

FIGURE 11-13. New dominant male lions will kill all the offspring of the previous dominant male lions.

But nature is not concerned with what we think and feel about approaches to reproduction. What proves adaptive in a given environment, for the given time, is what natural forces select for. Nature does not make judgments in the way that we do. It simply acts.

9.

Is there any way we can make monogamy work?

. . . .

But we humans are conscious beings driven by often unconscious elements from our past. And the ideals by which we live and that structure our lives do not always correspond with the ancestral ways of life that still call to us across the eons. Is monogamy doomed? No, not at all. As pointed out before, we are not slaves to our predispositions. There is enormous variation among all of us. It is just that knowing what we are up against when we make monogamy a condition of a relationship is essential. Not only to do we need to acknowledge the difficulty it imposes on others, we need to be aware of how hard it is for us.

FIGURE 11-14. We are not slaves to our ancestral impulses.

Sex does not need to occupy such a central position in our lives. But let's be honest: we are programmed to engage in reproductive behavior, pure and simple. For most people, removing sex from its position in their lives is a hard pill to swallow. Indeed, without this characteristic our species would very likely have gone extinct long ago, you would not be reading these words, and I would never have written them. But with the low rates of infant mortality that medical science has made possible, combined with the ever-increasing cost of raising a child to maturity—roughly a quarter million dollars without college (CNBC. com, 2012)—it is clear that producing large numbers of descendents is not required nor is it financially practical anymore. As a result, sex has been largely divorced from reproduction in our times.

The larger question is, do we have to live in a state of repressed sexual tension in which our old tendencies and our relatively new social conventions vie for control of our behavior? This is no trivial question. The wreckage of countless marriages, shattered households, and traumatized childhoods are the frightful consequent harvest of this conflict. How many psychopathologies have their roots in formative years lived in the shadow of parental discord and continual conflict? How many young people have grown up feeling deep ambivalence about their own sexuality because of what they witnessed?

FIGURE 11-15. We have had to change quite a lot to live in this world.

As a species, we began to pay quite a price ten thousand years ago for a property-owning materialist settled way of life, and we are still making payments today. Perhaps this is a conundrum that will force us to develop new adaptations that will allow us the opportunity to live in accord with our nature and our nurture. This conflict may serve to generate completely new social constructions that will begin to address our human needs rather than force us to bow to the needs of civilization. After all, does humanity serve civilization or does civilization serve humanity? Or we will continue to repress our evolved behavioral predispositions (with its terrible cost to individuals and to the young) until over many generations it becomes naturally selected out of our behavioral repertoire by the dictates of culture?

10.

What are we really looking for in our relationships?

A final note concerning sexual fidelity and interpersonal ties: all individuals, regardless of their gender, feel a rush of excitement at the beginning of new relationships. The sky seems bluer, the air is charged with a static energy that makes every touch electric, flavors are more intense, and feelings are more vivid. We feel alive. In the first weeks and months of such a relationship, the person we are involved with seems special and unique. But be aware that the heightened consciousness that accompanies this period is also the product of our biochemistry. As wonderful as the other person may be, the "aura" surrounding that individual is in our hormone-soaked brains.

If you find yourself constantly drawn to new people and have difficulty staying in a relationship for any length of time, it may help to ask yourself if you are simply searching for that one perfect partner—or if you are simply addicted to the "high" that accompanies new relationships.

FIGURE 11-16. Are we searching for that one true love, or are we in love with being in love?

It is difficult to take in all this information about our ancestral nature, our personal behavioral predispositions, and our socially constructed expectations and come to a conclusion about how we should manage our ties with others. Standing in our own shoes, let alone someone else's, and surveying the situation that finds us painted into a corner does not easily resolve anything. Perhaps the trick comes not in finding the right person in the world outside ourselves, but in finding a balance between what we need and what we want within ourselves. Then when the paint has dried we can objectively consider the conventions it imposes and make choices that we can truly live with.

MONEY AND THE GENDERS

 11.

Why is money such a confusing, contentious issue for so many people?

. . . .

As much as issues relating to sexual fidelity are a source of considerable conflict between gendered individuals, the matter of money also tends to complicate interpersonal relationships. The root of this problem stems largely from its novelty. That is to say, we humans did not evolve with it as a feature of the ancestral environment.

FIGURE 11-17. What captures our attention?

Think for a moment about the typical news of the day. A scandalous affair uncovered, a violent act of terrorism, a war brewing in some far-flung part of the world, political arguments about abortion rights, gun control, gay marriage—these are the things that tend to capture our attention. For most of us, a sudden spike in the bond yield on the debt of a sovereign nation, registers as a non-event.

Yet the decline of confidence in a nation's ability to pay its bills (which is what a sudden rise in bond yields usually indicates) could affect jobs, credit card interest rates, taxes, retirement funds, educational opportunities, and much more (Ferguson, 2008). These are things that can profoundly affect us, and the communities in which we live. Why then does news of a scandalous affair (which is extremely unlikely to directly affect us) stir such interest? Why does a conflict on the other side of the world catch our notice? Why does financial news tend to bore most people?

FIGURE 11-18. Why do we care about money so much yet understand so little about it?

Sex and violence—they are the staples of entertainment. And as much as we may decry them as signs of vulgarity and sensationalism, the reason they are part of so many of the movies and shows we tend to view, is that they light up our brains. Sex and violence are arousing because in the ancestral environment they were matters of life and death. Sex and violence have a long track record with our species.

We are certainly fascinated by money, but how many times have you heard someone say, "I am terrible at managing it." You maybe have read about individuals who win a huge lottery jackpot or inherit a vast sum of money, only to spend their windfall in a year or two and end up filing for bankruptcy. You would think that with all the financially savvy people in Wall Street there would never be billion dollar losses. Considering all the experienced economic advisors who occupy positions of influence in government, you would think there would never be recessions or depressions. And finally with the view that capitalists have of the perfect rationality and efficiency of markets, you would never imagine even the possibility of any financial hiccups in the global economy. Events like those that began in 2008, which rocked the world and affected billions of people, seem so contrary to what we would expect in light of our supposed concern for money.

There are lots of reasons offered for why we often find ourselves in trouble with money, but the most fundamental one is that we were not evolved to deal with it. As a species, we do not have a long history of living with it as a force that orders our lives. Females and males inflect their ancestral behavioral predispositions onto money matters and often discover that they come into conflict with each other in the process.

Like monogamy and fidelity, we did not evolve as a species with the social construct of money as a defining element in our lives. The guardian of eternity frame of reference that tends to order the female mindset inclines women to view resources as assets that can potentially enhance personal well-being and the long-term survival of children. As citizens of the present, the male outlook tends to focus on short-term gains as a means to attract potential mates. These differing perspectives tend to shape priorities and affect the way in which the genders respond to the presence or absence of money. And like the socially constructed use of monogamy as a criterion for the stability and durability of a relationship, we have come to use money as a measure of the suitability of potential mates. But it begs the question, is this a sound way of judging individuals?

FIGURE 11-20. Do we understand what these pieces of plastic really mean?

For as we have seen in the economic tumult of recent years, wealth by itself does not ensure well-being. It is how funds are deployed that determines long-term security not the aggregate amount itself. A person who has a million dollars but owes two million is far worse off than a person who has ten thousand

FIGURE 11-19. Why is money so often a contentious issue for couples?

dollars and owes nothing. Yet the luster of the former individual still outshines the latter. The person with a net worth of minus one million dollars is still more attractive than the person with a net worth of positive ten thousand dollars. We cannot easily get our minds around the real meaning of money's value (Lonergan, 2009). And how many individuals have been deceived, by this lack of experience with the social construction of money, into entering into a relationship with an individual who is actually deeply indebted?

12.

How can we realistically live with the complexities of money and relationships?

. . . .

So how do we navigate the added complication of money piled on monogamy to our relationships? Education helps. Though we may tell ourselves that we can override our impulse to engage in non-monogamous sexual activity and that we can resist the itch for uncontrolled self-destructive expenditure, it is important to understand that both these elements are new to our species. We do not have any evolved behavioral predispositions that can guide our behavior on these matters, which means that we must rely upon our ability to learn. Unlike our reflexive response to danger or our innate ability to discern the genetic suitability of potential mates, monogamy and money require the active use of our intelligence and our cognitive ability to judge, from situation to situation, the appropriate manner in which to proceed. The old recommendation to "follow your heart," which can be thought of as an invitation to fallback on ancestral impulses or to engage in non-cognitive intuitive processing of information, may not yield the optimal responses in relationships structured on capital and faithfulness.

FIGURE 11-21. We are far removed from the ancestral setting in which our behavioral predispositions evolved.

The behavioral predispositions we carry within us were shaped and tested on a windswept savanna long ago—an environment very different from our own. We need to make behavioral accommodations for the contrast that arises from the world in which we currently live and the one from which our kind originated. An active concern for long-term positive personal goals that ensure healthy outcomes, rather than a fixation on momentary gratification without regard for consequences, may offer a general approach from which to gain insight on how to navigate the complexities of the present. For males and females, this means being able to appreciate the needs and desires of the people in their lives and come to some equitable and reasonable resolution of these competing forces. Though such a way of determining how to respond to our surroundings may seem to run counter to the prevailing attitude of personal instant gratification, it may impart some broader meaning to the often confusing nature of money and consumption in the twenty-first century.

THE HISTORICAL CONTEXT OF GENDER EQUALITY

13.

Feminism and gender studies.

. . . .

In the last decades of the previous century, gender studies tended to gravitate toward the issue of women's rights and the struggle for liberation from the patriarchy that was perceived to control much of the Western world. The view presented from this interpretation of the interaction of the genders was of a controlling and repressive force that actively worked to prevent large segments of humanity from realizing their potential and achieving individual autonomy. Some commentators who addressed gender issues in this manner claimed that males and females were so different that they were essentially separate species—even metaphorically from different planets (Gray, 1994). On the other hand, some were proponents of the notion that the differences between females and males were not real but were socially constructed notions generated to maintain and further the dominance of one gender over another (Fausto-Sterling, 1985). Others went further and argued for a world free of one particular gender because behavioral findings indicated that gender was responsible for much of the unproductive and destructive activities that burdened whole societies (Gold, 2009). Far too much power, went the prevailing argument, lay in the hands of one gender, and the consequences of this imbalance resulted in costs to the individual and to the larger world, which could not and should not be borne any longer.

FIGURE 11-22. The struggle for equality has a long history.

As noted in Chapter 1, biological and epigenetic perspectives on gender issues were deemed essentialist. In other words, biology and genetics presented a view of the genders that were judged too deterministic, because the standard interpretation of findings derived from these approaches was that they rigidly dictated male and female behavior, and could be used to justify the power imbalance between the genders. The condemnation of essentialism reflected the desire for the belief that our biological natures contributed nothing to our personal qualities and potential. Indeed, some denied the existence of an inherent human nature. The orthodox social constructivist view was that we were all what we were taught to be—male and female were merely socially constructed gender concepts that could be altered in ways to ensure that children with XX and XY chromosomes could be taught to be whatever their parents chose or what was pronounced socially acceptable. If taken to its logical conclusion, it could be argued that there was nothing fundamentally male about XY chromosomes that functioned in the usual way and nothing essentially female about XX chromosomes. With the proper upbringing, any child could be made into whatever gender was desired.

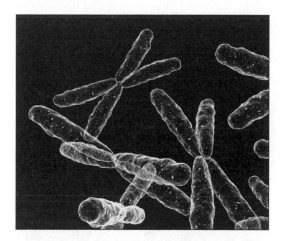

FIGURE 11-23. Are chromosomes really irrelevant to the matter of gender?

In such a setting, many males found gender studies during this period a perilous field, one in which they felt they were not welcomed to participate unless they stuck to the socially constructed position that dominated the discipline.

However, there were some feminists who realized that the conventional portrayal of all men as intentional oppressors of women and other gender groups was not entirely accurate. Some came to the realization that most males were subject to the same imbalances of power in the social environment as women (Faludi, 1999).

14.

How does feminism fit into the broad scheme of social change that has shaped our world?

Indeed, it is instructive to once again take a step back and take in a broader historical view. While women were fighting for their rights—for the right to vote, for the right to own and inherit property, for the power to control their own destinies during the nineteenth and twentieth centuries, other groups were also engaged with the struggle for equal rights. The Civil Rights movement, in which people of color sought to achieve equitable legal status and social justice, occurred during much the same time as the various women's rights movements. The effort among lesbians, gay men, bisexuals, and transsexuals for recognition and acceptance was an important twentieth century social movement as well. The rights of children, of individuals with certain medical conditions and disabilities, of ethnic groups, of veterans, of the poor and the homeless, have been the focus and concern of many other social movements. Advocates have argued for the well-being of animals and for the long-term health of the biosphere. In the wider historical context, the Women's movement can be understood as a part of a larger stream of social consciousness that sought to redress longstanding injustices and imbalances (Hirsch et al., 1993).

FIGURE 11-24. The signing of the Declaration of Independence was one of many historical efforts to correct the imbalances of power.

But if we look further into the past, there have been similar efforts to achieve these same goals by other groups. In 1789, the citizens of France rose up against the nobility to the rallying cry of liberty, equality, and brotherhood. In the American Revolution of 1776, the colonial yoke of Britain was violently cast aside. In the signing of Magna Carta in 1215, the first formal effort to limit the power of the king of England, was made law by consent. These were each in their own ways great struggles for liberation from the prevailing culturally created systems that locked people into roles and relationships that had come to be found unacceptable (Roberts, 1997).

There are many ways to categorize the various struggles of countless individuals to correct the imbalance between those with power and those without. From contemporary concerns about the treatment of the animals we eat to the long-sought universality of human rights, the drive to empower all people, and more recently, all Earthly life, has been, and continues to be, an arduous task.

By taking that step back and encompassing a wider perspective, it is possible to perceive a broad trend that has been sweeping through our species. All the people throughout history, who have engaged in the struggle for justice, equality, as well as rights and responsibilities, are part of a great wave that continues to advance across the story of our species. The effort to put right the disparities that exist between the genders is part of this long process.

BEYOND MERE TOLERANCE

15.

How does sexual orientation relate to the broad scheme of gender issues?

· ·

We currently live amid a tempest of competing social constructions that are vying for dominance. Nowhere is this more evident than in the variety of social responses to the issues of lesbian (female-female sexuality), gay (male-male sexuality), bisexual (male-male and male-female sexuality), transgender (individuals who are oriented to gender identities that differ from the one to which they were assigned), and transsexual (individuals who have either altered or intend to alter their physiology to better match their desired sex) rights. The degree to which some groups of individuals argue for the repression of what they regard

as aberrant gender and sexual orientations, reflects the threat that the push for open acceptance of individual differences poses to traditional social conventions.

There are many facets to this issue. It is by no means a simple matter.

FIGURE 11-25. There are many different views about sexuality and many opposing voices.

16.

What does biology tell us about diversity in sexual orientation?

· ·

From a biological essentialist frame of reference, variation is always present in any given population of individuals. Indeed, variation is a vital ingredient in the survival characteristics of any species. When environmental change occurs, such differences offer the possibility of adaptation that may prove advantageous in the long run. Since it is impossible to predict change, then selective criteria cannot be anticipated, which means no one can say with any certainty which variations are more desirable than others. In a nutshell, differences in sex and gender as well as sexual orientations, are from a biological point of view just that— different. And that is not a negative thing from a biological standpoint; on the contrary, it can be a highly beneficial quality.

If we remove the socially constructed bias that tends to color interpretations of biological essentialism, which places such priority on personal reproduction, and view sexuality as an element in human social contact that enhances group cohesion, a different light is cast on lesbian, gay and bisexual orientations. In other words, rather than consider sexuality as a means to achieve individual genetic survival by producing offspring and instead think about sexual contact as a means to facilitate group survival—which is certainly apt since we are social beings—by enhancing the variety of ties between individual group members, non-reproductive sexual orientations become important adaptations. As discussed in previous chapters, sex is more than a means to produce offspring. It is the means to foster group bonds and maintain a social setting conducive to raising healthy children. From this operational view of sex and sexuality, lesbian women, gay men, and bisexual individuals are essential parts of any large survival-oriented group. If this is the case, then the presence of individuals with non-reproductive sexual orientations in any population of humans should be commonplace and happen as a fairly consistent percentage of the total group population. In Chapter 8, it was noted that a bit less than ten percent of any group of humans is homosexual.

FIGURE 11-26. Why is it that we tend to disregard what statistics tell us about sexual orientation?

The fact that such a consistent proportion of individuals are gay suggests that this is an adaptation to the ancestral environment. In human prehistory, it may well be that those groups that did not have a certain percentage of homosexual members did not do as well as those that did. Over countless millennia, this varied population mix may have been selected for as an advantageous characteristic that persists into our time.

Consequently, if we adopt a broader criterion from which to apply biological views of sexuality, there is no indication that lesbian, gay, and bisexual orientations are in any way detrimental to the well-being of our species. Indeed, it may be a vital adaptation.

17.

What is the epigenetic perspective on sexual orientation diversity?

From an epigenetic perspective, it could be argued that different sexual orientations are merely the natural consequence of a species responding to the demands of the environment in which it evolved. The interaction of circumstance with inherent adaptive qualities produces our gender and sexual characteristics. If there is one thing that can be clearly discerned from examining gender matters through the lens of history, it is that we humans have had to make significant adjustments and adaptations both to changes in the natural world and to the new conditions we have created for ourselves. Socially constructed nurture interacting with our evolutionarily derived nature may well be the source from which most, if not all, gender and sexual variation issue. We have already seen how the social constructions of civilization have forced the repression and modification of ancient sexual impulses both in males and females and how the more recent technological and socioeconomic innovations of the last few decades have fueled the emergence of new relationship configurations (serial monogamy, blended families, etc.). Perhaps, from this point of view, the liberation of the individual that is afforded by the new social constructions have simply removed the repressive shackles that have forced so many to hide their inherent sexual and gender orientations for so long. Or it could be argued that the tensions of the new world unfolding before us are the trigger for genetic responses that underlie diverse orientations.

Either way, negatively stigmatizing the individual who is different is neither logical nor ethical in view of the epigenetic forces that tend to shape personal qualities.

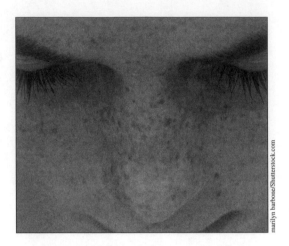

FIGURE 11-27. What is normal and abnormal today? Is it just a social construction?

18.

What does social constructivism reveal about sexual orientation diversity?

The view the social constructivist frame of reference offers is itself highly diverse. There are so many social constructions that order our interpretation of non-traditional sexual and gender orientations that it is not possible to make any generalizations. There are social constructions that condemn lesbian, gay, bisexual, transgender, and transsexual orientations; there are social constructions that are accepting of these manifestations of sexuality and gender. In the case of intersex individuals, for example, there is the view held by some in the medical community that if a child is born with ambiguous genitalia, that child should undergo corrective surgery to construct a penis, clitoris, or vagina that is deemed by prevailing social tastes acceptable. Others argue that the problem lies not with the intersex child but with the social constructions that judge this child's physical characteristics "abnormal."

The application of the essential social constructivist frame of reference is that homosexuality is a product of the prevailing cultural context and that the individual can choose to be straight or gay. In other words, lesbian, gay, and bisexual orientations are the products of learning and conditioning, and have no basis in biology. That varying sexual behavior occurs in other species of animals, and has been a feature of human cultures for as far back as we are able to discern, may be regarded by strict social constructivist thinking as just our socially constructed interpretation of behavioral phenomena.

The terms lesbian, gay, bisexual, transgender, transsexual, and heterosexual are themselves socially defined and constructed categories. It may well be the fact these classifications exist is more an indication of our tendency to categorize individuals in order to determine in-group and out-group status than anything else. Chimpanzees and bonobos probably do not apply such labels to themselves, but the reality is that they do engage in a variety of non-reproductive sexual behavior. Indeed, much of their sexual behavior is apparently for non-reproductive purposes—and this is certainly true for humans as well.

So, is there a definitive answer that can be derived from social constructivism? Yes, but any answer is conditionally correct only in the context from which it originates. Outside of a given culture, the norms so stridently defended as right may not be appropriate at all. And in view of the diversity of social constructions that inform our current cultural context, there is obviously no definitive answer that is forth coming. A kind of relativistic fog hangs over our worldview when we turn to social constructivism as a frame of reference. Many people, on all sides of these matters, find relativism disorienting, but it is a result of the lack of consensus about social constructions that are used to define sexual behavior, gender, and sexual orientations, not these matters themselves.

Is there any way of resolving this issue?

. . . .

History shows that men, women, and intersex individuals with varying sexual orientations have always been part of every human community. The implication of this fact is these behavioral characteristics are an adaptive feature of our species that have been honed over millions of years by the forces of natural selection. The conflict lies then not in our biology or our genetics but in our social constructions. Perhaps the most terrible personal tragedy of this conflict rests in the psyche of the lesbian, gay, bisexual, transgender, or transsexual person who cannot accept his or her (or whichever personal pronoun is applicable) own orientation because of the influence of social constructions that have shaped personal perceptions. The personal nightmare of being unable to accept the self is a terrible condition that arises from the mismatch between the qualities of the self and the conventions of the surrounding social context.

From a broader perspective, we need to get past this socially constructed notion that tolerance is an adequate response to diversity. Tolerance has become synonymous with "I don't care," as a kind of a very low-calorie version of acceptance. If the achievement of a truly peaceful, egalitarian social environment is to ever occur, we are going to have to learn to view all the different ways of being human in a positive light, and come to appreciate all the variations of gender, sex, and sexuality.

THE MATTER OF CIVILIZATION

How does gender fit into the scheme of hierarchy in civilization?

. . . .

FIGURE 11-28. What was life like before our ancestors created all this?

Imagine what it was like to live as most of our ancestors did before the rise of civilization and the establishment of the first cities. Though this way of life may seem remote from our own experience, many aspects of the nomadic tribal lifestyle still order our minds. You may recall from previous chapters that most of us can comfortably remember the faces and names of about a hundred and fifty people. According to the evolutionary psychological view of human behavior, this ability is a holdover from the way our distant foremothers and forefathers lived. The fact that we are inclined to want to live with dignity and with some measure of equality is a reflection of the social structure within which we evolved.

Much as in nomadic hunter-gatherer societies today, there were inequalities that existed between individuals in these groupings. Older men and women were revered for their knowledge and experience. The man who was a skilled hunter was regarded as a vital member of the tribe. The woman who had deep knowledge of plant life and their medicinal properties was also looked upon with great favor. The shaman, the spiritual leader among hunting and gathering people, was also an important tribal member. But no matter how exalted any individual might be, the difference between the status of the highest and the lowest person in a tribal grouping was insignificant compared to the distance that came with the rise of civilization.

For with the advent of agriculture and a settled way of life, the cities that coalesced out of a need for protection from those groups that still used raiding as a way to secure resources saw a much more elaborate hierarchy develop. Cities required leaders to maintain order. Civic heads organized all the activities that made it possible for such settlements to function, from matters as mundane as where the garbage was dumped to issues as significant as the law, taxation, and citizen participation in the defense of the city. The marketplaces that sprang from the trade in food and clothing within the first cities needed organizers. The merchants, the moneylenders, and the currency exchangers all added tier upon tier of complexity to the life of the city. The religious centers that emerged in city centers, which in ancient civilizations affirmed the right of rulers to hold office and to wield power, saw the formation of a special class of individuals whose lives were devoted entirely to spiritual matters. Priests and priestesses and other functionaries presided over ritual and ceremony. All this and much more sprang from what we would regard as small villages composed largely of hovels and mud huts.

Over time cities grew into city-states, provinces, and then nations. Two thousand years ago you could call yourself a citizen of Rome if you lived within the area that extended from Britain and Spain in the west, east to Iraq, Northern Africa and Egypt to the south, and to the borders of Central Asia to the north. In a few millennia after the formation of the first tiny town somewhere in what is now Iraq, the Roman Empire extended across what was then the entire known world.

Two thousand years ago, the social hierarchical distance between the loftiest, most powerful individual of Rome, the emperor (though as noted in Chapter 7, the real power in the imperial family may have sometimes been his wife) and the poorest person in the empire had grown enormously since the transition from a nomadic tribal way of life. The sheer size of human organization had grown from tribes that comprised a scant hundred and fifty individuals to empires populated by tens of millions.

If we conceive of the interconnected world we live in today as a global community, the distance between the most powerful person and the most impoverished dispossessed individual on the planet is even greater still. While the former can literally summon the attention and resources of whole nations and alter the destinies of billions of people, the latter anonymously struggles to have any control over his or her meager existence. The potential magnitude of the difference in status between these two end points in the current social hierarchy is incomparably greater today than it was before the dawn of human civilization ten millennia ago.

FIGURE 11-29. One consequence of civilization is the huge distance between the top and the bottom of the social hierarchy.

For our ancient forebears the social distance between the top of the social hierarchy and its bottom was insignificant. The leaders of the tribal family were elder men and women whose standard of living was little better than the lowest person on the social totem pole. Indeed, from the viewpoint of the tribal pecking order, the lowest person may have been a child whose survival would very likely have been held to be as important as the survival of its eldest member. Consequently, our ancient evolved outlook of our place in social structures was one in which we all perceived ourselves as living in a fairly egalitarian setting. In human prehistory, you were likely to personally know the most highly positioned person in the hierarchy—he or she may have been a relative. This is quite a contrast to the condition in which we live today.

Though we are apt to believe that social mobility—the possibility that any given individual can, through personal initiative, rise to a higher station in the social hierarchy—is a recent development that came with capitalism and democracy, the reality is that the status of our hunter-gatherer ancestors was much more fluid than our own. A person born as the most junior member of an ancient nomad community could, over time and with luck, become the head of a family or the leader of a tribe, simply by surviving into old age. The likelihood of any given individual reaching the stratospheric heights of power and status by simply reaching an advanced age is vanishingly small today.

Indeed, it could be argued that the reason we regard the ability to be upwardly socially mobile as a unique quality of our times stems from the fact that for the past ten thousand years, since the beginning of civilization, individuals have been far less able to change their place in the social hierarchy than in the mostly forgotten prehistoric past.

To study the life of the average man, woman, or child, from the time of the first civilizations to the present is a disturbing undertaking. Poverty, disease, hunger, and violence were constant companions in the lives of the vast majority of humanity. Both males and females were subject to rape and sexual exploitation. Men were obligated in many countries to answer the call of their masters and spiritual leaders, and provide the bulk of the fighting force of armies. They were the foot soldiers that were the fodder for spear and sword, musket, cannon and landmines. In the Western world, they were the throngs that sacrificed their lives for the imperial ambitions of kings and queens. For Rome, for the medieval crusades, for the ever-restless nation-states, and later empires that jostled for power across the Eurasian landmass, numberless anonymous men fought and died for crown and for country. This condition reached its apex in the last century when three hundred thousand men, women, and children died on average every day during the years of the Second World War (*The Economist*, 2012).

On the prehistoric grass-covered savannas or on the frozen tundra of previous ice ages, when a group of humans raided another group, there was no legal recourse available to those who had been victimized. No law enforcement existed to maintain the peace, protect individuals, and uphold property rights. No formal laws existed. For our nomad ancestors two alternatives were open to them, raid or be raided. If an individual was killed during an attack, no perpetrator was arrested, put on trial, judged, sentenced, and then incarcerated or executed. Revenge came either immediately after the killing or sought later. If an individual was abducted during a raid, that person became part of the raiding party's booty. There was no legal recourse for victims to compensated them for suffering and losses. The old saying "might makes right," was the closest thing to the rule of law between groups in prehistory.

FIGURE 11-30. There was no legal recourse available to our ancestors who lived during the last ice age.

Among many of the early civilizations, if a member of the nobility killed a slave or a peasant, it was usually a matter of little consequence. Slaves were property that could be bought, sold, and disposed of at the discretion of the owner (Veyne, 1987). Peasants were not seen as individual people, but as a class of humans that counted for little beyond a labor force in the fields where crops were grown. Disposing of one was no different than swatting a fly.

Until very recently, during times of war, manpower was not thought to be composed of individuals. An army is a single unit. New recruits are trained to put aside their sense of individuality and to conceive of themselves as merely part of a larger unity working as one for a single goal. The needs of the lone person are of no consequence in this context.

21.

What is the pivotal socially constructed concept that underlies the world we know?

Indeed, the concept of individualism itself is only a couple of centuries old. For nearly all of human history, unless a person was a member of the highest reaches of the social hierarchy, a man or woman was not conceived of as a person with rights and protections under a legal system that acknowledged his or her existence.

To put it simply, during the history of civilization the average individual did not matter until fairly recently. Our personal concerns, our individual needs and wants, did not figure into the grand scheme of civilizations through most of the past.

Yet as appalling as these historical realities are, there is a broader trend that can be made out against this backdrop of violence, murder, and social unrest. Gradually, the importance and the power of the lone individual person, irrespective of gender, have been growing. Technological and social innovations have brought improvements to standards of living and have empowered billions of females, males, and intersex individuals in the developed parts of the world to the level we currently enjoy today. The hope is that someday all the people of the world will know similar conditions in their lives.

We are living in a very unusual period.

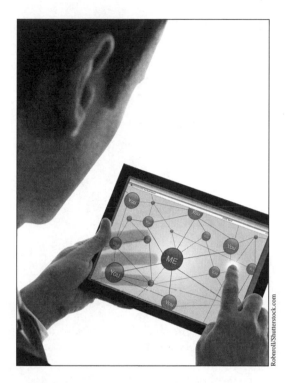

FIGURE 11-31. The power we have at our fingertips is unique in human history.

Think about the power you wield today. As an educated, literate individual reading these words, you probably know how to access the databases of the world for information. You can purchase goods made on the other side of the world. You can talk to nearly anyone within reach of contemporary communications technology. Transportation systems can whisk you to any point on the planet in a day, at hundreds of miles per hour. The electricity that lights your residence, runs your appliances, and powers your electronics would have seemed like magic to your ancestors whether they lived two million or two hundred years ago. Behind these tangible elements that empower you, there is a legal system and a body of law that in theory recognizes your personal right to live your life as you see fit (provided you do not adversely affect others), and to varying degrees protects you from the arbitrary behavior of others. It is not so easy for others to kill an individual now without having to face significant consequences that are enforced by the concept that no one is above the law.

This is not to say that we live in a completely fair and equitable cultural context. The fact that social movements still exist working to remedy imbalances and injustices is an indication that we are not yet close to achieving an entirely equal society. Yet we humans are slowly making our way forward, and in light of our recent history, we have made some progress.

For many who live in the developed nations of the world, each person has access to power and to capabilities no king or queen of the pre-industrial past could have imagined. The problem is that the summit of the social hierarchy has not remained static over the centuries but has continued to rise in potency and extent. A medieval monarch would arguably regard present day national and business leaders as wielders of power and resources he or she would attribute to the gods. And as a consequence, the distance between the average individual and a current head of state is incomparably greater than the loftiest prehistoric leader was to an average hunter-gatherer.

To realize the material standards of living that we enjoy today, we have come a long way. We have subjugated ourselves to a vast social hierarchy. Women have, as noted in Chapter 8, significantly altered their sexuality and their sexual behavior in response to the requirements of materialism and inheritance, with its priority on knowing the paternity of potential heirs. This obsession with reproduction has also placed great burdens on women and until recently has relegated females to roles largely limited by the demands of having children. It has also cast a stigmatizing shadow upon non-reproductive gender and sexual orientations. Individuals who were not perceived to be part of the reproductive in-group were consigned to a peripheral social status or worse. For males, the concern for power and resources in an ever increasingly hierarchical socioeconomic environment has also stifled their development and narrowed the field of their gender and sexual orientations.

Perhaps the principal questions, then, are how far will we bend our evolved gender tendencies in order to conform to the requirements of a social setting that has only recently emerged? How much of the conflict between the sexes and the genders—between males, females, and intersex individuals—is due to meaningful differences between individuals, and how much is actually the product of the new circumstances we find ourselves in? By this I mean, could it be that much of the conflict that seems to arise from differences between us are in reality a consequence of the novel settings that have come to order our lives?

FIGURE 11-32. How will we shape our world in the future?

The natural world of pre-agricultural Earth was a paradise for our prehistoric ancestors. Our species lived in harmony with this ancient Eden because we were an evolved part of it. When we ate of the fruit of knowledge, we embarked upon a developmental journey that carried our kind to new ways of living, thinking, feeling, and behaving. Our personal interests changed in a changing world—and perhaps an inevitable result of these changes was the conflict engendered by gender.

REFERENCES

CNBC.com (2012, May 5). "The inflation of life—cost of raising a child has soared." Retrieved from http://www.cnbc.com/id/46797268/

The Economist. (2012, June 9). "Counting the cost." vol 403, no 8788, p. 87.

Faludi, S. (1999). *Stiffed: the betrayal of the american man.* New York: William Morrow.

Fausto-Sterling, A. (1994). *Myths of gender: biological theories about women and men.* New York: Basic Books.

Ferguson, N. (2008). *The ascent of money: a financial history of the world.* New York: Penguin. pp. 65–118.

Fischer, A. & Stepleton, H. (2008). *The science of sex appeal.* [DVD] United States: Discovery Communications, LLC.

Freud, S. (1989). "Some psychical consequences of the anatomical distinction between the sexes." In Gay, P. ed. *The freud reader.* New York: W. W. Norton. pp. 670–678.

Gold, T. (2009, July 8). "Would a world without men be so bad?" *The Guardian.* G2, p. 6.

Gray, J. (1992). *Men are from mars, women are from venus: the classic guide to understanding the opposite sex.* New York: HarperCollins Publishers.

Hirsch, E. D., Kett, J. F. & Trefil, J. (1993). *The dictionary of cultural literacy, 2nd ed.* Boston: Houghton Mifflin.

Hrdy, S. B. (1999). *Mother nature: a history of mothers, infants, and natural selection.* New York: Pantheon. p. 236.

Lonergan, E. (2009). *Money*. Durham, UK: Acumen. pp. 50–53.

Pusey, A. E. & Packer, C. (1994) "Infanticide in lions." From Parmigiani, S. & von Saal, F. S. eds. *Infanticide and parental care*. Chur, Switzerland.

Roberts, J. M. (1997). *The penguin history of the world*. London: Penguin Books.

Roughgarden, J. (2009). *Evolution's rainbow: diversity, gender, and sexuality in nature and people*. Berkeley: University of California Press.

Ryan, C. & Jethá, C. (2010). *Sex at dawn: how we mate, why we stray, and what it means for modern relationships*. New York: Harper Perennial.

Saad, G. (2011). *The consuming instinct: what juicy burgers, ferraris, pornography, and gift giving reveal about human nature*. Amherst, New York: Prometheus Books. p. 91.

Shackelford, T. K. & Goetz, A. T. (2010). "Adaptation to sperm competition in humans." From Goldberg, W. A., ed. *Current directions in gender psychology*. Boston: Allyn & Bacon. pp. 148–154.

Sternberg, R. J. (1986). "Liking vs. loving: a comparative evaluation of theories. *Psychological Bulletin*. Vol. 102. Pp. 331–345.

Veyne, P. ed. (1987). *A history of private life: from pagan rome to byzantium*. Cambridge, Massachusetts: Belknap. pp. 51–70.

Name   Date

1. What is the difference between the "individualistic" approach to survival and the "group-centered" approach to survival?

2. How did the development of a settled way of life ten thousand years ago change the relationship between men and women, and in particular, how did this development affect female sexuality?

3. How did the more recent monetized approach to personal survival affect relationships between men and women?

4. What is meant by reproductive competition that occurs *after* sex instead of *before* it?

5. Why do we care so much about money but have such a difficult time managing it?

6. How does the female outlook on money tend to differ from the male outlook on money? Why is this critical?

7. What does "follow your heart" really mean? And why is it not always a good guide for making decisions?

8. Why do social constructivists condemn biological essentialism?

9. How does feminism fit into the broader scheme of Western history?

10. What does the biological essentialist frame of reference say about lesbian, gay, and bisexual orientations?

11. What does epigenetics say about lesbian, gay, and bisexual orientations?

12. How does social constructivism view lesbian, gay, and bisexual sexual orientations?

13. How did the relative social hierarchical position of the average individual change with the advent of civilization ten millennia ago?

14. During most of the last ten thousand years, did the average man have much control over his own life? Did the average woman?

15. What is the pivotal socially constructed concept that underlies the world we live in today?

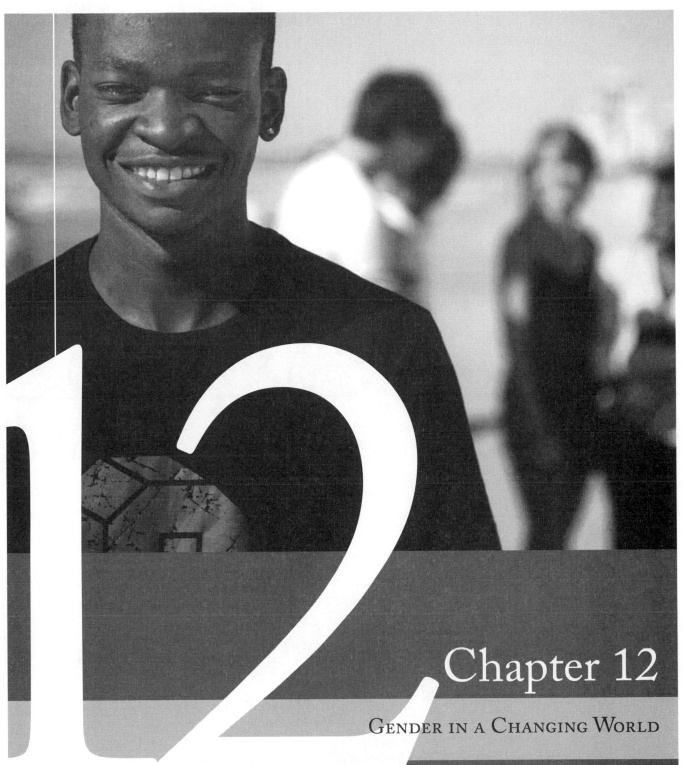

Chapter 12

GENDER IN A CHANGING WORLD

Juriah Mosin/Shutterstock.com;
Julien Tromeur/Shutterstock.com;
Shutterstock.com

UNINTENDED CONSEQUENCES

The economic downturn that began in late 2007, which we commonly refer to as the Great Recession, was one of many occurrences that contributed to the sense that the world around us is changing rapidly. The Presidential election of 2008, in which the first African American was chosen to occupy the highest office in the nation, was another signal event of change. The European debt crisis and the rise of China as a great power each altered our view of the world. The growing penetration of technology into our personal lives coupled with the loss of privacy and the increasing difficulty of maintaining control of our personal information are all new developments that have no precedent in our collective past.

FIGURE 12-1. Perhaps the most profound changes are the ones that won't be found in the pages of newspapers.

These are the obvious alterations to our perceptions and understanding of the world. But arguably, the most significant changes are ones that we cannot readily read as headlines or news updates. We ourselves are being altered by the changes occurring all around us.

The social aspect of gender means that though we are born intersex, female, or male, and our behavioral characteristics are nudged along by predispositions we inherited from our long-dead ancestors, how we are defined as individuals in the social setting that surrounds and informs us is increasingly shaped by culture. And as much as the old ways of life reach out of the past to influence current social constructions, the disruptive quality of technological and social innovation tends to push the older conventions in new epigenetic directions. This is certainly evident when it comes to gender issues.

What is definitively masculine behavior today? What is characteristically feminine anymore? Being androgynous, that is, having both male and female traits but not being distinctively one gender or another, is it becoming more acceptable? It is a confusing period in human history to be a gendered individual.

For better or worse, we once had clearly defined roles for being either male or female. There may have been ancient pre-agricultural societies that recognized intersex individuals, but for the most part the adage, "men were men and women were women," was the narrow norm for millions of years. Our biological nature once dictated our roles and our behavior. Now science, technology, economics, and new social constructions have largely swept aside the boundaries nature once imposed on us, and rigid gender roles have gone with them.

1.

Think about how historical developments have altered gender roles.

. . . .

The development of farming and of settled ways of life ended the old nomadic hunter-gatherer way of life for most people. The need for men to be fearless hunters of big game disappeared. For women, the habits of farming did not differ greatly from gathering. The invention of money and the appearance of markets made the risky habit of raiding less and less attractive. Men were increasingly not required to be active defenders of their households, nor was it as profitable to be a marauder anymore. Women and their children benefited from a safer, more stable environment. Interpersonal relationships changed to suit the requirements of materialism and the need to know the ancestry of offspring. Sexuality changed, and monogamy became the accepted norm in many money and market ordered cultures. The advances in labor that came with the application of power sources like fossil fuels, nuclear, and now renewable energy sources that began with the Industrial Revolution in eighteenth century England made brute physical strength unnecessary. Thousands of laboring men were no longer needed to build a road or a dam or a port now, just some fossil fuel-powered machines operated by trained individuals can do the job better, faster and more safely. Mechanization has made male physical strength increasingly irrelevant.

FIGURE 12-2. Machines are making physical strength meaningless in the workplace.

There is a certain irony in the progression of technological and social innovations that have changed the way we humans live. Though women tend to be more adept at dealing with change, the most fundamental, far-reaching modifications have had a greater effect on the roles that have informed the lives of males (Faludi, 1999). During the first two years of the Great Recession the American economy was in decline, though payrolls for both men and women declined sharply, males lost far more jobs than females (*The Economist*, 2011). The emphasis that technology places on communication skills and multi-tasking tends to favor attributes that women are more likely to possess. To put it simply, the more we have materially progressed, the more the abilities and tendencies males are more apt to possess have tended to be less needed.

But as transformative as the applications of new technologies and social innovations have been to men and women in the workplace, a far greater change is occurring within us. Our worldview is morphing.

2.

How have recent social developments affected your outlook for the future? Is your gender a factor?

. . . .

ALL YOU NEED IS MONEY—AND MARKETS?

In the early 1960s, the British rock band the Beatles declared in their similarly titled song that love was all that was required. The sentiment they expressed occurred at the cusp of a profound change that swept through Western civilization. For while we humans have been happily consuming the fruits of the marketplace since the rise of civilization a few thousand years ago, the late twentieth-century saw an explosion of mass-produced goods and services, accompanied by the means to purchased it all, widely available credit. Suddenly shopping was more than just an activity undertaken to acquire necessities, it was a preoccupation that for many was more fun than dating, or even sex (Barber, 2007). And with this development, the outlook the "Fab Four" espoused in their early 60s chart-topper became a quaint throwback to an earlier age.

FIGURE 12-3. More fun than sex?

The importance of love as an organizing principal of an individual's life reflects a period in human history in which we all depended on each other for survival. From the nomadic hunter-gatherers who lived and worked together in cohesive families and tribes, to the farming families who first adopted a settled way of life, to the city dwellers who each played a part in the functioning of the metropolis, we once relied upon face-to-face interpersonal contact to secure our place in a larger living system. Whether as husband or wife, family or tribal member, citizen of a community or a state, or intimate friend, we humans have a long history of belonging to social units that are bigger than us.

These relationships were based upon reciprocity—a mutual give and take—that ensured our place among other individuals. Just as we expect to be compensated for our labor, or understand that we must hand over our money for goods and services we wish to purchase; reciprocal relationships within friendships, families, and communities involve the exchange of things as seemingly insubstantial as goodwill or as tangible as food and shelter during times of need. Such informal give and take transactions between friends, family, and acquaintances helped to cement our place in social systems that greatly enhanced our chances for survival from prehistoric times to nearly the present.

That all changed when money and markets became an integral part of our lives. In the past we lived in cooperative groupings in which each person contributed something for the common good. Even in our own time, tasks like cooking, grocery shopping, household maintenance, childcare, errand running, and all the other labor-demanding activities that are required for a family to function were divided—often unequally—among its members. Now all tasks can be either delegated to a machine (like a robot vacuum cleaner) or hired out (as in a maid service).

In other words, an individual can now live perfectly well without relying on anyone else. People can depend entirely on fee-for-service helpers to accomplish tasks that were once carried out on an informal unpaid basis. Meals can be delivered ready to eat. Laundry can be farmed out to a pick-up and delivery cleaning service. Groceries can be ordered over the Internet and supplied directly to the household refrigerator and pantry. There are service providers that pay bills, arrange social events, purchase gifts, and raise children. All that is required is money (Hochschild, 2003).

One of the minor consequences of this new arrangement is that people need no longer behave in socially appropriate ways to get others to act in a cooperative manner. Being pleasant and affable to family and friends is unnecessary when all that is required is a swipe of a debit or credit card or an automatic withdrawal to get what is wanted. Thus the growing crudity of many people's behavior has been impelled by the increasingly buy-on-demand transactional nature of social interaction (Ericksen et al., 2010).

But by far the greatest effect of living in a commercialized environment, in which everything is for sale, is happening inside our psyches. Coupled with the expanding prevalence of advertising in our personal lives (as discussed in Chapter 7), more and more of us *feel* that we are the center of a vast consumption-oriented universe. Everything feeds into our needs, our wants; all we have to provide is cash or credit. And as we live year after year with the message that happiness is found in consumption ringing through our minds, we begin to perceive the world through this most recent social construction: that all things revolve around us (Ericksen et al., 2010). Our satisfaction is paramount—little else is of any consequence in this new cultural conception. Though communication devices and social networking sites connect us as never before, we are increasingly isolated, alone in our private worlds of consumption (Turkle, 2011). Fewer and fewer of us participate in social activities, attend public meetings, or engage in civic events (Putnam, 2000), while more of us sit entranced in front of a monitor, a smartphone, or a flat screen television. There is only the self. This is individualism taken to new extremes, in which everything is about "me," the give and take of traditional relationships is absent, face-to-face interpersonal relationships grow more rare, and loneliness is avoided through the obsessive use of social networking and consumption. This new psychological state is called hyper-individuation (Ericksen et al., 2010).

FIGURE 12-4. Gender becomes just another consumer choice...

In a world of hyper-individuated people, gender becomes more and more a matter of personal choice not social convention. Though the surrounding social context may inform individuals about the nature of the genders, it is the lone person who ultimately defines personal gender characteristics. The principal way gender is expressed is through consumption. Masculinity, femininity, intersexuality, heterosexuality, homosexuality, and any combination thereof is signaled to others by the goods and services that a person purchases. Thus the type of car, the mode of fashion, the preference in cuisine, the choices of lifestyle, and much else that can be bought, are arrayed in a manner that communicates, to the invisible audience the hyper-individuated person believes is always watching, specific gender characteristics. A high-powered muscle car may evoke a certain gender message, while preference for a particular fashion designer's line may suggest another. Life is structured as a reality-TV show. It forms the essential framework of the world of the hyper-individuated person (Ericksen et al., 2010).

In the late 1940s, the author George Orwell warned in his novel *1984* of a future in which video surveillance was omnipresent, with the consequent loss of privacy and personal freedom. The irony is that among the hyper-individuated, rather than fearing the watchful gaze of "Big Brother," the desire to be the celebrity of their own lives means that being watched all the time is perceived as a virtue, a means to achieve fame.

FIGURE 12-5. Being watched is now a virtue.

Unfortunately, the reliance on gender stereotypes—many of which are obsolete and dysfunctional—has a tendency to pervade the outlook of the hyper-individuated. Like advertising that attempts to capture the attention of as many potential customers as possible (as noted in Chapter 7), the hyper-individuated person is apt to employ default views of females and males that harkens back to pre-agricultural gender roles. The essential problem with the hyper-individuation outlook on gender matters is that by being the center of a consumer universe, the lone person may be commercially well connected but socially isolated. The isolation that accompanies this way of living means that individuals have little or no insight into the experiences of others. The very human capacity to empathize with others simply is not exercised when individuals have few face-to-face opportunities to interact.

The personal freedom that hyper-individuation affords is tempered by the relative loneliness that comes with this way of life. With this new extremely individualized social construction, the lone male, female, or intersex individual lives in a context that is shaped not by interaction with other people, but rather a personal space shaped by advertising and consumer preferences. Consequently, notions of gender are determined by advertising and personal choice. Due to advertising's reliance on ancient views of male and female that we are predisposed to possess, the hyper-individuated person has few other sources from which to draw gender references.

FIGURE 12-6. Advertising plays on our ancient predispositions.

This is the reason so many individuals—despite the efforts of members of feminist and gay, lesbian, transgender and transsexual communities to inform the general public of the limitations that constrain their outlook on sex and gender matters—continue to fall back on more traditional perspectives. The hyper-individuated outlook tends to reinforce ancient gender views because of the relative isolation of individuals who possess this worldview and the prominence of consumption in their lives.

3.

Do you know people who act like they are the center of the world?

· ·

DO WE NEED OUR EVOLVED MATES SELECTION ABILITIES IN THE 21ST CENTURY?

Ask yourself this question: What do I want in a relationship?

Then ask yourself: How much I am willing to sacrifice for such a relationship?

In the previous chapters, it is evident the evolutionary psychological perspective on interpersonal relationships between the genders is very much focused on reproduction. As we have seen, there are two approaches that have been defined by the evolutionary view of human reproductive behavior. The ancient practice of having children in a highly cohesive social environment in which all youngsters are regarded as everyone's offspring, and the more recent emphasis on the individual getting his or her genes into the future through children whose parentage is clearly known. The social context in which we currently live, particularly in view of the emergence of hyper-individuation, means that for now we will tend to define reproductive success in terms of the passage of an individual's genes into the future. Therefore, the search for a partner with resources and suitable genes will be of some priority in our mate selection choices, particularly if you are female.

Perhaps you are wondering if we can ever get past this tendency. Can we put aside the inclination to consciously or unconsciously fixate on getting our genes into the future and overcome the old motivations?

There are individuals who intentionally choose not to reproduce. Catholic priests and nuns take a vow of celibacy; that is, they commit themselves to a way of life in which sexual activity has no place. Other people for whom spirituality is a central part of their lives sometimes decide not to allow any aspect of reproduction to be a part of their lives. There are also couples that deliberately choose not to have children.

4.

Are you in charge of your life?

· ·

It is important to remember that evolutionarily derived behavioral predispositions are just that—predispositions. They are nudges that shape our behavior. These nudges can be ignored and overcome or, as most of us are apt do, we can fallback on them and use them as default guides to behavior. For some individuals the impulse to engage in sexual activity is subjectively felt to be a drive so strong that it compels them to pursue every opportunity that may lead to its achievement. For others it may be perceived as little more than an occasional twinge, an infrequent leaning, or may have no impact on their conscious choices. The degree of variation in any population of individuals is enormous.

It is also important to take into account the environment in which we live. Does the surrounding cultural context promote reproductive behavior? Does the social construction that informs our conception of ourselves encourage us to consciously or unconsciously seek relationships with others?

FIGURE 12-7. Are we really in conscious control of our lives?

We like to think of our conscious selves as being fully in charge of our behavior, that we exercise conscious choice all the time, but the reality is quite different. The conscious self is just a small part of our psyche. Largely hidden from us, the unconscious mind, shaped by millions of years of evolution, structures our view of the world, gathers the disparate sensory information we receive through our eyes, ears, nose, mouth, and skin, and arranges these elements into our sense of being alive and of being present in a particular environment. The unconscious also interprets all the data and directs our behavior in subtle ways that most of the time we are barely conscious of, in order to attain goals we may not consciously choose (Mlodinow, 2012).

For example, this may be explain why the person who voiced nothing but contempt for boorish chauvinist males ended up being swept off her feet by the very archetype of such a man and has four children with him. Her conscious self is the socially constructed side, rationally dedicated to a view of the world in which the old ways men and women relate to one another are no longer appropriate, but what her unconscious side "saw" may have been an opportunity to reproduce with an individual who has genes that complemented hers, who has the resources and the inclination to raise their offspring well. Her behavior may seem to

contradict her stated beliefs—but understand that this is one consequence of possessing an unconscious that was evolved to ensure reproductive success.

5.

Have you ever done something that seems out of character?

One of the interesting things about the way that our unconscious directs our behavior is that we often make a choice before we consciously know we have made one! And we tend to use our conscious intellectual faculties to come up with rationalizations to justify our unconscious decision after it has been made (Nørretranders, 1998). In other words, though we like to think our choices occur after conscious deliberation, the reality is that we unconsciously decide first and then conjure up justifications for our actions.

You may know a guy who seems to have all the right characteristics for being a parent but has never had any children. In other words, he chooses not to gamble. He possesses good genes, resources, and the behavioral predispositions necessary to raise children to healthy maturity, yet he does not engage in reproductive behavior. His unconscious may have evaluated his surroundings and come to the conclusion, for any number of possible reasons, that these conditions were not suitable for his potential offspring. Perhaps females with complementary genes and the right behavioral tendencies were not present, the environment was degraded in such a way that his descendents would be adversely affected, or some barely perceptible cue indicated that reproduction was not something to be undertaken. He may consciously have wanted to engage in sexual activity for the purposes of reproduction but his unconscious was sending the message, "Don't have kids." Through it all he may consciously shrug his shoulders and say, "I just haven't met the right gal."

Indeed, much like one evolutionary view of homosexuality, in which gay individuals contribute to the well-being of their siblings' children and so improve the likelihood of their genes being represented in the future in an indirect manner, heterosexuals who do not reproduce may similarly ensure their genetic future through their nieces and nephews rather than through potential sons and daughters. When resources grow scarce and population densities reach critical levels, what is the point of having offspring who will only end up taking resources from already living children who you are related to as an uncle or an aunt? Why diminish the survival chances of all your indirect descendents by adding more direct descendents to the environment? It may be better to contribute to the upbringing of your brother or sister's children than to have offspring of your own.

But to return to female, male, or intersex individuals who behave in ways that seem so contrary to their nature, how much of the seemingly inexplicable behavior of others can be accounted for by taking into consideration their unconscious, we may never know; however, it is a factor which often goes unconsidered.

FIGURE 12-8. Our unconscious is an important part of our psyche.

As mysterious and psychologically inaccessible as our unconscious may seem, we can affect it. We do not have to be mere puppets dancing at the end of strings that it manipulates. Though it is shaped by millions of years of evolution and apparently runs on predispositions geared to survival, it is not a fount of wisdom—it has its faults.

One of the key problems with our ancient unconscious is that—once again—it is tailored to a world we don't live in anymore. This is most evident when it comes to dealing with money. We like to think that we habitually gather all the available data about issues that affect our personal finances, crunch the numbers, weigh our choices, and make the best decision. However, more often than not, this is the last thing we are apt to do. Financial choices are made based on emotions, not rational thought (Mlodinow, 2012). This is why advertising is almost never directed at our intellectual side and is almost always an appeal to our emotions.

The ancient predispositions are also the cause of so many conflicts between the genders, as it tends to direct our behavior along paths that worked in the past but are often wholly dysfunctional in the present. A human male attempting to behave like a dominant primate guarding a harem of females is ridiculous in the current cultural context in which women may have as much overt power, and frequently more covert power, than men. Equally ridiculous is the emotion-driven negative reaction many heterosexual males have toward homosexual males. If you think about it, having lots of gay men around makes it easier for a straight guy to attract a potential female partner since there are fewer competitors present. But because we habitually categorize people into in-groups and out-groups and tend to demonize those who belong to the latter, we often react in ways that make no logical sense and are detrimental not only to others, but also to ourselves.

As discussed in the third chapter, as old as Aristotle's approach to thinking about the Universe may seem from a historical perspective, the habit of responding not in accord with reason but to the rush of feelings is so much more ancient, and so much stronger, that most of us tend not to rely upon our intellect to make decisions. However, emotion-driven decisions may have been a perfectly adaptive behavioral predisposition on the savannas of the last ice age when a pack of carnivores threatened or a neighboring tribe launched a raid, but in the twenty-first century such judgment-making tendencies can be disastrous.

6.

Can we really take charge of our lives?

FIGURE 12-9. Pilots are trained to maintain their rational faculties and think logically no matter the circumstance.

We can override the unconscious predispositions. Pilots are trained not to respond to ancestral impulses and react with panic in times of emergency, but to maintain their intellectual faculties and situational awareness no matter the circumstances they find themselves. Naval crewmembers aboard submarines are trained not to run from the sound or sight of water but to seek out its source and deal with the problem immediately. When an earthquake occurs, people are taught to seek safety under a strong table or a structurally resilient part of a building where they can find protection from falling objects, rather than reflexively run out of a building where the likelihood of being

injured or killed is greater. We can train our conscious selves to inhibit the old unconscious behavioral patterns and adopt new ones.

It requires a lot of effort, but it is essentially part of the educative process into which we invest so much of our time, money, and energy. Learning about the systems that form the foundation of the world in which we currently live is at the heart of all formal education.

You are attempting to learn how to go about being a gendered individual in a world that changes with startling speed. You are trying to learn how to function effectively in a social context in which the ancestral definitions of male, female, and intersex are losing much of their adaptive qualities. This is no small feat. To borrow a term from computer science, you are attempting to over-write several million years worth of behavioral programming.

7.

Developing our unconscious...

FIGURE 12-10. With training we can overcome our innate fear of heights and climb to the summit of such peaks.

In essence, part of the goal of education is to add to the interpretative power of the unconscious. For example, the innate fear of heights that we all possess as children can be overcome through learning and experience. Some of us master this predisposition to such a degree that we are able to climb mountains or work on towering construction sites. The inborn fear of falling can be channeled through learning into a concern for safety that makes scaling a cliff or building a skyscraper an exhilarating yet manageable activity. We can develop our ancestral unconscious predispositions in such a way that they enhance our capabilities.

So do we need our evolutionarily derived ability to sense which person is a good mate? Until genetic science completely understands the ways in which genes interact, how heredity in every detail works, we will have to rely to some degree upon our ancestral sensibilities about mate selection. We are not even close to fully comprehending the dance of DNA. Making the best match that your gut tells you is for now one way to find a mate with whom to have offspring. However, it is important to be mindful of this unconscious selective inclination.

Listen up, guys. The problem is that we tend to let the unconscious mate selection part of our psyche rule all our social interactions. We are not going to potentially have children with every person we meet; yet for heterosexual males the fixation on attractiveness can become so obsessive that every female they encounter is judged along such criteria. There is much more to life—and survival—than just having sex and possibly having children. How many significant social ties that may enhance our lives go undeveloped because the old inborn standards for mate selection are being overly utilized is probably beyond count. The loss to ourselves and to the larger society of which we are a part is immeasurable.

Likewise to the girls—the tendency to evaluate all males along reproductive concerns for resources and genetic quality, also greatly limits the scope of our personal development. Some of the most significant aspects of the people around us cannot be measured by relative material wealth or apparent health. Our ability to survive and prosper in a world that is changing rapidly means that the effective use of our intellects will play a larger and larger role in personal well-being as the older evolutionarily derived characteristics become increasingly obsolete and out of step.

The problem with our evolved mate selection abilities is that we tend to allow this part of our unconscious too much latitude. Indeed, the case can be made that we are too prone to let the entire repertoire of our ancestral predispositions control our behavior. From in-group/out-group prejudices to all too frequent emotionally driven financial choices, from an excessive reliance on ancient gender stereotypes to an obsessive concern with reproductive behavior, we need to find ways to place appropriate boundaries on predispositions that were born so long ago. We no longer live nomadic lives on a windswept savanna. For better or worse, we are citizens of a complex, highly changeable, technology and market-driven society. The old ways may serve as rough guides, but to blindly adhere to them without conscious consideration of current conditions is to court disaster.

MYOPIC FORESIGHT

If we could travel back in time say fifty thousand years and hang out with our hunter-gatherer ancestors (after we persuaded them not to regard us as threatening outsiders) and have a meaningful chat (after we had become fluent in their language), it would be interesting to ask them what they thought their future would bring (after we taught them the concept of progress).

Knowing how most humans are inclined to think, our distant forefathers and foremothers would probably imagine a future world that would be just a better, faster version of their current circumstances.

"Bigger fatter mammoth, larger more effective spears, a hand ax that never gets dull—and wood that never stops burning!" a hunter would declare, thinking of a possible future.

"Bigger sweeter berries, more plentiful nuts, plants that grow in the winter, and meat that dries more quickly—and painless childbirth," a gatherer would suggest.

The hunter would nod in agreement.

Can you imagine the unimaginable?

. . . .

Predicting the future is difficult because we are limited by our current worldview, by our own experiences. It is very unlikely that our ancient ancestors would have imagined a future in which houses, television—or even formal wedding ceremonies—existed. Such things were entirely outside their experience. They lived nomadic lives. The closest thing they ever encountered to what we would call a dwelling was a cave or a tent made of animal skins; consequently, an artificially heated or cooled structure made of wood and glass in which people could live year after year was simply beyond their imagination. Similarly, a modern wedding party would represent an outlay of resources beyond our forebears' wildest dreams.

And it is not just the material things our ancient predecessors would probably have never imagined when speculating of the future. How about something abstract like money? Could our Paleolithic kin have ever conceived of stock exchanges, bond markets, or even banks? How about human rights, the rule of law, or the concept of sovereignty?

FIGURE 12-11. Could our ancestors have ever imagined the world we live in?

Then again, how many people today really comprehend compound interest and what it does to credit card debt?

How good are we at anticipating the future?

. . . .

Predicting the future is difficult because our personal outlook narrows the scope of our imagination. It is hard to conceive of things that are completely new and, in unforeseen ways, alter the way we live. In 1968, when the movie *2001: A Space Odyssey* was released, the authors, Arthur C. Clarke and Stanley Kubrick, conceived of a future only a little over three decades away in which orbiting hotels and journeys to the moon were commonplace, yet the phone booth still existed. They did not foresee the cell phone, the Internet, or palm-sized computers. In their version of the year 2001, the Cold War was still going on. They did not foresee that the Soviet Union would be gone by 1991. The astronauts who manned the spaceship going to Jupiter were all male. Female astronauts were not part of their worldview. That the zeal for human space exploration would decline and that men would land on the moon but not return after the early 1970s was inconceivable to Clarke and Kubrick. It is also interesting to note how skinny everyone was in the view of 2001 they conceived (Clarke, 1968).

When we look to the future we are constrained by the same limitations as our ancestors, both ancient and recent. For example, we might conceive of smartphones becoming small enough that they are implanted directly to the auditory and visual centers of our brains. Smartphones could essentially de-materialize, handheld units would be a thing of the past, and our brains would be wirelessly connected to the web. We would never be disconnected.

10.

How are we changed by technological and social innovations?

. . . .

FIGURE 12-12. Are we shaping technology or is it shaping us?

But can we imagine how this would change us? What does it mean when all of us are permanently part of a worldwide, interconnected system that runs all the time? Would we be able to "turn off" our implants—and by

"turn off" I do not mean "power down" these devices—I mean, would we be able to psychologically stand not being part of the network? What would happen to our sense of being an individual person when we are electronically connected to everyone else? Would a bad date ever really end? Would we ever get any sleep? Would others be able to hack into our thoughts, our feelings, and our dreams? Would we know after a while which thoughts were ours, and which belonged to someone else?

And this is just one obvious technological change that could have many unforeseen sociological and psychological consequences. The elements of the future that make it so difficult to predict are those that are outside of our experience—elements that disrupt the old systems that order our present world.

11.

Imagine how much more rapidly change will occur in the future.

. . . .

FIGURE 12-13. Have you ever used a machine like this?

If you were a parent in the 1960s, what would you tell your young daughter if she announced that she was thinking of becoming a typist? A typist? Once upon a time before desktop computers existed, vast legions of office workers, usually women, banged away on typewriters producing the documents word processing programs now routinely generate. Countless women once made a career of tapping out letters and memos. Today, to use an equally antiquated saying, typists are as common as hen's teeth. Likewise, would you advise your daughter or son to study computer science if in a few years computers develop the ability to write their own software as well as take over the design and manufacter of hardware? Or should we buy a gasoline/electric hybrid car today when some unforeseen technology or geopolitical event could make such a means of conveyance obsolete overnight?

12.

The three frames of reference and the changing nature of gender.

. . . .

Then there is the social constructivist aspect of change that needs to be considered. Social constructions are collective creations. The psychologist Lev Vygotsky, one of the proponents of social constructivism, lived through Lenin's Bolshevik Revolution of 1917 that brought both Socialism and Communism to the Russian people and saw the formation of the Soviet Union. Contemporaneous to Vygotsky's intellectual development was the rise of the art movement known as Constructivism (Wood et al., 1989). These currents of thought proceeded from the view that the old ways should be swept aside by the new constructions of Marxism. This is one of the key historical events that underlie social constructivism. It is relevant because it reveals the revolutionary ideological foundations of this frame of reference.

As noted in the third chapter, race is an example of a social construction. It came into creation because enough people shared the view that small differences between groups of people were perceived to be so glaringly obvious as to justify the classification of these groups as significant subsets of humanity. The characteristics of those within these subsets were supposedly so distinct that it was possible to generalize all members of a race accordingly. So, the claim could be made that all members of Race A were thieves or all members of Race B were smart. Of course we know this is nonsense. Within any so-called race there is enormous variation, and if these variations are averaged out and compared with other so-called races, no meaningful differences are discernible. If there are no differences then race is product of culture, not of objective evaluation. Yet the social construction of race persists.

Gender is a social construction, too. Our culture recognizes sex differences, those biological essentialist characteristics that make males, females, and intersex individuals distinct from each other, but these traits figure less and less in our cultural understanding of men, women, and intersex individuals. Think about the freedom women now enjoy compared to what females only a hundred years ago knew. There may come a day when "anything goes" may truly be the social construction that informs the lives of all people irrespective of gender. In such a future the notion of distinct genders may disappear completely and gender studies may be a course offered solely in the history department—a field of inquiry that is entirely retrospective. On the other hand, there could be a backlash against a completely open-ended cultural view of gender, and a new social construct could develop in which rigid essentialist gender roles may reestablish themselves. Perhaps gender roles will be mixed together so that traditional ways of being female are incorporated into new schemes of being male and vice versa. Being intersex may become the new norm. Or circumstances could arise that nudge us into completely new roles that bear no reference to the past. Imagine a genderless world in which we teach our children not to give in to any of their innate gender identities. But whatever happens, the degree of flexibility inherent in these roles makes it clear that biology is for now becoming less and less a factor in determining the specific attributes of a particular gender.

FIGURE 12-14. What happens when social constructions can shape biology?

From the biological essentialist view, change in the future will also make itself felt. Technology is no longer limited to affecting us at the cultural level; it can now reach into the biological essence of being male, female, and intersex. In the future we could conceivably develop genetic technologies that could allow us to determine not only the sex of our children but change our own sex at will. Why not be a female in early life, a male later, and finish off as an intersex person? How about being a groom in your first marriage, a bride in your second, and a "broom" (bride/groom) in your third? With reproductive technologies like in vitro fertilization, surrogacy, cryogenic sperm freezing, and genetic screening, are

separate sexes really necessary from a biological standpoint? As we become more and more concerned with economic efficiency, why not have a world populated with just one sex but a rainbow of genders? Separate bathrooms will no longer have to be provided in public buildings. When any individual can have the means to raise children without a partner, do we need to exercise our evolved mate selection strategies? When technology makes it possible to transcend the biological boundaries of sex, do we even need gender? Why not be biologically genderless? The point is that when technology makes it possible to change us at the biological level, the few remaining boundaries that once constrained individuals into specific roles could largely disappear. Men will not have to be male, women will not have to be female, and intersex individuals will not have to be intersex. Transgender or non-gender could become real options for everyone. The larger question is whether we can truly overcome our evolved gender sensibilities. Then again, would we want to? Of particular concern for the future is whether individuals can put aside the old tendency to categorize others into in-group or out-group and stop demonizing those who are deemed members of the out-group.

Epigenetics, the nature via nurture perspective on gender and change, would be revolutionized if we adopt technologies that affect us at the biological essentialist level because nature itself would be altered. What was once a physiologically determined characteristic—a person's sex—would truly become a social construction. Both sex and gender would come into our control and become entirely personally defined attributes. The only aspect of our humanity that would still tend to shape our sense of being gendered individuals would be our evolutionarily derived predispositions. This would be the last remaining nudge from nature in the epigenetic view.

13.

When nearly every aspect of our gender identity becomes a social construct, what choices will we make?

If we do become a populace of wirelessly connected brains, will virtual sexual contact become common as our old predispositions for reproductive behavior inflect through new technologies? Could cyber-rape become a possibility? And if this happens, would the perpetrators tend to be of one gender? If we make both our biological sex and our socially constructed gender matters of personal choice, how will we exercise the power we will possess to shape our sense of who we are? Will we leave behind our evolved gender tendencies, or will we retain the old ways of defining men, women, and intersex?

A future of flying cars and space colonies seems terribly naïve when we consider the scope of our inability to imagine, let alone predict, the nature of tomorrow.

THE FUTURE

The idea that tomorrow will be better than today has been part of the Western cultural construct for a few hundred years now. However, the socioeconomic and environmental conditions that are enfolding before us as the twenty-first century advances causes many people to feel somewhat pessimistic about the prospect of ever-rising standards of living being a permanent feature of human development. No doubt, gender will be at the leading edge of change. The hope is that justice and equality remain organizing principles in gender relationships.

When the author John Steinbeck received the Nobel Prize for literature, he made the point in his acceptance speech that when we acquire new abilities and new powers, it is not enough for us to use them, we must also take responsibility for their use (1971). In the twentieth century we were offered choice. In the twenty-first century, we must take responsibility for the choices we have made and for the choices that are still left to us.

FIGURE 12-15. A better world for us all...

REFERENCES

Barber, B. R. (2007). *Consumed: how markets corrupt children, infantilize adults, and swallow citizens whole.* New York: W. W. Norton.

Clarke, A. C. (1968). *2001: a space odyssey.* New York: New American Library.

The Economist: Special Report: Women and Work. "Female labor markets: the cashier and the carpenter." Vol. 401. No. 8761. Nov 26 2011. p. 6.

Ericksen, L. & Shimazu, M. (2010). *Nations of one: the emerging psychology of the 21st century.* Xlibris.

Faludi, S. (1999). *Stiffed: the betrayal of the american man.* New York: William Morrow and Company, Inc.

Hochschild, A. R. (2003). *The commercialization of intimate life: notes from home and work.* Berkeley: University of California Press. pp. 30–44.

Mlodinow, L. (2012). *Subliminal: how your unconscious mind rules your behavior.* New York: Pantheon.

Nørretranders, T. (1998). *The user illusion: cutting consciousness down to size.* New York: Penguin Books. pp. 213–250.

Putnam, R. D. (2000). *Bowling alone: the collapse and revival of american community.* New York: Simon & Schuster.

Steinbeck, J. (1971). *The viking portable Steinbeck.* New York: Viking Press. pp. 690–692.

Turkle, S. (2011). *Alone together: why we expect more from technology and less from each other.* New York: Basic Books.

Wood, M., Cole, B.. & Gealt, A. (1989). *Art of the western world: from ancient greece to postmodernism.* New York: Touchstone. p. 287, 317.

Questions

Name   Date

1. What important changes have gendered individuals had to cope with over the last ten millennia?

2. Do we really need to actively cooperate with other people in our lives today to ensure personal survival and well-being or can we rely upon money and markets?

3. How are we psychologically responding to a world in which everything needed for survival can be purchased?

4. What is the consumer relationship between gender and personal choice in the twenty-first century?

5. Why is loneliness such a common feature of contemporary life?

6. Can we overcome our ancestral evolutionarily derived behavioral predispositions?

7. If you observe a person you know well doing something that seems distinctly out of character, what role might that person's unconscious be playing in his or her decision-making?

8. How might not having children be adaptive if you already have nieces and nephews?

9. What is meant by myopic foresight?

10. How might gender be affected by technological developments in the future? What does it mean that technology can now affect us at the level of our biology as well as at the social construction level?

Glossary of Terms

· ·

Adaptation: the process by which the characteristics of an individual or a group of individuals or a species is fitted to the particular circumstances that prevail.

Adaptive: a characteristic that an individual or a group of individuals or a species possesses that confers some advantage that enhances well-being or survival in a given environment.

Agricultural: the practice begun roughly ten thousand years ago of producing food through the growing of plants and collecting the edible portion of such produce (can also include the raising of livestock).

Alloparent: derived from *allo-* (from the Greek for "other than"), refers to adults who assist in the care and nurture of children.

Ancestors: all those individuals from whom the current population of humans is either directly or indirectly descended.

Ancestral environment: refers to the natural pre-agricultural setting in which our ancestors lived as nomadic hunter-gatherers. It was in such a setting that many of our innate behavioral predispositions evolved as an adaptation to the specific conditions that prevailed more than ten thousand years ago.

Androgen: any group of hormones that promote the development of male physical characteristics.

Androgen insensitivity syndrome: a condition in XY males whose physiology does not respond to the presence of androgens (male hormones), consequently at birth such an individual will appear female.

Androgynous: possessing both male and female characteristics.

Anthropology: the science of humanity. It is concerned with our physical evolution as well as our cultural adaptations, consequently there are two broad divisions of this field of study: physical anthropology and cultural anthropology.

Archetype: in Jung's view, it is a primary image that emerges from the unconscious, which structures and informs our understanding of all things. For example, our struggle with fear and darkness makes it possible for us to emotionally engage in movies like *Star Wars*. From an evolutionary perspective, an archetype is an idea shaped by the ancestral environment and the experiences of our ancestors.

Asexual reproduction: a method of producing offspring in which no sexual exchange of genetic information takes place. A clone is the product of asexual reproduction.

Behavior: the observable actions of an organism.

Behavioral predisposition: an inborn tendency to act in a certain way in response to a given stimuli or situation. For example, we are all inclined to behave with caution when we find ourselves in completely novel surroundings.

Behavioral sciences: psychology, sociology, anthropology, economics, political science, and many more new disciplines (like behavioral genetics) are all sciences concerned with behavior. Each has its own sphere of study (psychology focuses on the individual, while sociology studies groups of individuals).

Biodiversity: the degree of variety among the living things in a given environment or across the entire planet. It is a measure of the health of ecosystems (the community of living and non-living elements, and their interaction).

Biological essentialist: A frame of reference that emphasizes the biological origins of our behavior. Our biological nature, which is the product of billions of years of evolution, is the primary source from which our behavioral tendencies spring.

Biology: the scientific study of all living organisms and their interaction.

Bisexual: a sexual orientation in which an individual is inclined to engage in male-female as well as male-male sexual behavior.

Bonobo: one of two primates to whom humans are closely related. More than 98% of our DNA is identical.

CAH (congenital adrenal hyperplasia): a prenatal hormonal condition in which the presence of excessive androgens (hormones that promote male development) produces the masculinization of external genitalia in female fetuses. In particular, the clitoris appears to resemble a small penis.

Catholic Church (Roman Catholic Church): according to doctrine, it is the original Christian faith. Founded by Jesus Christ in the first century A.D., during the time of the Roman Empire, it is one of the key elements that structure the Western cultural tradition.

Certainty: a condition in which there can be no doubt. Certainty is a trap because it closes the human mind from the possibility that there may be other ways of interpreting things. Physics also shows that certainty does not exist in this Universe. Consequently, all knowledge is provisional—our current best understanding of phenomena.

Chauvinism: an excessive or blind adherence to, or acceptance of, a particular view or position (see certainty).

Chimerism: in this condition two separate fertilized eggs fuse to form a single individual.

Chimpanzee: one of two primates to whom humans are closely related. More than 98% of our DNA is identical.

Chromosome: an organized collective of DNA and proteins located in cells. We humans have 23 pairs of chromosomes. The critical pair in the study of gender is the XX (usually female in humans, but not always in other living things) and the XY (usually male in humans, but not always in other living things) chromosomes.

Civilization: a level of social organization that emerges when a sufficiently large number of individuals live in settlements and engage in complex social, economic, political, religious, and other collective activities, with some degree of cultural cohesion

Clitoris: button-shaped sexual organ found only in female mammals, located above the opening of the urethra and the vagina.

Clone: offspring derived from asexual reproduction. Its DNA is identical to its parent.

Common ancestor: a species from which different species emerge. A common misunderstanding of evolutionary is that humans are descended from chimpanzees and bonobos. The reality is that humans, chimpanzees, and bonobos share a common ancestor who existed before humans, chimpanzees, bonobos existed. It is rather like saying that you share a common ancestor with your brother or sister. That common ancestor is your mother or father. You are not descended from your sibling.

Convention: norms, values, behaviors, and other socially constructed aspects of a social system that are widely accepted.

Correlation: an apparent relationship between two things that may or may not be causally connected.

Covert power: the indirect assertion of will (as opposed to the direct application of force). Persuasion and seduction are examples of covert power.

Cultural anthropology: (see anthropology) the sub-discipline of anthropology concerned with the cultural manifestations of humanity. Customs, mythology, religious beliefs, moral, values and social conventions of a particular group of people are of interest in this field of study.

Cultural context: the background culture that informs and structures the thoughts, feelings, attitudes, values, and behaviors of people.

Culture: the emergent customs, conventions, attitudes, values, behaviors, arts, sciences, religions, etc. that result from the interaction of individuals within a cohesive group.

de la Chapelle syndrome: a genetic condition in which an individual whose genotype is XX (female) but whose physical characteristics are male. This happens when the father's contribution of an X chromosome has the active genes of a Y chromosome in it. So despite the presence of two Xs, development follows the male pattern.

Default view: a frame of reference that we rely upon when we choose not to employ more recently developed ways of dealing with the world in which we live. Default views come from the past and are often based upon ancestral ways of thinking. Our strong inclination to pigeonhole people into in-group/out-group categories based upon mere appearances is a default view applied to diversity.

Descendants: the offspring of an individual or individuals. We are the descendants of our ancestors.

Determinism: a view of the world in which the cause and effect relationship is limited and narrow. Thus if A is the state of a particular thing: then only B can result. Other results (C, D, E, etc.) are not possible.

Discrimination: the prejudicial treatment of an individual or individuals based upon membership—or perceived membership—in a particular out-group or category.

Disruptive technologies: new developments from which new processes emerge that fundamentally change the way things are done. Digital transmission of music has completely remade the way music is bought and sold, for example.

DNA: the hugely complex molecule (**d**eoxyribo**n**ucleic **a**cid) that encodes the information required for the generation, function, and replication of life on the Earth.

Economic: the collective or individual use of resources as it relates to the production, distribution, and consumption of goods and services.

Environment: the physical, biological, and social context in which we live.

Eon: an extremely long period of time.

Epigenetic: also referred to as nature via nurture, the term translates as "upon genes." From the frame of reference of epigenetics, the characteristics of an individual, or a group of individuals, or a species are shaped by the interaction of the environment through the potentialities that genes offer.

Essentialist: (as applied in biological essentialism) sex and gender characteristics (behavioral and physical) are determined by biology.

Estrogen: the female sex hormone.

European Dark Ages: the period of time in Western Europe that began with the fall of the Roman Empire, in the mid to late fifth century, and the re-establishment of some semblance of social order in the eleventh century.

Evolution: the process of change through differential selection of random mutations. The prevailing conditions an organism or entity finds itself either selects for or against its continued survival through the interaction of its characteristics with the environment, thus resulting in gradual or sometimes abrupt change. Evolution is not a conscious force. It does not seek perfection. It acts upon organisms in terms of the conditions, as they exist at the time. A characteristic that is adaptive today may not be suitable tomorrow.

Evolutionary psychology: the behavioral science that focuses on individual behavior, which seeks to understand the roots of such behavior in the context of evolution.

Evolutionary theory: Darwin's theory that explains the development of all the diverse forms of life present on Earth. Its use has been extended into non-biological areas as well.

Female: from a purely biological point of view, females are the subset of a sexually reproducing species that produces the large gametes (eggs) as opposed to the small gametes (sperm). From our socially constructed point of view, typically human females are those individuals who either choose to identify themselves as women or girls, or are perceived to possess those attributes that are collectively regarded as female.

Feminine: among humans, those characteristics and qualities associated with being female.

Fidelity: within the context of the text, the practice of an individual engaging in sexual activity with only one other individual.

Fractional fatherhood: the condition found in the group-breeding social configuration in which the multiple male sexual partners of a receptive female are uncertain of the exact paternity of her children and thus may be the father of any given child she might bear. This uncertainty promotes the generalized care of all children present in a particular group.

Frame of reference: the view offered by a particular philosophical or scientific approach to interpreting information.

Gametes: sperm and eggs in humans.

Gay: generally a term used to describe a homosexual individual.

Gender: the socially constructed set of specifications that inform personal identity with reference to be being female, male, intersex, or some other sex.

Gender identity: the personal sense of being intersex, male, female or other sex.

Gender neutral: not possessing a sex designation.

Genes: the unit of heredity (within DNA) that when expressed confers onto an organism a particular trait or traits.

Genetics: the scientific study of genes and heredity.

Genocide: the intentional and systematic destruction of a particular group of individuals based upon a shared characteristic that all members possess.

Genotype: the actual genetic makeup of an organism or set of instructions that reside in the genetic code of an organism. Genotype is often compared to phenotype (which is the observable characteristics or traits of an organism) because of the interesting contrast that might exist between the two.

Gonads: the organs (testes in males and ovaries in females) that make gametes (eggs and sperm).

Gossip: the conversational form of grooming behavior adopted according to evolutionary psychologists as a means to maintain interpersonal relationships and group cohesion.

Greece (Greek civilization): the Northern Mediterranean civilization whose early history begins in the eighth century B.C. Plato and Aristotle are among many noted thinkers of Greek antiquity.

Grooming: the physical act of picking at the skin and hair in order to remove debris and parasites, but is principally meant to maintain interpersonal ties between individuals and enhance group cohesion.

Group cohesion: the social bonds between individuals that act to keep a larger collective of individuals together and functioning in a manner that promotes the well-being of its members.

Heterosexual: sexual behavior between males and females. The term is also used to describe an individual whose sexual orientation is to engage in sexual behavior with those individuals who are not the same sex (*hetero-* means "different").

Homo sapiens: taxonomic name of our species.

Homosexual: sexual behavior between individuals who are of the same sex or gender. The term is also used to describe an individual whose sexual orientation is to engage in sexual behavior with those individuals who are the same sex (homo means "the same").

Hormone: a chemical released by a cell or gland that affects other cells in the body. Thus when testosterone, which is a hormone, is secreted, other cells and organs in the body are affected.

Human: broad term used to describe all members of our species.

Human sexual response: the four stages of physiological reaction (as determined by researchers Masters and Johnson) that we characteristically experience when sexually stimulated.

Hunter-gatherer: term used to describe our ancestors who lived before the development of the settled agricultural lifestyle that spawned civilization ten thousand years ago. It refers also to the methods used to secure food: the hunting of game and the gathering of edible vegetation.

Hunter-gatherer societies: those socially cohesive groupings that tended to number roughly 150 individuals, which existed during the millions of years before the rise of agriculture and civilization.

Hyper-individuation: a psychological world-view from which the individual perceives the self as existing at the center of a consumption-oriented universe. All things revolve around the individual. It is individualism taken to extreme.

Hypothesis: attentive assumption or guess used to attempt to explain a particular phenomenon.

In-group: a socially constructed designation that encompasses all those individuals a person regards as being allied with or as being a member of.

Inborn: those qualities and characteristics an individual is born with.

Individual: the basic unit of any social group: a lone person.

Industrial Revolution: term used to describe the transition from a largely agricultural economy to one in which the large-scale manufacture and production of goods became the dominant feature.

Infidelity: when a person engages in sexual contact with more than one individual when that person claims that sexual contact is restricted to one individual.

Inherent: qualities and characteristics that are inherited aspects of an individual or individuals.

Innate: qualities and characteristics that are present in an individual or individuals from birth.

Intelligence: vague term used to describe the aptitudes of an individual along many different abilities and knowledge bases.

Intersex: an individual who possesses characteristics that is intermediate or atypical along a spectrum of traits between male and female.

Intimate relationship: a degree of connectedness between individuals that is exceeds the merely superficial and at minimum involves some measure of attachment, affiliation, and at least a modicum of trust.

Klinefelter's syndrome: a genetic condition in which an individual has an XXY chromosomal configuration. Such a person appears male.

Lesbian: a term used to describe female homosexual orientation. The term is also used as a designation for a female who regards herself as a female homosexual.

Major histological complex: corresponds to a group of genes that defines a person's immune system and the way in which that person's physiology responds to infections and disease.

Male: from a purely biological point of view, males are the subset of a sexually reproducing species that produces the small gametes (sperm) as opposed to the large gametes (eggs). From our socially constructed point of view, typically human males are those individuals who either choose to identify themselves as men or boys, or are perceived to possess those attributes that are collectively regarded as male.

Mammal: all members of the class of animals called mammalia. All mammals are animals that breathe air, have spines, have hair, three middle ear bones, control their internal body temperature and have mammary glands, which, in females with young, produce milk. Humans are mammals.

Markets: those socially constructed institutions through which goods and services are traded.

Masculine: among humans, those characteristics and qualities associated with being male.

Materialism: within the context of the text, it is the priority placed upon the acquisition and consumption of goods. In particular, the perception that happiness and well-being are measured by the amount of "stuff" an individual has access to through the use of money and markets.

Mega-fauna: large animals.

Menarche: the onset of menstruation in females and the initial physiological sign of reproductive viability.

Menopause: the end of menstruation and the onset phase in a woman's life in which reproduction is no longer possible without medical intervention.

Menstruation: the roughly monthly cycle of the shedding of the uterine lining in reproductive-aged women.

Millennia: a period of a thousand years.

Models: representations of phenomena that are so designed as to mimic every important aspect of the phenomena under investigation.

Monetize: in the context of the text, the process by which all those elements required for personal survival have been made into commodities that are widely available for purchase, thus making money the sole requirement for material well-being.

Monogamy: the practice of having only one sexual partner.

Middle Ages: the roughly thousand year period in Western history extending from the fall of the Roman Empire in the mid- to late-fifth century to the beginning of the European Renaissance in the mid-fifteen century.

Mutation: changes in the DNA or an organism.

Myth: an expression of the worldview of a people that informs their understanding of their place in the universe. It is the subjective counterpart to the objective view offered by such approaches to knowledge as science.

Natural selection: the process by which the traits found in any given population of individuals is made more or less common through interaction with the environment.

Nature via nurture: see Epigenetic.

Nomad: people who move from place to place, and have no fixed settlement.

Non-reproducing sexual orientation: in the text, it is a blanket term for sexual orientations that do not directly result, nor can result, in the production of offspring.

Objectivity: the approach to understanding the Universe that eliminates bias, preconceived notions, and emotional involvement in the outcome of investigation. The accuracy of the findings must be wholly independent from the individual or individuals who make the finding and stated with unambiguous clarity.

Offspring: the children of a parent.

Out-group: a socially constructed designation that encompasses all those individuals a person regards as being outside the confines of the in-group.

Ovaries: organs that produce eggs; the female gonads.

Overt power: the direct assertion of will (as opposed to the indirect application of force). Commands and orders given as a function of authority are examples of the application of overt power.

Patriarchy: a socially constructed system of control in which males are the principal authority figure.

Penis: male external sex organ.

Perspective: the "point of view," from which an issue is considered.

Phenotype: the observable characteristics or traits that an organism possesses, and results from the interaction of genes and environmental conditions.

Pre-agricultural: that period before the advent of agriculture.

Prehistoric: in the text, the period before the recording of history either in written or spoken (as in folklore or storytelling) form.

Prenatal: the period in pregnancy between the fertilization of the egg and birth.

Polyandry: the practice of one woman mated to more than one man.

Polygamy: the practice of having multiple sex partners.

Polygyny: the practice of one man mated to more than one woman.

Post-industrial: when a culture has moved beyond the production of goods as the principal economic activity to one in which services are dominant.

Postmodern: is a broad term that encompasses the view that widely accepted social constructions like values, customs, standards, etc. are not constants. We live in a relativistic Universe in which the personal frames of reference of the individual must be taken into account and accepted.

Prejudice: preconceived judgment about an individual or group of individuals based upon gender, age, religious affiliation, sexual orientation, race/ethnicity, nationality, or other out-group designation.

Psychology: the behavioral science concerned with the individual.

Puberty: the period during which a child's body transitions into physical and reproductive maturity.

Quantum mechanics: the branch of physics concerned with phenomena scaled at the level of atoms and subatomic particles, and encompasses the wave-like and particle-like behavior of matter and energy. It also makes clear the limits of measurement and certainty.

Race: a socially constructed way of sub-classifying humans based upon superficial physical differences.

Racial-ethnic: a socially constructed way of sub-classifying human based upon superficial physical differences and cultural-linguistic-lineage differences.

Reification: the act of turning an abstraction or a concept into a measureable, concrete thing. For example, turning the vague abstraction of intelligence into a numerically measureable entity.

Relativity (Special and General): Einstein's theories published in 1905 and 1915 that revolutionized our understanding of the universe. Principally, for the purposes of understanding gender, it emphasizes the importance of an individual's personal frame of reference.

Reproduction: the generation of offspring.

Roman Empire: the first major European empire; it encircled the Mediterranean Sea from 27 B.C. to 476 A.D. In many ways it is the founding template for Western civilization.

Same-sex marriage: a legally accepted union between two individuals who each are of the same sex.

Science: a human activity that builds, structures and systematizes knowledge in the form of explanation and makes possible the ability to predict. Its field of concern is everything in the Universe.

Sex: the designation determined by the biological nature of an individual, or one defined by the conventions of a given culture.

Sex: engaging in activity that is defined by a given culture as being sexual in its nature.

Sexist: like the term racist, it refers to discrimination based upon sex or gender.

Sexual: when anything relates to sex.

Sexual dimorphism: the phenotypic difference between males and females of the same species.

Sexual reproduction: the generation of offspring through the mixing of the genes of two individuals.

Social constructivist: knowledge that is generated through group interaction is elaborated into a complete system of understanding the environment. Culture is a social construction. Social constructions order our sense of reality. For example, some people claim that PMS is a social construction—a phenomenon that has no basis in objective science and is created by the collective agreement of a critical population of individuals, thus making it a commonly accepted reality. Strict social constructivism makes the claim that reality itself is a social construction and has no objective basis.

Social convention: a set of generally accepted standards, norms, altitudes, values, customs, etc. that is widely held by a population of individuals.

Socioeconomic: contraction of *social* and *economic*; a term that collectively indicates the dynamics of social elements and economic elements.

Sociology: the behavioral science concerned with groups of individuals.

Species: the basic unit of the taxonomic system through which all life is classified. All humans are members of the species *Homo sapiens*.

Sperm competition: the process by which the sperm of more than one male in the reproductive tract of a woman competes to fertilize the egg.

Stereotype: a preconceived notion about a group of individuals that is used to prejudge all individuals who are perceived to be members of that group.

Straight: heterosexual.

Subjectivity: a frame of reference that is not objective, but based upon the personal view of an individual.

Swyer's syndrome: a condition in which an individual has the XY male genotype and is female in appearance. A range of different genes on the Y chromosome may not activate the formation of fetal testes; as a result, no androgens are produced.

Testes: organs that produce sperm: the male gonads.

Testosterone: the principle male sex hormone.

Theory: a provisional explanation of observed phenomena.

Transgender: a blanket term for individuals who diverge from their assigned gender. Included in the term are intersex individuals, transsexuals, cross-dressers, transvestites, gender queens, etc.

Transsexual: a blanket term for individuals who have altered, or intend to alter, their anatomy through surgical, hormonal, or other means, in order to achieve a match with their chosen gender identity.

Turner's syndrome: an individual whose genotype is X0; that is, she has only one X chromosome.

Vagina: female sex organ.

West, The: a broad term used to characterize those cultures that have their origin in Western Europe, specifically some connection to the Greek-Roman cultural tradition.

Worldview: derived from the German word weltanschauung, it is the framework of concepts, ideas, values and beliefs that informs an individual's perception of the surrounding world.

XX chromosome: the typical human female chromosomal configuration.

XY chromosome: the typical human male chromosomal configuration.

Zygote: the initial cell formed by the fusion of the egg with a sperm.